THE FOURTH LESSON
in the Daily Office

THE
FOURTH
LESSON
in the Daily Office

BOOK TWO

Readings from outside Scripture for the Weekdays
and Holy Days of a year; designed for use with the
three Lessons in the Daily Office of the Joint Liturgical Group ('Series II, Revised')

Edited by
Christopher Campling

Darton, Longman & Todd
London

NOTE

The 'Fourth Lessons' for Holy Days, which are the same in both years of the liturgical cycle, will be found in BOOK ONE, and are not repeated here.

INTRODUCTION

This is the second volume of *The Fourth Lesson*, giving a second year's cycle of readings to supplement the second year of biblical readings in the Joint Liturgical Group's Daily Office, Series II (Revised). The purpose of the book, therefore, is to provide a reading from a Christian source outside the Bible that can be used with the revised Daily Office for every week-day of a second year. In the Office three lessons from the Bible are suggested for Matins and Evensong, one from the Old Testament, one from the Gospels and one from the rest of the New Testament. Here then is a 'fourth lesson', not from the Bible, but Christian and (I hope) edifying.

I see no need to write an apologia for this book, as I explained the principles behind it in the Introduction to Book One. Only a little indignation has come my way for proposing the introduction of readings from Christian literature into the Daily Office. After all, we clergy preach what we dare to call 'the word of God' to our congregations. Why should we not read and listen to other people's 'word of God'? The Bible remains unique, and no one could claim that these readings can have the same kind of authority as lessons taken from it. They have, perhaps, the nature of short homilies, and I do not think it can be wrong to call them Lessons. It would be odd to claim that the Bible alone contains words of divine inspiration and that with the closing of the canon of the New Testament, the Holy Spirit ceased to speak.

Some people have criticized the choice of readings – and I cannot complain about that. However I derive some comfort from the fact that the critics here nicely balance one another. There are those who would have welcomed a much wider selection of readings culled from novels and from non-Christian sources. I believe that a stimulating book of this sort waits to be compiled – but not for regular use in the Christian liturgy at the present time. There should be a measure of authority, of Christian given-ness, in what we read for edification in the course of worship, and I claim that the readings I have chosen have this quality for the reason that they were consciously written as witness to Christian truth. Others mind that I have included so much contemporary writing and that I have not found more room for ancient authors especially the early Fathers. I could say to this that if a book of readings from patristic sources were required, I should not be the person to edit it; and add that I was led to believe that the Roman Catholic Church was producing just such a book. But I would rather be bold and positive about this particular criticism. I believe that God the Holy Spirit is at work in the minds of Christian writers today – creatively, wonderfully, giving direct, startling, life-giving inspiration, as fine and penetrating as anything ever written. This book is for use today and onwards; and an editor in my seat would be making an extraordinary judgment if he were to exclude modern writers and confine himself to writers of the ancient past. We are worshipping God today. We need guidance from today's scholars, priests and prophets.

The most difficult problem has been the literary one, and there are many excellent authors of all ages whose writing is not suitable for daily readings because (most inconsiderately) they write paragraphs of the wrong length, or their argument is so packed that it cannot be broken up, or so stately and slow that short excerpts seem to contain nothing. So – I have done my best; and I can boast gratefully that the experience of editing these books has been very stimulating to me personally. If I add that at the end of it all I go back to the Bible with even more astonished joy than before, can anyone say that that is a bad thing? My prayer is that those who use this book will be edified by its contents; and if they also find new joy in the Bible, then that will be no bad thing either.

One small technical point needs to be explained. The Sundays of the year are named as they are in the Series Three Communion Service; and the scheme of themes comes originally from the Church of England Liturgical Commission's orange book, *The Calendar and Lessons of the Church's Year*. But alterations were made in the scheme of themes and lessons in that book for the first few Sundays of the year; and I have followed the new scheme as it is in Series Three Holy Communion.

CHRISTOPHER R. CAMPLING

ACKNOWLEDGEMENTS

The Editor and Publishers acknowledge the courtesy of the following persons and companies in permitting the use of copyright material:

Hodder & Stoughton Ltd. for BURY ME IN MY BOOTS by Sally Trench; GOD'S SMUGGLER by Brother Andrew.

John Murray Ltd. for STUDIES OF ENGLISH MYSTICS by W. R. Inge; LUX MUNDI ed. by Charles Gore.

Collins Fontana Ltd. for THE HUMANITY OF GOD by Karl Barth; SELF-ABANDONMENT TO DIVINE PROVIDENCE by Jean-Pierre Caussade; THE RESURRECTION OF CHRIST by A. M. Ramsey; UNDECEPTIONS by C. S. Lewis.

SCM Press Ltd. for THE SECULAR CITY by Harvey Cox; THE ETERNAL NOW by Paul Tillich; THE FUTURE OF THE CHRISTIAN CHURCH by Leon Joseph Suenens; A DICTIONARY OF CHRISTIAN ETHICS ed. by John Macquarrie; THE GO-BETWEEN GOD by John V. Taylor; A BUNDLE OF MEMORIES by H. Scott Holland quoted in THE CHURCH OF ENGLAND 1900–1965 by Roger Lloyd.

Macmillan & Co. Ltd. for THE FULLNESS OF SACRIFICE by F. C. N. Hicks; READINGS IN ST. JOHN'S GOSPEL by William Temple.

Longman Group Ltd. for THE GLORY OF GOD AND THE TRANSFIGUR-ATION OF CHRIST by A. M. Ramsey; OUTSPOKEN ESSAYS by W. R. Inge.

J. M. Dent & Sons Ltd. for ESSAYS AND ADDRESSES by Baron Friedrich von Hügel.

Penguin Books Ltd. for THE LADDER OF PERFECTION by Walter Hilton; THE CLOUD OF UNKNOWING by Clifton Wolters; A RUMOUR OF ANGELS by Peter L. Berger; ST. LUKE by G. B. Caird.

Victor Gollancz Ltd. for THE THEOLOGY OF AUSCHWITZ by Ulrich E. Simon.

S.P.C.K. for THE CALL OF THE CLOISTER by Peter F. Anson; THE CHRISTIAN PRIEST TODAY by A. M. Ramsey; DEVOTION AND DISCIPLESHIP by A. H. McNeile.

James Nisbet & Co. Ltd. for THE CHRISTIAN UNDERSTANDING OF ATONEMENT by F. W. Dillistone; THE DOCTRINE OF THE TRINITY by L. Hodgson.

A. P. Watt & Sons for ST. FRANCIS OF ASSISI by G. K. Chesterton; PAST-ORAL SERMONS by Ronald Knox.

David Higham Associates Ltd. for HE CAME DOWN FROM HEAVEN by Charles Williams.

Geoffrey Chapman Ltd. for JOURNAL OF A SOUL by Pope John XXIII.

Revd A. G. Hebert for THE THRONE OF DAVID.

The Faith Press Ltd. for TRANSFIGURATION by J. W. C. Wand.

Anthony Sheil Associates Ltd. for CONTEMPLATING NOW by Monica Furlong.

Oxford University Press and Princeton Press for CHRISTIAN DISCOURSES by Søren Kierkegaard.

Revd Mother St. George for MATER CHRISTI by Mother St. Paul.

The Clarendon Press for THE GOSPEL MESSAGE OF ST. MARK by R. H. Lightfoot.

Augsburg Publishing House for THE GOSPEL OF SUFFERING by Søren Kierkegaard.

CONTENTS

CONTENTS

CONTENTS

CONTENTS

CONTENTS

CONTENTS

CONTENTS

CONTENTS

CONTENTS

FIFTH SUNDAY BEFORE ADVENT
(Ninth Sunday before Christmas)

Monday

The Secular City

HARVEY COX

Presecular man lives in an enchanted forest. Its glens and groves swarm with spirits. Its rocks and streams are alive with friendly or fiendish demons. Reality is charged with a magical power that erupts here and there to threaten or benefit man. Properly managed and utilized, this invisible energy can be supplicated, warded off, or channelled. If real skill and esoteric knowledge are called into play, the energies of the unseen world can be used against a family foe or an enemy of the tribe.

Anthropologists now concede that magic is not simply one aspect of primitive life. It is a world-view. 'Everything is alive', reported a Pit Indian to his scholarly interrogator; 'that's what we Indians believe. White people think everything is dead.' Magic constitutes the style of presecular, tribal man. Furthermore, the bushes and beasts are his brothers. He perceives the world as an inclusive cosmological system in which his own kinship groups extend out to encompass every phenomenon in one way or another. Totemism . . . is a vast network of kinship ties by which the creatures of the natural world are incorporated into the basically familial organization of the tribe.

Many historians of religion believe that this magical world-view, although developed and organized in a very sophisticated way, was never really broken through until the advent of biblical faith. The Sumerian, Egyptian, and Babylonian religious systems, despite their fantastically complicated theologies and their enormously refined symbol systems, remained a form of high magic, relying for their cohesion on the intergal relation between man and the cosmos. Thus the annual flooding of the Nile, the predictable revolution of the stars, and the commanding presence of the sun and moon provided the framework by which the society was held together. Sun gods, river goddesses, and astral deities abounded. History was subsumed under cosmology, society under nature, time under space. Both god and man were part of nature.

This is why the Hebrew view of Creation signals such a marked departure. It separates nature from God and distinguishes man from nature. This is the beginning of the disenchantment process. True, the Hebrews freely borrowed the material of the Creation story from their mythologically oriented neighbours of the ancient Near East. The themes and motifs are in no sense original. But what the Hebrews did with these myths, how they modified them, is the important thing to notice. Whereas in the Babylonian accounts, the sun, moon, and stars are semidivine beings, partaking in the divinity of the gods themselves, their religious status is totally rejected by the Hebrews. In Genesis, the sun and moon become creations of Yahweh, hung in the sky to light the world for man; they are neither gods nor semidivine beings. The stars have no control over man's life. They too are made by Yahweh. None of the heavenly bodies can claim any right to religious awe or worship.

From: *The Secular City* by Harvey Cox

(SCM, 1966, pp. 21–2)

Tuesday

The Secular City

HARVEY COX

The Genesis account of Creation is really a form of 'atheistic propaganda'. It is designed to teach the Hebrews that the magical vision, by which nature is seen as a semidivine force, has no basis in fact. Yahweh, the Creator, whose being is centred outside the natural process, who calls it into existence and names its parts, allows man to perceive nature itself in a matter-of-fact way. It is true, as some modern writers have pointed out, that modern man's attitude toward disenchanted nature has sometimes shown elements of vindictiveness. Like a child suddenly released from parental constraints, he takes savage pride in smashing nature and brutalizing it. This is perhaps a kind of revenge pressed by a former prisoner against his captor, but it is essentially childish and is unquestionably a passing phase. The mature secular man neither reverences nor ravages nature. His task is to tend it and make use of it, to assume the responsibility assigned to The Man, Adam.

Nor is man tied to nature by kinship ties. The lines of kinship in the Bible are temporal, not spatial. Instead of reaching out to encompass kangaroos and totem shrubs, they reach back to the sagas of the fathers and forward to the fortunes of the children's children. The structure of Hebrew kinship is linear; it is historical, not cosmological. The Bible, with one or two quaint exceptions (Eve's serpent and Balaam's ass), is devoid of the animal fables which abound in the legends and myths of magical peoples. Just after his creation man is given the crucial responsibility of naming the animals. He is their master and commander. It is his task to subdue the earth. Nature is neither his brother nor his god. As such it offers him no salvation. When he looks up to the hills, Hebrew man turns from them and asks where he can gain strength. The answer is: Not from the hills, but from Yahweh, who *made* heaven and earth. For the Bible, neither man nor God is defined by his relationship to nature. This not only frees both of them for history, it also makes nature itself available for man's use.

From: *The Secular City* by Harvey Cox

(SCM, 1966, p. 23)

Wednesday

The Secular City

HARVEY COX

Max Weber has called this freeing of nature from its religious overtones 'disenchantment'. The word is intended to connote not disillusionment but matter-of-factness. Man becomes in effect a subject facing nature. He can still enjoy it and delight in it, perhaps even more so since its terrors have been reduced for him. But man is not a mere expression of nature, and nature is not a divine entity.

This disenchantment of the natural world provides an absolute precondition for the development of natural science. Since we have already shown that technopolis, today's technical city, would not have been possible without modern science, disenchantment is also an essential precondition for modern urbanization. Science is basically a point of view. However highly developed a culture's powers of observation, however refined its equipment for measuring, no real scientific breakthrough is possible until man can face the natural world unafraid. Wherever nature is perceived as an extension of himself or his group, or as the embodiment of the divine, science as we know it is precluded. This is evident in Assyrian culture, where an uncanny accuracy in astronomical observation developed, but in which the heavenly bodies were still experienced as the determinants of human destiny; hence no real scientific astronomy emerged.

It remains true in so-called underdeveloped cultures today that the mere introduction of modern technological devices and procedures will never suffice to produce a scientific culture. Somehow nature must be disenchanted, which means the destruction of many traditional religions. This destruction took place in the past century mainly under the auspices of Christian missions. More recently it occurred as a result of the spread of communist ideology. In this instance, Christianity and communism, despite their differences, played nearly identical roles in the removal of traditional religious restraints to scientific and technological change. Both are historically oriented ways of perceiving natural reality. Both exorcize the magical demons and open nature for science. More recently still, less precise socialistic ideologies of a vague planned welfare state have had the same influence. The disenchantment of nature is one of the essential components of secularization.

From: *The Secular City* by Harvey Cox

(SCM, 1966, p. 23–4)

Thursday

Dogma and the Universe

C. S. LEWIS

In popular thought . . . the origin of the universe has counted (I think) for less than its character – its immense size and its apparent indifference, if not hostility, to human life. And very often this impresses people all the more because it is supposed to be a modern discovery – an excellent example of those things which our ancestors did not know and which, if they had known them, would have prevented the very beginnings of Christianity. Here there is a simple historical falsehood. Ptolemy knew just as well as Eddington that the earth was infinitesimal in comparison with the whole content of space. There is no question here of knowledge having grown until the frame of archaic thought is no longer able to contain it. The real question is why the spatial insignificance of the earth, after being known for centuries, should suddenly in the last century have become an argument against Christianity. I do not know why this has happened; but I am sure it does not mark an increased clarity of thought, for the argument from size is, in my opinion, very feeble.

When the doctor at a post-mortem diagnoses poison, pointing to the state of the dead man's organs, his argument is rational because he has a clear idea of that opposite state in which the organs would have been found if no poison were present. In the same way, if we use the vastness of space and the smallness of earth to disprove the existence of God, we ought to have a clear idea of the sort of universe we should expect if God did exist. But have we? Whatever space may be in itself – and, of course, some moderns think it finite – we certainly perceive it as three-dimensional, and to three-dimensional space we can conceive no boundaries. By the very forms of our perceptions, therefore, we must feel as if we lived somewhere in infinite space. If we discovered no objects in this infinite space except those which are of use to man (our own sun and moon), then this vast emptiness would certainly be used as a strong argument against the existence of God. If we discover other bodies, they must be habitable or uninhabitable: and the odd thing is that both these hypotheses are used as grounds for rejecting Christianity. If the universe is teeming with life, this, we are told, reduces to absurdity the Christian claim – or what is thought to be the Christian claim – that man is unique, and the Christian doctrine that to this one planet God came down and was incarnate for us men and our salvation. If, on the other hand, the earth is really unique, then that proves that life is only an accidental by-product in the universe, and so again disproves our religion. Really, we are hard to please. We treat God as the police treat a man when he is arrested; whatever He does will be used in evidence against Him. I do not think this is due to our wickedness. I suspect there is something in our very mode of thought which makes it inevitable that we should always be baffled by actual existence, *whatever* character actual existence may have. Perhaps a finite and contingent creature – a creature that might not have existed – will always find it hard to acquiesce in the brute fact that it is, here and now, attached to an actual order of things.

From: *Undeceptions* by C. S. Lewis

(Geoffrey Bles, 1971, pp. 18–19)

Friday

Dogma and the Universe

C. S. LEWIS

. . . It is certain that the whole argument from size rests on the assumption that differences of size ought to coincide with differences of value: for unless they do, there is, of course, no reason why the minute earth and the yet smaller human creatures upon it should not be the most important things in a universe that contains the spiral nebulae. Now, is this assumption rational or emotional? I feel, as well as anyone else, the absurdity of supposing that the galaxy could be of less moment in God's eyes than such an atom as a human being. But I notice that I feel no similar absurdity in supposing that a man of five-feet high may be more important than another man who is five-feet three and a half – nor that a man may matter more than a tree, or a brain more than a leg. In other words, the feeling of absurdity arises only if the differences of size are very great. But where a relation is perceived by reason it holds good universally. If size and value had any real connexion, small differences in size would accompany small differences in value as surely as large differences in size accompany large differences in value. But no sane man could suppose that this is so. I don't think the taller man *slightly* more valuable than the shorter one. I don't allow a slight superiority to trees over men, and then neglect it because it is too small to bother about. I perceive, as long as I am dealing with the small differences of size, that they have no connexion with value whatsoever. I therefor conclude that the importance attached to the great differences of size is an affair, not of reason but of emotion – of that peculiar emotion which superiorities in size produce only after a certain point of absolute size has been reached.

We are inveterate poets. When a quantity is very great, we cease to regard it as mere quantity. Our imaginations awake. Instead of mere quantity, we now have a quality – the sublime. Unless this were so, the merely arithmetical greatness of the galaxy would be no more impressive than the figures in a telephone directory. It is thus, in a sense, from ourselves that the material universe derives its power to over-awe us. To a mind which did not share our emotions, and lacked our imaginative energies, the argument from size would be sheerly meaningless. Men look on the starry heavens with reverence: monkeys do not. The silence of the eternal spaces terrified Pascal, but it was the greatness of Pascal that enabled them to do so. When we are frightened by the greatness of the universe, we are (almost literally) frightened by our own shadows: for these light years and billions of centuries are mere arithmetic until the shadow of man, the poet, the maker of myth, falls upon them. I do not say we are wrong to tremble at his shadow; it is a shadow of an image of God. But if ever the vastness of matter threatens to overcross our spirits, one must remember that it is matter spiritualized which does so. To puny man, the great nebula in Andromeda owes in a sense its greatness.

From: *Undeceptions* by C. S. Lewis

(Geoffrey Bles, 1971, pp. 19–20)

Saturday

Dogma and the Universe

C. S. LEWIS

. . . If the world in which we found ourselves were not vast and strange enough to give us Pascal's terror, what poor creatures we should be! Being what we are, rational but also animate, amphibians who start from the world of sense and proceed through myth and metaphor to the world of spirit, I do not see how we could have come to know the greatness of God without that hint furnished by the greatness of the material universe. Once again, what sort of universe do we demand? If it were small enough to be cosy, it would not be big enough to be sublime. If it is large enough for us to stretch our spiritual limbs in, it must be large enough to baffle us. Cramped or terrified, we must, in any conceivable world, be one or the other. I prefer terror. I should be suffocated in a universe that I could see to the end of. Have you never, when walking in a wood, turned back deliberately for fear you should come out at the other side and thus make it ever after in your imagination a mere beggarly strip of trees?

I hope you do not think I am suggesting that God made the spiral nebulae solely or chiefly in order to give me the experience of awe and bewilderment. I have not the faintest idea why He made them; on the whole, I think it would be rather surprising if I had. As far as I understand the matter, Christianity is not wedded to an anthropocentric view of the universe as a whole. The first chapters of Genesis, no doubt, give the story of creation in the form of a folk-tale – a fact recognized as early as the time of St. Jerome – and if you take them alone you might get that impression. But it is not confirmed by the Bible as a whole. There are few places in literature where we are more sternly warned against making man the measure of all things than in the Book of Job: 'Canst thou draw out leviathan with an hook? Will he make a covenant with thee? wilt thou take him for a servant? Shall not one be sat down even at the sight of him?'[1] In St. Paul, the powers of the skies seem usually to be hostile to man. It is, of course, the essence of Christianity that God loves man and for his sake became man and died. But that does not prove that man is the sole end of nature. In the parable, it was the one lost sheep that the shepherd went in search of:[2] it was not the only sheep in the flock, and we are not told that it was the most valuable – save in so far as the most desperately in need has, while the need lasts, a peculiar value in the eyes of Love. The doctrine of the Incarnation would conflict with what we know of this vast universe only if we knew also that there were other rational species in it who had, like us, fallen, and who needed redemption in the same mode, and that they had not been vouchsafed it. But we know none of these things. It may be full of life that needs no redemption. It may be full of life that has been redeemed. It may be full of things quite other than life which satisfy the Divine Wisdom in fashions one cannot conceive. We are in no position to draw up maps of God's psychology, and prescribe limits to His interests. We would not do so even for a man whom we knew to be greater than ourselves. The doctrines that God is Love and that He delights in men, are positive doctrines, not limiting doctrines. He is not less than this. What more He may be, we do not know; we know only that He must be more than we can conceive. It is to be expected that His creation should be, in the main, unintelligible to us.

From: *Undeceptions* by C. S. Lewis

(Geoffrey Bles, 1971, pp. 20–1)

---

[1] Job 41:4, 9.
[2] Matthew 18:12; Luke 15:4.

Monday

He Came Down from Heaven

CHARLES WILLIAMS

The Church has never defined the nature of the aboriginal catastrophe [of the Fall] the tale of which it accepts. It has traditionally rather accepted the view that this catastrophe was the second of its kind, the first having occurred in the 'heavens' themselves, and among those creatures whom we call angels. Our own awareness of this explanation is generally referred to the genius of Milton, who certainly shaped it for us in great poetry and made use of it to express his own tender knowledge of the infinite capacity of man's spirit for foolish defiance of the God. But long before Milton the strange tale recedes, and long before Milton the prayers of Christendom implore aid against the malignity of fallen spirits. The popularity of the legend has perhaps been assisted by the excuse it has seemed to offer for mankind, by the pseudo-answer it has appeared to offer to the difficulty of the philosophical imagination concerning a revolt in the good against the good, and by its provision of a figure or figures against whom men can, on the highest principles, launch their capacities of indignant hate and romantic fear. The devil, even if he is a fact, has been an indulgence; he has, on occasion, been encouraged to reintroduce into Christian emotions the dualism which the Christian intellect has denied, and we have relieved our own sense of moral submission by contemplating, even disapprovingly, something which was neither moral nor submissive. An 'inferiority complex', in the slang of our day, is not the same thing as humility; the devil has often been the figure of the first, a reverse from the second, and the frontier between the two. While he exists there is always something to which we can be superior.

Of all this, however, the book of Genesis knows nothing (unless, indeed, in the sentence about the mist). The myth of the Fall there is formally limited to the Adam, and to the creature 'of the field', an immense subtlety twining into speech. There is not much difference apparently between the Adam and the beasts, except that he (or they) control them. There is nothing about intellectual power; in fact, so far as their activities in Genesis are concerned, the intelligence of the Adam is limited to preserving their lives by obtaining food, by a capacity for agriculture, and by a clear moral sense, though behind these things lies the final incantation of the creation: 'Let us make man in Our image, after Our likeness', and the decision upon that, as upon the earliest rift of light: 'Behold, it was very good.'

From: *He Came Down from Heaven* by Charles Williams

(Heinemann, 1938, pp. 15–16)

Tuesday

He Came Down from Heaven

CHARLES WILLIAMS

The nature of the Fall – both while possible and when actual – is clearly defined. The 'fruit of the tree' is to bring an increase of knowledge. That increase, however, is, and is desired as being, of a particular kind. It is not merely to know more, but to know in another method. It is primarily the advance (if it can be so called) from knowing good to knowing good and evil; it is (secondarily) the knowing 'as gods'. A certain knowledge was, by its nature, confined to divine beings. Its communication to man would be, by its nature, disastrous to man. The Adam had been created and were existing in a state of knowledge of good and nothing but good. They knew that there was some kind of alternative, and they knew that the rejection of the alternative was part of their relation to the Omnipotence that created them. That relation was part of the good they enjoyed. But they knew also that the knowledge in the Omnipotence was greater than their own; they understood that in some way it knew 'evil'.

It was, in future ages, declared by Aquinas that it was of the nature of God to know all possibilities, and to determine which possibility should become fact. 'God would not know good things perfectly, unless he also knew evil things. . . .' It is therefore part of that knowledge that he should understand good in its deprivation, the identity of heaven in its opposite identity of hell, but without 'approbation', without calling it into being at all.

It was not so possible for man, and the myth is the tale of that impossibility. However solemn and intellectual the exposition of the act sounds, the act itself is simple enough. It is easy for us now, after the terrible and prolonged habit of mankind; it was not, perhaps, very different then – as easy as picking a fruit from a tree. It was merely to wish to know an antagonism in the good, to find out what the good would be like if a contradiction were introduced into it. Man desired to know schism in the universe. It was a knowledge reserved to God; man had been warned that he could not bear it – 'in the day that thou eatest thereof thou shalt surely die'. A serpentine subtlety overwhelmed that statement with a grander promise – 'Ye shall be as gods, knowing good and evil.' Unfortunately to be as gods meant, for the Adam, to die, for to know evil, for them, was to know it not by pure intelligence but by experience. It was, precisely, to experience the opposite of good, that is the deprivation of the good, the slow destruction of the good, and of themselves with the good.

From: *He Came Down From Heaven* by Charles Williams

(Heinemann, 1938, pp. 16–18)

Wednesday

The Theology of Auschwitz

ULRICH E. SIMON

Theology is the science of divine reality, Auschwitz (Oswiecim) is a place in Poland where millions of human beings were killed between 1942 and 1945. This *Konzentrationslager* occupied about fifteen square miles and consisted of three main and thirty-nine subsidiary camps. The first prisoner arrived on July 14th, 1940. The camp was evacuated and for the most part destroyed by January 27th, 1945, before Russian troops liberated what was left of it. There were only 40,000 registered prisoners among the millions who perished there without leaving a name.

At first sight Theology and Auschwitz have nothing in common. The former articulates a joyful tradition, the latter evokes the memory of untold suffering. Theology speaks of eternal light, Auschwitz perpetuates the horror of darkness. Nevertheless, as light and darkness are complementary in our experience, and as the Glory and the shame must be apprehended together, so the momentous outrage of Auschwitz cannot be allowed to stand, as it has done, in an isolation such as the leprous outcast used to inspire in the past. 'The evils that men do live after them'; unless they are understood they may recur.

Such an understanding meets with endless obstacles. It is easy enough to present the documentation of what happened in Auschwitz between 1942 and 1945. The facts, which will only briefly figure here, are available to all who care to open the files. The lawyers have put us in their debt by enabling us to see the scene of unprecedented crime in as unemotional light as possible. The pictures of the tormented, the dying, and the dead, as well as of the death factories, have become the exhibits in the many trials which have been held to bring guilty men to justice. The subject has thus been frozen with the unemotional air of the dispassionate procedure of justice. These cases were listed, heard, and concluded under criminal law. . . .

The theologian's enquiry goes beyond the terms of criminal investigation and the sifting of evidence. Unlike the court he is not satisfied by the elucidation of the facts. He must ask the great 'Why?', rather than be content to know how and when certain crimes were perpetrated. He extends the 'Why?' to the root of the historical drama and to the actors in it. He will compare and contrast his findings with the declared Christian doctrines. How does Auschwitz stand in the light of the Fatherhood of God, the Person and Work of Christ, and the Coming of the Holy Ghost? These norms of Christian theology govern our enquiry and rule out an untidy or hysterical survey. They exclude a morbid fascination with facts which the human eye finds too repuslive to see and which the mind cannot fathom. . . .

Auschwitz belongs to the past, thank God. But its multi-dimensional range of evil extends to the present and throws its shadow over the future. It is for our purpose the comprehensive and realistic symbol of the greatest possible evil which still threatens mankind. A theology of Auschwitz is, therefore, an attempt to interpret this evil responsibly for the present.

From: *A Theology of Auschwitz* by Ulrich E. Simon

(Gollancz, 1967, pp. 9–12)

The Theology of Auschwitz

ULRICH E. SIMON

The experience of political evil is the very stuff of Christian theology. The story of what Austin Farrar calls 'Love Almighty and Ills Unlimited', comes to man through the reading of history, first of Israel and then of Christ and his Church. The Babylonian Exile, the spoliation of the Temple, the Crucifixion, the Fall of Jerusalem, are links on the continuous chain of events which, despite, or because of, its catastrophic import, grants us the insight into God's dealings with man which nature and speculation cannot supply.

Auschwitz must, therefore, be seen against the canvas of tradition, even if, as we maintain, a new element of evil will have to be comprehended. Auschwitz can be seen to recapitulate the impressive array of all the ills as they were known to Christian theology before 1942. The hostility of the forces of nature, such as heat and cold, drought and rain, wind and snow; the rule of accident and chance, as manifested in the grotesque 'order' of the camp; the war between man and other life, such as dogs and insects; the alienation between groups, classes, nations, races, generations – all these and more destructive forces, open or hidden, general or particular, contributed to the climax of lawlessness of which pain, agony, death, decomposition, and cremation may be cited as the apex of an incontestable logic of evil.

Auschwitz gives a new note to this tradition by removing from it every vestige of theory. In general our natural reaction to pain succeeds in reducing the ache to manageable proportions. We seek to be spectators without being involved in loss. We know that until it happens to be my pain, or it is 'my son Absalom' whose death I lament, we can erect castles in the air against the reality of suffering. Remote plagues, earthquakes, explosions, or wrecked ships do not touch our existential core. But this disaster, once grasped in its immensity, tolls the bell for the whole world. Its impact is that of a personal bereavement, which, as C. S. Lewis showed with a searing insight, spells out the end of theories.

From: *A Theology of Auschwitz* by Ulrich E. Simon

(Gollancz, 1967, pp. 15–16)

B

The Theology of Auschwitz

ULRICH E. SIMON

Now the traditional arguments, which have been put forward in the past to justify God's ways with man, have never given complete, or even a great deal of, satisfaction. These so called theodicies endeavoured to rationalize the irrational. Under the glaring light of a concentration camp they still command respect, if only by pinpointing the nature of the conflict.

We must first pass in review the ancient theory that suffering is the result of sin. It can be supported by a host of texts, is not confined to Christian thinking, but may almost be said to come from any marketplace. It is the slogan of a healthy common-sense: 'as a man sows, so shall he reap'. The formula x sin = x suffering states not only the cause and effect but also the content of sin and suffering in proportionate terms.

Our survey of Auschwitz confirms that a law of cause and effect governs sin and suffering. It must also acknowledge that degrees of suffering exist and that these are related to the degree of evil intended and performed. For example, even in the general greyness of unutterable gloom greater shades of horror must be attributed to certain outrageous institutions, such as the punishment blocks.

On other counts, however, the calculation fails. Here the agent of sin certainly does not suffer for his own sin, except possibly in ways which he would not register as suffering. The prophets in the Old Testament had already seen that the victims suffer for another's sins. The teaching and the example of Christ ruled out a crude rule of thumb by which to measure any man's share in sin by assessing his suffering. The formula x sin = x suffering had to be dismissed even then as an absurd simplification.

The picture which we are forced to look at is highly complex, not only because the victims are clearly not reaping their own, but other men's, rewards, but also because the content of the sin cannot be measured. We can no longer speak conveniently of recognizable deadly sins, since gluttony, covetousness, lust, envy, anger, sloth, and pride – though never far absent – do not explain, or account for, the total indifference or sadistic pleasure which prevailed in the camp.

From: *A Theology of Auschwitz* by Ulrich E. Simon

(Gollancz, 1967, pp. 16–17)

Saturday

The Theology of Auschwitz

ULRICH E. SIMON

The absence of a measurable crime was noted in particular when the war-criminals were tried before the courts. The question at issue could never be, as in ancient laws, that of fixing the amount of guilt so that the accused could make restitution to his victims or their legal heirs. This procedure has in any case become impossible in serious cases. But in dealing with war crimes all punishments seemed irrelevant just because the nature of the evil could not be assessed in a normal manner. Even the sentences that were passed could hardly be regarded as deterrents, let alone as means of restitution, reparation, or satisfaction.

Yet these trials also brought out a positive revaluation of the moral conflict. The court could not arrogate for itself the office of God, or of a Supreme Being, and weigh up the immeasurable proportions of sin and suffering. But the judges gave expression to the commonly felt conviction that, so far as humanly possible, justice cannot remain passive alongside unatoned and unexpiated outrages. Thus the judges stressed on many occasions that human retribution, though wholly inadequate, pertained to the very function of justice, even when face to face with an intrinsically impossible case. Even if the execution of a commander of Auschwitz may not deter future commanders from committing similar atrocities, and brings satisfaction to no one, it shows, if only by articulating the impotence of the law, the imperishable challenge of the moral law and its vindication.

This legal approach never failed to stress that the point of the accusation, and thus of the conflict, concerned not so much the nature of the offence but the degree of responsibility to be attached to the accused. The defence, quite rightly, seized upon this point as vital. The theologian, too, must find in the degrees of freedom a key to the multi-dimensional chaos of evil at Auschwitz. What matters to us – since nothing can now be altered – is who did what to whom, and why, and with what degree of accountability.

This multi-dimensional view helps us to come to closer quarters with the problem of the nature of evil itself. It takes us out of the world of bazaars, where one thing is changed for another (so much sin, so much suffering), and opens to us the vast universe of human relationships. Auschwitz may warn us not to go too far in this respect, for in that infernal world material things matter almost more than relationships, for a piece of bread keeps alive, whereas friendship may not. But even this realistic note reinforces the paramount question: What is evil? Is it a real thing? To what extent is Auschwitz real? Is it not its unreality which is its evil? It is not for nothing that so many prisoners despaired of understanding it and admonished themselves not even to seek a rational explanation.

From: *A Theology of Auschwitz* by Ulrich E. Simon

(Gollancz, 1967, pp. 17–19)

Monday

The Gift of Freedom

KARL BARTH

God's freedom is not merely unlimited possibility or formal majesty and omnipotence, that is to say empty, naked sovereignty. Nor is this true of the God-given freedom of man. If we so misinterpret human freedom, it irreconcilably clashes with divine freedom and becomes the false freedom of sin, reducing man to a prisoner. God Himself, if conceived of as unconditioned power, would be a demon and as such His own prisoner. In the light of His revelation, God is free in word and deed; He is the source and measure of all freedom, insofar as He is the Lord, choosing and determining Himself first of all. In His own freedom, as the source of human freedom, God above all willed and determined Himself to be the Father and the Son in the unity of the Spirit. This is not abstract freedom. Nor is it the freedom of aloof isolation. Likewise, man's God-given freedom is not to be sought and found in any solitary detachment from God. In God's own freedom there is encounter and communion; there is order and, consequently, dominion and subordination; there is majesty and humility, absolute authority and absolute obedience; there is offer and response.

God's freedom is the freedom of the Father and the Son in the unity of the Spirit. Again, man's freedom is a far cry from the self-assertion of one or many solitary individuals. It has nothing to do with division and disorder. God's own freedom is trinitarian, embracing grace, thankfulness, and peace. It is the freedom of the living God. Only in this relational freedom is God sovereign, almighty, the Lord of all.

From: *The Humanity of God* by Karl Barth

(Collins Fontana, 1967, pp. 67–8)

Tuesday

The Gift of Freedom

KARL BARTH

In His free grace, God is for man in every respect; He surrounds man from all sides. He is man's Lord who is before him, above him, after him, and thence also with him in history, the locus of man's existence. Despite man's insignificance, God is with him as his Creator who intended and made mankind to be very good. Despite man's sin, God is with him, the One who was in Jesus Christ reconciling the world, drawing man unto Himself in merciful judgement. Man's evil past is not merely crossed out because of its irrelevancy. Rather, it is in the good care of God. Despite man's life in the flesh, corrupt and ephemeral, God is with him. The victor in Christ is here and now present through His Spirit, man's strength, companion, and comfort. Despite man's death God is with him, meeting him as redeemer and perfecter at the threshold of the future to show him the totality of existence in the true light in which the eyes of God beheld it from the beginning and will behold it evermore. In what He is for man and does for man, God ushers in the history leading to the ultimate salvation of man.

Though in a different way, God is beyond doubt also before, above, after, and with all of His other creatures. However, we may best venture some ideas of this difference in the meaning of God's freedom for these creatures, of the gift of freedom to them. In reality we have no precise knowledge about this. Through His revelation God is known in His loving-kindness to us as the God of *man*. However, God was not and is not bound to choose and to decide Himself for man alone and to show His loving-kindness to him alone. The thought of any insignificant being outside the human cosmos being far more worthy of divine attention than man is deeply edifying and should not be lightly dismissed. But it remains true that God who gave His Son to become and to remain our brother assures us that He willed to love *man*, that He loved us and still loves us and shall love us because He chose and determined Himself to be our God.

From: *The Humanity of God* by Karl Barth

(Collins Fontana, 1967, pp. 69–70)

Wednesday

The Gift of Freedom

KARL BARTH

This freedom of God as it is expressed in His being, word, and deed is the content of the *Gospel*. Receiving this good news from those who witness to it, the Christian *community* in the world is called to acknowledge it in faith, to respond to it in love, to set on it its hope and trust, and to proclaim it to the world which belongs to this free God. It is the privilege and the mission of the Christian community to acknowledge and to confess the Gospel. By acknowledging and confessing Jesus Christ as the creation and revelation of God's freedom, this community is incorporated into the body of Christ and becomes the earthly and historical form of His existence. He is in its midst.

We do well to keep remembering that the existence of the Christian community, through its preaching and its works, is already an expression of man's God-given freedom. Let us therefore respect the difference in perspective! The existence of the Christian community in its faith, love, and hope, and in its proclamation, is unmistakably part of the divinely inaugurated *Heilsgeschichte*.* It is part of it in so far as to acknowledge and confess God's freedom is an act of freedom bestowed upon man in the course of this history. But it is and remains an act of human freedom. The divine freedom was not initiated in and by this act of human freedom. Nor is it accomplished and somehow encompassed in it. Rather, God's freedom is and remains above and beyond human freedom. Measured against the act of divine freedom, the act of human freedom has its own beginning, its own course, and its own preliminary and relative ends. None of these coincide or are to be confounded with those of the *Heilsgeschichte*.* It remains the prerogative of the divine freedom to set the end of this history, the beginning of which it set also.

God's own freedom and its realizations is the source and object of every Christian act of recognition and confession. It is sufficient that this human act takes place in the context of the freedom of God to which it bears witness. Yahweh lives and will live in solidarity, but not in identity, with Israel. The same holds true for Jesus Christ, the word and deed of God, with regard to His community, to the task it

* history of salvation

has to perform in response to the gift of freedom, and to its *kerygma*. The head does not become the body and the body does not become the head. The king does not become his own messenger, and the messenger does not become king. It is sufficient that the community be called into being, be created, protected, and sustained by Jesus Christ, and that it may confess Him who came into the world, is present now, and shall come in glory. It may confess Him who was, is, and shall be the word and deed of God's freedom and of His all-embracing loving-kindness.

From: *The Humanity of God* by Karl Barth

(Collins Fontana, 1967, pp. 70–1)

Thursday

The Gift of Freedom

KARL BARTH

As a gift of God, human freedom cannot contradict divine freedom. This leads to certain limitations regarding human freedom which are similar to those mentioned in our earlier attempts to define the freedom of God. We now make bold to say:

(1) Human freedom as a gift of God does not allow for any vague choices between various possibilities. The reign of chance and ambiguity is excluded. For the free God Himself, the giver of man's freedom, is no blind accident, no tyrant. He is the Lord, choosing and determining Himself unmistakably once and for all. He is His own law.

(2) Human freedom is not realized in the solitary detachment of an individual in isolation from his fellow men. God is . . . *for Himself*, but He is . . . *for us*. For us! It is true that He who gave man freedom because He is man's friend, is also . . . *for me*. But I am not Man, I am only *a man*, and I am a man only in relation to my fellow men. Only in encounter and in communion with them may I receive the gift of freedom. God is *for me* because He is *for us*.

(3) Human freedom is only secondarily freedom *from* limitations and threats. Primarily it is freedom *for*.

(4) Human freedom is not to be understood as freedom to assert, to preserve, to justify and save oneself. God is primarily free *for*; the Father is free for the Son, the Son for the Father in the unity of the Spirit. The one God is free for man as his Creator, as the Lord of the

covenant, as the beginner and perfecter of his history, his *Heilsge-schichte*. God says 'Yes'. Only once this 'Yes' is said, He also says 'No'. Thereby He reveals Himself to be *free from* all that is alien and hostile to His nature. Only once this 'Yes' is said, is He free for Himself and for His own glory. Human freedom is freedom only within the limitations of God's own freedom.

From: *The Humanity of God* by Karl Barth

(Collins Fontana, 1967, pp. 74–5)

Friday

The Gift of Freedom

KARL BARTH

Freedom is *being joyful*. Freedom is the great gift, totally unmerited and wondrous beyond understanding. It awakens the receiver to true selfhood and new life. It is a gift from *God*, from the source of all goodness, an ever-new token of His faithfulness and mercy. The gift is unambiguous and cannot fail. Through this gift man who was irretrievably separated and alienated from God is called into discipleship. This is why freedom is joy! Certainly, man does not live up to this freedom. Even worse, he fails in every respect. It is true enough that he does not know any longer the natural freedom which was bestowed upon him in creation; he does not know as yet the ultimate freedom in store for him at the completion of his journey, in the ultimate fulfilment of his existence. It is true enough that man may presently know and enjoy this freedom through the abiding Spirit of the Father and the Son only in spite of sin, flesh, and death; in spite of the world, his earthly anxiety and his worldly nature; and in spite of himself in his persistent temptation. This, however, does not prevent man from being enabled to know and to live out this freedom in incomparable and inexhaustible joy, limited as his own awareness may be. Some may not want any part of it, and at times we all feel this way. But this does not change anything. God's gift is there for all. It is poured out at the beginning of our journey, at its destination, and most certainly also in our present plight. Freedom is waiting here and now to be received and lived out in joy, albeit a joy that is not without travail.

From *The Humanity of God* by Karl Barth

(Collins Fontana, 1967, pp. 75–6)

Saturday

The Gift of Freedom

KARL BARTH

Human freedom is the joy whereby man appropriates for himself God's election. God has elected Himself in His Son to be the God, Lord, Shepherd, Saviour, and Redeemer of mankind. Through His own election, He willed man to be His creature, His partner, and His son, He, the God of the community of men, and we, the community of men, His people! Freedom is the joy whereby man acknowledges and confesses this divine election by willing, deciding, and determining himself to be the echo and mirror of the divine act. Each individual is called to this commitment in the midst of the community of men, not as the first disciple but as a follower in the visible and invisible footsteps of many; not as the only one but together with many known and unknown fellow Christians. He may be accompanied by the comforting help of several or by at least a few. He may be a rather sad member of the rearguard or he may be away ahead of the crowd where he is temporarily alone. He lives for himself, but not only for himself. He is constantly in living relationship to others, as a member of the people of God who appropriates for himself God's election and is responsible for the brothers. Each individual is called by his own name as a member of the people of God. Each one is responsible for his relationship with God and his fellow men. He is free because he chooses, decides, and determines himself to be this person. His freedom is the joy of that obedience which is given to him. This is a daring venture whenever it is undertaken. A venture at one's own risk and peril? Never! It is the venture of responsibility in the presence of the Giver and the fellow receivers of the gift – past, present, and future. It is the venture of obedience whereby man reflects in his own life God's offer and his own response. This is the life of obedience, allowed for by man's freedom: to will himself to be that member of God's household which God willed him to be.

From: *The Humanity of God* by Karl Barth

(Collins Fontana, 1967, pp. 76–7)

Monday

The Fullness of Sacrifice

F. C. N. HICKS

'The origin and rationale of sacrifice are nowhere fully explained'
in the Old Testament. Like other fundamental beliefs and institutions, it is taken for granted. But the beginning illustrates the end,
just as the end often reveals the beginning. There may survive in a
later system traces of what was originally there, or atrophied parts,
which seem to have lost the capacity of being used again, until some
new force revivifies and reinterprets the whole. Further, it is not
always to be expected that with primitive forms, and with survivals
from them, we should find conscious expressions of their meaning.
Robertson Smith pointed out that here, as so often is the case, we
tend to apply our own ideas, or to expect to find them applied, to
circumstances entirely different from those of the age in which we
live. We think more of the inward meaning than of the outward act:
ceremonial only has value to us as interpreted. We go further, 'religious duties being presented to the learner as flowing from the
dogmatic truths he is taught to accept'. That is no doubt true enough
of the modern attitude; I should add only too true. We do, in fact,
tend to damage our own religion by assuming as its foundation
principle the intellectual acceptance of a given intellectual position:
quite unconsciously in most cases, no doubt, but none the less truly,
we try to erect a religion on the basis of a philosophy. And we are
surprised that the religion, in its devotional expression or as a motive
force for character, is all the time cold and lifeless in itself, and has
lost the power of stimulating. It is not infectious. And with this dis-
qualification unrecognized, and indeed misread as an actual advantage, we try to form opinions about earlier and less advanced religions.
The truth often is that where we assume the power to criticize we
ought really to be learners. Ancient religions were crude, barbarous;
from our standpoint, immoral or non-moral; based at the best on a

perilous admixture of the false with the true: but they were religions, and ours may have gained all the advantages which they had not but have lost itself.

From: *The Fullness of Sacrifice* by F. C. N. Hicks

(Macmillan, 1930, pp. 25–6)

Tuesday

The Fullness of Sacrifice

F. C. N. HICKS

We need to remind ourselves, therefore, both of the inevitable difference of standpoint and of our own disadvantages before we can estimate the meaning of ancient religious institutions; and, in the first place, as I have suggested, it is not always right to expect to find meanings for actions such as we instinctively expect. For religion – whatever its form – is a life: a way of living. It rests, not upon abstract definitions, but upon a felt contact between man and God. No one would estimate the goodness of a child by the things which he says about his parents – nor even by the things which he says to them: we observe what he does, and the feelings and dispositions which he shows. So in religion, whether primitive or developed, what matters is what a man is; and what he does shows what he is and what he feels. The earlier we go in human history, the less self-conscious the stage of human development that we are studying, the less shall we expect to find men expressing, or able to express, or even thinking of expressing, the meaning of their acts. And a large part of the value of the study of primitive religion lies in just this, that in the old age, or disillusioned middle life, of human history we can put ourselves to school with its childhood. Because we shall find there crudities and ineptitudes it does not follow that we shall not also find something that we may well recapture for ourselves. The grown-up man has his lessons to learn from the nursery. 'Except ye turn, and become as little children, ye shall in no wise enter into the kingdom of heaven.'

Such considerations as these apply to most of the ancient observances; but there are others that have an especial bearing on the question of the value of survivals such as that of the sacrificial meal. At every point, on a question of survival, we have to bear in mind the contrast of ancient and of modern life. To the duration of traditions and observances such contrasts make all the difference. The habits of modern life destroy memory; not only its hurry, its multiplicity of experiences, its loss of the vacant spaces for quiet thinking, but the instinct for written memoranda in private affairs, and for the making of careful records in public life, all tend to destroy our belief in tradition. No one can fail to recognize this who observes the difference even in our own day between the life of towns and the life of the more or less untouched parts of the country: there tradition still lives, and with an accuracy at which, when it can be unexpectedly tested, we are innocently surprised. And in the East memory and tradition hold a place which no child of a European civilization of yesterday can easily picture for himself. We cannot measure the survival force of Eastern customs and institutions by our Western standards. Our tendency in the West is easily to think that things must be too old to be true. There, in the East, nothing seems too old to be true. Which of these, after all, is the greater or the more damaging superstition?

From: *The Fullness of Sacrifice* by F. C. N. Hicks

(Macmillan, 1930, pp. 26–8)

Wednesday

The Fullness of Sacrifice

F. C. N. HICKS

In all probability the key to the development of sacrifice is the development of society. The primitive Semitic unit according to Robertson Smith is the kin unit of the clan – originally reckoning its descent from the mother and later from the father, just as in some cases the Semitic deities appear to change from the female sex to the male. The bond of unity was the blood which made them of one flesh. And within this unit there were included, certainly the god of the clan, and probably its domestic animals. The evidence for the latter is of various kinds: there are creation legends which represent the creating god as making both men and animals out of a mixture of clay with his own blood: there is the undoubted sacredness of the animals, and their ownership, not by private individuals but by the clan as a whole. With this went the limitations on their killing. The clan-blood might only be shed by the clan (thus the Hebrew method of execution, when an offender had to be separated from the com-

munity, was by stoning, every member taking his part in the act):
and the animals were only killed by a corporate act to which the god
was made a party. Thus sacrifices are, in the first place, acts of fellowship between the god and members of the clan; and – later – are used
for covenants, to create a blood brotherhood with individuals to be
admitted into the clan or with other clans, though this second covenant use may only belong to the time when the original clan-unit
system was breaking down. In every case the blood is life released in
order to be communicated. This connection of blood with life appears
in the case of water: for in a largely waterless country perennial
springs and streams were parts of the divine manifestation due to
divine agency, and the life-giving character of the water was ascribed
in many cases to the blood of the god having mingled with it. Thus
the familiar idea of 'living water' in the Bible has a subconscious
connection from the first with the idea of the community life, both
divine and human, as blood: it is part of the circle of ideas out of
which, from its ultimate beginnings, the later religion grew, with its
characteristic principle of the communication of a single life to the
whole community.

From: *The Fullness of Sacrifice* by F. C. N. Hicks

(Macmillan, 1930, pp. 34–5)

Thursday

The Fullness of Sacrifice

F. C. N. HICKS

The fundamental feature in the sin-and-guilt-offerings is undoubtedly the use of the blood. It is not the death that atones, but
the life.[1] The death is vital to the sacrifice, because it sets free the
blood, which is the life. But the victim is, in a true sense, operative,
not as dead, but as alive 'as it had been slain'.[2]

Once more, in this connection, we meet the limitations of the system. An element of the communion meal remained in the sin-offering
and still more in the peace-offering. But it was severely restricted. In
all sacrifices the blood – the life itself of the divine food – was wholly
forbidden to the Israelites. Here and there, as when on some occa-

---

[1] Lev. 17:11 above.
[2] Not as νεκρόν but ὡς ἐσφαγμένον

sions the priest dipped his finger in the blood or in the putting of the blood on the door-posts at the Passover, there is perhaps an un-acknowledged survival of the unrestricted personal appropriation of the blood of primitive times. But the eating of the flesh alone made that stage of the sacrifice, as communion, almost wholly inoperative. And, in the sin-offerings, even this was restricted, as stated above.

The reason for this is significant. The flesh of the sin-offering is holy. What was eaten by the priests was to be eaten 'in the place of the sanctuary, seeing it is most holy'.[1] The part which was not eaten, or burnt, was to be carried without the camp, and burnt there, but the bearer was to wash his clothes and his person – under the rule for contact with what was holy.[2] It is this principle which makes it clear that the victim does not become sinful by the imposition of the offer-er's hands. On the Day of Atonement two goats are used. One is taken by lot as the sin-offering, and, as we have seen, is holy. It is the other over which the High Priest confesses the sins of the people; and this is the scapegoat which is sent to Azazel in the wilderness, to carry the sins away.[3]

From: *The Fullness of Sacrifice* by F. C. N. Hicks

(Macmillan, 1930, pp. 18–19)

Friday

The Fullness of Sacrifice

F. C. N. HICKS

Just as in the sin-offering the characteristic feature is not the death of the victim but the liberation of its life, so in the burnt-offering the significance lies not in its destruction but in its transformation. It is difficult to over-estimate the harm that has been done to the ordinary ideas about sacrifice by the use in the translations of the Hebrew text for this offering of the words *holokautoma*,[4] holocaust, 'burnt-offering'. These familiar words, interpreted inevitably by the over-whelming later association of burning with the purpose of destruc-tion, suggest exactly the wrong conception of *'óláh*. Provided, how-ever, that the character of the burning is understood, 'burnt-offering',

[1] Lev. 10:17.
[2] Lev. 16:27 f.
[3] Lev. 16:21, 22.
[4] ὁλοκαύτωμα.

and, still more, the comparatively rare term *kālil*[1] translated 'whole burnt-offering', do suggest another important feature, viz. that the whole of the flesh was in this case consumed on the altar. There was nothing left over for a sacrificial meal. The significance of this emerges in the study of the historical development of the various sacrifices.

The significance of the peace-offering lies in the fact that it is a meal. Its various forms were the votive offering, the free-will offering and the thank-offering . . . There can be little doubt that as it is the oldest of the Hebrew sacrifices, so it carried with it, at least in its history, the tradition of an original purpose of communion with the deity. How far, if at all, the idea of communion remained explicit in the later period will be considered later. What does remain is the fact that it is inseparably bound up with the idea of praise[2] and thanksgiving. In fact, in Philo and in Aquila the word *eucharist*[2] is frequently used to describe it. Whatever it had lost, it preserved and emphasized the old spirit of joyfulness in the worship of God in contrast to the more sombre feelings of penitence and guilt which belonged to the piacular sacrifices, and the thought of fear, of securing the Divine favour, and of self-surrender, in the burnt-offering.

From: *The Fullness of Sacrifice* by F. C. N. Hicks

(Macmillan, 1930, pp. 19–20)

Saturday

The Fullness of Sacrifice

F. C. N. HICKS

. . . The classical case of a covenant, with express information about its ratification, is that of the covenant at Sinai. Here[3] the account is precise. The blood is sprinkled – the regular technical term for the use of the blood in sacrifice – spirted – upon the altar and upon the people. Moses offers burnt-offerings and peace-offerings: 'and they beheld God, and did eat and drink'.

The Passover, again, in some of its features a sacrifice of a primitive type, is essentially a sacrificial meal. And its primary purpose is to

[1] Dt. 33:10; Ps. 51:19.
[2] εὐχαριστία.
[3] Ex. 24:1-11.

commemorate the deliverance from Egypt, the beginning in history
of the covenant relationship between God and His people.

One further point should be mentioned. In all the sacrifices there
is one constant element. The animals to be offered were limited to the
domestic – those which shared man's life, and into the tending of
which he put his work. Similarly there were no wild products of the
earth in the non-animal offerings. Here again they must be something into which man's own life had passed – in the form, at least, to
which he had contributed by his labour. There is, therefore, in every
offering an ethical element. So David says to Araunah:[1] 'neither will
I offer burnt-offerings unto the Lord my God which cost me nothing'.
Cost is the essential of sacrifice; and with all the failures of the Old
Testament system, alike by historical precedent and by sacrificial
rule, there was a sense in which man, in offering, offered himself.

From: *The Fullness of Sacrifice* by F. C. N. Hicks

(Macmillan, 1930, p. 24)

[1] 2 Sam. 24:24.

TRINITY 27
SUNDAY NEXT BEFORE ADVENT

Monday

The Messianic Hope – The Son of David

A. G. HEBERT

It is in the first Isaiah that the figure of a personal Messiah, a King of David's line, is clearly sketched out, in two or three prophecies which had a decisive influence on the whole subsequent development. . . .

It is not difficult to see why the name of David . . . comes in. It was not merely that politically the reigns of David and Solomon formed the high-water mark of Israel's prosperity, as the time when the whole nation was unified and had one King, and exercised a suzerainty over the Syrian tribes to the north as far as the Euphrates, and over Moab and Edom to the south, controlling the export of ores from Ezion-geber and the corresponding imports that made Solomon rich. More important than these political and economic considerations was the thought that now at last Yahweh had accomplished that for which He had redeemed Israel out of Egypt four centuries earlier, and brought them into the Promised Land. There had not failed one word of all His good promise.

But was it really so? From that time onwards nothing seems to go right. Solomon's reign is followed by the schism, the result of his tyrannical rule. It is not long before the suzerainty over the tribes to north and south disappears; Moab[1] and Edom[2] regain their independence, and soon Ahab is fighting to keep hold on the last remains of Israel's own territory to the east of Jordan. There is a temporary revival under Jeroboam II; but soon Assyrian aggression brings not merely loss but disaster and captivity. Samaria goes into exile, and a similar fate hangs over Jerusalem.

What was God doing? For what had He brought them out of Egypt? . . .

[1] 2 Kings:3.
[2] 2 Kings:8, 20.

> Why hast thou then broken down her hedge,
> That all they that go by pluck off her grapes?[1]

They look back to the reign of David as the ideal time, and they long
– how they long! – for it to return. Why does it not? The answer of
the eighth-century prophets is that they are being punished for their
sins: sins of the paganizing of the worship of Yahweh in the high-
places, or going after the Canaanite Baals and the Tyrian Astarte,
and of darker superstitions still under the terrible strain of the war of
nerves; sins, too, of oppression of the poor, especially since the increased use of currency had put the small farmer in the power of the
landowners. It is in these circumstances that Isaiah promises that the
Reign of David shall indeed return. There must be judgment first, a
terrible chastisement, which only a Remnant will survive. But when
Yahweh has performed His whole work upon Mount Zion and upon
Jerusalem,[2] it is His Purpose to send a Davidic King, who shall rule
in righteousness: . . .

A Prince shall be born, whose name shall be Immanuel,[3] and:

> 'Wonderful, Counsellor,
> Mighty God, Everlasting Father, Prince of Peace:
> Of the increase of his government and of peace there shall be no
>   end,
> Upon the Throne of David, and upon his Kingdom,
> To establish it and to uphold it,
> With judgment and with righteousness,
> From henceforth even for ever.'[4]

From: *The Throne of David* by A. G. Hebert

(Faber & Faber, 1941, pp. 39–43)

---

[1] Psalm 80:4 ff.
[2] Isaiah 10:12.
[3] Isaiah 9:6-7.
[4] Isaiah 7:14.

Tuesday

The Messianic Hope – Paradise Restored

A. G. HEBERT

'With righteousness shall he judge the poor,
And reprove with equity for the meek of the earth; . . .'

But the marvel of these prophecies of Isaiah is that he combines these promises of a redemption of politics with imagery drawn from older sources. The passage which we have been quoting continues:

'And the wolf shall dwell with the lamb,
And the leopard shall lie down with the kid,
And the calf and the young lion and the fatling together;
And a little child shall lead them . . .
They shall not hurt nor destroy in all my holy Mountain.
For the earth shall be full of the knowledge of the Lord,
As the waters cover the sea.'[1]

This is the Garden of Eden, where according to Genesis the animals came to Adam and received their names. There is, however, no sign that Isaiah is referring to the story as told in Genesis; we seem rather to be in touch with the same popular folklore which underlies the Genesis-story. Oesterley, in his book *The Evolution of the Messianic Idea*, shows how this folklore is the common property of many nations, who have had dreams of a Golden Age in the past when men lived with the gods in happiness, peace and plenty, free from the fear of wild animals, enjoying universal peace, and a supernatural fertility of the soil; frequently too there is the thought of a *Heilbringer*, a divine Friend and Helper of man. The greatness of Isaiah is not only that he can clothe these thoughts with the most wonderful poetical imagery, but that he can combine this vision of Paradise Restored with that of a transformed Jerusalem. He speaks no longer of a Garden but of a City. The gifts of civilization are all to be brought into the Messianic Reign of God. He is not indulging in phantasies, but envisaging the redemption of the city life which he knows. The combination of these two sides makes this the first glimpse of *Urbs coelestis Jerusalem*. . . .

The idea of an earth transformed so that it becomes supernaturally

[1] Isaiah 11:6, 9.

fruitful, water being poured on the dry ground, the wilderness becoming fertile, mountains levelled and valleys lifted up, occurs in many places through the whole period of the Old Testament, and down to the Rabbinic period: till at last we reach the extravagant picture of vines with 10,000 shoots, each with 10,000 branches, each with 10,000 twigs, each with 10,000 clusters, each with 10,000 grapes, which would appear in the Messianic Age.

A typical prophetic expression of the idea of a transformed earth, where the Messiah, if he were mentioned (but he is not) would be the *Heilbringer* of the ancient myths, is Isaiah 35:

> 'The wilderness and the parched land shall be glad;
> And the desert shall rejoice, and blossom as the rose.'

There will be supernatural healing also for men:

> 'Then shall the eyes of the blind be opened,
> And the ears of the deaf shall be unstopped;
> Then shall the lame man leap as a hart,
> And the tongue of the dumb shall sing . . .'[1]

Our Lord is almost quoting this passage when He replies to the messengers sent from John the Baptist, that they are to go and tell him how

> 'The blind receive their sight,
> And the lame walk
> The lepers are cleansed,
> The deaf hear,
> And the dead are raised up,
> And the poor have Good Tidings preached to them.'[2]

From: *The Throne of David* by A. G. Hebert

(Faber & Faber, 1941, 44–7)

Wednesday

The Messianic Hope – The Remnant

A. G. HEBERT

It was the work of the eighth-century prophets to bring to Israel conviction of sin. The lesson was learnt, and has never been forgotten; at the same time it is one of those lessons that the People

[1] Isaiah 35:5 ff.   [2] Matthew 11:5,

and each individual have continually to learn, over and over again.

Amos was sent to castigate a nation that was delighting in shallow hopes of a Golden Age when Yahweh would come to inaugurate for His People a Golden Age of material well-being:

> 'Woe unto you that desire the Day of the LORD!
> Wherefore would ye have the Day of the LORD?
> It is darkness, and not light.'[1]

How much will be left after the judgment? His answer is that as good as nothing will remain; 'as when a shepherd rescues from a lion two legs, or a piece of an ear'.[2] No word of consolation has been given to Amos to say.

But Isaiah looks for a radical purging:

> 'I will turn my hand upon thee,
> And thoroughly purge away thy dross
> And will take away all thy alloy:
> And I will restore thy judges as at the first,
> And thy counsellors as at the beginning.'[3] . . .

The purging is to be very radical; it will be

> 'As a terebinth, and as an oak,
> Whose stock remaineth, when they are felled.'[4]

But from the stump a living growth would yet spring:

> 'There shall come a shoot out of the stock of Jesse,
> And a branch out of his roots shall bear fruit.'[5]

This doctrine of the Remnant was so central to Isaiah's thought that he called his son Shear-jashub;[6] and it has ever since remained as a permanent element in the idea of the Church. It was Jeremiah's mission to watch over the Remnant in the hour of its passion. Ezekiel pushed the idea so far as to believe that every righteous person would survive the fall of the city; thus in the symbolical account which he gives of the capture of the city, the Man with the writer's inkhorn by his side is told to go through the city and put a mark on the foreheads of all who sigh and cry for the abominations done in it; when the slaughter begins, none of these may be touched.[7]

[1] Amos 6:18.
[2] Amos 3:12.
[3] Isaiah 1:25–6.
[4] Isaiah 6:13.
[5] Isaiah 11:1.
[6] Isaiah 7:3; 10:20–2.   [7] Ezekiel 9:2–6.

The idea of the Remnant comes again in the 'poor' of whom the Psalms so often speak; 'the faithful and God-fearing' Israelites, who held together and formed an *ecclesiola in ecclesia*, as opposed to the worldly and indifferent, often also paganizing and persecuting, majority.

It comes again in the great 'Son of Man' prophecy in Daniel. There appear four beast-figures, symbolizing four militaristic empires, the last of which is the Syrian kingdom of Antiochus Epiphanes, who set himself to exterminate the faith of Israel and establish everywhere a cosmopolitan Hellenism; and then the Son of Man, a human figure, which is interpreted as signifying the 'kingdom of the saints of the Most High'. These are the Remnant; to them Daniel speaks . . . [and] tells the Remnant of Israel that they will have to suffer for a long time, but yet a limited time; and at the last they will prevail.

All through the story, it is a Remnant who keep the faith alive; seven thousand who have not bowed the knee to Baal in Elijah's day; a Remnant who listen to Isaiah, and the other prophets who come after him; a Remnant who restore the liturgical worship of the Second Temple; a Remnant who endure persecution under Antiochus Epiphanes. And when the Messiah comes, it is a Remnant who believe in Him.

From: *The Throne of David* by A. G. Herbert

(Faber & Faber, 1941, pp. 53–5)

Thursday

The Messianic Hope – The Bride

A. G. HEBERT

The theme of Israel as the Bride of Yahweh starts from the same point as that of the Remnant: God's judgment on sinful Israel.

As Hosea's wife Gomer had been unfaithful to him, so, he came to see, had Israel been unfaithful to Yahweh. Israel then, must be put under penance, stripped of all her fine apparel, the gifts of civilization, and put out again in the wilderness:

'And she shall make answer there,
As in the days of her youth,
And as in the day when she came up out of the land of Egypt.'[1]

[1] Hosea 2:15.

'For the children of Israel shall abide many days without king, and without prince, and without sacrifice, and without pillar, and without ephod or terraphim. Afterward shall the children of Israel return, and seek the Lord their God, and David their king.'[1]

This beautiful image is taken up by Jeremiah, and notably by Ezekiel, who in chapter 16 tells the story of Israel as of a foundling child, whom Yahweh had found in the wilderness; he took her and cared for her, and educated her, and gave her raiment, bracelets, rings, fine flour, honey, and oil:

> 'And thy renown went forth among the nations for thy
> > beauty,
> For it was perfect,
> Through my majesty which I had put upon thee
> Saith the Lord God.'[2]

But she has been unfaithful and committed fornication; now therefore all these good gifts must be taken away, till she repents and returns again.

The latter part of the Book of Isaiah is dominated by the thought of the fulfilment of Yahweh's purpose for Israel, and is thus predominantly Messianic. Here Israel is seen as the Faithful Wife. So in the fiftieth chapter:

> 'Thus saith the Lord,
> Where is the bill of your Mother's divorcement,
> Wherewith I have put her away?'[3]

She had indeed been divorced, 'for your transgressions'. But now she is restored: Zion, once desolate and childless, is seen rejoicing over a multitude of children.

> 'Sing, O barren, thou that didst not bear;
> Break forth into singing, and cry aloud, thou that
> > didst not travail with child:
> For more are the children of the desolate
> Than the children of the married wife,
> > Saith the Lord.[4]

> For thy Maker is thy Husband . . .
> For the Lord hath called thee as a Wife forsaken and
> > grieved in spirit,

[1] Hosea 3:4-5.
[2] Ezekiel 16:14.
[3] Isaiah 50:1.
[4] Isaiah 54:1.

Even a wife of youth, when she is cast off,
    Saith the Lord.'[1]

But now He has had mercy on her. In chapter 61 : 10 she is seen as
a Bride clothed in bridal garments of righteousness; and in chapter
62 : 4–5 her name is to be called Hephzi-bah, 'My delight is in her',
and her land Beulah, 'Married':

'For as a young man marrieth a virgin,
So shall thy Builder marry thee,
And as a bridegroom rejoiceth over the bride,
So shall thy God rejoice over thee.'[2]

Finally she is seen as the Mother:

'Rejoice ye with Jerusalem, and be glad for her,
    All ye that love her:
Rejoice for joy with her,
    All ye that mourn over her:
That ye may suck, and be satisfied with the breasts of her
    consolations.
Ye shall be borne upon the side,
And shall be dandled upon the knees.
As one whom his mother comforteth, so will I comfort you,
And ye shall be comforted in Jerusalem.'[3]

From: *The Throne of David* by A. G. Hebert

(Faber & Faber, 1941, pp. 56–8)

Friday

The Messianic Hope – A New Heart and a New Spirit: The Spirit of Yahweh

A. G. HEBERT

No account of the Messianic Idea either in the Old Testament or
in the New can be other than misleading which confines itself to its
'institutional' aspect and describes simply the outward form which
the Divine redemptive action will take; whether it be the advent of a

[1] Isaiah 54:5–6.
[2] Isaiah 62:5.
[3] Isaiah 66:10–13.

King on David's throne, the establishment of a Remnant here in this world, the restoration of Paradise, or the espousal of the Bride. There must be an inward change, a change in men themselves. This is not fully explicit in Isaiah; with all the mighty power of his call to faith in God, he still thinks of the process of purging as a removal of the dross,[1] an elimination of the unworthy citizens who are 'not written among the living in Jerusalem'.[2] But in Jeremiah it is an inward change that constitutes the essence of the New Covenant which Yahweh will make in place of the Old:

> 'This is the Covenant which I will make with the house of
>   Israel after those days, saith the Lord:
> I will put my law in their inward parts,
> And in their heart will I write it,
>   And I will be their God,
>   And they shall be my People;
> And they shall teach no more every man his neighbour,
>   And every man his brother,
>   Saying, Know the Lord:
> For they shall all know me,
> From the least of them unto the greatest of them,
>   Saith the Lord:
> For I will forgive their iniquity,
> And their sin will I remember no more.'[3]

Other writers go deeper still, and speak of an inward cleansing in terms which give the idea of the *metanoia* of the New Testament:

> 'Create in me a clean heart, O God,
> And renew a right spirit within me;
> Cast me not away from thy presence,
> And take not thy holy Spirit from me.'[4]

Above all, there is the great passage in Ezekiel:

> '. . . For I will take you from among the nations,
> And gather you out of all the countries,
> And will bring you into your own land.
>   And I will sprinkle clean water upon you,
>   And ye shall be clean:
>   From all your filthiness, and from all your idols
>   Will I cleanse you.

[1] Isaiah 1:25.   [2] Isaiah 4:3.
[3] Jeremiah 31:33–6.   [4] Psalm 51:10–11.

A new heart also will I give you,
And a new spirit will I put within you:
And I will take away the stony heart out of your
  flesh,
And I will give you an heart of flesh.
And I will put my Spirit within you,
And cause you to walk in my statutes,
And ye shall keep my judgments, and do them.
And ye shall dwell in the land that I gave to your fathers;
  And ye shall be My People,
  And I will be your God.'[1]

Both the fifty-first psalm and Ezekiel's prophecy put side by side
'a right [steadfast] spirit' or 'a new spirit' in man, and the presence in
man of God's own Spirit. The following chapter of Ezekiel contains
the Vision of the Dry Bones. The bones as of the slain on a battlefield, symbolize the house of Israel, defeated, dispirited, scattered and
hopeless; but as in the vision the bones are seen to come together,
and to become covered again with flesh, and then animated by the
'breath', the 'wind', the 'spirit' of life, so Yahweh will raise the
People to life again:

'And I will put my Spirit within you,
  And ye shall live,
And I will place you in your own land;
And ye shall know that I the Lord have spoken it, and
  performed it,
      Saith the Lord.'[2]

From: *The Throne of David* by A. G. Hebert

(Faber & Faber, 1941)

Saturday

The Messianic Hope–The Servant of Yahweh

A. G. HEBERT

. . . If we take a wider view of the Messianic Hope, and view it
theologically, as the prophet's vision of the manner in which Yahweh
would complete His Purpose which He had begun, then we cannot

[1] Ezekiel 36:23–8.
[2] Ezekiel 37:14.

fail to include within it the picture of the Servant. In these songs the poet is expressing in a concrete form what Jeremiah and Ezekiel had said in more abstract language in their prophecies of the New Covenant and the New Spirit. And if it is the great contribution of these two prophets to the Messianic Hope, that they think not merely of what God will do *for* His People, but of the change that He will bring to pass *in* them, then there is nothing in the Old Testament so deeply Messianic as the picture given in these four poems of what St. Paul calls the New Man . . .

The Mission of Israel to the Gentiles is mentioned in two, or perhaps three, of the four poems: the Servant is to bring forth judgment to the Gentiles,[1] to be set for a light to the Gentiles,[2] to 'sprinkle', or 'startle', many nations.[3] Only when Israel truly is the Lord's Servant will it be able to accomplish the humanly impossible duty, which He has nevertheless laid on it, of bringing the nations in.

The Servant is also shown as the Sufferer and Martyr;[4] bruised for our iniquities, say the People: Yahweh hath laid on him the iniquity of us all; he has borne the sin of many; his life has been given as a sacrifice for sin; and his martyrdom leads through to victory and peace. With these two Songs go two Psalms which translate the same theme into the form of supplication and thanksgiving: 'My God, my God, look upon me, why hast thou forsaken me?'[5] and 'Save me, O God, for the waters are come in, even unto my soul'.[6]

These poems were not reckoned by the Jews as Messianic. No one dared to think of the Messiah as suffering and dying, till He Himself did so. It is He who broadens out the Messianic Idea, till it is seen to gather up in itself all Old Testament theology. When we view it so, we must bring into it not only the sufferings thus ascribed to the Servant, but those which were actually endured by 'prophets, wise men and scribes',[7] by the long line of servants sent by the Lord of the Vineyard to claim the fruits that were due,[8] in whom our Lord sees the principle of victory-through-suffering which finds its supreme exemplification in His own passion. Again, among the nations of the world Israel is the martyr-nation, from the Exile onwards; there were spiritual lessons which it was called upon to learn, with the loss of

[1] Psalm 42:1.
[2] Psalm 49:6.
[3] Isaiah 52:15.
[4] Isaiah 50:4–9; 52:13–Ch. 53.
[5] Psalm 22.
[6] Psalm 69.
[7] Matt. 23:34, Luke 11:49.
[8] Mark 12:1–5.

the temporal power. There is the echo of the passion of Israel in the literature; in the long endurance of saint Jeremiah; in the Book of Job; in the many psalms 'of complaint' in which an afflicted People (the 'Poor') cries to God for help; above all, in the Servant-poems. Yet again, we can think, how the action of the Sacrifices, with their costliness to the worshipper, with their ritual of blood-shedding and death, pointed the same way, and indicated that suffering must at last have a redemptive meaning; but of this the Old Testament gives scarcely a hint, and there is little more than that one verse[1] where it is said that the Servant's life is made an offering for sin.

In the wide and true sense, all these things that we have mentioned are Messianic. But their Messianic significance could not come to light till it was interpreted by the creative wisdom of Him who in 'fulfilling' it all, gathered it all into one, at the central point in the history of the world.

From: *The Throne of David* by A. G. Hebert

(Faber & Faber, 1941, pp. 68–70)

---

[1] Isaiah 53:10.

ADVENT 1

Monday

The Eternal Now

PAUL TILLICH

It is our destiny and the destiny of everything in our world that we must come to an end. Every end that we experience in nature and mankind speaks to us with a loud voice: you also will come to an end! It may reveal itself in the farewell to a place where we have lived for a long time, the separation from the fellowship of intimate associates, the death of someone near to us. Or it may become apparent to us in the failure of a work that gave meaning to us, the end of a whole period of life, the approach of old age, or even in the melancholy side of nature visible in autumn. All this tells us: you will also come to an end.

Whenever we are shaken by this voice reminding us of our end, we ask anxiously – what does it mean that we have a beginning and an end, that we come from the darkness of the 'not yet' and rush ahead towards the darkness of the 'no more'? When Augustine asked this question, he began his attempt to answer it with a prayer. And it is right to do so, because praying means elevating oneself to the eternal. In fact, there is no other way of judging time than to see it in the light of the eternal. In order to judge something, one must be partly within it, partly out of it. If we were totally within time, we would not be able to elevate ourselves in prayer, meditation and thought, to the eternal. We would be children of time like all other creatures and could not ask the question of the meaning of time. But as men we are aware of the eternal to which we belong and from which we are estranged by the bondage of time.

From: *The Eternal Now* by Paul Tillich

(SCM, 1963, pp. 103–4)

Tuesday

The Eternal Now

PAUL TILLICH

We speak of time in three ways or modes – the past, present and future. Every child is aware of them, but no wise man has ever penetrated their mystery. We become aware of them when we hear a voice telling us: you also will come to an end. It is the future that awakens us to the mystery of time. Time runs from the beginning to the end, but our awareness of time goes in the opposite direction. It starts with the anxious anticipation of the end. In the light of the future we see the past and present. So let us first consider our going into the future and towards the end that is the last point that we can anticipate in our future.

The image of the future produces contrasting feelings in man. The expectation of the future gives one a feeling of joy. It is a great thing to have a future in which one can actualize one's possibilities, in which one can experience the abundance of life, in which one can create something new – be it new work, a new living being, a new way of life, or the regeneration of one's own being. Courageously one goes ahead towards the new, especially in the earlier part of one's life. But this feeling struggles with other ones: the anxiety about what is hidden in the future, the ambiguity of everything it will bring us, the shortness of its duration that decreases with every year of our life and becomes shorter the nearer we come to the unavoidable end. And finally the end itself, with its impenetrable darkness and the threat that one's whole existence in time will be judged as a failure.

How do men, how do *you*, react to this image of the future with its hope and threat and inescapable end? Probably most of us react by looking at the immediate future, anticipating it, working for it, hoping for it, being anxious about it, while cutting off from our awareness the future which is farther away, and above all, by cutting off from our consciousness the end, the last moment of our future. Perhaps we could not live without doing so most of our time. But perhaps we will not be able to die if we *always* do so. And if one is not able to die, is he really able to live?

From: *The Eternal Now* by Paul Tillich

(SCM, 1963, pp. 104–5)

Wednesday

The Eternal Now

PAUL TILLICH

How do we react if we become aware of the inescapable end contained in our future? Are we able to bear it, to take its anxiety into a courage that faces ultimate darkness? Or are we thrown into utter hopelessness? Do we hope against hope, or do we repress our awareness of the end because we cannot stand it? Repressing the consciousness of our end expresses itself in several ways.

Many try to do so by putting the expectation of a long life between now and the end. For them it is decisive that the end be delayed. Even old people who are near the end do this, for they cannot endure the fact that the end will not be delayed much longer.

Many people realize this deception and hope for a continuation of this life after death. They expect an endless future in which they may achieve or possess what has been denied them in this life. This is a prevalent attitude about the future, and also a very simple one. It denies that there *is* an end. It refuses to accept that we are creatures, that we come from the eternal ground of time and return to the eternal ground of time and have received a limited span of time as *our* time. It replaces eternity by endless future.

But endless future is without a final aim; it repeats itself and could well be described as an image of hell. This is not the Christian way of dealing with the end. The Christian message says that the eternal stands above past and future. 'I am the Alpha and the Omega, the beginning and the end.'

The Christian message acknowledges that time runs towards an end, and that we move towards the end of that time which is our time. Many people – but not the Bible – speak loosely of the 'hereafter' or of the 'life after death'. Even in our liturgies eternity is translated by 'world without end'. But the world, by its very nature, is that which comes to an end. If we want to speak in truth without foolish, wishful thinking, we should speak about the eternal that is neither timelessness nor endless time. The mystery of the future is answered in the eternal of which we may speak in images taken from time. But if we forget that the images are images, we fall into absurdities and self-deceptions. There is not time *after* time, but there is eternity *above* time.

From *The Eternal Now* by Paul Tillich

(SCM, 1963, pp. 105–6)

The Eternal Now

PAUL TILLICH

We go towards something that is not yet, and we come from something that is no more. We are what we are by what we came from. We have a beginning as we have an end. There was a time that was not *our* time. We hear of it from those who are older than we; we read about it in history books; we try to envision the unimaginable billions of years in which neither we nor anyone was who could tell us of them. It is hard for us to imagine our 'being-no-more'. It is equally difficult to imagine our 'being-not-yet'. But we usually don't care about our not yet being, about the indefinite time before our birth in which we were not. We think: *now* we are; this is *our* time – and we do not want to lose it. We are not concerned about what lies before our beginning. We ask about life after death, yet seldom do we ask about our being before birth. But is it possible to do one without the other? The fourth gospel does not think so. When it speaks of the eternity of the Christ, it does not only point to his return to eternity, but also his coming *from* eternity. 'Truly, truly, I say to you, before Abraham was, I *am*.' He comes from another dimension than that in which the past lies. Those to whom he speaks misunderstand him because they think of the historical past. They believe that he makes himself hundreds of years old and they rightly take offence at this absurdity. Yet he does not say, 'I *was*' before Abraham; but he says, 'I *am*' before Abraham was. He speaks of his beginning out of eternity. And this is the beginning of everything that is – not the uncounted billions of years but the eternal as the ultimate point in our past.

The mystery of the past from which we come is that it is and is not in every moment of our lives. It is, in so far as we are what the past has made of us. In every cell of our body, in every trait of our face, in every movement of our soul, our past is the present.

Few periods knew more about the continuous working of the past in the present than ours. We know about the influence of childhood experiences on our character. We know about the scars left by events in early years. We have rediscovered what the Greek tragedians and the Jewish prophets knew, that the past is present in us, both as a curse and as a blessing. For 'past' always means both a curse and a

C

blessing, not only for individuals, but also for nations and even continents.

History lives from the past, from its heritage. The glory of the European nations is their long, inexhaustibly rich tradition. But the blessings of this tradition are mixed with curses resulting from early splits into separated nations whose bloody struggles have filled century after century and brought Europe again and again to the edge of self-destruction. Great are the blessings *this* nation has received in the course of its short history. But from earliest days, elements have been at work that have been and will remain a curse for many years to come. I could refer, for instance, to racial consciousness, not only within the nation itself, but also in its dealings with races and nations outside its own boundaries. 'The American way of life' is a blessing that comes from the past; but it is also a curse, threatening the future.

From: *The Eternal Now* by Paul Tillich

(SCM Press, 1963, pp. 106–8)

Friday

The Eternal Now

PAUL TILLICH

In each human life a struggle is going on about the past. Blessings battle with curses. Often we do not recognize what are blessings and what are curses. Today, in the light of the discovery of our unconscious strivings, we are more inclined to see curses than blessings in our past. The remembrance of our parents, which in the Old Testament is so inseparably connected with their blessings, is now much more connected with the curse they have unconsciously and against their will brought upon us. Many of those who suffer under mental afflictions see their past, especially their childhood, only as the source of curses. We know how often this is true. But we should not forget that we would not be able to live and to face the future if there were not blessings that support us and which come from the same source as the curses. A pathetic struggle over their past is going on almost without interruption in many men and women in our time. No medical healing can solve *this* conflict, because no medical healing can change the past. Only a blessing that lives above the conflict of blessing and

curse can heal. It is the blessing that changes what seems to be unchangeable – the past. It cannot change the facts; what has happened has happened and remains so in all eternity! But the *meaning*
of the facts can be changed by the eternal, and the name of this
change is the experience of 'forgiveness'. If the meaning of the past
is changed by forgiveness, its influence on the future is also changed.
The character of curse is taken away from it. It becomes a blessing
by the transforming power of forgiveness.

There are not always blessings and curses in the past. There is also
emptiness in it. We remember experiences that, at the time, were
seemingly filled with an abundant content. Now we remember them,
and their abundance has vanished, their ecstasy is gone, their fullness
has turned into a void. Pleasures, successes, vanities have this
character. We do not feel them as curses; we do not feel them as
blessings. They have been swallowed by the past. They did not con-
tribute to the eternal. Let us ask ourselves how little in our lives
escapes this judgment.

From: *The Eternal Now* by Paul Tillich

(SCM Press, 1963, pp. 109–10)

Saturday

The Eternal Now

PAUL TILLICH

The mystery of the future and the mystery of the past are united
in the mystery of the present. Our time, the time we have, is the time
in which we have 'presence'. But how can we have 'presence'? Is not
the present moment gone when we think of it? Is not the present the
ever-moving boundary line between past and future? But a moving
boundary is not a place to stand upon. If nothing were given to us
except the 'no more' of the past and the 'not yet' of the future, we
would not have anything. We could not speak of the time that is *our*
time; we would not have 'presence'.

The mystery is that we *have* a present; and, even more, that we
have *our* future also because we anticipate it in the present; and that
we have *our* past also, because we remember it in the present. In the
present our future and our past are *ours*. But there is no 'present' if
we think of the never-ending flux of time. The riddle of the present

is the deepest of all the riddles of time. Again, there is no answer except from that which comprises all time and lies beyond it – the eternal. Whenever we say 'now' or 'today', we stop the flux of time for us. We accept the present and do not care that it is gone in the moment that we accept it. We live in it and it is renewed for us in every new 'present'. This is possible because every moment of time reaches into the eternal. It is the eternal that stops the flux of time for us. It is the eternal 'now' which provides for us a temporal 'now'. We live so long as 'it is still today' – in the words of the letter to the Hebrews. Not everybody, and nobody all the time, is aware of this 'eternal now' in the temporal 'now'. But sometimes it breaks powerfully into our consciousness and gives us the certainty of the eternal, of a dimension of time which cuts into time and gives us our time.

People who are never aware of this dimension lose the possibility of resting in the present. As the letter to the Hebrews describes it, they never enter into the divine rest. They are held by the past and cannot separate themselves from it, or they escape towards the future, unable to rest in the present. They have not entered the eternal rest which stops the flux of time and gives us the blessing of the present. Perhaps this is the most conspicuous characteristic of our period, especially in the western world and particularly in this country. It lacks the courage to accept 'presence' because it has lost the dimension of the eternal.

'I am the beginning and the end.' This is said to us who live in the bondage of time, who have to face the end, who cannot escape the past, who need a present to stand upon. Each of the modes of time has its peculiar mystery, each of them carries its peculiar anxiety. Each of them drives us to an ultimate question. There is *one* answer to these questions – the eternal. There is *one* power that surpasses the all consuming power of time – the eternal: He who was and is and is to come, the beginning and the end. He gives us forgiveness for what has passed. He gives us courage for what is to come. He gives us rest in his eternal Presence.

From: *The Eternal Now* by Paul Tillich

(SCM Press, 1963, pp. 110–11)

ADVENT 2

The Throne of David

A. G. HEBERT

The Epistle to the Hebrews begins at once with the statement[1] that God, who of old spoke to the fathers through the prophets in many fragmentary ways, has at the close of the pre-Messianic age spoken to us in His Son. We notice first that it is one and the same God who spoke both in the Old Covenant and in the New; when we join with the Church to confess the truth of the Gospel concerning Jesus the Messiah, we are thereby confessing that the Messianic Hope of the Old Testament was a true hope. It is quite insufficient to say that the prophecies which express that Hope are religiously valuable. It is necessary to affirm that God was preparing a Messianic Kingdom, and that the prophets were right in looking for such a Kingdom, to be established by His Act.

We notice secondly that He is said to have spoken by the prophets, in many fragments and in many modes. It was not only that different prophets had different styles, and that God also spoke through laws and rites and liturgical poems; but that the visions conveyed by these various modes were fragmentary and incomplete. Thus Isaiah saw one vision, and Ezekiel another, and there was the testimony both of the sacrificial rituals and of the prophets' criticisms of sacrifice. It is only in the Son of God that there is an integral embodiment of the Messianic Idea, so that it can be seen as a whole; He who fulfils the Messianic expectation gathers up all the strands in one. We have seen how from a survey of the Old Testament alone it would be impossible to produce a satisfactory statement of the Messianic Idea, since it would be impossible to know certainly which elements in it were primary and which secondary, and it is not till the Fulfilment has come that the various elements fall into place.

Thus the Old Testament is at once the word of God and not the final word of God. It is an imperfect, provisional, preparatory Covenant, needing to be made complete in the Messiah. It represents

[1] Hebrews 1:1–2.

a stage in the education of the People of God; we have seen instance after instance of the imperfection which attaches to it. This view of the Old Testament as at once Divine and incomplete is altogether fundamental to the New Testament's view of things, and is indeed implied in the Old Testament itself, by the fact that it looks forward to a future Messiah; and to assert that because the Old Testament is Divine, therefore it is inerrant and perfect in every part, is to be the victim of a false logic.

From: *The Throne of David* by A. G. Hebert

(Faber & Faber, 1941, pp. 240–1)

Tuesday

The Throne of David

A. G. HEBERT

Thus the conceptions of the Old Testament writers are imperfect and incomplete, not only because of the necessary imperfection which attaches to the human mind and its limited understanding, but also because the word which God was speaking through each of them was, as is stated in this verse of Hebrews, fragmentary and partial. The Messianic Idea in its wholeness is complete and true, but it is only when the Messiah comes that it can be seen as a whole. When He has come, the contribution of each prophet can be seen as fitting into its place and as true, in the context of the whole Biblical interpretation of His Person and His saving work and His Kingdom. But if we insist on taking the teaching of each writer separately, in isolation from the rest, and without any reference to its Fulfilment, then it will become to us one-sided and erroneous. It would be easy to quote passages from the Old Testament about the Messianic King which Christians love and treasure, in support of the conception of the Messianic King in the Psalms of Solomon: that is to say, of the very conception which our Lord rejected on the Mount as a tempta-tion of Satan. Yet, as we have seen, He did not reject the idea of the Davidic King, but only this debased form of it. He who makes all things new wove the strands together into a new pattern, not destroy-ing but fulfilling. . . .

We may conclude this section with a particular instance to show how, when they are thus judged as individuals, the Old Testament writers are found saying things that are one-sided and quite plainly erroneous in matters of faith and morals. The belief that a good life will always be rewarded by worldly prosperity is asserted in Deuteronomy, and is pushed almost to an extreme by Ezekiel: 'the soul that sinneth, it shall die'. But this belief is confronted in the Old Testament on one side with the teaching that God visits the sins of the fathers upon the children unto the third and fourth generation of them that hate Him, and on another side with the impassioned pleading of Job. It is a problem which is no less acute now, in these days of war. But, while each of the opposed beliefs has a measure of truth, no satisfactory reconciliation of them was possible for Israel till the Messiah came, or is possible now on any other basis. But when He has come and in fulfilling the Messianic Hope has creatively transformed it, we find the New Testament writers asserting on the one hand the final responsibility of every soul before God: 'We must all be made manifest before the judgment-seat of Christ, that each one may receive the things done in the body, according to what he hath done, whether it be good or bad',[1] and on the other hand the solidarity of men one with another in this life, both in sin and in suffering and in redemption: 'All have sinned, and fall short of the glory of God',[2] and 'If one member suffer, all the members suffer with it',[3] and 'I fill up on my part that which is lacking of the afflictions of the Messiah in my flesh for his Body's sake, which is the Church'.[4] Thus, while the Old Testament is Divine, it is incomplete. The several writers are incomplete when taken as individuals and isolated from the whole which is Israel; and Israel as a whole is incomplete, apart from its Fulfilment in the Messiah and His *Ecclesia*.

From: *The Throne of David* by A. G. Hebert

(Faber & Faber, 1941, pp. 242–4)

[1] 2 Cor: 5, 10
[2] 2 Rom. 3: 23.
[3] 1 Cor: 12, 26.
[4] Col. 1: 24.

The Throne of David

A. G. HEBERT

It should be possible, after what has been said, to reach some satisfactory conclusion about the vexed questions of Revelation, Inspiration, and Inerrancy. The last of these words is made specially difficult by its ambiguity: clearly we need to distinguish between Error in the schoolmaster's sense, of mistakes in matters of fact, dates and the like, or exaggerated estimates of the number of casualties in Old Testament battles, and Error in the theological sense, where it concerns matters of faith and morals, and is equivalent to material heresy, or at least some one-sided and misleading presentation of Divine truth. There is little difficulty in acknowledging Error in the Bible in the former sense, with the proviso that since the Revelation of God has come in history, there must be certain points at least where matters of great moment are involved; and here those who believe that the Christian Faith is true will believe that honest investigation will vindicate the truth of the Gospel message. With regard to the second sense, we have seen that, if we insist on treating Biblical writers as individuals, in isolation from Israel as a whole, we may find in them teaching even on matters of faith and morals which must be called erroneous. And yet the Bible, as the book of the People of God, is the supreme safeguard against Error and Heresy and Unbelief.

With regard to Revelation, two opposed or complementary views confront one another and each can be stated in such a way as to be unsatisfactory. On the one hand, it is plainly unsatisfactory to think of the Revelation as consisting in bare Acts of God, without any hint of their significance. In this case all theology, including that of the Bible and of the Creeds, will have to consist of purely human formulations of the meaning of these Acts of God; formulations which must be more or less provisional and subject to revision, being conceived in the thought-forms of some particular age. But the complex Act of God which consists in the saving work of Jesus the Messiah includes not only the Events of His birth, death, resurrection and ascension, but also His ministry and teaching. He died for us; but He also explained the meaning of His death in a series of sayings, and in the sacrificial rite which He gave us at the Last Supper. Clearly then

Revelation cannot consist solely in the Acts of God, bare and un-explained; we must think of them as coming to us with some meaning attached.

On the other hand, it cannot be satisfactory to think of the Revela-tion as being simply a revealing of truths, ideas, or doctrines about God, and consequently of Faith as being solely an act of intellectual assent; for in this case it becomes peculiarly difficult to say in what the Revelation consists. To the Apostles a 'deposit of faith' is said to have been committed; but no one can point us to an apostolic form of words containing this primitive deposit. Even where it is believed that the Pope speaks infallibly, it is notoriously uncertain on what occasions he has spoken infallibly. With regard to the Bible the position is peculiarly difficult, since on this view it is hard to allow any mistakes anywhere, even in quite trivial matters of fact; while with regard to Error in matters of faith and morals, it would be difficult, for instance, to maintain the soundness of the dogmatic teaching of Ecclesiastes, on the assumption that we must treat each book and indeed each sentence as revealed truth, in isolation from all the rest of the Bible.

From: *The Throne of David* by A. G. Hebert

(Faber & Faber, 1941, pp. 244–6)

Thursday

The Throne of David

A. G. HEBERT

. . . We must look at the Bible as a whole, and see the parts in the context of the whole. We have said of the Old Testament – and it is equally true of the New Testament – that it has two fundamental dogmas: the Reality of God, and the Divine Election of Israel to be His People. We are compelled therefore to think of Revelation as primarily and essentially the making-known to man of GOD HIMSELF by means of Acts such as those recorded in the Bible, whereby a first Covenant is inaugurated under Moses, and a New Covenant by the Messiah. We insisted that the Reality of God is to be clearly distinguished from the metaphysical doctrine of Monotheism, but also that it has this doctrine as its necessary corollary; the monotheistic doctrine is the interpretation to the human mind of what the Reality of God involves. Similarly the Divine Acts whereby He makes His Covenant with man do not come to man bare and unexplained; for the making of the Covenant will demand a response of faith on the part of the men who receive it. In other words, there needs to be also a Divine Inspiration interpreting to men His action, and enabling them to understand, not indeed completely, but yet sufficiently.

It is common for the word 'Revelation' to be used to mean both the Divine Acts and the interpretation of their meaning. But we shall hope to show that it is better and clearer to keep the word Revelation for the former, and Inspiration for the latter, provided it is understood that the two are inseparable; and we shall draw a parallel with the respective functions of the Divine Son and the Holy Spirit in making known to us God and His Truth. Here too we must distinguish, but we may not separate.

Let us set this out. Revelation happens in a series of Events, in which God's Arm is bared; in the one case, after the preparation of the patriarchal period, the series consists of the events of the Exodus and the inauguration of the Covenant, in the other, of the events which centre round the crucifixion and the resurrection of the Messiah. But then, Revelation is not unaccompanied by Inspiration. In the case of our Lord, this is abundantly clear. The Holy Spirit descends on Him at His baptism, to 'abide on Him'[1] and speak in Him, so that His words are spirit and are life,[2] and is bestowed by Him at Pentecost, that men may know who He is:

> 'He shall glorify me;
> For he shall take of mine, and shall declare it unto you.
> All things that the Father hath are mine;
> Therefore said I, that he taketh of mine, and shall
>   declare it unto you.'[3]

But it is no less clear in the case of the Old Covenant. Yahweh does not simply deliver Israel out of Egypt; He sends a prophet, Moses, whom the Old Testament always regards as having been the greatest of all the prophets: 'There hath not arisen a prophet since in Israel like unto Moses, whom the Lord knew face to face.'[4] It was his function to interpret to Israel the mighty Acts of God, and make plain what He was doing with her. Moses was inspired by God to do this.

[1] John 1:33.
[2] John 6:63.
[3] John 16:14–15.
[4] Deut. 34:10.

But that is not the whole story. The Events of the Incarnation and the Redemption are followed by the work of the Holy Spirit in the Christian centuries; and it is just the same with Israel. After the manifestation of the Name of Yahweh in the Exodus, Israel is enabled to see His continual presence in her midst as her Lord and Judge and Saviour, through various means of grace, and in particular through the succession of the prophets, by whom, as we confess in the Creed, the Holy Ghost spake. When we think of the prophets, we must of course avoid the foolish mistake of beginning with Amos, as if Samuel and Elijah had not been prophets of the first rank; and we should remember further that the Jews always reckoned among the prophetic books the books of Samuel and Kings, which were written to relate the history as the story of God's dealings with His People.

From: *The Throne of David* by A. G. Hebert

(Faber & Faber, 1941, pp. 246–8)

Friday

The Throne of David

A. G. HEBERT

Now this distinction which we have made between Revelation and Inspiration corresponds with the broad lines of the doctrine of the Holy Trinity. God the Father, the *principium* or Fount of Deity, reveals Himself through the Word and the Spirit, whom St. Irenaeus calls the two 'hands' of God: the Word uttered from His Mind, wherein the Divine Glory has full and perfect utterance and expression, and the Spirit who is the Will, the Power, the Love, whereby God loves the Good which is Himself.

St. John has distinguished for us the respective activities of the Word-made-flesh and the Spirit in the work of Redemption, as we have seen. He has omitted to do so in the Prologue to his gospel, which mainly describes the general operation of the Word in the world; but the activity which is there ascribed to the Word must of course cover the activities proper to the Third Person as well as to the Second. 'All things were made by him'; by the Son as the *exemplar* or pattern, by the Spirit as the efficient cause reproducing the pattern in things. The Son is the Image of the Father, out of which have proceeded the created works of God which manifest His glory; the Spirit is the operative power bringing the works of God into being. 'And God [the Father] said [the Word], Let there be Light; and there was light [by the operation of the Spirit].' 'In him was life': the Son is the Life, but the Spirit is the life-giver to men. And while the Son is the Light of the world, it is properly the Spirit who 'lighteneth every man that cometh into the world', and through whom those who believed on the Son 'were born not of the flesh . . . but of God'. Thus in the Prologue, the operations of the Son and of the Spirit are described together without being explicitly distinguished, as they are distinguished when we come to the redemptive work.

Already then in the general operation of God in the world we can discern a clear difference between the Word and the Spirit. It becomes explicit in the Incarnation. The Word becomes incarnate once for all, at a definite place and time, and was capable of being seen, heard, touched, described. Hence the symbols used for Him are ordinarily definite concepts such as King, Shepherd, Priest, Victim. But the Spirit is pictured in symbols of movement: the flying Dove, the running Water, the Wind, the Fire, the Tongues; symbols which do not, so to speak, stand still while we look at them, since He is the principle of Life and the Life-giver to all that lives.

From: *The Throne of David* by A. G. Hebert

(Faber & Faber, 1941, pp. 248–50)

Saturday

The Throne of David

A. G. HEBERT

This distinction between the Word and the Spirit corresponds exactly to that which we have made between Revelation and Inspiration. Revelation is the manifestation of God Himself in His action, and it is accompanied by Inspiration which declares the meaning of what God is doing. Consequently, the act of faith *in* God who takes Israel for His People, and who through the Messiah reconciles the world to Himself, is necessarily also an act of belief in certain truths *about* God. Revelation comes in a closed series of Events; Inspiration declares the meaning of those Events at the time and after, showing to succeeding generations how the Divine Intervention in the Acts
í Revelation reveals Him as active also throughout all history.

What does it mean, then, to say that the Bible is 'inspired'? Simply that, in many fragments and in various modes, God is speaking in it. Each writer says what he, with his limited vision, has been given to see. At the same time, it is more than a mere story of religious development; to say that God is speaking through the writers implies that there is an initiative which rests with Him. And is the Bible inspired in a different way from other books? Yes; but it is not that the Holy Ghost does not speak in other books; it is that this book is different because it interprets the Revelation. That is why it ends with the Apostolic testimony to the completion of God's saving Purpose in the coming of the Messiah and the establishment of His Ecclesia, and does not go on to describe the Christian centuries. Why then does not the Old Testament end with the Entry into Canaan? Because God's Purpose was not then complete, and the Old Testament had to look forward to the Messiah and prepare His way.

What then are we to say of the word Inerrancy? Principally this: that it is so confused and confusing a word that it is best avoided. It has a truth in it, namely that the Bible is the supreme witness to the Truth of God against Error. But it is an ambiguous word, since it covers two quite different kinds of Error. It is also a negative word, since it does not affirm that the Bible is true, but denies that it contains Error. But this involves the attribution of freedom-from-error not to the Bible as a whole, but to each several part taken in isolation; and to take the books and the teachings of the Bible in isolation from the rest is an error which is common to the Liberal critic and to the scholastic-minded theologian. The Bible is not 'true' in the sense of containing two or three hundred thousand true propositions, but because 'both in the Old and New Testaments everlasting life is offered to Mankind by Christ, who is the only Mediator between God and Man, being both God and Man'. The Old Testament Scriptures are imperfect because the writers can only apprehend in diverse ways various fragments of His truth; they are true because they do nevertheless apprehend it. Abraham rejoiced to see His Day. Moses wrote of Him. Isaiah saw His Glory.

From: *The Throne of David* by A. G. Hebert

(Faber & Faber, 1941, pp. 251–2)

ADVENT 3

Monday

The Christian Priest Today

MICHAEL RAMSEY

The priest is the teacher and preacher, and as such he is the *man of theology*. He is pledged to be a dedicated student of theology; and his study need not be vast in extent but it will be deep in its integrity, not in order that he may be erudite but in order that he may be simple. It is those whose studies are shallow who are confused and confusing. The Church's hold upon the faith requires those who in theology are 'learned', concentrated, dedicated, and deep; and by his service of the laity in this role the priest will be helping them to be better witnesses. But this work will be a partnership; and the contrast between *discens* and *docens* [learning and teaching] melts away as the priest learns from the laity much about the contemporary world and about the meaning of divine truth in its human context. Together they, from their several kinds of knowledge, will work out the meaning of the Word of God as it bears upon life's problems and upon the various spheres of the Church's witness. It can be a wonderful partnership, and within it ordained priesthood finds its role. Thus in new guises the old 'didactic' and 'kerygmatic' roles of the priest are carried on. The 'kerygmatic' role still stands, for it is the presence of the divine Word and its proclamation to, and with, and by, the Church that the Church is still *ecclesia Dei*.

From: *The Christian Priest Today* by Michael Ramsey

(SPCK, 1972, pp. 7–8)

Tuesday

The Christian Priest Today

MICHAEL RAMSEY

The priest is the minister of reconciliation; and by this office he links the common life of the Church to the gospel of divine forgiveness upon which its common life depends.

Now the priest today is only one among many skills and agencies designed to help people in their troubles. The psychiatrist, the doctor, the welfare officer, the marriage guidance counsellor, and many kinds of social worker bring relief to the problems with which people get entangled. The parson's monopoly has long ceased, and the confessional no longer stands pre-eminent as the seat of counsel and direction. Yet amidst all the various activities for the putting right of human ills there is so often a whole dimension missing, the dimension of sin and forgiveness. It not seldom happens that psychiatry, instead of liberating the patient into the realm of moral responsibility and the issues of conscious sin and forgiveness, can substitute medicine for moral responsibility. It is this dimension of sin and forgiveness which the priest keeps alive by an office which represents the forgiving Church and the forgiving Lord Jesus. He will do this by his ministry in Confession and Absolution and by his preaching of the gospel of God's reconciliation. He will bear witness to the cost of forgiveness to the divine holiness, and he will remember that the familiar phrase in 2 Corinthians 5:20 which we translate 'the ministry of reconciliation' means 'the ministry of *the reconciliation*',[1] the reconciliation once for all wrought on the hill of Calvary and subsequently to be applied through the centuries to every penitent heart. 'Whose sins thou dost forgive they are forgiven.'

From: *The Christian Priest Today* by Michael Ramsey

(SPCK, 1972, pp. 8–9)

[1] τῆς καταλλαγῆς

Wednesday

The Christian Priest Today

MICHAEL RAMSEY

The priest, in the Church and for the Church, is the *man of prayer*. Do not all Christians pray? They do indeed, and from many of them we priests can learn to pray and to pray better. Yet 'man of prayer' is in a special way the role of the priest, and because it is so the Church's prayer will be the stronger. As the teacher of theology, the priest must pray, as theology which is alive includes not only book-work but the authentic knowledge of God which comes through prayer alone. So too as the minister of reconciliation the priest will pray, for he is one with those who are sinful in the bitter estrangement of their sin and in the hopeful grief of their penitence; and at the same time he is one with Christ in his sorrow for sinners and his joy at sin's conquest. As absolver and pastor, no less than as theologian and teacher, the priest has a prayer which focuses the Church's prayer. In him the Church's prayer is expressed in strength, and it thereby becomes the stronger.

From: *The Christian Priest Today* by Michael Ramsey

(SPCK, 1972, p. 9)

Thursday

The Christian Priest Today

MICHAEL RAMSEY

When we say [of Jesus] 'he lives to make intercession' we note that the verb entychanein [ἐντυμχανεῖν] which we habitually translate 'intercede' means literally not to make petitions or indeed to utter words at all but to *meet*, to *encounter*, to *be with* someone on behalf of or in relation to others. Jesus is *with* the Father; with him in the intimate response of perfect humanity; with him in the power of Calvary and Easter; with him as one who bears us all upon his heart, our Son of Man, our friend, our priest; with him as our own. That is the continuing intercession of Jesus the high priest.

Now we can begin to see what is our own role as men of prayer, as priestly intercessors. We are called, near to Jesus and with Jesus and in Jesus, *to be with God with the people on our heart*. That is what you will be promising when I say to you 'will you be diligent in prayers?'. You will be promising to be daily with God with the people on your heart.

Your prayer then will be a rhythmic movement of all your powers, moving into the divine presence in contemplation and moving into the needs of the people in intercession. In contemplation you will reach into the peace and stillness of God's eternity, in intercession you will reach into the rough and tumble of the world of time and change.

The Godward movement has many aspects. It includes the use of mind and imagination which we call meditation, it includes the counting of God's mercies which we call praise and thanksgiving, and self-abasement which we call confession. But try to think of it more simply: it means putting yourself near God, with God, in a time of quietness every day. You put yourself with him just as you are, in the feebleness of your concentration, in your lack of warmth and desire, not trying to manufacture pious thoughts or phrases. You put yourself with God, empty perhaps, but hungry and thirsty for him; and if in sincerity you cannot say that you want God you can perhaps tell him that you want to want him; and if you cannot say even that perhaps you can say that you want to want to want him! Thus you can be very near him in your naked sincerity; and *he* will do the rest, drawing out from you longings deeper than you knew were there and pouring into you a trust and a love like that of the psalmist – whose words may soon come to your lips. Forgive me for putting this so clumsily. I am trying to say that you find you are 'with God' not by achieving certain devotional exercises in his presence but by daring to be your own self as you reach towards him.

From: *The Christian Priest Today* by Michael Ramsey

(SPCK, 1972, pp. 13–15)

Friday

The Christian Priest Today

MICHAEL RAMSEY

... 'To be with God with the people on your heart' will be your role beyond the ordered times of prayer because it will be a part of your life. Since Bonhoeffer's influence has been felt, and his lessons have been learnt and unlearnt, and since the negative concept of 'religionless Christianity' has in turn given place to the more positive concept sometimes called 'the new spirituality', we have been realizing how transcendence is to be found in the midst of secular experience and not apart from it, and how prayer is not only for the closet but for all the ups and downs of life. If we knew that before, or thought we did, we have been discovering it in a new vividness.

Amidst our contemporary tensions between traditional modes of prayer and the newer forms of secular spirituality, it helps greatly to recapture the simplest meaning of our Lord's high-priestly intercession: to be with God for the people. Anywhere, everywhere, God is to be found. In your daily encounters with people, God is there: you can recollect him, you can be with him, you can share your doings with him, you can shoot arrows of desire from your heart to his: and all this will be for the people's sake. You can be on the Godward side of every human situation; for the Godward side is a part of every human situation. But you are unlikely to have the power to be on the Godward side of human situations if you think that it can be done by a kind of shallow secularized activism. That is the fallacy which does so much damage at the present time. The truth is that you will have the awareness of God and the power to be on the Godward side of human situations only if you carry with you into the day's ups and downs an 'interior castle' of recollection drawn from your times of quietness and eucharist and scripture. There is no by-passing the Psalmist's wisdom, 'Be still and know that I am God', and there is no by-passing the example of our Lord whom Simon Peter found praying alone in a desert place a great while before day. You will not try to be wiser than the Psalmist, or wiser than our Lord.

In the coming years your prayer will not be a sort of specialized activity. Rather will your prayer be, in a hundred ways, *you* – you with God for the people, and you with the people in God's strength. Your prayer will change much through the years, it will be free and flexible, an exciting adventure. There will be many ups and downs, times when you pray badly and times when you pray well, times when prayer is a slogging discipline and times when it is a spontaneous joy. Think of it simply as 'God, myself, and the people', being with him for them, and with them for him. And the supreme fact is the prayer of Jesus himself: throughout your ministry he will be there, praying and wanting you to have a little share with him in his prayer. So tomorrow I shall ask you confidently, 'Will you be diligent in prayers?', and you will answer joyfully, 'I will endeavour myself so to do, the Lord being my helper.'

From: *The Christian Priest Today* by Michael Ramsey

(SPCK, 1972, pp. 17–18)

Saturday

The Christian Priest Today

MICHAEL RAMSEY

So too the priest is the *man of the Eucharist*. The liturgy indeed belongs to all the people. We being many are the one bread, one body. We take, we break, we offer, we receive; and the more vivid realization of this has been one of the exciting marks of liturgical renewal in our time. Where then, and why then, the priest? As celebrant he is more than the people's representative. In taking, breaking, and consecrating he acts in Christ's name and in the name not only of the particular congregation but of the Holy Catholic Church down the ages. By his office as celebrant he symbolizes the focusing of the Eucharist and the givenness of the historic gospel and the continuing life of the Church as rooted in that gospel. He finds that at the altar he is drawn terribly and wonderfully near not only to the benefits of Christ's redemption but to the redemptive act itself.

Man of theology, man of reconciliation, man of prayer, man of the Eucharist; displaying, enabling, involving the life of the Church – such is the ordained priest. I have not made 'pastor' one of the categories, because pastor describes the whole. In describing the priest's office in this way I have followed an empirical approach, beginning with the Church's practical experience and working back from this to an understanding of the ministry. This way of approach may help where a purely *a priori* or deductive approach is found unhelpful. Yet it is far from true that while the Church is our Lord's creation the ministry is only a device whereby the Church can be effective. Both Church and ministry are gifts of the divine Lord Jesus. He appointed twelve that they might be with him, and that he might send them forth. When he ascended on high he gave gifts to men. The apostle draws his commission and authority from Christ alone, and he uses an authority given to him when in Christ's name he ordains and commissions the presbyters. 'Take thou authority for the office and work of a priest in the Church of God now committed unto thee by the imposition of these hands . . . and be thou a faithful dispenser of the word of God and of his holy sacraments.'

'Are we then beginning to commend ourselves?' It is impossible for us to commend priesthood as something 'in itself', and attempts to do so by propaganda court failure. Yet 'as servants of God we commend ourselves in every way' if our consciousness is not of our own status but of Christ whose commission we hold and of the people we serve in his name. See the matter thus, and you could find the old words are true:

> O Sacerdos, quid es tu?
> Non es a te, quia de nihilo,
> Non es ad te, quia mediator ad Deum,
> Non es tibi, quia sponsus ecclesiae,
> Non es tui, quia servus omnium,
> Non es tu, quia Dei minister,
> Quid es ergo? Nihil et omnia,
> O Sacerdos.

From: *The Christian Priest Today* by Michael Ramsey

(SPCK, 1972, pp. 9–11)

ADVENT 4

(It is suggested that Saturday's reading be used on Christmas Day, whichever day of the week Christmas is)

Monday

Self-abandonment to Divine Providence

JEAN-PIERRE DE CAUSSADE

Sanctity consists in fidelity to the order established by God and in self-abandonment to his action . . .

God still speaks to us today as he spoke to our fathers, when there were no spiritual directors or set methods. Then, spirituality consisted in fidelity to the designs of God. . . . Then it was enough for those who led a spiritual life to see that each moment brought with it a duty to be faithfully fulfilled. On that duty the whole of their attention was fixed at each successive moment, like the hand of a clock which marked each moment of the hour. Under God's unceasing guidance their spirit turned without conscious effort to each new duty as it was presented to them by God each hour of the day.

Such were the hidden springs of Mary's conduct, for she was of all creatures the most utterly submissive to God. Her reply to the angel when she said simply: *Fiat mihi secundum verbum tuum* [Be it unto me according to thy word], contained all the mystical theology of our ancestors. Everything was reduced, as indeed it is today, to the complete and utter self-abandonment of the soul to God's will under whatever form it was manifested.

This beautiful and lofty disposition of Mary's soul is admirably revealed in those simple words: *Fiat mihi* [Be it unto me.] Note how perfectly they agree with those words which our Lord wishes us to have always on our lips and in our hearts: *Fiat voluntas tua* [Thy will be done]. It is true that what was asked of Mary at that moment was something very glorious for her. But all the splendour of that glory would have had no effect on her had she not seen in it the will of God which alone was able to move her.

It was this divine will which ruled her every act. Whatever her occupations, commonplace or lofty, they were in her eyes but external signs, sometimes clear, sometimes obscure, under which she saw the means both of glorifying God and of acknowledging the action of the Almighty. Her spirit, transported with joy, looked on everything she had to do or to suffer at each moment as a gift from him who fills with good things the hearts which hunger for him alone and not for created things.

From: *Self-Abandonment to Divine Providence* by Jean-Pierre de Caussade, translated from the standard French Edition of *Father P. H. Ramière, S.J.* by Algar Thorold

(Collins Fontana, 1971, pp. 31–2)

Tuesday

Self-abandonment to Divine Providence

JEAN-PIERRE DE CAUSSADE

The duties of each moment are shadows beneath which the divine action lies concealed.

'The power of the Most High shall overshadow thee,' said the angel to Mary. This shadow beneath which the power of God conceals itself in order to bring Jesus Christ to souls, is the duty, attraction or cross which every moment brings. These are in fact but shadows similar to those in nature which spread themselves like a veil over visible objects and hide them from us. Thus in the moral and supernatural order the duties of each moment conceal under their outward appearances the true reality of the divine will which alone is worthy of our attention. It was in this light that Mary regarded them. As these shadows spread over her faculties, far from causing her any illusion, they filled her with faith in him who is unchanging. Draw back, archangel, you are only a shadow; your moment passes and you disappear. Mary moves beyond you; Mary goes forward unceasingly. From now on you are left far behind her. But the Holy Spirit, who under the visible form of this mission has entered into her, will never leave her.

There are few extraordinary features in the external life of the Blessed Virgin. At least Holy Scripture does not record any. Her life is represented as externally very simple and ordinary. She does and experiences the same things as other people in her state of life. She goes to visit her cousin Elizabeth, as her other relations do. She takes shelter in a stable; a natural consequence of her poverty. She returns to Nazareth after having fled from the persecution of Herod; Jesus and Joseph live there with her, supporting themselves by the work of their hands. This provides their daily bread, but what is the divine food with which this material bread feeds the faith of Mary and Joseph? What is the sacrament of each of their sacred moments? What treasures of grace are contained in each of these moments underneath the commonplace appearance of the events that fill them? Outwardly these events are no different from those which happen to everyone, but the interior invisible element discerned by faith is nothing less than God himself performing great works. O bread of angels, heavenly manna, the pearl of the Gospels, the sacrament of the present moment! You present God in such lowly forms as the manger, the hay and straw! But to whom do you give him? *Esurientes reples bonis*. 'You fill the hungry with good things.' God reveals himself to the humble in the humblest things, while the great who never penetrate beneath the surface do not discover him even in great events.

From: *Self-Abandonment to Divine Providence* by Jean-Pierre de Caussade, translated from the standard French Edition of *Father P. H. Ramière, S.J.* by Algar Thorold

(Collins Fontana, 1971, pp. 32–3)

Wednesday

Self-abandonment to Divine Providence

JEAN-PIERRE DE CAUSSADE

A soul comes under the divine action as soon as goodwill springs up in its heart, and God's action has more or less influence on it according to the degree of its self-abandonment. The art of self-abandonment is nothing but the art of loving, and divine action is the action of divine love. How can these two loves which seek each other fail to agree when they meet? How could divine love refuse anything to the soul whose every desire it directs? And how could God meet with a refusal from a soul that lives only by him? . . . Love can but ask for what love wishes, and is it possible for love not to desire what it desires?

God pays attention to nothing but goodwill. It is not the capacity of the other faculties which attract him, nor their incapacity which repels him. All he demands is a good, pure, upright, simple, submissive, filial and respectful heart. If he finds such a heart, he takes possession of it and of all its faculties and disposes so well all things for its good that it will find materials for its sanctification in everything. . . .

Divine love is, then, for the souls who give themselves wholly to it, the principle of all good. And in order to acquire this inestimable good it is sufficient to will it firmly.

Yes, dear souls, God asks for your heart only; if you are seeking this treasure, this Kingdom in which God reigns alone, you will find it. For if your heart is wholly devoted to God, it forthwith becomes this treasure, this very kingdom that you are desiring and seeking. From the moment that we desire God and his will we enjoy God and his will, and our enjoyment corresponds to the ardour of our desire. To love God is to desire sincerely to love him; because we love him, we wish to be the instrument of his action, so that his love may exercise itself in and through us.

From: *Self-Abandonment to Divine Providence* by Jean-Pierre de Caussade, translated from the standard French edition of *Father P. H. Ramière, S.J.* by Algar Thorold

(Collins Fontana, 1971, pp. 152–4)

Thursday

A Christmas Meditation

RONALD KNOX

There is nothing irreverent, I think, in comparing man's search for God to a game of hide-and-seek. A child's game with its father, all the skill and foresight on the one side, all the romance and excitement on the other! . . .

In the history of our race, it was man first that hid himself from God. We know the story; Adam and his wife hid themselves among the trees of the garden. 'The woman Thou gavest me' – you gave her to be a help-meet, to look after me, to restrain me, and she has been no help here. No resource for Adam in the mother-wit of Mother Eve; she has only dragged him down and cowers there beside him, ineffectively ambushed, to avoid the scrutiny of a God. Man began it; man issued the challenge; and thenceforward, through long centuries, he was like a frightened child feeling its way alone through the darkness, racked by a thousand causeless terrors, searching for the God who had left so many proofs of his presence, but remained always hidden from sight. 'Show us the Father, and it is enough' – yes, but the Wisdom God had bestowed on us was only a rushlight in the darkness, not a mother to draw aside the curtain and tell us, 'See, he is here!'

And then, in the fullness of time, God changed his hiding-place. Suddenly, while all was quiet around, with the deep stillness of a winter night, he came and hid in a manger, came and hid in the form of man. Not quite so silently but he betrayed himself; just a movement among the stars, just the brush of angels' wings, was enough to raise the hue and cry among a few searchers, shepherd folk with their keen ears, stargazers with their sharp eyes. And so the hunt started afresh: Tell us, where is he born, the King of the Jews? The question, repeated to one passer-by after another, begins to sound like the chorus of some children's game. What, this tumble-down house in a back street, this draughty cellar underneath it – it's no good looking in there! He wouldn't hide in a place like that! And then the door opens, and a woman stands there, a finger pressed to her lips; our Mother, come out to help in the search. 'Yes, he's in there; but come in quietly; he's asleep.' The God who does not dwell in temples made with hands, asleep in there! The God who neither sleeps nor slumbers, watching over Israel, in there asleep!

From: *Pastoral Sermons* by Ronald Knox

(Burns & Oates, London, 1960, pp. 359, 360–1)

Friday

A Christmas Meditation

RONALD KNOX

I think you can say that there are three qualities, I won't say which have been made known to us, but which show up in a new light, as the result of the Christian revelation: humility, charity, and purity. They are all words derived from the Latin; but if a Roman of Julius Caesar's time could come back to earth, I don't think we could mention them to him without finding ourselves at cross purposes.

Humility – if you look up that word in the Latin dictionary, you will get a surprise. You will find that it means 'lowness, meanness, insignificance, littleness of mind, baseness, abjectness', and it has no other sense until you come on to the Christian authors. And yet how instinctively we recognize the worth of it today, even those of us who wouldn't call ourselves Christians! To be sure, there are all sorts of inferior substitutes for it which owe little or nothing to the influence of Bethlehem; there is the mock modesty which prompts us to under-rate our own achievements simply as a matter of good manners; we don't want to make a bad impression of boastfulness on the people we meet. There is the calculating, affected humility of Uriah Heep; you demean yourself before important people because you know which side your bread is buttered. But real humility, how it shines when it catches the light! The man who can take an affront and feel it is no more than he deserves; who takes it for granted that his successful rival was the better candidate; who can work to other men's plans when they run contrary to his own advice, the advice which was not asked for, or went unregarded – how we admire such a man, even when we think that he carries his good qualities to a fault! And the reason for our admiration – the historical reason for our admiration – is because we have been told about a God who for us men and for our salvation came down from heaven, and took upon himself the nature of a slave for our sakes.

And charity – if you look that up in the Latin dictionary, you find that it means affection for your family or your close friends. How should it mean more, to people who hadn't read the parable of the good Samaritan? Once again, not everything that is done in the name of charity is real charity. There is the ostentatiousness which likes to see its name on a subscription-list; there is the love of interference which is ever eager to manage other people's lives for them. But, when you have made all allowances for that, charity towards com-plete strangers has become a habit with us. It has filled the world with hospitals and orphanages and almshouses, all because of Bethlehem; there was no name for such things before Jesus Christ came. Because Jesus Christ came to redeem us when we were stran-gers who had no claim on him, brought redemption to everybody far and near, we too, even you and I, are ashamed to button up our pockets.

And then – purity. The Romans, of course, use the word often enough, but I don't think they meant any more by it than cleanness of body; no one seems to have bothered much about purity of mind. And yet our Lord tells us that all sins, even the sins of sense, take their origin in the mind. How hard it is, nowadays, to persuade people that there is such a thing as purity! They get it mixed up with mere ignorance about sex; or with prudery, that loves the sensation of being shocked; or with the morbid terror of sex which is found, sometimes, in ill-adjusted natures. But there is such a thing as real purity, which sees the facts of life as they are, and has too much sense of the rich, living thing marriage is, of the bright, delicate thing virginity is, to sully either with brooding thoughts, or with sniggering jocularity. That, too, we owe to Bethlehem; to the memory of that virgin motherhood which saved us all.

All that we owe to Christmas. Whatever difference it may have made in our behaviour, as compared with that of our pagan fore-fathers, it has altered the standards of behaviour which we reverence and desire. . . . No new voice which speaks to us in the name of religion will have any appeal for us, if it does not bring us back to the stable at Bethlehem – there to humble our pride, and enlarge our charity, and deepen our sense of reverence with the sight of a dazzling purity.

From: *Pastoral Sermons* by Ronald Knox

(Burns & Oates, London, 1960, pp. 366–8)

Saturday or Christmas Day

The Nativity

DEAN FARRAR

In the Gospel of St. James there is a really striking chapter, des-cribing how, at the awful moment of the nativity, the pole of the heaven stood motionless, and the birds were still, and there were workmen lying on the earth with their hands in a vessel, 'and those who handled did not handle it, and those who took did not lift, and those who presented it to their mouth did not present it, but the faces of all were looking up; and I saw the sheep scattered and the sheep stood, and the shepherd lifted up his hand to strike, and his hand remained up; and I looked at the stream of the river, and the mouths of the kids were down, and were not drinking; and everything which was being propelled forward was intercepted in its course.' But of this sudden hush and pause of awe-struck Nature, of the parhelions and mysterious splendours which blazed in many places of the world, of the painless childbirth, of the perpetual virginity, of the ox and the ass kneeling to worship Him in the manger, of the voice with which immediately after His birth He told His mother that He was the Son of God, and of many another wonder which rooted itself in the earliest traditions, there is no trace whatever in the New Testament. The inventions of man differ wholly from the dealings of God. In His designs there is no haste, no rest, no weariness, no discontinuity; all things are done by Him in the majesty of silence, and they are seen under a light that shineth quietly in the darkenss, 'showing all things in the slow history of their ripening'. 'The unfathomable depths of the Divine counsels,' it has been said, 'were moved; the fountains of the great deep were broken up; the healing of the nations was issuing forth; but nothing was seen on the surface of human society but this slight rippling of the water: the course of human things went on as usual, while each was taken up with little projects of his own.'

From: *The Life of Christ* by Dean Farrar

(Cassell, 1963, pp. 10–12)

CHRISTMAS 1

(If the Feast of the Epiphany occurs in this week, it is suggested that the readings for Christmas 2 be used.)

Monday

The Nativity

DEAN FARRAR

One mile from Bethlehem is a little plain, in which, under a grove of olives, stands the bare and neglected chapel known by the name of 'the Angel to the Shepherds'. It is built over the traditional site of the fields where, in the beautiful language of St. Luke 'there were shepherds keeping watch over their flock by night, when, lo, the angel of the Lord came upon them, and the glory of the Lord shone round about them', and to their happy ears were uttered the good tidings of great joy that unto them was born that day in the city of David a Saviour, which was Christ the Lord.

The associations of our Lord's nativity were all of the humblest character, and the very scenery of His birthplace was connected with memories of poverty and toil. On that night, indeed, it seemed as though the heavens must burst to disclose their radiant minstrelsies. The stars, and the feeding sheep, and the 'light and sound in the darkness and stillness', and the rapture of faithful hearts, combine to furnish us with a picture painted in the colours of heaven. But in the brief and thrilling verses of the Evangelist we are not told that those angel songs were heard by any except the wakeful shepherds of an obscure village; – and those shepherds, amid the chill dews of a winter night, were guarding their flocks from the wolf and the robber, in fields where Ruth, their Saviour's ancestress, had 'gleaned, sick at heart, amid the alien corn', and David, the despised and youngest son of a numerous family, had followed the ewes great with young.

'And suddenly,' adds the sole Evangelist who has narrated the circumstances of that memorable night in which Jesus was born, amid the indifference of a world unconscious of its Deliverer, 'there was with the angel a multitude of the heavenly host, praising God, and saying, Glory to God in the highest, and on earth peace among men of good will.'

From: *The Life of Christ* by Dean Farrar

(Cassell, 1963, pp. 1–2)

Tuesday

The Nativity

DEAN FARRAR

It might have been expected that Christian piety would have marked the spot by splendid memorials, and enshrined the rude grotto of the shepherds in the marbles and mosaics of some stately church. But, instead of this, the Chapel of the Herald Angel is a mere rude crypt; and as the traveller descends down the broken steps which lead from the olive grove into its dim recess, he can hardly persuade himself that he is in a consecrated place. Yet a half-unconscious sense of fitness has, perhaps, contributed to this apparent neglect. The poverty of the chapel harmonizes well with the humble toil of those whose radiant vision it is intended to commemorate.

'Come now! let us go into Bethlehem, and see this thing which has come to pass, which the Lord made known to us,' said the shepherds, when those angel songs had ceased to break the starry silence. Their way would lead them up the terraced hill, and through the moonlit gardens of Bethlehem, until they reached the summit of the grey ridge on which the little town is built. On that summit stood the village inn. The khan (or caravanserai) of a Syrian village, at that day, was probably identical, in its appearance and accommodation, with those which still exist in modern Palestine. A khan is a low structure, built of rough stones, and generally only a single storey in height. It consists for the most part of a square enclosure, in which the cattle can be tied up in safety for the night, and an arched recess for the accommodation of travellers. The *leewan*, or paved floor of the recess, is raised a foot or two above the level of the court-yard. A large khan – such, for instance, as that of which the ruins may still be seen at Khan Minyeh, on the shore of the Sea of Galilee – might contain a series of such recesses, which are, in fact, low small rooms with no front wall to them. They are, of course, perfectly public; everything that takes place in them is visible to every person in the khan. They are also totally devoid of even the most ordinary furniture. The traveller may bring his own carpet if he likes, may sit cross-legged upon it for his meals, and may lie upon it at night. As a rule, too, he must bring his own food, attend to his own cattle, and draw his own water from the neighbouring spring. He would neither expect nor require attendance, and would pay only the merest trifle for the advantage of shelter, safety, and a floor on which to lie. But if he chanced to arrive late, and the *leewans* were all occupied by earlier guests, he would have no choice but to be content with such accommodation as he could find in the court-yard below, and to secure for himself and his family such small amount of cleanliness and decency as are compatible with an unoccupied corner of the filthy area, which he would be obliged to share with horses, mules, and camels. The litter, the closeness, the unpleasant smell of the crowded animals, the unwelcome intrusion of the pariah dogs, the necessary society of the very lowest hangers-on of the caravanserai, are adjuncts to such a position which can only be realized by any traveller in the East who happens to have been placed in similar circumstances.

From: *The Life of Christ* by Dean Farrar

(Cassell, 1963, pp. 3–4)

Wednesday

The Nativity

DEAN FARRAR

Guided by the lamp which usually swings from the centre of a rope hung across the entrance of the khan, the shepherds found their way to the inn of Bethlehem, and found Mary, and Joseph, and the Babe lying in the manger. The fancy of poet and painter has revelled in the imaginary glories of the scene. They have sung of the 'bright harnessed angels' who hovered there, and of the stars lingering beyond their time to shed their sweet influences upon that smiling infancy. They have painted the radiation of light from His manger-cradle, illuminating all the place till the bystanders are forced to shade their eyes from that heavenly splendour. But all this is wide of the reality. Such glories as the simple shepherds saw were seen only by the eye of faith; and all which met their gaze was a peasant of Galilee, already beyond the prime of life, and a young mother, of whom *they* could not know that she was wedded maid and virgin wife, with an Infant Child, whom, since there were none to help her, her own hands had wrapped in swaddling-clothes. The light that shined in the darkness was no physical, but a spiritual beam; the Dayspring from on high, which had now visited mankind, dawned only in a few faithful and humble hearts.

From: *The Life of Christ* by Dean Farrar

(Cassell, 1963, p. 10)

Thursday

Christmas

H. P. LIDDON

[Why was God manifested in human form?]

Many answers in detail may be given, to instruct us, to redeem us, to sanctify us. But the general answer is, To bring God near to the heart and thought of His intelligent and moral creatures. Certainly He is already, by virtue of His Omnipresence, very near each one of us. He is the atmosphere in which we live; 'in Him we live, and move, and have our being'. But although thus near us in fact, He is remote from our thought. When we try to think constantly of an Infinite Being, Whose Power has no limits, Whose Knowledge has no limits, Whose Love has no limits, we soon, if we are trying to attach meaning to our words, find our minds straining more and more despairingly towards the inaccessible. And when doing this, we are sometimes tempted to reject truths which elude the comprehension – I do not say the apprehension – of finite minds, in the vain hope of reaching some truth that, although higher, will be entirely within our grasp. The popular but shallow maxim, that nothing is to be believed which is not perfectly intelligible, cannot be adopted, in the field of religious thought, without grave consequences. . . .

And it is to be observed that the greatest stumbling-blocks in the life of God which Deistic reason has made for itself, have turned . . . *not so much* upon His Majesty, His Almightiness, His Awfulness, as upon His Love and Condescension. Those who believe in God at all have felt that to say He was Almighty was the least they could say about Him. But they have been often unwilling to recognize in Him any traces of real Love. They would put up with a passive, unproductive Benevolence, smiling from some corner of the Universe over the tears of a creation which was too impotent or too sublime to reach. But an active, helping, interfering, practical Love; a Love studying sorrow in detail and assuaging it, or making of it a discipline, that should train men for perfect consolation in the mighty future; – this has Deism ever rejected even with scorn.

From: *Christmastide in St. Paul's* by H. P. Liddon

(Rivingtons, 1889, pp. 115–16)

Friday

Christmas

H. P. LIDDON

Christianity has ever been what it was in the Manger of Bethlehem. It has had two sides; one meeting the bodily eye; another, the eye of faith. To those who have failed to understand its Divine character, the visible, earthly side of Christianity has seemed to be its all. Throughout the ages of Christendom the eye of flesh, if we may so speak, has gazed exclusively at the Infant lying in the Manger; while faith has heard the angels chanting the *Gloria in Excelsis* around their Lord. Look at Christian literature – the Bible most of all. To sight, it is only an interesting collection of histories, and poems, and moral precepts, coming down to us from a long-past age, and entitled on literary grounds to our homage and admiration; but not at all exempt from error, or above criticism. To faith, it is the Word of God, Who has thus unveiled His Mind to His creatures by means of a series of organs of His Will, continued through many ages, until at last He spoke to us in His Son. Look, again, at Christian worship. Natural sight sees in it only the employment of certain words, the observance of particular forms, obedience to a rule which has come down from past ages; the partaking publicly of a little bread and wine; the sprinkling a little water on an infant's brow. To faith, all is lighted up by the sense of His Presence to Whom worship is offered, and apart from Whom it is unmeaning. . . .

And yet that which is outward in Christianity is addressed, not only or chiefly to our senses or natural reason, but also, and especially, to our hearts. Ever since the Everlasting Wisdom of the Father lay in the Manger, 'manifest in the Flesh', His religion has been tangible as well as spiritual, popular as well as philosophical. It has had an earthly form as well as a heavenly spirit; it has made provision for affection and imagination as well as for reason and conscience. Its Scriptures have been not merely thought, but poetry; its worship not merely the harmonious movement of souls towards the Invisible and Infinite Being, but the beauty of outward reverence and order; its life, outward duties of love as well as love's inward temper. Men have constantly endeavoured to suppress one side of Christianity in the supposed honour of the other; to ignore its provisions for intellect in order to exalt those which it makes for affection; or to reject

D

the visible ministries and expressions of love, with the object of making religion and worship more spiritual. But Christianity holds on its way, with its twofold character intact, as a Revelation of God, thus manifested in the Flesh, among the scenes of time.

From: *Christmastide in St. Paul's* by H. P. Liddon

(Rivingtons, 1889, pp. 119–20)

Saturday

Christmas

H. P. LIDDON

This bright festival itself, like the Infant in the Manger, has a human side as well as a Divine. It is an occasion for kindly greetings and courtesies, such as does not recur in the year. It has a joy all its own, some rays of which fall even on those who know nothing of its higher claims upon Christian faith. Let us not despise this lower aspect of Christmas; but let us not overestimate it. Christmas has its true meaning only for those who are leading new lives; for whom God's manifestation in the Flesh is, in their daily thoughts, an event with the importance of which nothing else can possibly compare.

If we thus know anything of the happiness of Christmas, let us turn our knowledge to practical account. We may each of us, on this day of the Kindness and Love of God our Saviour, do some act of kindness in His honour to some one of our poor or suffering brethren. There must be many natural recipients of such bounty known to very many of us; there must be some known to all. There must be some service which all can do in honour of Jesus Christ; all, even the youngest and the poorest. We can give, if not time, then food; if not food, then money, or clothes; we can pay a welcome visit, or offer the sympathy which is needed by those who get little of it. Only let each one in this congregation resolve to do something tomorrow in honour of Jesus Christ, and how much happiness will be diffused! The more we can do, the better. The more cheerfully we can do what we do, the better. Above all, the more unostentatiously we do what we do, the better; since we are doing it in His honour Who for our sakes veiled His Divine Glory beneath a servant's form.

From: *Christmastide in St. Paul's* by H. P. Liddon

(Rivingtons, 1889, pp. 121–2)

CHRISTMAS 2

(It is recommended that the readings suggested for this week be used for the week in which the Feast of the Epiphany occurs.)

Monday

The Glory of God

MICHAEL RAMSEY

In the previous chapters of this book the Biblical conception of the glory of God has been traced in every part of the Old Testament and the New. We have seen how the *kabod* of Yahveh includes ideas of power, character, radiance and physical accessibility which can be neither wholly disentangled nor set in historical sequence. We have seen how the Greek word *Doxa* finds a new meaning to express the Biblical conception in its variety and unity, and to provide a pattern upon which the New Testament writers could work. Then came the revelation of glory in the Gospel. Still the ideas of power, character, radiance and physical accessibility are included, for if the physical suggestions of glory are now made utterly subordinate to its ethical and transcendental aspects they never wholly disappear. To the last man's quest remains what it was in the days of Moses – the *seeing* of God. The Christian does not despise as carnal the ancient longing: 'Shew me, I pray thee, thy glory.'

In tracing the doctrine of the glory we have, almost unwittingly, been disclosing the pattern of the faith of the Bible. The God of the Bible is manifested in His created works, and yet He transcends them all. He rules in history with the sovereignty of His righteous purpose: He shewed His glory in delivering Israel to be His people, and though His glory cannot be circumscribed in time or place He set it in the midst of Israel as a tabernacling presence. Again and again He judged Israel for ascribing glory not to Him but to herself; and in the fullness of the times, He manifested His glory decisively in the birth, life, death and Resurrection of His Son. Once more He redeemed a people and set the glory of His presence in their midst, a glory which faith alone can discern. Again and again He has judged the new Israel for ascribing glory not to Him but to herself. And our present discerning of the glory of God by faith is not worthy to be compared to the vision of glory when we shall see Him as He is. In this glory not only redeemed humanity but all creation will share, though it now groans in bondage and awaits its deliverance into the liberty of the glory of God's children. In His glory righteousness and power are inseparably one; together with a radiance – bright so that men may receive knowledge of the truth, yet so bright that the truth is beyond their understanding.

From: *The Glory of God and the Transfiguration of Christ* by A. M. Ramsey

(Longmans, 1949, pp. 82–3)

Tuesday

The Glory of God

MICHAEL RAMSEY

The conception of glory illuminates every part of the structure of the Christian faith.

[Thus:]

God

The glory of God has been disclosed in His created works. 'The heavens declare the glory of God; and the firmanemt sheweth his handywork.'[1] In the things that are made the everlasting power and divinity of God are discernible by man, who is without excuse if he fails to give glory to Him.[2] But although God is known in His creation He transcends it utterly. Without Him, it cannot be: without it, His being is perfect. It is not that the existence of creatures is necessary to His glory, but that His creating them is the utterance or overflowing of a glory which eternally lacks nothing. The Biblical doctrine condemns the recurring sin whereby we worship some creature in place of the Creator, and it denies two recurring errors; the error of neglecting the *testimonia gloriae* in nature, in man and in history, and the error of treating God and the created world as co-partners mutually necessary. To glorify God is both to rejoice in His works, and to own their absolute dependence upon the Creator.

From: *The Glory of God and the Transfiguration of Christ* by A. M. Ramsey

(Longmans, 1949, p. 83)

[1] Ps. xix:1.
[2] Rom. i:20.

Wednesday

The Glory of God

MICHAEL RAMSEY

Glory and God

It is perhaps surprising that the word *glory* does not occur in the
Synoptic record of the teaching of Jesus about God. But in all that
He taught about the providence, graciousness, Fatherhood and
judgment of God, Jesus was implicitly speaking of the divine glory.
Above all, He brought into particular prominence the Fatherhood
of God: 'Father' became not one title amongst many, but *the* title by
which God is named. In the Lord's Prayer the 'name', the 'kingdom'
and the 'will' of the Father comprise the Father's glory. But Jesus
reveals the Father not by expounding a doctrine of universal
Fatherhood, but by executing His own mission as the Son . . .
Only when the mission of the Son has reached its climax in the
Passion and when the Spirit of the Son has been sent into the hearts
of the disciples crying 'Abba, Father', can they come to know the
Father's glory.

It is thus in the revelation of the Son and in the gift of the Spirit
that the Father's glory is fully disclosed. And it is disclosed in an
inseparable union with the glory of the one God, Father, Son, Spirit.
The obedience of Jesus to the Father in His life and death and the
vindication of Jesus by the Father in the Resurrection are the disclosure within time of a glory of self-giving love which belongs to
God from all eternity. 'The doctrine of the Trinity is the projection
into eternity of this essential relationship, the assertion that eternally
the divine life is a life of mutual self-giving to one another of Father
and Son through the Spirit who is the *vinculum* or bond of love
between them.' 'He lives in a human way the replica of a previous
mystery, without which the historic mystery would not exist. The
marvels of Galilee and Judaea are possible only because God has an
eternal Son.' The worship finally evoked by the events of the Gospel
is neither a cult of Jesus nor a reformed prophetic Judaism with the
Fatherhood in a new prominence, but the adoration of the triune
God.

From: *The Glory of God and the Transfiguration of Christ* by
   A. M. Ramsey

(Longmans, 1949, pp. 83–4)

The Glory of God

MICHAEL RAMSEY

Incarnation

'The Word became flesh and dwelt among us; and we beheld his glory.' Not all who saw Jesus saw the glory, but only those with faith to discern it. From the rest it was hidden. If the rulers of the world had known it, 'they would not have crucified the Lord of glory'.[1]

It was in humiliation that the glory was revealed on earth. There was the humiliation whereby the eternal Word took upon Himself the particularity of historical existence with all the limitations which that particularity involved. There was the humiliation involved in the 'messianic secret' which the Synoptists describe: for Jesus could not express His messianic claims outright to all and sundry without the continual danger of the distortion of claims which no human language and no contemporary categories sufficed to convey. There was the humiliation whereby His mission was completed only in suffering and death. But if this threefold humiliation was, viewed from one angle, a concealment of the glory, it was, viewed from another angle, only an aspect of the glory. That the Son of God could thus make His own the frustrations of human life and death was a signal manifestation of the glory of the divine self-giving. This point, which is independent of formal doctrines of Kenosis, has been made both by ancient and modern writers. Thus Gregory of Nyssa: 'That the omnipotence of the Divine nature should have had strength to descend to the lowliness of humanity, furnishes a more manifest proof of power than even the greatness and supernatural character of the miracles. . . . It is not the vastness of the heavens and the bright shining of the constellations, the order of the universe and the administration over all existence that so manifestly displays the transcendent power of the Deity, as this condescension to the weakness of our nature – the way in which sublimity is actually seen in lowliness, and yet the loftiness descends not.'[2] The mission of the Lord was at once the descent of one who trod the road of frustration, ignorance,

---

[1] 1 Cor. ii:8.

[2] Oratio Catechetica Magna, xxiv. cf. P.PT. Forsyth: *The Person and Place of Jesus Christ,* chs. XI, XII, for a powerful modern exposition of a similar line of thought.

pain and death and the ascent of one who was realizing in humiliation a glory which had been His from all eternity.

From: *The Glory of God and the Transfiguration of Christ* by A. M. Ramsey

(Longmans, 1949, pp. 84–5)

Friday

The Glory of God

MICHAEL RAMSEY

Glory and Incarnation

This paradox of the Incarnation is apparent in the Johannine language. On the one hand the Son retains on earth the glory which He ever had with the Father: 'the heavenly Word proceeding forth, yet leaving not the Father's side'. On the other hand the Son prays that the Father will bestow glory upon Him in the Passion and in the exaltation which will follow. There has been no abandonment of glory: yet the Son prays for glory and awaits the day when He will receive it. The right solution of this problem of Johannine exegesis seems to be that it is in His *human nature* that the Son receives glory from the Father, and He asks that through the Passion and Resurrection the human nature may be exalted into the eternal glory of the Godhead. Yet these two data – the Son's abiding glory, the Son's reception of glory through death and resurrection – are as two facets of a single mystery. It is by the humiliation of the Son's winning of glory in the toils of history that the eternal glory of the divine self-giving is most signally disclosed.

Such is the glory of the Incarnate life. We read of it in the narratives of the ministry and the Passion. But behind it is the glory of the act of Incarnation itself. *Verbum caro factum*: it is not only in the story of the Incarnate Lord but in the fact that He became Incarnate that the glory is made known, evoking the worship of angels and men. 'The Christian, then, looks out upon a metaphysical landscape of almost unbearable grandeur which compels him to awestruck adoration. But within that landscape, bathed in the light of charity, he sees in its full and touching beauty the specific object of his worship. This specific object is not simply the human figure of the Incarnate, the "historic Jesus", but the Eternal Godhead who here utters His word within the human arena and stoops to the human level; and whose inmost nature that figure reveals to men. . . . The real splendour of catholic devotion, its mingling of spaciousness and transcendence with homely love, is missed unless there is a remembrance of that unconditioned glory, which enters our conditioned world through that lowly door.'

From: *The Glory of God and the Transfiguration of Christ* by A. M. Ramsey

(Longmans, 1949, pp. 85–6)

Saturday

The Glory and the Christian Faith

MICHAEL RAMSEY

Atonement

It might be thought that the conception of glory, linked as it is with the Incarnation, had less to do with the doctrine of Atonement. But closer study shews that the glory not only provides a pattern of the doctrine of Atonement but illuminates the inner unity of some aspects of that doctrine which have been too often separated.

Primarily and obviously glory suggests that aspect of the Atonement which is described in the phrase *Christus Victor*. The glory shewn forth on Calvary was a kingly power mightier than the human and cosmic evil which was ranged against it. The prince of this world was defeated and judged: the world was overcome. But the *Christus Victor* doctrine does not stand alone: it includes, in the Fourth Gospel, the doctrine of a godward offering whereby sin is expiated. The Passion is a glorifying of the Father inasmuch as it is the laying down of the Son's life as a sacrificial offering.[1] The prayer for glory is also the prayer for Christ's self-consecration as a victim on behalf of the disciples.[2] Hence in the story of the Passion the imagery of the victorious king who reigns from the tree is blended with the imagery of the sacrificial victim who expiates sin and brings communion between God and man, slain as he is at the passover time[3] and slain as a peace-offering without the breaking of a bone.[4] The victory and the expiation are inseparable, and the *doxa* expresses this. The *doxa*

[1] John cf. vi:51; x:18.
[2] John xvii:1,19.
[3] John xix:14.
[4] John xix:36.

is the utter self-giving of Christ to the Father which, released by His death and brought into touch with human lives by His Spirit, can become the new principle of self-giving within them, and can banish from them the old principle of self-centred selfishness. Just as in Hebrews the sacrifice of Christ, through the sprinkling of the blood of sacrificial self-giving upon the consciences of men, breaks the power of sin, so in Saint John the glory of Christ's self-giving breaks the power of men's sinful glory of self-esteem. Christ's godward sacrifice for sin, Christ's victory over sin, Christ's sanctification of men by the Spirit: these aspects of Atonement are held together within the doctrine of the glory.

From: *The Glory of God and the Transfiguration of Christ* by A. M. Ramsey

(Longmans, 1949, pp. 86–7)

EPIPHANY 1

The Glory and the Christian Faith

MICHAEL RAMSEY

Church

'And the glory which thou has given me, I have given unto them; that they may be one, even as we are one.'[1] Herein lies the meaning of the Church. It is the mystery of the participation of men and women in the glory which is Christ's. Baptized into His death and made sharers in His resurrection they are members of the Body which is Christ's, branches of the vine who is Christ. Here the Spirit glorifies *Christ*, taking the things that are Christ's and declaring them to men.[2] Here the *Father* is glorified by the fruitfulness of the disciples.[3] Here too *men* are glorified, even as they are called and justified.[4] Here they are being transformed into Christ's image from glory to glory as from a sovereign Spirit.[5] But beneath every act in the Church whereby this many-sided work of glory is being wrought there is the truth about the Church's essential being, namely that the glory of Christ *is there*. The glory which Christians are to grow into and to manifest by the practical response of the Christian life is a glory which *is theirs* already.

Inasmuch as the glory dwells in it, the Church is the temple of God. In the post-exilic temple built by Zerubbabel and in the later temple built by Herod the glory had not returned. But now Christ's people, coming to Him 'a living stone, rejected indeed of men, but with God elect, precious', are built up 'as God's true temple'.[6] 'Know ye not', says Saint Paul, 'that ye are the temple of God, and that the Spirit of God dwelleth in you? If any man defile the temple of God, him shall God destroy; for the temple of God is holy, which temple ye are.'[7] Again, 'what agreement hath the temple of God with idols? For ye are the temple of the living God; as God hath said, I will dwell in them, and walk in them; and I will be their God, and they shall be my people.'[8] The Christians are 'an holy temple unto the Lord: in

[1] John xvii:22.
[2] John xvi:14.
[3] John xv:8.
[4] Rom. viii:30.
[5] 2 Cor. iii:18.
[6] 1 Peter ii:4–5.
[7] 1 Cor. iii:16–17.
[8] 2 Cor. vi:16.

whom ye also are builded together for an habitation of God through the Spirit'.[1]

From: *The Glory of God and the Transfiguration of Christ* by A. M. Ramsey

(Longmans, 1949, pp. 87–8)

Tuesday

The Glory and the Christian Faith

MICHAEL RAMSEY

Glory and The Church

... The knowledge that the glory dwells already in the Church may betray its members into the ancient sin whereby Israel ascribed the glory to itself, unless they are mindful of two warning truths of the apostolic teaching. (1) The first of these truths is that the glory in the church is an invisible glory. Though the Church is visible the glory is not to be confused with earthly majesty and splendour, for it is a glory discernible without and realized within – only through faith. It is hidden from the eyes of the unbelieving world and can never be displayed for that world's admiration; and it is hidden also from the members of the Church and can never be enjoyed by them in a quasi-worldly manner. 'Ye died, and your life is hid with Christ in God.'[2] Only at the Parousia will the glory become visible, and meanwhile *'neque Christum neque Christianos novit mundus; ac ne Christiani quidem plane seipsos.*[3] [Neither Christ nor Christians are known by the world: and Christians do not even clearly know one another.]' (2) The second of these truths is that the glory in the Church is but a foretaste of the glory that is to come, and therefore the Church's sense of possession is mingled with the Church's sense of incompleteness. *Here* the powers of the age to come are at work within the Church's humiliation: *there* the open vision of a glory awaits the Church in the day when judgment will begin at the house of God. It follows that the Church's claims are ratified by the Church's humility, and the Church's riches by the Church's hunger for what she lacks. Torn from this eschatological context the doctrine of the Church becomes the doctrine of an institution among other institu-

[1] Eph. ii:21–2.
[2] Col. iii:3.
[3] Bengal: Gnomon Novi Testamenti on Col. 3. 1–4.

tions upon the plane of history. Set in this eschatological context it
is the doctrine of a Church filled already with glory, yet humbled by
the command to await both a glory and a judgment hereafter.

From: *The Glory of God and the Transfiguration of Christ* by
A. M. Ramsey

(Longmans, 1949, pp. 88–9)

Wednesday

The Glory and the Christian Faith

MICHAEL RAMSEY

Eschatology

Throughout the investigation of the glory it has again and again
been apparent that the 'last things' are not a far-off outwork of the
structure of the Christian faith, but a determining factor within the
structure. If there is already 'salvation', 'redemption', 'life', 'glory',
it is so only because, through the agency of the Holy Spirit, an
anticipation has been given to us of 'salvation', 'redemption', 'life',
'glory' that belong to the age to come. Of the powers of that age we
have been allowed to taste.

The idea of the 'last things' has often been presented in terms of the
destiny of the individual: 'what happens to me when I die?'. But the
Christian doctrine sees the destiny of the individual as one part of the
pattern of the divine design for mankind and for all creation. God,
who created the world for His glory, will glorify His creatures and
lead them to glorify Him. The end is a new creation, forged from out
of the broken pieces of a fallen creation, filled with glory and giving
glory to its maker.

The crown of God's creation is man, made in the Creator's own
image and possessing an affinity to Him in virtue of which he may
come to know Him, to obey Him, to love Him and in the end to see
Him. The service of God in the reflection of God's holiness and love
is subsumed in the worship of God: and both the worship and the
service are subsumed finally in the seeing of God as He is. The seeing
of God amid the shadows of history in the Incarnate Life of the Son
is far less than the seeing of God which will be 'face to face'[1] and 'as

[1] 1 Cor. xiii:12.

he is'.[1] And this perfect seeing awaits the transforming of mankind into the image of Christ and their being made 'like Him'.

From: *The Glory of God and the Transfiguration of Christ* by
    A. M. Ramsey

(Longmans, 1949, pp. 89–90)

Thursday

The Glory and the Christian Faith

MICHAEL RAMSEY

Glory and Eschatology

. . . Besides his affinity to the Creator, in whose image he is made to and whose vision he strives to attain, Man has his place in relation to the rest of creation. He is set to rule over it as God's vicegerent, 'crowned with glory and honour' and with all things put in subjection under his feet;[2] and in his worship of God he is the spokesman of all created things. The mystery of evil afflicts not man alone, but all creation too. The sufferings of men at this present time,[3] the bondage of corruption in nature,[4] the fact that we see not yet all things made subject to man,[5] all betoken the frustration of the divine design by the fall. But by the Cross and Resurrection of Christ the inauguration of a new creation has begun, and this new creation will include both mankind brought to sonship and to glory,[6] and nature renewed in union with man in the worship and praise of God.[7] The Christian hope is therefore far more than the salvaging of human souls into a spiritual salvation: it is the re-creation of the world, through the power of the Resurrection of Christ.

Thus the hope of the beatific vision is crossed by the hope of the vindication of the divine design not only in man but in all things. And the hope of the resurrection of the body, when the body of our low estate is transformed into the body of Christ's glory,[8] is the reminder of our kinship with the created world which the God of glory will redeem in a new world wherein the old is not lost but fulfilled.

From: *The Glory of God and the Transfiguration of Christ* by
    A. M. Ramsey

(Longmans, 1949, p. 90)

[1] John iii:2.   [2] Ps. viii:3–8.   [3] Rom. viii:18.   [4] Rom. viii:21.
[5] Heb.ii:8.   [6] Rom. viii:21; Heb. ii:10.   [7] Rom. viii:21.   [8] Phil. iii:21.

Friday

The Praise of His Glory

MICHAEL RAMSEY

At the heart of the Church's glorifying of God there is however the new rite of the Eucharist. Here the Church is united to the glory of Christ on Calvary and in heaven, and finds the focus of the glorifying of God by all created things.

In the upper room our Lord (i) gave thanks to God over the loaf at the beginning of the supper and over the cup at the end of the supper, (ii) identified the loaf with His body and the wine with His blood – that is with His life surrendered in sacrificial offering, (iii) bade His disciples partake of both the body and the blood, (iv) predicted a feasting with them in the messianic age. This eucharistic action may be interpreted by the language of the Fourth Gospel. Inasmuch as our Lord, by His actions and words with the loaf and the cup, is declaring Himself to be dedicated to a sacrificial death, He is indeed glorifying the Father[1] and consecrating Himself on behalf of the disciples.[2] Inasmuch as He bids the disciples to feed upon His life surrendered as a sacrifice it is here that 'the glory which thou gavest me I have given unto them'.[3] The food which they receive is the life of Christ laid down in godward offering: the glory which they are given is the glory wherewith Christ glorified the Father.

Thus the subsequent eucharistic worship of the Church is on its godward side a participation in Christ's glorifying of the Father, and on its manward side a receiving of Christ's glory – the glory of the Cross. Inasmuch as the rite is a shewing-forth of Christ's death[4] it recalls the glory of Calvary. Inasmuch as it is a sharing in the body of Christ and in the blood of Christ[5] it unites those who partake with the glory of Christ as He now is – risen, ascended and glorifying the Father. Inasmuch as it employs God's common gifts of bread and wine and brings them to be blessed, it is a glorifying of the Creator by the giving back of His own created gifts to Him. And inasmuch as it points forward to the coming of Christ again[6] it is an anticipation of that feasting with Christ in the world to come, when Him Whom we now perceive by faith we shall behold with open face.

[1] John xvii:I.   [2] John xvii:19.
[3] John xvii:22.   [4] 1 Cor. xi:26.
[5] 1 Cor. x:16.   [6] 1 Cor. xi:26.

Inasmuch as the glory is the glory of Father and Son in the bond of love, the eucharistic gift of glory to the disciples is tested in their unity. The Pauline 'we being many are one bread, one body, for we all partake of the one bread' is tested in the Johannine, 'the glory which thou has given me I have given unto them; that they may be one, even as we are one'.[1] The new covenant in the blood of Christ is inseparable from the new commandment of mutual love in the manifestation of Christ's own love.[2] Hence the common life of the Christian fellowship is not only a witness to the glory, but is itself the glory of the Father and the Son shewn forth to the world. Without this common life – *ichabod*, the glory is departed.

From: *The Glory of God and the Transfiguration of Christ* by A. M. Ramsey

(Longmans, 1949, pp. 98–9)

Saturday

The Praise of His Glory

MICHAEL RAMSEY

The godward life of the Church includes the manward mission of the Church, not merely as a close corollary but as a very part of that life. Christ's own proclamation of the word to the disciples[3] was a part of His glorifying of the Father;[4] and the disciples' own ministry of the word[5] is the means whereby men are led to share in the glory.[6] Saint Paul likewise after describing the Christians as beholding the glory and being transformed into it from glory unto glory[7] goes on to tell of the preaching by the apostles of the gospel of the glory of Christ.[8]

The preaching of the glory of Christ, if it is guided by the New Testament use of *doxa*, has as its centre the Resurrection with the Cross as its prelude, and it leads men to see the significance of the ministry and teaching of our Lord with the light of Calvary and Easter upon it. The preaching will appeal to the affinity between the gospel and mankind as created in the divine image, and its preachers will commend themselves 'to every man's conscience in the sight of

---

[1] John xvii:22.
[2] John xiii:31–5.
[3] John xvii:6.
[4] John xvii:4.
[5] John xvii:20.
[6] John xvii:22.
[7] 2 Cor. iii:17.
[8] 2 Cor. iv:3–6.

God'.[1] But the warning of Saint Paul must be heeded: 'But and if our gospel is veiled, it is veiled in them that are perishing: in whom the god of this world hath blinded the minds of the unbelieving, that the light of the gospel of the glory of Christ who is the image of God, should not dawn upon them'.[2] It is not to be thought that the gospel will be made simple to the worldly and the impenitent, and the attempt to make it simple to them may corrupt or distort it.

For, as has been wisely said[3]: 'the simplicity of the gospel lies in the simplicity of the moral issues which it raises, and not in the ease with which its teaching can be explained to the careless and the hardened.' The injunction to let our light so shine before men that they may see our good works and so be led to glorify God[4] does not mean that a programme of good works can commend the gospel by meeting men's ideals upon their own level, without any challenge to the assumptions on which those ideals often rest. The fellowship of the Church can indeed manifest the glory of God to the consciences of men; but it does so not by providing something for impenitent men to like and admire, but by being a fellowship so filled with God Himself that the conscience is pierced by God's love and judgment. Thus the Gospel of the Glory of God is always very near to mankind, and yet always very far from them: near, because the divine image is in mankind and the Gospel is the true meaning of man; far, because it is heard only by a faith and a repentance which overthrow all man's glorying in himself and his works.

'And I saw another angel flying in mid heaven, having an eternal Gospel to proclaim unto them that dwell on the earth, and unto every nation and tribe and tongue and people; and he saith with a great voice, Fear God, and give Him glory; for the hour of his judgment is come: and worship him that made the heaven and the earth and sea and fountains of waters.'[5]

From: *The Glory of God and the Transfiguration of Christ* by A. M. Ramsey

(Longmans, 1949, pp. 99–100)

[1] 2 Cor. iv:2.
[2] 2 Cor. iv:3–4.
[3] H. L. Goudge, *The Second Epistle to the Corinthians.*
[4] Matt. v:16.
[5] Rev. xiv:6–7.

EPIPHANY 2

Monday

Pastor Pastorum

H. LATHAM

I have spoken of the 'Schooling of the Apostles' for want of a better phrase, but the mental changes wrought in the disciples by their Master's company constitute a very different sort of schooling from what commonly goes by the name. They receive no doctrinal instruction in dogmatic form, they obtain nothing which they can display, they are shewn no new system for dealing with the problems of life, nor are they given fresh views about the Messiah. Those who come asking 'What they are to do?' are always told that they already know, or should know, this very well of themselves. Among the great Teachers of the world there is hardly one, whose chosen pupils have received so few tenets in a formulated shape as those of Christ; and yet the Apostles at the time of the Ascension have undergone a transformation, compared with what they were when our Lord first found them, greater than was ever wrought in men in the same time before.

One special function was assigned to the Apostles which sets them apart from all other men. In them was engendered a new quality belonging to spiritual life; they were the trustess of mankind for a new capacity; they were the depositaries of the faculty for realizing 'the assurance of things hoped for, the proving of things not seen'. In them Faith, which elsewhere existed only in the germ, was brought to perfection and bore fruit, and scattered seed. Their progress in this quality proceeds by certain steps; these are roughly indicated in the first chapter of this book, but I will name them here again.

First of all, the men who were chosen for the work had a more than usual power of savouring the things of God. They are brought under the influence of One whom they regard as the Messiah but about whom something of mystery hangs. They conceive for him a passionate loyalty, and an affection, of which that inspired by the highest human natures will only serve to give a bare idea; they are with him day by day; they look on his Signs and Wonders, but it seems to them so natural that a Man like Him should work wonders, that they scarcely marvel at them. Inward evil, selfish thoughts and all, disappear when He is by.

From: *Pastor Pastorum* by Rev. Henry Latham

(Deighton Bell, Cambridge, 1897, pp. 272–4)

Tuesday

Pastor Pastorum

H. LATHAM

[The Apostles] are educated to feel that in His company they are safe against outward dangers. This growing confidence was tried and found wanting when they were with their Master on the Lake and the storm arose; the lesson had to be studied a little longer. As soon as it was fully learned they were advanced another stage; the Apostles, in the great practical lesson which is the leading matter of this chapter, were taught that Christ's power reached beyond His presence, that it could even be delegated to them, and that His shelter could be spread over them, though He might be far away. They are sent forth without purse and scrip that they may better feel that they are in Christ's hand and need give no thought to petty daily cares. The same lesson is afterwards given to the Seventy disciples. The Crucifixion brought about an education of a very different kind, that of affliction and trial; but the Apostles do not, at once, wholly lose their Master, He is withdrawn from them by degrees. After the Resurrection though He no longer lives on the earth a common life with men, yet His disciples feel that He is not absolutely gone; He seems to be still close by, and they may at any moment see His loved and honoured form and hear the words 'Peace be unto you'. The stranger who joins them on the road may prove to be He; they may catch sight of the Lord's features as He vanishes away. Then comes the last stage of separation when He is completely lost to eye and ear, and Spiritual Communion only is maintained. Most carefully and by wisely ordered

degrees had they been brought to apprehend this Spiritual Communion, and they were actuated by the inner sense of His presence
during all the rest of their lives. This it was, this realization of our
Lord's words 'Lo, I am always with you unto the end of the world',
which rendered – and still is rendering – the Christian Church a
body living and organic, and not a mere exponent or depository of
doctrines, and of traditions about the Lord.

From: *Pastor Pastorum* by Rev. Henry Latham

(Deighton Bell, Cambridge, 1897, pp. 274–5)

Wednesday

Pastor Pastorum

H. LATHAM

Our Lord left his fixed home at Capernaum, and He and the
Twelve adopted a wandering life. These journeys taken in company
supplied a need which in all education is a foremost one, that of
discipline. They were given duties to perform. When men travel together, faring hardly on rough mountain ways, bound to start together and to keep up each with the rest, whether disposed to do so
or not, they soon come to set inclination on one side and to learn
what obligation means. There is no kind of companionship which
binds men in a closer and heartier fellowship than this journeying
together. Thus the Schooling of the Twelve went on, without their
guessing it, as they went with their Master, sometimes on foot over
the hills, sometimes rowing the boat on the Lake, sometimes providing for His reception in the cities, or marshalling hearers to listen to
the word; and sometimes, when multitudes had to be fed, arranging
them, plot by plot, so that they might be reached by those who
distributed the food.

This work afforded the very training required. Nothing is more
remarkable in the Apostles than their unbroken mental health. The
histories of religious communities are full of instances of ecstasies
and hysterical delusions; but never do we find among our Lord's
followers anything approaching to a spiritual craze. Such crazes are
commonly the growth of solitude, and no Apostle while the new ideas

are working in him is suffered to be long alone. This health of theirs came in great measure from their being constantly employed about matters of which their hearts were full. The training of the Apostles fulfils all the conditions for sound spiritual health; the Twelve lead lives of out-door labour, with constant change of scene, with varied interests, with occupations to engage their minds; some had the provisioning to see to, some the contributions, some were sent on in advance to secure lodging, and some wrought works of healing in their Master's name. All this was conducive to their becoming self-helpful, fertile in practical resource, as well as earnestly devoted to their Master, confident both of His power and of that delegated to themselves. Their way of life brought them also in acquaintance with the various dispositions and ways of men: all of this was essential for their work.

From: *Pastor Pastorum* by Rev. Henry Latham

(Deighton Bell, Cambridge, 1897, pp. 277–9)

Thursday

Pastor Pastorum

H. LATHAM

'And as they went in the way, a certain man said unto him, I will follow thee whithersoever thou goest. And Jesus said unto him, The foxes have holes, and the birds of the heaven *have* nests; but the Son of man hath not where to lay his head. And he said unto another, Follow me. But he said, Lord, suffer me first to go and bury my father. But he said unto him, Leave the dead to bury their own dead; but go thou and publish abroad the kingdom of God. And another also said, I will follow thee, Lord; but first suffer me to bid farewell to them that are at my house. But Jesus said unto him, No man, having put his hand to the plough, and looking back, is fit for the kingdom of God.'[1]

What caught attention and led to the collocation of these two (and in St. Luke three) instances was the diversity of our Lord's treatment of cases apparently similar. The disciples saw that our Lord repelled one who was willing to follow him at once, and imperatively sum-

[1] Luke ix:57–62.

moned two others who asked for delay. But though they might be puzzled at this inconsistency, they felt sure that there was a purpose and a meaning in it; so they transcribed these contrasting cases side by side, to show that for different conditions of soul Christ had different treatment ready. The second and third of these colloquies probably took place at a different time from the first. They seem to have been held between our Lord and some of the disciples who were summoned to go out on the mission of the seventy, for St. Luke inserts this document in his history just before his account of the mission. Thus St. Matthew in his narrative puts the passage where the first incident occurs, while St. Luke fixes its place by the second and third.

This *individualizing* in our Lord's treatment of men struck the disciples as something new; they do not indeed point it out as a novel feature, for they never remark upon our Lord's ways, but the care of the Evangelists in preserving the most striking instances of this diversity of treatment shews that it caught their notice. To our Lord's eye every human being had a moral and spiritual physiognomy of his own. He saw at once, what it was in each man which went to make him emphatically and distinctly his very self, and He addressed Himself largely to this.

From: *Pastor Pastorum* by Rev. Henry Latham

(Deighton Bell, Cambridge, 1897, pp. 373–5)

Friday

Pastor Pastorum

H. LATHAM

What most particularizes the scribe is his impulsiveness. We have here another example of that mistrust of emotional fervour which our Lord uniformly shews. The woman who cried 'Blessed is the womb that bare thee', the scribe in the case before us, and St. Peter, when he said, 'I am ready to go with thee both to prison and to death', all are answered by our Lord in the same tone of repression.

Sudden transports and ebullitions of feeling like those just named, come mainly of temperament and of passing physical conditions which subjugate the agent, and our Lord does not regard them as betokening a character on which he can depend.

It speaks well for the right feeling of this scribe, that he forbears to press his suit. He divined, with the delicacy of a well bred Oriental, that our Lord's reply, though apparently only discouraging him from following for his own sake, shewed that He held it best that he should stay behind. He is satisfied that our Lord's judgment will be right and he yields at once. A man with less perception might have protested against the imputation on his endurance, and have declared that he would go with the Master though he should have to lie on the bare earth.

That, however genuine his devotion may have been, it was best for the scribe to stay at home is easy to understand; he had been used to an indoors life and under hardships and exposure he would have broken down; besides, while being a burden to the rest, he could, as a jaded man, have gained little in moral or spiritual growth. He was moreover, both as to culture and social caste, of a different type from the rest, and his presence would have made the party less homogeneous. Another important consideration was this: by remaining where he was, he might do that particular kind of good for which he was suited by temper and condition better than by following our Lord. The course which had taken hold of his imagination may not have been that in which he could do the best work. By remaining in Galilee and mixing with other educated men, he, like Joseph of Arimathea and Nicodemus, might help to spread tolerance and leaven the mass.

From: *Pastor Pastorum* by Rev. Henry Latham

(Deighton Bell, Cambridge, 1897, pp. 375–7)

Saturday

Pastor Pastorum

H. LATHAM

It has commonly been taken for granted, that the father of the spokesman in the first of these cases was lying dead when our Lord met him and bade him follow; but Eastern usages almost preclude this view, for the Jews buried within twenty-four hours of the death, and for a son to be seen in public while his father was lying dead would to their minds have been highly indecent. Some think that, the father being in extreme age, the son asked to be allowed to stay with him till he died; what seems to me more likely is that the completion of the ten days of strict mourning was regarded as part of the obsequies, and that the word 'buried' applies to this. The father might have been laid in the ground, but the ten days not having expired, the funeral solemnities were not considered over.

I think that our Lord meant in this case to leave a lesson, and that the lesson was this. Family ties and duties, blessed though they usually are, must not be turned into idols or suffered to hamper the 'clear spirit' in its ascent to God. There is such a thing as the tyranny of family just as there is of social usage or public opinion, and from each and all of these our Lord would set men free. This kind of freedom would cost a struggle as other kinds also would, and owing to divisions caused by change of Faith even parents might be set against children and children against parents – a heavy price indeed, but one that vanishes compared with the opening of eternal life to mankind. Supposing, as I do, that these disciples were summoned by our Lord to go forth with the seventy, I find in this inflexibility which our Lord displays something quite of a piece with the order to 'salute no man by the way', and to wipe off the dust from their feet when not received; all this is consistent, when taken together, and viewed as a lesson in the dignity of consecration to God and the imperative character of the charge imposed.

From: *Pastor Pastorum* by Rev. Henry Latham

(Deighton Bell, Cambridge, 1897, pp. 377–9)

(If the Feast of St. Paul occurs in this week of Epiphany 3, the reading for St. Paul should be used on that day, the reading for Friday omitted, and the rest adjusted accordingly.)

Monday

St. Paul

W. R. INGE

Saul of Tarsus was a Benjamite of pure Israelite descent, but also a Roman citizen by birth. His famous old Jewish name was Latinized or Graecized as Paulos (*Saulos* means 'waddling', and would have been a ridiculous name); he doubtless bore both names from boyhood. Tarsus is situated in the plain of Cilicia, and is now about ten miles from the sea. It is backed by a range of hills, on which the wealthier residents had villas, while the high glens of Taurus, nine or ten miles further inland, provided a summer residence for those who could afford it, and a fortified acropolis in time of war. . . .

St. Paul did not belong to the upper class. . . . But he was well educated because he was the son of a strict Jew. A child in such a home would learn by heart large pieces of the Old Testament, and, at the Synagogue school, all the minutiae of the Jewish Law. The pupil was not allowed to write anything down; all was committed to the memory, which in consequence became extremely retentive. The perfect pupil 'lost not a drop from his teacher's cistern'. At the age of about fourteen the boy would be sent to Jerusalem, to study under one of the great Rabbis; in St. Paul's case it was Gamaliel. Under his tuition the young Pharisee would learn to be a 'strong Churchman'. The Rabbis viewed everything from an ecclesiastical standpoint. The interests of the Priesthood, the Altar, and the Temple overshadowed everything else. The Priestly Code, says Mr. Cohu, practically resolves itself into one idea: Everything in Israel belongs to God; all places, all times, all persons, and all property are His. But God accepts a part of His due; and, if this part is scrupulously paid, He will send His blessing upon the remainder. Besides the written law, the Pharisee had to take on himself the still heavier burden of the oral law, which was equally binding. It was a seminary education of the

most rigorous kind. St. Paul cannot reproach himself with any slack-
ness during his novitiate. He threw himself into the system with
characteristic ardour. Probably he meant to be a Jerusalem Rabbi
himself, still practising his trade, as the Rabbis usually did. For he
was unmarried; and every Jew except a Rabbi was expected to marry
at or before the age of twenty-one.

From: *Outspoken Essays* by William Ralph Inge

(Longmans, 1919, pp. 209–11)

Tuesday

St. Paul

W. R. INGE

We must bear in mind his terrible record of suffering if we wish to
estimate fairly the character of the man. During his whole life after
his conversion he was exposed not only to the hardships of travel,
sometimes in half-civilized districts, but to 'all the cruelty of the
fanaticism which rages like a consuming fire through the religious
history of the East from the slaughter of Baal's priests to the slaughter
of St. Stephen, and from the butcheries of Jews at Alexandria under
Caligula to the massacres of Christians at Adama, Tarsus, and
Antioch in the year 1909'.[1] It is one evil result of such furious bigotry
that it kindles hatred and resentment in its victims, and tempts them
to reprisals. St. Paul does speak bitterly of his opponents, though
chiefly when he finds that they have injured his converts, as in the
letter to the Galatians. Modern critics have exaggerated this element
in a character which does not seem to have been fierce or implacable.
He writes like a man engaged in a stern conflict against enemies who
will give no quarter, and who shrink from no treachery. But the
sharpest expression that can be laid to his charge is the impatient,
perhaps half humorous wish that the Judaizers who want to circum-
cise the Galatians might be subjected to a severer operation themselves.[2] The dominant impression that he makes upon us is that he
was cast in a heroic mould. He is serenely indifferent to criticism and
calumny; no power on earth can turn him from his purpose. He has
made once for all a complete sacrifice of all earthly joys and all

[1] Deissmann.
[2] Gal. v:12.

earthly ties; he has broken (he, the devout Jewish Catholic) with his Church and braved her thunders; he has faced the opprobrium of being called traitor, heretic, and apostate; he has 'withstood to the face' the Palestinian apostles who were chosen by Jesus and held His commission; he has set his face to achieve, almost single-handed, the conquest of the Roman Empire, a thing never dreamed of by the Jerusalem Church; he is absolutely indifferent whether his mission will cost him his life, or only involve a continuation of almost intolerable hardship. It is this indomitable courage, complete self-sacrifice, and single-minded devotion to a magnificently audacious but not impracticable idea, which constitute the greatness of St. Paul's character. He was, with all this, a warm-hearted and affectionate man, as he proved abundantly by the tone of his letters. His personal religion was, in essence, a pure mysticism; he worships a Christ whom he has experienced as a living presence in his soul. The mystic who is also a man of action, and a man of action because he is a mystic, wields a tremendous power over other men. He is like an invulnerable knight, fighting in magic armour.

From: *Outspoken Essays* by William Ralph Inge

(Longmans, 1919, pp. 213–14)

Wednesday

St. Paul

W. R. INGE

The distinctive feature of the Jewish religion is not, as is often supposed, its monotheism. Hebrew religion in its golden age was monolatry rather than monotheism; and when Jahveh became more strictly 'the only God', the cult of intermediate beings came in, and restored a quasi-polytheism. The distinctive feature in Jewish faith is its historical and teleological character. The God of the Jew is not natural law. If the idea of necessary causation ever forced itself upon his mind, he at once gave it the form of predestination. The whole of history is an unfolding of the divine purpose; and so history as a whole has for the Jew an importance which it never had for a Greek thinker, nor for the Hellenized Jew Philo. The Hebrew idea of God is dynamic and ethical; it is therefore rooted in the idea of Time. The Pharisaic school modified this prophetic teaching in two ways. It became more spiritual; anthropomorphisms were removed, and the transcendence of God above the world was more strictly maintained. On the other hand, the religious relationship became in their hands narrower and more external. The notion of a covenant was defined more rigorously; the Law was practically exalted above God, so that the Rabbis even represent the Deity as studying the Law. With this legalism went a spirit of intense exclusiveness and narrow ecclesiasticism. As God was raised above direct contact with men, the old animistic belief in angels and demons, which had lasted on in the popular mind by the side of the worship of Jahveh, was extended in a new way. A celestial hierarchy was invented, with names, and an infernal hierarchy too; the malevolent ghosts of animism became fallen angels. Satan, who in Job is the crown-prosecutor, one of God's retinue, becomes God's adversary; and the angels, formerly manifestations of God Himself, are now quite separated from Him. A supramundane physics or cosmology was evolved at the same time. Above Zion, the centre of the earth, rise seven heavens, in the highest of which the Deity has His throne. The underworld is now first divided into Paradise and Gehenna. The doctrine of the fall of man, through his participation in the representative guilt of his first parents, is Pharisaic; as is the strange legend, which St. Paul seems to have believed,[1] that the Serpent carnally seduced Eve, and so infected the race with spiritual poison. Justification, in Pharisaism as for St. Paul, means the verdict of acquittal. The bad receive in this life the reward for any small merits which they may possess; the sins of the good must be atoned for; but merits . . . may be stored and transferred. Martyrdoms especially augment the spiritual bank-balance of the whole nation. There was no official Messianic doctrine, only a mass of vague fancies and beliefs, grouped round the central idea of the appearance on earth of a supernatural Being, who should establish a theocracy of some kind at Jerusalem. The righteous dead will be raised to take part in this kingdom. The course of the world is thus divided into two epochs – 'this age' and 'the age to come'. A catastrophe will end the former and inaugurate the latter. The promised deliverer is now waiting in heaven with God, until his hour comes; and it will come very soon. All this St. Paul must have learned from Gamaliel. It formed the framework of his theology as a Christian for many years after his conversion, and was only partially thrown off, under the influence of mystical experience and of Greek ideas, during the period covered by the letters. The lore of good and bad spirits (the latter are 'the princes of this world' in 1 Cor. ii. 6, 8)

[1] 2 Cor. xi:3.

pervades the Epistles more than modern readers are willing to admit. It is part of the heritage of the Pharisaic school.

From: *Outspoken Essays* by William Ralph Inge

(Longmans, 1919, pp. 215–16)

Thursday

St. Paul

W. R. INGE

Philo gives important testimony to the existence of a 'liberal' school among the Jews of the Dispersion, who, under pretext of spiritualizing the traditional law, left off keeping the Sabbath and the great festivals, and even dispensed with the rite of circumcision. Thus the admission of Gentiles on very easy terms into the Church was no new idea to the Palestinian Jews; it was known to them as part of the shocking laxity which prevailed among their brethren of the Dispersion. With Stephen, this kind of liberalism seemed to have entered the group of 'disciples'. He was accused of saying that Jesus was to destroy the temple and change the customs of Moses. In his bold defence he admitted that in his view the Law was valid only for a limited period, which would expire so soon as Jesus returned as Messiah. This was quite enough for the Sanhedrin. They stoned Stephen, and compelled the 'disciples' to disperse and fly for their lives. Only the Apostles, whose devotion to the Law was well known, were allowed to remain. This last fact, briefly recorded in Acts, is important as an indication that the persecution was directed only against the liberalizing Christians, and that these were the great majority. Saul, it seems, had no quarrel with the Twelve; his hatred and fanaticism were aroused against a sect of Hellenist Jews who openly proclaimed that the Law had been abrogated in advance by their Master, who, as Saul observed with horror, had incurred the curse of the Law by dying on a gibbet. All the Pharisee in him was revolted; and he led the savage heretic-hunt which followed the execution of Stephen.

What caused the sudden change which so astonished the survivors among his victims? To suppose that nothing prepared for the vision near Damascus, that the apparition in the sky was a mere 'bolt from the blue', is an impossible theory. The best explanation is furnished by a study of the Apostle's character, which we really know very well.

The author of the Epistles was certainly not a man who could watch a young saint being battered to death by howling fanatics, and feel no emotion. Stephen's speech may have made him indignant; his heroic death, the very ideal of a martyrdom, must have awakened very different feelings. An undercurrent of dissatisfaction, almost of disgust, at the arid and unspiritual seminary teaching of the Pharisees now surged up and came very near the surface. His bigotry sustained him as a persecutor for a few weeks more; but how if he could himself see what the dying Stephen said that he saw? Would not that be a welcome liberation? The vision came in the desert, where men see visions and hear voices to this day. They were very common in the desert of Gobi when Marco Polo traversed it. 'The Spirit of Jesus', as he came to call it, spoke to his heart, and the form of Jesus flashed before his eyes. Stephen had been right; the Crucified was indeed the Lord from heaven. So Saul became a Christian; and it was to the Christianity of Stephen, not to that of James the Lord's brother, that he was converted. The Pharisee in him was killed.

From: *Outspoken Essays* by William Ralph Inge
(Longmans, 1919, pp. 216–18)

Friday

St. Paul

W. R. INGE

The travelling missionary was as familiar a figure in the Levant as the travelling lecturer on philosophy. The Greek language brought all nationalities together. The Hellenizing of the East had gone on steadily since the conquests of Alexander; and Greek was already as useful as Latin in many parts of the West. A century later, Marcus Aurelius wrote his Confessions in Greek; and even in the middle of the third century, when the tide was beginning to turn in favour of Latin, Plotinus lectured in Greek at Rome. Christianity, within a few years after the Crucifixion, had allied itself definitely with the speech, and therefore inevitably with the spirit, of Hellenism. At no time since have travel and trade been so free between the West of Europe and the West of Asia. A Phrygian merchant (according to the inscription on his tomb) made seventy-two journeys to Rome in the course of his business-life. The decomposition of nationalities, and the destruction of civic exclusiveness, led naturally to the formation of voluntary associations of all kinds, from religious sects to trade unions; sometimes a single association combined these two functions. The Oriental religions appealed strongly to the unprivileged classes, among which genuine religious faith was growing, while the official cults of the Roman Empire were unsatisfying in themselves and associated with tyranny. The attempt of Augustus to resuscitate the old religion was artificial and unfruitful. The living movement was towards a syncretism of religious ideas and practices, all of which came from the Eastern provinces and beyond them. The prominent features in this new devotion were the removal of the supreme Godhead from the world to a transcendental sphere; contempt for the world and ascetic abnegation of 'the flesh'; a longing for healing and redemption, and a close identification of salvation with individual immortality; and, finally, trust in sacraments ('mysteries', in Greek) as indispensable means of grace or redemption. This was the Paganism with which Christianity had to reckon, as well as with the official cult and its guardians. The established church it conquered and destroyed; the living syncretistic beliefs it cleansed, simplified, and disciplined, but only absorbed by becoming itself a syncretistic religion. But besides Christians and Pagans, there were the Jews, dispersed over the whole Empire. There were at least a million in Egypt, a country which St. Paul, for reasons unknown to us, left severely alone; there were still more in Syria, and perhaps five millions in the whole Empire. In spite of the fecundity of Jewish women, it is impossible that the Hebrew stock should have multiplied to this extent. There must have been a very large number of converts, who were admitted, sometimes without circumcision, on their profession of monotheism and acceptance of the Jewish moral code. The majority of these remained in the class technically called 'God-fearers', who never took upon themselves the whole yoke of the Law. These half-Jews were the most promising field for Christian missionaries; and nothing exasperated the Jews more than to see St. Paul fishing so successfully in their waters. The spirit of propagandism almost disappeared from Judaism after the middle of the second century. Judaism shrank again into a purely Eastern religion, and renounced the dangerous compromise with Western ideas. The labour of St. Paul made an all-important parting of the ways. Their result was that Christianity became a European religion, while Judaism fell back upon its old traditions.

From: *Outspoken Essays* by William Ralph Inge

(Longmans, 1919, pp. 218–20)

Saturday

St. Paul

W. R. INGE

'There is hardly any fact' (says Harnack) 'which deserves to be turned over and pondered so much as this, that the religion of Jesus has never been able to root itself in Jewish or even upon Semitic soil.' This extraordinary result is the judgment of history upon the life and work of St. Paul. Jewish Christianity rapidly withered and died. According to Justin, who must have known the facts, Jesus was rejected by the whole Jewish nation 'with a few exceptions'. In Galilee especially, few, if any, Christian Churches existed. There are other examples, of which Buddhism is the most notable, of a religion gaining its widest acceptance outside the borders of the country which gave it birth. But history offers no parallel to the complete vindication of St. Paul's policy in carrying Christianity over into the Graeco-Roman world, where alone, as the event proved, it could live. This is a complete answer to those who maintain that Christ made no break with Judaism. Such a statement is only tenable if it is made in the sense of Harnack's words, that 'what Gentile Christianity did was to carry out a process which had in fact commenced long before in Judaism itself, viz. the process by which the Jewish religion was inwardly emancipated and turned into a religion for the world'. But the true account would be that Judaism, like other great ideas, had to 'die to live'. It died in its old form, in giving birth to the religion of civilized humanity, as the Greek nation perished in giving birth to Hellenism, and the Roman in creating the Mediterranean empire of the Caesars and the Catholic Church of the Popes. The Jewish people were unable to make so great a sacrifice of their national hopes. With the matchless tenacity which characterizes their race they clung to their tribal God and their temporal and local millennium. The disasters of A.D. 70 and of the revolt under Hadrian destroyed a great part of the race, and at last uprooted it from the soil of Palestine. But conservatism, as usual, has had its partial justification. Judaism has refused to acknowledge the religion of the civilized world as her legitimate child; but the nation has refused also to surrender its life. There are no more Greeks and Romans; but the Jews we have always with us.

St. Paul saw that the Gospel was a far greater and more revolutionary scheme than the Galilean apostles had dreamed of. In principle he committed himself from the first to the complete emancipation of Christianity from Judaism. But it was inevitable that he did not at first realize all that he had undertaken. And, fortunately for us, the most rapid evolution in his thought took place during the ten years to which his extant letters belong. It is exceedingly interesting to trace his gradual progress away from Apocalyptic Messianism to a position very near that of the Fourth Gospel. The evangelist whom we call St. John is the best commentator on Paulinism.

From: *Outspoken Essays* by William Ralph Inge

(Longmans, 1919, pp. 222-4)

Monday

The Birds and the Lilies

SØREN KIERKEGAARD

It was on the summit of Sinai the Law was given, amidst the thunders of heaven; every beast that approached the holy mountain (alas, innocently and unawares) must be put to death – according to the Law. It is at the foot of the mountain the Sermon on the Mount is preached. Thus it is the Law is related to the Gospel, which is the heavenly come down to earth. . . . It is at the foot of the mountain; yea, what is more, the birds and the lilies are in the company . . . and what is more they are there to teach; for it is true enough that the Gospel itself is the real teacher, that He is 'the Teacher' – and the Way and the Truth and the Life in the instruction, and yet the birds and the lilies come along as assistant teachers of a sort.

How is this possible? Well, really, the thing is not so difficult. For the fact is that neither the lilies nor the birds are *heathen*, but neither are the lilies and the birds *Christians*, and just for this reason they could be especially helpful by way of giving instruction in Christianity. Consider the lilies and the birds, and then thou dost discover how the heathen live, for it is precisely not like the lilies and the birds that they live; if thou dost live like the lilies and the birds, thou art a Christian – which the lilies and the birds neither are nor can become. Paganism stands in opposition to Christianity, but the lilies and the birds stand in no opposition to any of these contending parties; if one may say so, they play apart by themselves, keep shrewdly aloof from all oppositions. So then, the Gospel, in order not to condemn and denounce, uses the lilies and the birds to show what paganism is, but also at the same time to show what is required of Christians. In order to avoid a tone of condemnation the lilies and the birds are thrust in between; for the lilies and the birds condemn nobody – and as for thee, thou shalt not condemn the heathen, thou shalt learn from the lilies and the birds. Yes, it is a difficult task the lilies and the birds have, a difficult position they are in as instructors; there was nobody else could do it, every other teacher would so easily be tempted to accuse and condemn the heathen and praise the Christians (instead of imparting instruction), or mockingly to condemn the so-called Christians who do not live as they ought. But the lilies and the birds, which are engaged solely in teaching and are absorbed in it, do not express any opinions, look neither to the right hand nor to the left, neither commend nor reprove, as teachers generally are wont to do. Like Him, 'the Teacher', of whom it is said, that He 'careth not for any man',[1] so they care not for any man, or rather they care for themselves. And yet, and yet it is almost an impossibility not to learn something from them, if one considers them.

From: *Christian Discourses* by Søren Kierkegaard

(Princeton Paperbacks, 1971, pp. 13–14)

Tuesday

The Birds and the Lilies

SØREN KIERKEGAARD

Ah, a man may do all he is capable of doing, and yet it sometimes may be doubtful whether the pupil learns anything from him; but the lilies and the birds do nothing whatever, and yet it is almost an impossibility not to learn something from them. Surely one can learn from them in the very first instance what it is to teach, what it is to teach in a Christian sense, can learn from them the great art of teaching, namely, to be careless about it, to care for oneself, and yet to do this in such an arousing way, so arrestingly, so ingratiatingly, and, so far as expense is concerned, so cheaply, and withal so persuasively, that it is impossible not to learn something from it. For doubtless when a human teacher has done everything and the pupil has learned nothing, he can say, 'It is not owing to me!' Oh, but when thou hast learnt so much from the lilies and the birds, is it not as though they said, 'It is not owing to us'? So benevolent are these teachers towards the pupil, so benevolent, so humane, so worthy of their divine commission. If thou hast forgotten something, they are willing at once to repeat it to thee, and to repeat and repeat, so that at last thou mightest learn it; if thou dost learn nothing from them, they do not reproach thee, but merely continue with rare zeal to go on with the instruction, concerned only with teaching; and if thou dost learn something from them they attribute it all to thee, act as if

[1] Mark xii:14.

they had no part in it, as if it were not to them thou owest it. They despair of no one, however indocile he may be, and they do not require slavish dependence upon them, even of him who has learnt the most. Ah, ye marvellous teachers, if one were to learn from you nothing else, if only he learned to teach, how much he would have learnt! It is already a great thing if a human teacher put into effect some part of his own teaching, since usually one makes much ado and does little – ah, but also this observation about others the lilies and the birds never made! But, you marvellous teachers – well in a certain sense you do not do what you say; you do it without saying anything. Yet this laconic silence of yours and this faithfulness towards yourselves, year in and year out, long as the day may be, whether you are appreciated or unappreciated, understood or misunderstood, seen or unseen, doing the same thing – oh, marvellous masters of the art of teaching!

From: *Christian Discourses* by Søren Kierkegaard

(Princeton Paperbacks, 1971, pp. 14–15)

Wednesday

The Birds and the Lilies

SØREN KIERKEGAARD

Be not therefore anxious, saying, what shall we eat? or, What shall we drink? – after all these things do the heathen seek.

This anxiety the bird has not. What does the bird live on – for about the lily we will say nothing, it can get along of course, for it lives on air – but what does the bird live on? . . . Surely not on what it gathers into barns, for it does not gather into barns – and really a man never lives on what he has laid up in the barn. But what does the bird live on? The bird cannot give an account of itself; in case it were to be summoned, it would have to answer like the man born blind, who was interrogated about Him who had given him his sight, and said, 'I know not, but this I know, that I, the blind man, see.' So the bird must make answer, 'I know not, but this I know, that I live.' On what does it live? The bird lives on the *'daily bread'*, this heavenly food which cannot be too long kept,[1] this immense store of provision which is in such good custody that no one can steal it; for only that

[1] The allusion here and hereafter is to the manna (Exodus xvi).

which is kept over the night can the thief steal, that which is used during the day no one can steal.

So then the daily bread is the bird's living. The daily bread is the most scantily measured supply, it is exactly enough, but not the least bit more, it is that little which poverty needs.

From: *Christian Discourses* by Soren Kierkegaard

(Princeton Paperbacks, 1971, pp. 17–18)

Thursday

The Birds and the Lilies

SØREN KIERKEGAARD

What then does the poor Christian live on? On the *daily bread*. Therein he resembles the bird. But the bird which true enough is not a heathen, is yet not a Christian either – for the Christian *prays* for the daily bread. But then is he not even poorer than the bird, for the fact that he must pray for it, whereas the bird gets it without praying? Yes, so the heathen thinks. The Christian prays for the daily bread, by praying for it he receives it, yet without having anything to keep over night; he prays for it, and by praying for it he keeps away the anxiety at night, while he sleeps soundly, to awaken the next day to the daily bread which he prays for. The Christian therefore does not live on the daily bread like the bird or like a character in a fairy-tale who takes it where he finds it; for the Christian finds it where he seeks it, and he seeks it by praying. But therefore he has also, however poor he may be, something more to live on than the daily bread, which to him has an added flavour, a value, a satisfying quality, which it does not have for the bird; for the Christian indeed prays for it, and so he knows that the daily bread is *from God*. And in another sphere, does not a trifling gift, a little insignificance, possess infinite value for the lover because he knows that it comes from the beloved? Therefore the Christian does not say merely that the daily bread is enough for him, in so far as it supplies his earthly want and need, but he speaks also of something else (and no bird and no heathen knows what it is he is talking about) when he says, 'For me it is enough, it is from Him', that is, from God. Like the simple wise man[1] who talked constantly about food and drink, yet talked profoundly of the highest

[1] Socrates.

things, so does the poor Christian, when he talks about food, talk with simplicity of the highest things; for when he says, 'the daily bread', he is not thinking so much about food as of the fact that he receives it from God's table. So also the bird does not live on the daily bread; it surely does not, like the heathen, live to eat, it eats to live – and yet does it really *live*?

From: *Christian Discourses* by Søren Kierkegaard

(Princeton Paperbacks, 1971, pp. 18–19)

Friday

The Birds and the Lilies

SØREN KIERKEGAARD

The poor Christian does not question about all such things as the heathen seek after. On the other hand, there is something else he seeks, and therefore he *lives* (for indeed it seemed doubtful in how far one can properly say that the bird 'lives') – he lives therefore, or it is for this he lives, and it is for this reason he can say that he lives. He believes that he has a Father in heaven who every day openeth His bountiful hand and filleth all things living (him included) with blessing; yet what he seeks is not the satisfaction of his appetite, it is the heavenly Father. He believes that man is not distinguished from the birds for the fact that he cannot live on so little, but for the fact that he cannot live 'on bread alone'; he believes that it is the blessing which satisfies; yet what he seeks is not to be satisfied, but the blessing. He believes (what no sparrow knows anything of – and what does it help a sparrow that it is so?) that no sparrow falls to the ground without the will of the heavenly Father. He believes that so long as he has to live here on earth he surely will receive the daily bread, and that then some day he shall live blessedly in the hereafter. Thus it is he explains the saying that 'the life is more than food'; for no doubt the temporal life is more than food, but an eternal life is surely beyond comparison with food and drink, wherein a *man's* life does no more consist than does the kingdom of God! He constantly bears in mind that a life of holiness was led here on earth in poverty, that 'He' was hungry in the desert and thirsted upon the cross; so that not only can one live in poverty, but in poverty one can *live*. – Hence he prays, it is true, for the daily bread, and gives thanks for it, but to pray and give thanks is to him more important than the food, and is indeed his meat, as it was Christ's 'meat to do the Father's will'.

From: *Christian Discourses* by Søren Kierkegaard

(Princeton Paperbacks, 1971, pp. 19–20)

Saturday

The Birds and the Lilies

SØREN KIERKEGAARD

Think in conclusion of the bird, which has its place in the Gospel, and should have its place in the discourse. In comparison with the ungodly melancholy of the heathen, the bird, which in poverty is without the anxiety of poverty, is carefree; in comparison with the pious faith of the Christian, the carefreeness of the bird is light-mindedness. In comparison with the lightness of the bird, the heathen is as heavily weighted as a stone; in comparison with the freedom of the Christian, the bird too, however, is subjected to the law of gravity. In comparison with the bird, which is alive, the heathen is dead; in comparison with the Christian, however, one cannot properly say that the bird lives. In comparison with the bird, which keeps silent, the heathen is garrulous; in comparison with the Christian, however, the heathen is dumb, he neither prays nor gives thanks, and that in the deepest sense is human language; everything else, everything the heathen says, is related to this as a bird which has learnt to talk is related to a man. The bird is poor and yet not poor; the Christian is poor yet not poor, rich; the heathen is poor, and poor, and poor, and poorer than the poorest bird. *Who* is *that* poor man who is so poor that this is the only thing one can say about him, just as it is the only thing he himself can talk about? It is the heathen. According to the teaching of Christianity, no one else, no one is poor, neither the bird nor the Christian. It is a long road – in poverty to desire to be rich. The bird's short cut is the shortest, the Christian's way the most blessed.

From: *Christian Discourses* by Søren Kierkegaard

(Princeton Paperbacks, 1971, pp. 25–6)

EPIPHANY 5

Studies of English Mystics

W. R. INGE

God has spoken by the prophets at sundry times and in divers manners. He fulfils Himself in many ways, lest one good custom should corrupt the world. Revelation – the *unveiling* of the Divine to human apprehension – should not be regarded as a particular mode of communicating Divine truth, differing from other modes by its immediacy or externality. The antithesis between natural and revealed is misleading, for the religion of nature, so far as it is true, is one kind of revealed religion. The antithesis of 'natural' is not 'revealed', but non-natural or supernatural; the classification implies an exclusive claim on behalf of certain facts to be unique and incommensurable with other facts. But in the truest sense, all religion is natural, and all religion is revealed. Our nature is what God intended us to grow into; and since, in the beautiful words of Augustine, He 'made us for Himself, our hearts are unquiet until they rest in Him'. But if we thus claim for our nature its royal rights, if we say that our nature is to be like God, to attain the stature of the fullness of Christ; if we assert that the whole law may be briefly comprehended in the old sayings 'know thyself' and 'be thyself', we are at once confronted with the paradox that the self-centred life is spiritual death. As individuals we are not self-sufficing, we are not independent. Our minds are no pure mirrors in which the beauty and wisdom of the Divine mind may shine reflected. We cannot, for the most part, find God unaided. He has spoken to the prophets, not to us. This is why we have needed, and still need, the word revelation. Revelation is the unveiling of some Divine truth which we could not have discovered for ourselves, but which when it is shown to us by others to whom God has spoken, we can recognize as Divine. There can be no revelation which is purely external; such a communication would be partly unnoticed, and partly misunderstood. There must be the answering witness of the Spirit within us that this is the voice of God; but the voice comes to us first from without, through the mouth of those whom God has

honoured by making them His spokesmen. A 'mystery', in the New
Testament, is always something which has been revealed, but in this
manner.

From: *Studies of English Mystics* by William Ralph Inge

(John Murray, 1907, pp. 1–3)

Tuesday

Studies of English Mystics

W. R. INGE

It is necessary for us, who are neither saints nor prophets, to sit at
the feet of those who have seen the mysteries of the Kingdom of God.
It may be that we shall never share their higher experiences. Strictly
speaking, visions of Divine truth are not communicable. What can
be described and handed on is not the vision itself, but the inadequate
symbols in which the seer tries to represent what he has experienced,
to preserve it in his memory, and to impart it to others. . . . The lives
of the saints are thus a very important part of religious literature.
Hagiology has fallen into discredit because in time past it was written
for edification, and not for truth. Any story that the biographer
thought honourable to the saint, and conducive to faith and devotion,
was inserted without investigation. What Newman called the 'illative'
faculty was allowed to run riot. We desire no more religious romances
of the old sort. The strict truth is good enough for us. If we can arrive
at it, we shall find a reinforcement to Christian faith of enormous
value. For Christianity is a very concerete practical thing. It is, as
John Smith, the Cambridge Platonist, said, a Divine life, not a Divine
science. It is embodied in great personalities more adequately than in
any philosophical systems or doctrinal formulas. It found its complete expression in the Person of the Incarnate Christ; and, after the
Gospels, it is in the lives of His best disciples that we shall find its
brightest illustrations. Those who have the privilege of knowing a
living saint in the flesh have the best opportunities of all, of understanding what Christianity is. The great saints of the past can only be
known by their books, or by the books of others about them; and
those books will be most valuable which more fully and clearly
reveal the personality of their authors.

From: *Studies of English Mystics* by William Ralph Inge

(John Murray, 1907, pp. 3–6)

Wednesday

Studies of English Mystics

W. R. INGE

Since the vision of God is the culminating point, not of any one faculty, even of the moral conscience, but of our whole nature, transfigured into the likeness of Him whom, unless we are like Him, we cannot see as He is; and since the diverse faculties, which in their several ways bear witness to God, are developed in very different proportions by different individuals, we should expect to find that there are many paths up God's holy hill, though all meet at the top. The conditions laid down in Psalm xv are no doubt inexorable. Only he who has clean hands and a pure heart, who is humble and sincere, charitable and upright, can ascend into the hill of the Lord, or rise up in His holy place. But the intuition of eternal truth is no monopoly of the contemplative recluse, or of the philosopher, or of the poet, or of the man of action. The perfect Christian would cultivate and consecrate heart, intellect, imagination, practical energy, in an harmonious manner, and would be brought near to God by all parts of his nature acting together. But *non omnia possumus omnes* [we cannot all do everything]. God gave some apostles, some prophets, some evangelists, some pastors and teachers. All these worketh one and the self-same Spirit, dividing to every man severally as He will.

The life of devotion has its mystical state, when the God whom the saint has striven to love with all his heart and mind and soul and strength, for whom he has renounced all dear domestic ties, all ambition, and all pleasure, reveals Himself, in mysterious intercourse to the inner consciousness, in a vision, perhaps, of the suffering Redeemer or as an unseen presence, speaking words of love and comfort.

The intellectual life has its mystical state, when the religious philosopher, whose thoughts have long been concentrated upon the deeper problems of existence, endeavouring to find the unity which underlies all diversity, the harmony which reconciles all contradictions, seems to behold what he sought in a blank trance which imposes silence on all the faculties, even the restless discursive intellect, and unites the thinker for a few moments with the primal source of all thought, the ineffable One. Such was the goal of the 'intellect in love' of Plotinus, and the *amor intellectualis Dei* of Spinoza.

From: *Studies of English Mystics* by William Ralph Inge

(John Murray, 1907, pp. 6–8)

Studies of English Mystics

W. R. INGE

The poet's worship of nature has its mystical state, when in Platonic fashion the admiration of beautiful forms, either human or in God's other handiwork, has led him up to a vision of Divine beauty. The scientific worship of nature has its mystical state. Science is a patient conversion of insight into sight, and the investigator is lighted throughout his labours by the torch of the imagination, without which natural phenomena are disconnected, dull, and spiritless. The scientific imagination creates a religion – not the old religion of nature, which peopled the woods with Dryads, and saw 'old Proteus rising from the sea', but a pure, humble, disinterested reverence and worship for the vastness and splendour and majesty of the universe. This worship may daunt and oppress the spirit, . . . or it may awaken a sense of sublimity and magnificence such as the cramped universe of pre-scientific thought and imagination could hardly inspire. . . .

The immanent pantheism, or 'monism' as its votaries prefer to call it, which is the creed of most scientists who are religious, is a real religion, which only ignorance and prejudice can stigmatize as 'infidelity'. In so far as it culminates in an immediate *feeling* of being enveloped by the all-embracing Spirit of the cosmos, or, in Huxley's words, 'in the sense of growing oneness with the great Spirit of abstract truth', it is a mystical religion.

From: *Studies of English Mystics* by William Ralph Inge

(John Murray, 1907, pp. 8–11)

Friday

Studies of English Mystics

W. R. INGE

The active life also may issue in a thoroughly mystical faith, as may be seen in the lives of soldier-mystics like Colonel Gardiner, who was slain at Prestonpans in 1745, and Charles Gordon, the knight without fear and without reproach, who fell at Khartoum. Men of this type see the hand of God everywhere. Life for them is as sacramental, as full of 'mysteries' in the Greek sense of the word, as to the Platonic philosopher or the poet of nature. But there is a very striking difference in the kind of sacramental symbolism which these two classes of mystics seek and find in the external world. The active, practical worker demands a spiritual world-order in which spiritual facts *happen in time,* just as his own spiritual activites are devoted to making things happen in time. The philosopher and the poet do not want to make anything happen, but to discover and understand and set a value upon what always happens. Hence their religious symbols are quite different. The active man craves for evidence of Divine intervention – for supernaturalism in some form; the philosopher and poet make no such demand, and the religious man of science regards belief in miracles as a kind of blasphemy. Amiel says that 'miracle is a vision of the Divine behind nature'. Yes; but of the Divine *energizing* and altering the face of nature, even as the active man would fain leave his mark on the world, as a unique force acting upon it. This is no place for a discussion upon miracles, a subject which lies quite outside the scope of these lectures; but for those who are interested in current controversies I would suggest that much light is thrown upon the attitude of the two parties by the considerations which I have just suggested. The man who wishes to understand the world will have different religious symbols from him who wishes to leave his mark upon it.

From: *Studies of English Mystics* by William Ralph Inge

(John Murray, 1907, pp. 11–13)

Saturday

Studies of English Mystics

W. R. INGE

A recent writer on the psychology of religion gives us the following definition. 'Mysticism is that attitude of mind which divines and moves toward the spiritual in the common things of life, not a partial and occasional operation of the mind under the guidance of far-fetched analogies.' The definition is a good one, and is valuable as claiming for the trivial round, the common task, the power to waft us upward to the very footstool of God's throne. It is most important that we should recognize the sacramental value of mere right action, even of the most commonplace kind. Not, of course, that the action itself has this value; it is valuable because it is the expression of our habitual view of things and events and men and ourselves. Our habitual point of view is fatally incomplete unless it finds expression in habitual action. 'The intellect by itself moves nothing', as Aristotle said. Beautiful thoughts hardly bring us any nearer to God until they are acted upon. 'No one,' says Martineau, 'can have a true idea of right, until he does it; any genuine reverence for it, till he does it often, and with cost; any peace ineffable in it, till he does it always and with alacrity.' The religion of right conduct is no doubt frequently contrasted with the mystical type. The religious man who begins and ends with obedience to his conscience, and devotion to duty, is not a mystic. There are many noble characters who have little or no affinity to mystical religion. Such persons will echo the words of Christina Rossetti:

> We are of those who tremble at thy Word,
> Who faltering walk in darkness towards our close
> Of mortal life, by terrors curbed and spurred, –
>   We are of those.
> Not ours the heart thy loftiest love hath stirred,
> Not such as we thy lily and thy rose,
> Yet, Hope of those who hope with hope deferred,
>   We are those.

Nevertheless it is the fact that the habitual performance of the humblest daily duties has often developed the highest spirituality of character, with a vivid consciousness of the presence of God within and around us, a profound conviction that communion with Him takes place by prayer, and an intuitive certainty of Divine truth which is essentially mystical.

From: *Studies of English Mystics* by William Ralph Inge

(John Murray, 1907, pp. 13–15)

Monday

Studies of English Mystics

W. R. INGE

The life of the recluse is now seldom chosen and never respected. It is difficult for us to realize that it was once a career, and not the abdication of all careers. The professional saint almost disappeared from Northern Europe at or before the Reformation. In the earlier Middle Ages, however, his was a recognized manner of life which, however austere, did not at all condemn him who had chosen it to obscurity or contempt. The hermit becomes an important figure in Church history in the half century which followed the Decian persecution, when many thousands in Northern Africa alone fled to the deserts, renouncing all domestic and civic ties. In ecclesiastical circles, at any rate, it was the shortest road to a high reputation. Pilgrims who visited the caves and huts in which the hermits found shelter, spread far and wide accounts of their austerities and their miracles. They described how some lived in dried-up wells, others among the tombs, others on pillars. The macerations to which they subjected themselves – their abstinence from food, sleep, and ablutions – made them heroes at a time when mortification of the flesh was considered the highest virtue. They were consulted on problems of theology, and even on practical questions. This movement, one of the most difficult in history for moderns to comprehend, was on its saner side a great purity crusade, combined with a desire to cultivate to the utmost the spiritual life by sacrificing all else to it. To call the hermits selfish is a mistake. There is room for this kind of specialization as well as for others. If the hermits 'produced' nothing, in the economic sense, they consumed next to nothing; and even those who are most sceptical about the value of intercessory prayer may admit that the true saint, who can bring his example and influence to bear on the social life of his generation, is a useful member of the community.

From: *Studies of English Mystics* by William Ralph Inge

(John Murray, 1907, pp. 38–9)

Studies of English Mystics

W. R. INGE

In the Middle Ages, England was full of persons who in one form or another had taken religious vows. Besides the larger monasteries and convents, there were numerous 'anchorages' for solitary women, some in the open country, but more in the vicinity of a church. The cell of the anchoress, which was often built against the church wall or in a churchyard, sometimes contained more than one apartment, for the recluse usually had one, or even two, servants to attend upon her. She herself never left the walls of her cell, which had no means of egress, except by the windows. Even the window which opened towards the outside was generally covered by a heavy curtain, and those who wished for an audience with the recluse would kneel before the window until she chose to draw back the screen.

The Ancren Riwle, a precious specimen of early English, was written for three anchoresses, sisters, who had retired from the world for pious exercises, and lived together with their domestic servants or lay sisters. They were not, it seems, connected with any religious community. They lived at Tarrant Kaines, Dorsetshire. The reputed author of the *Ancren Riwle* is Simon de Ghent, Archdeacon of Oxford in 1284, and Bishop of Salisbury 1297–1315. But the style is said to be earlier, and it is more probable that it was written by Bishop Poore, who was born and buried there. The author of the *Ancren Riwle* was certainly a learned man; he quotes the Christian Fathers, and even Pagan poets, such as Horace and Ovid. His treatise is just what it professes to be, a compendium of rules and good advice for anchoresses. . . .

The author begins by saying: 'My dear sisters, you have asked me for a Rule. But I will only give you two rules. One rules the heart, and makes it even and smooth, without any knot or scar of evil. This is charity out of a pure heart, and love unfeigned. The other is all external. It is bodily exercise or discipline, which, the apostle says, profiteth little. This rule is only to serve the other. The rule of love is as lady, the rule of discipline as handmaid. The rule of love is always the same, the rule of discipline may be changed and varied.'

From: *Studies of English Mystics* by William Ralph Inge

(John Murray, 1907, pp. 40–3)

Wednesday

Studies of English Mystics

W. R. INGE

The ancient prayer which they are ordered to say at the Holy Communion is remarkable for the spiritual and unsuperstitious doctrine of the Eucharist which it implies: 'Grant, we beseech thee, almighty God, that Him whom we see darkly, and under a different form, and on whom we feed sacramentally on earth, we may see face to face, and may be thought worthy to enjoy Him truly and really as He is in heaven through the same Jesus Christ our Lord.'

The chapter on the 'Guard of the Senses' contains some amusing admonitions. The young ladies are cautioned severely against looking out of the parlour window, 'like the staring anchoresses'. And they are not to be always chattering with visitors, 'like the cackling anchoresses' (*kakelinde ancren*). Silence is always to be observed at meals, and throughout Friday, and during Holy Week. It is permissible, however, to say 'a few words' to your maid during silent times. But talking is a snare. 'More slayeth word than sword.'

Gossip was evidently a temptation to the recluse. 'People say,' writes our author, 'that an anchoress has always a magpie to chatter to her; so that men have a proverb: "From miln and market, from smith and nunnery, men bring tidings." Christ knows, this is a sad tale.'

Our Lord's words, 'Foxes have holes, and birds of the air have nests', may be allegorically applied to true and false anchoresses. 'The true anchoresses are indeed birds of heaven, that fly aloft and sit on the green boughs singing merrily. That is, they meditate enraptured upon the blessedness of heaven that never fadeth and is ever green. A bird, however, sometimes alighteth on earth to seek food, but never feels secure there, and often turns herself about', on her guard against danger. Even so should the anchoress be wary when she is obliged to busy herself with earthly things.

From: *Studies of English Mystics* by William Ralph Inge

(John Murray, 1907, pp. 43–5)

Thursday

Studies of English Mystics

W. R. INGE

The seven deadly sins are then compared to animals – pride to the lion, envy to the serpent, and so forth. The noxious beasts all have 'whelps' – seven, twelve, or six particular vices which all belong to the deadly sin in question. The best worth quoting of these somewhat arbitrary classifications is the paragraph about *accidie*, that besetting sin of the cloister:

'The bear of heavy sloth hath these whelps. Torpor is the first – that is, a lukewarm heart. Next is pusillanimity, which is too faint-hearted and too reluctant withal to undertake any high thing in hope of God's help and trust in His grace. The third is dullness of heart. Who doeth good, but with a dead and sluggish heart, he hath this whelp. Fourth is idleness. Whoso stands still, doing no good at all, he hath this whelp. Fifth is a grudging and grumbling heart. Sixth is sorrow for anything except sin. Seventh is negligence in saying or doing or providing or remembering or taking care. The eighth is despair, the grimmest bear's whelp of all, which cheweth and wasteth God's mild kindness and much mercy and boundless grace.'

The sow of greediness and her pigs are very briefly disposed of, 'for I am nought afeard, my beloved sisters, that ye feed them'.

There is a remarkable passage about the consolations which an anchoress experiences at first, but which she must not expect to enjoy always. This caution, which we find in almost all who have written with intimate knowledge about the life of devotion, is psychologically and practically of great interest. 'An anchoress thinks [beforehand] that she shall be most strongly tempted in the first twelve months. Nay, it is not so. In the first years, it is nothing but ball-play.' 'In the beginning it is only courtship, to draw you into love.' Afterwards, you must expect to be treated with 'less forbearance', but 'in the end cometh great joy'.

From: *Studies of English Mystics* by William Ralph Inge

(John Murray, 1907, pp. 46–7)

Friday

Studies of English Mystics

W. R. INGE

The exhortation to sisterly affection is written with great delicacy, and a sort of quaint tenderness which is very charming.

'My dear sisters, let your dear noses always be turned to each other with sweet love, fair semblance, and with sweet cheer, that ye may be ever with oneness of one heart, and of one will united together. While you are united, the fiend cannot harm you. . . . And if the fiend blow up any resentment between you, which may Jesus Christ forbid, until it is appeased none ought to receive Jesus Christ's flesh and blood. . . . But let each send word to the other, that she hath humbly asked her forgiveness, as if she were present.'

We obtain little glimpses into the minor troubles and arrangements of the household when we read special admonitions like the following: 'Be glad in your hearts if ye suffer insolence from Slurry the cook's knave, who washes the dishes in the kitchen.' 'My dear sisters, ye shall have no beast but one cat.'

Lastly, the good man is distressed to find his spiritual daughters treating themselves too hardly. 'Dear sisters, your meat and drink have seemed to me less than I would have it.' He forbade them to wear hedgehog skins as a discipline, or iron or haircloth, and to beat themselves with leathern thongs, or with a leaded lash, or with holly or briars till the blood comes, at least without leave from their confessor. Their clothes are to be warm and well made, 'and as many as you need, both for bed and back.' They are allowed to wash, we are glad to find 'as often as you please'.

From: *Studies of English Mystics* by William Ralph Inge

(John Murray, 1907, pp. 47–9)

Saturday

Studies of English Mystics

W. R. INGE

With all of us, the range of spiritual vision is extremely limited. We are like persons gazing at the moonlight on the sea. Every wave and wavelet reflects the light, but each spectator sees only one narrow silvery path, that which stretches to the horizon straight out from his own feet. Only those who lean entirely on external authority are likely to be disappointed with, and to disapprove of, *all* the mystics. And to them I will read, in conclusion, a few wise words from a very eminent and thoughtful philosopher, the late Professor Wallace.

'In the Kingdom of God are many mansions; and while some are content, as it were, to live on tradition and authority, to believe on trust, to repose on the common strength, it is necessary that there should also be from time to time a few, a select number, who resolve, or rather are compelled by a necessity naturally laid upon them, to see for themselves. Theirs also is faith; but it is the faith of insight and of knowledge, the faith which is gnosis. Hard things have been said of gnosis, and harder things of gnosticism; but it cannot be too clearly seen that gnosis is the very life of the Church, the blood of religion. It is the faith which is not merely hearsay and dependence, but which really envisages the unseen for itself. It does not believe *on* a Person; it believes in and into Him: it becomes, by an act at once voluntary and impelled from without (as all human action that is really entitled to that name), participant with Him and through Him of a force of life and conduct.'

From: *Studies of English Mystics* by William Ralph Inge

(John Murray, 1907, pp. 36–7)

SEPTUAGESIMA

Monday

The Foolishness of God

J. A. BAKER

There is no reason to question that one of the most prominent themes in Jesus' preaching was that of the kingdom or sovereignty of God. The phrase occurs thirteen times in Mark's record of his words, and far more often in *Matthew* and *Luke*. This kingdom is at once something active, which draws near to Man and impinges on his life here and now and specifically in the activity of Jesus, and also a goal which men seek, an order into which they strive to enter. It is said that John the Baptist also proclaimed the imminence of the Kingdom;[1] and as the fact of God's ultimate sovereignty over all creation it was a concept familiar to the Judaism of the time. Jesus, however, saw the implementation of this sovereignty with eyes rather different from those of his contemporaries.

First, he seems to have rejected the idea that God showed his sovereignty by intervening in the details of life to reward or protect the good and to punish the wicked. It was a feature of his picture of God that 'your Father who is in heaven . . . makes his sun to rise on the evil and on the good, and sends rain on the just and on the unjust'.[2]

He rejects the idea that the victims of tyranny or of natural disaster were by their fate shown to be worse sinners than other men.[3] He clearly regarded the poor, the bereaved, the hungry, and the persecuted as God's special favourites.[4] In taking up these positions he was to some extent expressing his own mind, to some extent voicing attitudes found in sectarian Judaism, but he had little or nothing in common with the official and orthodox assumptions of his time.

Secondly, he put forward a radically different doctrine of God's forgiveness. He repeatedly taught that only one condition was necessary to obtain forgiveness from God, and that was a readiness

[1] Matthew 3:2.
[2] Matthew 5:45.
[3] Luke 13:1–5.
[4] Luke 6:20–2.

to forgive other people. This principle is set out in the Lord's Prayer, and in many other passages.[1] The views of Judaism on this subject were both more complicated and more restrictive. Forgiveness could be secured by expiatory sacrifice, or by good works undertaken as a kind of penance to cancel out the guilt which had been incurred. At the Last Judgment God would forgive the unexpiated sins of those who on balance had lived a good life, keeping the divine commandments. Moreover, when God did forgive a man's sins here and now, this fact would be confirmed by manifest signs of his blessing.

From: *The Foolishness of God* by John Austin Baker

(Darton, Longman & Todd, 1970, pp. 188–9)

Tuesday

The Foolishness of God

J. A. BAKER

A counterpart in practice of Jesus' general doctrine of forgiveness is to be found in his association with the outcasts of society. The note sounded early in *Mark* by the Pharisees' question to his followers:

Why does he eat with tax-collectors and sinners?[2]

recurs.[3] The tax-collectors have even supplied the 'hero' of one of the most famous passages in the Gospels, 'the Pharisee and the Publican'.[4] This story is one which could almost have been written by a conventional Jew (or by a conventional early Christian) – almost, but not quite. In a Jewish version or in one, let us say, by the Evangelists themselves the Pharisee's unacknowledged faults would have had to be made explicit in order to show why the tax-collector was the better man. The greater penetration of the present version suggests that here we have a good tradition going back to Jesus himself. It is true that faults on the part of the Pharisee are implied; but then the tax-collector will have had serious faults too. The crucial difference does not lie here at all, but in the attitude of mind. The Pharisee cannot even cast a mental glance around to see whether he has any faults; he is lost in admiration of his own rectitude, while the Publican

[1] Matthew 6:14–15; 18:35; Mark 11:25–6; Luke 17:3–4.
[2] Mark 2:16.
[3] Luke 15:1.
[4] Luke 18:9–14.

can only beat his breast and say, 'God be merciful to me, a sinner!' This, and this alone, is why the latter is accounted righteous by God.[1]

To be *accounted* righteous, however, is not the same thing as to *be* righteous. It is noteworthy that Jesus never expresses the sentimental view that the tax-collectors, prostitutes, and other undesirables with whom he associated were 'good at heart', or 'not such bad sorts after all'. When he flays the devout with the warning:

> The tax-collectors and harlots go into the kingdom of God before you[2]

he means to shame them. It is because the woman who weeps over him *is* a sinner that his respectable host ought to be all the more conscience-stricken over his lack of proper courtesy.[3] The reference to the interest shown by the same class of people in John the Baptist[4] uses the same technique of censure by contrast. This link with John the Baptist is illuminating in another way. John, like Jesus, turned no one away from God's forgiveness, provided that they were penitent; and he too demanded reform of life. The difference between him and Jesus lies simply in the fact that Jesus did not scruple to be friends with such people in the context of ordinary daily living; and this is an attitude so distinct from that of everyone around him – scribes, Pharisees, John, the common people – that it must have a basis in fact.

From: *The Foolishness of God* by John Austin Baker

(Darton, Longman & Todd, 1970, pp. 191–2)

Wednesday

The Foolishness of God

J. A. BAKER

The same two elements – the 'tax-collectors and sinners' and John the Baptist – reappear in a delightful passage deriving from the non-Markan source common to *Matthew* and *Luke*, in which a wry allusion is made to Jesus' non-ascetic manner of life:

[1] Luke 18:14a.
[2] Matthew 21:31.
[3] Luke 7:36–50.
[4] Matthew 21:32.

But to what shall I compare this generation? It is like children sitting in the market places and calling to their playmates,

> 'We piped to you, and you did not dance;
> we wailed, and you did not mourn.'

For John came neither eating nor drinking, and they say, 'He has a demon'; the Son of man came eating and drinking, and they say, 'Behold, a glutton and a drunkard, a friend of tax-collectors and sinners!' Yet wisdom is justified by her deeds.[1]

Ascetic practices as a rule of life came late to Judaism. Fasting, sack-cloth and ashes, abstention from wine and sexual intercourse, are all to be found in Old Testament times, but only for use on special occasions or for limited periods, and for particular reasons – public or private days of mourning and repentance, vows, and so on. Later, fasting as a regular devotional discipline became a mark of certain groups;[2] and some Rabbis carried mortification to extremes. Neither John the Baptist nor Jesus, however, fit easily into any of these categories. John is an example of the desert hermit,[3] whose manner of life is devoid of every pleasure and comfort which the average person enjoys. Jesus moves in ordinary society, but is celibate and has no home of his own.[4] His life is hard and exhausting to a degree,[5] Jesus and his disciples cannot find time even for a meal;[6] but this is due to the demands of his mission, not to any voluntary disciplines undertaken for self-improvement. Nothing could be more absurd, therefore, than to see in the passage we are considering evidence that Jesus was a *bon vivant*. The humorous exasperation with which he rebukes the detractors is aimed at the narrow conventionalism which will allow only one strictly defined way of life to be appropriate to the good and pious man, and which, because it never stops to think that different vocations may call for different patterns of conduct, condemns people for utterly superficial reasons. The incident may well have been seen in the early Church as relevant to the variety of rules among Christians. James, the Lord's brother, head of the Jerusalem church, is traditionally reported to have been an ascetic; and very severe ideals of life were put forward in some Syrian churches. Equally, however, a more relaxed tone is discernible in Pauline congregations, and in stories of Peter and others. But though the

[1] Matthew 11:16–19; Luke 7:31–5.
[2] cf. Luke 18:12, 'I fast twice a week'.
[3] Luke 1:80.
[4] Luke 9:58.
[5] Mark 3:20.
[6] cf. also John 4:6–8.

Christian situation may have been the reason for preserving the story, just as it has made Jesus refer to himself as 'the Son of Man',[1] the nuances and the delightful comparison taken from the games of children in the streets have the distinctive ring of Jesus' own words, and make it another reliable glimpse of him as he was.

From: *The Foolishness of God* by John Austin Baker

(Darton, Longman & Todd, 1970, pp. 192–3)

Thursday

The Foolishness of God

J. A. BAKER

We must return to the question of Jesus' authority as the agent of God's coming kingdom. His claim to forgive sins is but one example of a general attitude detectable in the narratives. Another is his approach to the question of sabbath observance. Judaism developed a most elaborate code of regulations relating to the sabbath, following her practice of putting 'fences round the Law'. The basic principle here is that the best way to ensure that scriptural commandments are not broken is to allow a margin for error. How, for example, is the command to do 'no manner of work' on the sabbath to be obeyed? What constitutes work? Some things have to be done, unless one is to remain in complete immobility for twenty-four hours. By establishing a maximum of permitted activity, both in quantity and in kind, which is well below the amount that might still be within the spirit of the Law laid down by God, one can make doubly sure that no offence is committed. Thus, harvesting is work; but what constitutes harvesting? Jesus' disciples, walking through a cornfield on the sabbath, pluck some ears of corn, husk them, and eat them – is not this an offence?[2] There was also a strict limit on travel, about two miles,[3] and even such journeys should be undertaken only if strictly necessary. When sick people come on the sabbath to the synagogue where Jesus is, in order to be healed by him, their journey is not strictly necessary because they could equally well have visited Jesus for that purpose on some other day.[4] The narratives are unanimous

[1] Matthew 11:19; Luke 7:34.
[2] Mark 2:23–4; Matthew 12:1–2.
[3] cf. Acts 1:12, Olivet is a 'sabbath day's journey' from Jerusalem.
[4] Luke 13:14.

in their picture of Jesus' indignant impatience with this kind of pettifogging. If David's men could appease their hunger by eating the holy bread set out in the sanctuary,[1] could not Jesus' followers pick a few grains of corn in the open field? Which was the greater invasion of the rights of a holy God? If the rules allowed one for humanity's sake to untie an animal and to lead it out to feed and water it on the sabbath, why was it wrong to do the even more humane act of healing the sick, and for the sick themselves to make a journey for that purpose?

From: *The Foolishness of God* by John Austin Baker

(Darton, Longman & Todd, 1970, pp. 193-4)

Friday

The Foolishness of God

J. A. BAKER

. . . Is there a hint of more to the matter [of Sabbath observance] than just moral priorities? It seems at times to be Jesus' very act of healing on the sabbath which is the chief offence, not such incidentals as unnecessary travelling. A story in *Mark* [the story of Jesus, healing the man with a withered hand in the synagogue on the sabbath], which has been incorporated by Matthew and Luke raises the question.[2] There were indeed rules about how much medical assistance might be given to the sick or in an emergency on the sabbath; but is this the point? Is a miracle 'work' anyway?

The answer, phrased somewhat flippantly, is that it may not be work for Man, but it certainly is for God. Although, it is true, the Evangelists sometimes express the view that the healings were effected by a power in Jesus himself, the relevant recorded words of Jesus

---

[1]Mark 2:25-6; cf. I Samuel, 21:1-6.

[2] Again he entered the synagogue, and a man was there who had a withered hand. And they watched him, to see whether he would heal him on the sabbath, so that they might accuse him. And he said to the man who had the withered hand, 'Come here.' And he said to them, 'Is it lawful on the sabbath to do good or do harm, to save life or to kill?' But they were silent And he looked around at them with anger, grieved at their hardness of heart, and said to the man, 'Stretch out your hand.' He stretched it out and his hand was restored. The Pharisees went out, and immediately held counsel with the Herodians against him how to destroy him. (Mark 3:1-6; cf. Matthew 12:9-14; Luke 6:6-11.

himself offer no such explanation. In his view the power resides in God. In Mark 3:22-30 he scornfully exposes the weak argument of those who attribute his cures to the Devil, and claims that the Holy Spirit, that is, the spirit of God, is responsible.[1] If, however, this was his conviction then clearly he thought it right to call on the help of God on the sabbath, even though God had not merely ordained a sabbath rest for men but had himself rested on the seventh day from all his work in creation.[2] Trained theologians, therefore, might be pardoned for suspecting that Jesus, by performing miracles on the sabbath, was pretending to dictate to God in direct opposition to God's own revealed intentions. (The argumentation seems strange to us, but it is entirely in the spirit of the times.) Such a man was a blasphemer, and obviously any apparent good he did was really the work of the powers of evil.

The Fourth Gospel makes this conclusion explicit:

The man went away and told the Jews that it was Jesus who had healed him. And this was why the Jews persecuted Jesus, because he did this on the sabbath. But Jesus answered them, 'My Father is working still, and I am working.' This was why the Jews sought all the more to kill him, because he not only broke the sabbath but also called God his Father, making himself equal with God.[3]

– and *John*, as we have already seen, is often good evidence for Jewish anti-Christian polemic. In view of the belief of the early Church about the identity of Jesus such stories would clearly be regarded as of signal significance; but it is notable that Jesus' own understanding of the matter, as recorded, does not demand a developed doctrinal interpretation. For him healing was a work of divine mercy, and was in season at any time. To restrict it by appeal to regulations of human invention showed a totally perverted scale of values which no one who, like himself, was the appointed agent of God's kingship could adopt for one moment. In this essential standpoint we may take it that the Gospels faithfully reflect his historical attitude.

From: *The Foolishness of God* by John Austin Baker

(Darton, Longman & Todd, 1970, pp. 194–6)

---

[1] cf. Luke 11:20.
[2] Genesis 2:2; cf. Heb. 4:10.
[3] John 5:15–18; cf. 10:32–3.

Saturday

The Foolishness of God

J. A. BAKER

One thing that cannot rationally be doubted is that Jesus did teach, anywhere and everywhere. What kind of a teacher was he? Can he, for example, be classified as a rabbi on the contemporary Jewish model? In this respect the language of the Gospels is interesting. Mark has three instances of Jesus' being addressed as 'Rabbi', using the actual Aramaic word transliterated into Greek,[1] and in each of them the speaker is one of Jesus' inner circle of disciples. Matthew follows the same principle. Luke never uses the actual Aramaic preferring the Greek word for 'teacher'. This may simply be meant as a translation of 'Rabbi' for Gentile readers, not an avoidance of it on principle; but it is interesting that only one out of his six instances coincides with those of *Mark*. Again, all are in the mouths of Jesus' closest disciples. John uses it only slightly more often, and makes it a form of address from interested Jews as well.[2] How far he is, however, from giving it a strict technical sense may be seen from the fact that he has John the Baptist's disciples using it to their own master – and anyone less like a conventional Rabbi than the Baptist it would be hard to find. So far as Jesus is concerned, it may safely be said that the only feature which he had in common with the true rabbi was a circle of personal disciples. There is no evidence that he had ever received the essential qualification of an academic religious training as the pupil of another rabbi; indeed, the Fourth Gospel flatly excludes such a thing.[3] The essence of the rabbinic calling was to develop and hand on the tradition that one had received, taking scrupulous care to name one's authorities; of this, Jesus' method is the exact opposite. When, therefore, we find the title accorded to him in the earliest sources only by his own equally unprofessional followers it is hard to resist the impression that this is another accurate element. Amateur Galilean enthusiasts may have liked to think of him as 'Rabbi'; the authorized leaders of Judaism would never have dreamed of doing so. On the whole, it suited the early Church to leave it at that.

From: *The Foolishness of God* by John Austin Baker

(Darton, Longman & Todd, 1970, pp. 197–8)

[1] Mark 9:5; 11:21; 14:45.   [2] John 3:2; 6:25; 9:2.
[3] John 7:15.

SEXAGESIMA

Monday

The Foolishness of God

J. A. BAKER

It is this fundamental approach by Jesus to the task of teaching which was new and refreshing, and which made a vivid impression on those who heard him:

> And when Jesus finished these sayings, the crowd were astonished at his teaching, for he taught them as one who had authority, and not as their scribes.[1]

What he said was clear, comprehensible, and patently his own conviction. But that was not all. He presented his teaching as God's will for men, but at the same time he never attributed it to a direct communication from God like that given to Moses or to the prophets. It is significant that one of the most characteristic mannerisms of his speaking style, attested in all the sources, is the phrase, 'I tell you', often given special solemnity by the introductory word, 'Amen', 'Truly', or 'Indeed'. The authority with which he speaks rests not on training, qualifications, or position as rabbi or sage, not on direct prophetic inspiration, not on the ultimate authority of Scripture, but on himself; and yet what he speaks comes to the listener with the authority of God.

This quality in Jesus is not confirmed only by an examination of his teaching, such as we have just made, and by the fury which he aroused in the orthodox religious leaders. It also explains more convincingly than anything else another feature of the Gospel portrait, his refusal to differentiate between himself and his message. His call to his first disciples (with the affectionately remembered and surely authentic joke, 'I will make you fishers of men') is a personal one, to follow him.[2] The rich young man is told to give all his wealth to the poor and to follow Jesus.[3] In Matthew and Luke's common source there was a story that John the Baptist, when in prison, sent two of his

[1] Matthew 7:28–9. [2] Mark 1:17, 20; 2:14.
[3] Mark 10:21.

followers to Jesus to ask whether he was indeed 'the one who is to come', and received from Jesus the following reply:

> Go and tell John what you hear and see: the blind receive their sight and the lame walk, lepers are cleansed and the deaf hear, and the dead are raised up, and the poor have good news preached to them. And blessed is he who takes no offence at me.[1]

The preaching of the Gospel and the mighty works that accompany it are inseparable from the person of Jesus; response to them must include acceptance of Jesus. He himself is part and parcel of the good news.

From: *The Foolishness of God* by John Austin Baker

(Darton, Longman & Todd, 1970, pp. 218–19)

Tuesday

The Foolishness of God

J. A. BAKER

The preaching of the Gospel and the mighty works that accompany it are inseparable from the person of Jesus; response to them must include acceptance of Jesus. He himself is part and parcel of the good news.

How far is this tradition authentic? One or two incidents suggest very strongly that it is. It has often been remarked that a unique trait of Jesus was the value which he set upon childhood and the innocence of children. This is, so far as we know, unexampled in the ancient world. In paganism a child was essentially something immature, valuable only for what it might become. The practice of killing unwanted infants by exposing them at birth was widespread and taken for granted. Judaism had always valued and cherished children as a precious gift of God (as it does to this day), but it did not see in the state of childhood any special quality which would be desirable in an adult. Nor, to judge from the frequent references in the New Testament to immature Christians as 'babes', did the early church. We may therefore take it that Jesus' idiosyncrasy in this respect is a genuine historical memory. This gives especial interest in our present context to such passages as the following:

[1] Matthew 11:4–6.

And they were bringing children to him, that he might touch them; and the disciples rebuked them. But when Jesus saw it he was indignant, and said to them, 'Let the children come to me, do not hinder them; for to such belongs the kingdom of God. Truly, I say to you, whoever does not receive the kingdom of God like a child shall not enter it.[1]

Or again:

And he took a child, and put him in the midst of them; and taking him in his arms, he said to them, 'Whoever receives one such child in my name receives me; and whoever receives me, receives not me but him who sent me.'[2]

Trust and innocence like that of childhood are needed if men are to be open to the kingdom of God, and are the mark of those who are at home in it. Care for those who supremely embody these qualities is acceptance of God – but it is also acceptance of Jesus, and this element is too deeply embedded in such stories to be excised by any critical scalpel.

From: *The Foolishness of God* by John Austin Baker

(Darton, Longman & Todd, 1970, pp. 219–20)

Wednesday

The Foolishness of God

J. A. BAKER

It would be nothing very extraordinary, indeed, that the preacher of a new gospel should couple loyalty to that gospel with loyalty to himself; but this is not quite what Jesus would seem to have done. In the case, let us say, of a prophet, the hearer might respond to the message without needing to pay any particular attention to the messenger; the inhabitants of Jerusalem could have repented at the preaching of Isaiah or Jeremiah, and then forgotten about these men as such, without in any way impairing their repentance. But in the Gospels an attitude to Jesus in person is an integral part of the right response. This comes out in a different way in another saying:

[1] Mark 10:13–15.
[2] Mark 9:36–7.

And I tell you, every one who acknowledges me before men, the
Son of man also will acknowledge before the angels of God; but
he who denies me before men will be denied before the angels of
God.[1]

It will be remembered from our earlier discussion of this verse that,
while the early Church undoubtedly took this as identifying Jesus
with the heavenly 'Son of Man' who was to judge the world at the
Last Day, the phrasing could perhaps more naturally be held to
distinguish between them. If the original meaning was the second,
the saying could easily be authentic, and would testify to the point
in question: the great criterion by which men will be judged is their
attitude to Jesus. Mark, whose additional clause, 'when he comes in
the glory of his Father with the holy angels', indicates his version as
secondary, has included a reference to the teaching – 'ashamed of
me and of my words'. But the simpler form concentrates on Jesus
himself. How are we to interpret this?

There is no need to recapitulate here arguments already set out in
detail in a previous chapter. A summary of conclusions will be
sufficient. Jesus thought of himself as God's human agent whose
death would usher in the end of the present age and the resurrection
of the saints, with himself as their first fruits. He did not identify himself with the heavenly Son of Man. This is an equation which has
been retrojected on to the tradition by the faith of the early Church,
stimulated by certain sayings ('The son of man is lord even of the
sabbath', 'The son of man has power on earth to forgive sins') which
were originally statements about the privileges of all men who chose
to live truly under the sovereignty of God.

In the light of these conclusions a number of factors in the story
take on a new significance. We must take seriously the tradition that
Jesus supplemented his own ministry by sending out his followers to
preach the news of the coming kingdom of God.[2] These accounts
have been considerably elaborated to make them models for the
behaviour of missionaries in the early Church. Luke, moreover, with
his special interest in the preaching of the gospel to the Gentiles, has
foreshadowed this by having two such missions. In the first, the
Twelve are sent out, symbolizing the preaching to the twelve tribes
of Israel; in the second, seventy disciples are engaged, in accordance
with the Jewish belief that the population of the world was divided
into seventy nations. But behind all this it is not unlikely that there
is a hard fact. The reason for this step on the part of Jesus can be

[1] Luke 12:8–9; cf. Mark 8:38.
[2] Matthew 10:5–23; Luke 9:1–6; 10:1–20.

glimpsed in Matthew 10:23, a prediction which was falsified in the event, and may for that very reason be regarded as authentic:

> When they persecute you in one town, flee to the next; for truly, I say to you, you will not have gone through all the towns of Israel, before the Son of man comes.

How did Jesus react when this expectation was disappointed? Did he become convinced that something more was required of him than simply to preach? – that he had to die as well?

From: *The Foolishness of God* by John Austin Baker

(Darton, Longman & Todd, 1970, pp. 218–20)

Thursday

The Foolishness of God

J. A. BAKER

We are now approaching the heart of the historical problem of Jesus. We may note or deduce with some certainty any number of characteristics about him: the carpenter, son of a carpenter, with the quick and powerful intellect, the commanding personality, the unforgettable speech, the urgent compassion for the suffering, the eye for natural beauty, the tough physique coupled with abnormal psychological capacities for endurance. Here was a man who deliberately identified with the poor and the oppressed, who without compromising his own standards made the weak and the sinful feel that there was no barrier to friendship between him and them, but who demanded above all that men be open and genuine. There is the shrewd sense of humour, the reverence for children, the gift of poetry, the devastating anger, and yet the rejection of solutions imposed by force. We then begin to feel as if we 'know' him, in the way that we might know a great figure of our own times whom we have heard and seen on television or in the papers, perhaps in the flesh, or whose biography we have read. We observe that he apparently possesses exceptional gifts, such as the power of healing. We can go on to study his ethical teaching and his belief about God, to note its simplicity, its radical demands, its coherence, its insight into human nature; and we begin to know him a little better, in rather more depth. We come to understand how he was able to inspire loyalty in his friends, but at the same time intense and enduring loyalty only in a few, and that even these might at times find the relationship almost too demanding, though once they had enjoyed it, everything else might seem insipid by comparison. Finally, we can watch and marvel at his bearing under persecution and injustice, his noble endurance of a cruel death, and feel that this was all of a piece with his life. It is what we would have expected of him. But at the very heart of him there is a mystery, one question of absolutely overriding importance to which we must have an answer, for as yet he has eluded us. We may have a fair idea what we think of him, but our final verdict will depend on something much more significant: what did he think of himself?

It is obvious that Jesus did have a clear vision of his own role in history, and that he believed it essential for others to understand what this was. As we turn to examine the evidence on this crucial issue, we have some general guidelines already laid down to help us as a result of our examination of the various facets of his public presence. We are not dealing with a neurotic, or with a man whose moral values are perverse. He is not someone, for instance, who would try to force the hand of God or man by virtual suicide. If he walks straight up to death, it is because he is following the path of his duty, and death has chosen to bar his way. He is not someone who prides himself on one hundred per cent moral perfection. He does not 'thank God that he is not as other men are', for he is more interested in other men than in himself. He joins the crowd to receive a 'baptism of repentance for the remission of sins', and when an enthusiastic admirer calls him 'good' he takes him to task. Yet he sees his own mission as unique, and specifically as a unique work for God.

From: *The Foolishness of God* by John Austin Baker

(Darton, Longman & Todd, 1970, pp. 222–3)

Friday

The Foolishness of God

J. A. BAKER

... In the case of Jesus, the picture we have tried to present is this. He was convinced that God, the Father for whom he had absolute love and trust, and whose will he took as the absolute directive of his own life, had called him to be the Messiah of Israel, and so eventually to establish and rule in the Messianic kingdom on earth. But this kingdom lay on the far side of a time of crisis and distress culminating in a divine judgment of the whole world, to be carried out by a heavenly being, the Son of Man. His immediate task, therefore, was not to proceed directly to the setting up of the kingdom. In the prevailing circumstances this could be done only by means of force, propaganda, and political intrigue, which was as much as to say that it could not be set up at all, since God's sovereignty could never be implemented by anti-God methods. In the meantime, therefore, he could only prepare, by enlisting men who as the servants of mankind were to head the new order, by training them in those values and principles of God on which the kingdom was to be built, and by preparing them for the coming period of crisis, which they were to meet in that same spirit and with that same perfection of human conduct. This meant first of all that his Messiahship had to remain a secret to all except those who had been initiated into its new and revolutionary ethical nature. It could not be revealed to the generality of men, who would interpret it in terms of their own violent, nationalist, and anti-God aspirations. It also meant, however, that he was bound to criticize and challenge the assumptions of Israel at large, and to confine himself to Israel, since it was Israel, purged and converted, which would have to be the central, foundation community of the new world order. It could not be otherwise, since they were the only people who knew that human life must be based on total love for the one universal God and for all men as his children. This challenge to Israel was therefore a recall to the basic principles of her own heritage, and a critique of the ways in which they had perverted it. As such it inevitably meant hostility, danger, and death for himself and his friends. Hence he finally decided if possible to draw down all this enmity on himself, and as the hidden Messiah to take the full brunt of the Messianic woes, thereby opening the way for the divine judg-

F

ment and for the resurrection which would usher in the kingdom of God on earth.

From: *The Foolishness of God* by John Austin Baker

(Darton, Longman & Todd, 1970, p. 238)

Saturday

The Foolishness of God

J. A. BAKER

After the crucifixion and resurrection the Church proclaimed the imminent fulfilment of this plan [of Jesus]:

> Let all the house of Israel therefore know assuredly that God has made him both Lord and Christ, this Jesus whom you crucified.[1]

They set up in Jerusalem a community of complete sharing and brotherly love,[2] attracted many converts[3] and widespread admiration.[4] But this only brought down upon them increasing persecution, first of the Christian leaders,[5] and then of the whole body.[6] This, by dispersing the new sect, helped the spread of their gospel.[7] But it must also have led to a reassessment of the point they had reached in God's programme. Clearly the time of the Messianic woes had not yet passed. Jesus' predictions of danger and persecution for his followers, therefore, were now seen as applying to their present stage, and his instructions on the subject of missionary preaching were also expanded and adapted to guide the Church's current activities.

Likewise, the judgment by the Son of Man must be still in the future; and here what is perhaps the most crucial creative change is made – the identification of the Messiah with the Son of Man. The Fourth Evangelist has recorded this identification as clearly as anyone could wish:

> For as the Father has life in himself, so he has granted the Son also to have life in himself, and has given him authority to execute judgment, because he is the Son of man.[8]

The effects of this change on the wording of the tradition have already

[1] Acts 2:36.
[2] Acts 2:44–5; 4:32–5.
[3] Acts 6:7.
[4] Acts 2:46–7; 5:12–13.
[5] Acts 4:1–22; 5:17–42.
[6] Acts 7:54–8:3.
[7] Acts 8:4.
[8] John 5:26–7; cf. also 12:34.

been studied in some detail; all that we need to remark here is the naturalness of it. In the first place, there were, as we have seen, sayings of Jesus which could spark off the identification; secondly, Jesus had spoken of his earthly mission, with its criticism of the existing order, in the imagery of judgment and division:

> Do not think that I have come to bring peace on earth; I have not come to bring peace, but a sword.[1]

Thirdly, having 'ascended to his Father' after the resurrection, he must return if he was to reign in the Messianic kingdom; and if that kingdom was to be preceded by the judgment, then the conclusion shouted for acceptance that the return of Jesus and the judgment by the Son of Man, would prove to be one and the same event.

From *The Foolishness of God* by John Austin Baker

(Darton, Longman & Todd, 1970, pp. 239–40)

---

[1] Matt. 10:34.

QUINQUAGESIMA

Monday

The Foolishness of God

J. A. BAKER

It is interesting to note the wording of another passage in one of Peter's early speeches in *Acts*, where he is referring to the return of Jesus:

> Repent therefore, and turn again, that your sins may be blotted out, that times of refreshing may come from the presence of the Lord, and that he may send the Christ appointed for you, Jesus, whom heaven must receive until the time for establishing all that God spoke by the mouth of his holy prophets from of old.[1]

Here we have, on the present hypothesis, a very early form indeed of the Christian hope. The ultimate vision is of the setting up of the Messianic kingdom on earth, predicted (as it undoubtedly was) by the Old Testament prophets. In preparation for this, the believer is to repent, to receive God's forgiveness, and by his new manner of life to hasten the return of the 'Messiah appointed for you, Jesus', for citizenship of whose kingdom he will now be fitted. No identification here of Jesus with the coming Judge – indeed, no mention of the latter at all. Other passages in these chapters seem to imply a judgment of some kind,[2] but the allusion is oblique, and this element clearly not a primary concern. The purpose of Jesus' exaltation to heaven is to make repentance and forgiveness freely available.[3]

This sunny and hopeful atmosphere did not, however, last long. Rejection of the Gospel and persecution of its messengers made it clear that the battle was far from over; and the continuing vigour of the evils which Jesus had denounced brought into prominence his sayings about the seriousness of decision, the inevitability of an ultimate separation of wheat from tares, of the children of the kingdom from the hypocrites – and with these sayings, of course,

---

[1] Acts 2:19–21.
[2] Acts 2:40; 4:12.
[3] Acts 5:31.

the role of the Son of Man. It was beneath the louring skies of conflict and persecution that the vision of judgment, and of Jesus' part in it, came to the fore – sometimes, alas, from motives of bitterness and revenge[1] but sometimes from a sad but accurate realization of the power in men of those evil forces which were personalized in popular myth as the ape and enemy of the Messiah: the Antichrist.[2] Not unnaturally in such circumstances, Christians gradually ceased to believe in the possibility that the times of the Church might be the Messianic age. Jesus had not returned, the apostles were dead.[3] The hope of future blessedness now moves wholly into an other-worldly existence in the eternal presence of God.

From: *The Foolishess of God* by John Austin Baker

(Darton, Longman & Todd, 1970, pp. 241–3)

Tuesday

The Foolishness of God

J. A. BAKER

In seeking to recover the portrait of Jesus as he was, we have made no attempt in the currently fashionable way to indulge in generalized ethical assessments, or to highlight only those pieces of evidence which can be easily distilled into abstract principles – 'freedom to give oneself in sacrificial love', 'the Man for Others', and so forth. It is not that such phrases are false to Jesus; indeed, they are necessary and useful. But they are also dangerous, because they disguise the fact that he was a distinct and distinctive individual, with specific beliefs and hopes and values expressed in the thought and imagery of a particular time and society, and that it is this historical man to whom we are asked to respond, and who stands over against all the generations of those who seek to follow him, as a challenge, a judgment, and an eternal inspiration. Jesus did not see himself just as Everyman, nor as the Saviour of the World, even less as a divine pre-existent being from heaven. His whole life was directed to the task of bringing men to see that their only

[1] cf. Rev. 18.
[2] I John 2:18; 4:3; cf. II Thess. 2:1–12.
[3] II Peter 3:4.

Saviour was God, who was in very truth their Father in heaven. But he did see himself as the Messiah of Israel, appointed by God to bring in his kingdom on earth through service, suffering, and death. This, in the classic phrase, is the 'scandal of particularity' in the faith that proclaims him also as universal Lord. How such a man can justly be accorded supreme and saving significance for all men in all times will be the subject of the next chapters. Our final thought here must be simply this: that even though faith has hailed him as in the deepest sense both Son of Man and Son of God, it is in the end the role to which he himself felt that he was called by which he and his followers have been and will always be known – 'Messiah', the 'Anointed One', in Greek, 'Christos,' the Christ of the Christian Church.

From: *The Foolishness of God* by John Austin Baker

(Darton, Longman & Todd, 1970 pp. 242–3)

Ash Wednesday

Holiness

JEAN-PIERRE DE CAUSSADE

If the work of our sanctification presents us with difficulties apparently so insurmountable, it is because we do not look at it in the right way. In reality holiness consists in one thing alone, namely, fidelity to God's plan. And this fidelity is equally within everyone's capacity in both its active and passive practice.

The active practice of fidelity consists in accomplishing the duties imposed on us by the general laws of God and the Church, and by the particular state of life which we have embraced. Passive fidelity consists in the loving acceptance of all that God sends us at every moment.

Which of these two requirements of holiness is beyond our strength? Not active fidelity, since the duties imposed by it cease to be such when they are really beyond our powers. If the state of your health does not allow you to hear Mass, you are under no obligation to do so. It is the same with all positive precepts, namely, those which prescribe duties to be done. The only precepts to which no exceptions can be permitted are those which forbid the doing of things that are evil in themselves, for it is never permissible to do evil.

Can anything be easier or more reasonable? What excuse can we plead? Yet this is all that God demands of the soul in the work of its sanctification. He demands it from the high and the low, from the strong and the weak; in a word, from all, always and everywhere. It is true then that he asks from us only what is simple and easy, for it is sufficient to possess this simple fund of goodwill in order to attain to eminent holiness.

If over and above the commandments he puts before us the counsels as a more perfect goal of our endeavour, he is always careful to accomodate the practice of the counsels to our position and character. The attractions of grace which facilitate the practice of the counsels are the chief sign that he is calling us to follow them. He never presses anyone beyond his strength or aptitudes. Once more, what could be more just?

From: *Self-Abandonment to Divine Providence* by Jean-Pierre de Caussade, translated from the Standard French Edition of *Father P. H. Ramière, S.J.* by Algar Thorold

(Collins Fontana, 1971, pp. 34–5)

Thursday

Holiness

JEAN-PIERRE DE CAUSSADE

Perfection does not consist in understanding God's designs but in submitting to them.

God's designs, God's good pleasure, the will of God, the action of God and his grace are all one and the same thing in this life. They are God working in the soul to make it like himself. Perfection is nothing else than the faithful co-operation of the soul with the work of God, and it begins, grows and is consummated in our souls secretly and without our being aware of it.

Theology is full of ideas and expressions explaining the marvels of this ultimate state in each soul in accordance with its capacity. A man may know all the theory of it, may speak and write admirably on the subject, and instruct and direct souls, but if his knowledge remains merely theoretical, then compared with those who attain the goal of God's design without knowing the theory of it in whole or in part, or without being able to discourse on it, he is like a sick doctor in comparison with simple people who are in perfect health.

When God's designs and will are embraced with simplicity by a faithful soul, they produce this divine state in it without its knowing it; just as medicine taken obediently by a sick man effects his cure though he neither knows nor is capable of knowing anything about medicine. Similarly, as it is fire and not the philosophy or scientific knowledge of fire that warms us, so it is the will and designs of God that produce sanctity in our souls and not intellectual speculation about this principle and its effects. If we wish to quench our thirst, we must lay aside books which explain thirst, and take a drink. By itself, curiosity for knowledge can only make one thirstier. Thus, when we thirst for holiness, curiosity for theoretical knowledge of it can only drive it further from us. We must put speculation on one side, and with simplicity drink everything that God's designs present to us in actions and sufferings. What happens to us each moment by God's design is for us the holiest, best and most divine thing.

From: *Self-Abandonment to Divine Providence* by Jean-Pierre de Caussade, translated from the Standard French Edition of *Father P. H. Ramière, S.J.* by Algar Thorold

(Collins Fontana, 1971, pp. 37–8)

Friday

Holiness

JEAN-PIERRE DE CAUSSADE

The whole essence of the spiritual life consists in recognizing the designs of God for us at the present moment. All reading that is chosen by us apart from God's designs is harmful to us; the designs and will of God are the grace which works in the depths of our hearts through the books we read as through everything else we do. Apart from God, books are merely useless externals, and being devoid for us of the life-giving power of God's plan, they succeed only in emptying the heart by the very satisfaction which they give to the mind.

This divine will, working in the soul of a simple ignorant girl by means of a few ordinary sufferings and actions, produces in the depths of her heart this mysterious fulfilment of supernatural life without putting into her mind ideas which might make her conceited. While on the contrary, a proud man who reads spiritual books only from curiosity and without any regard for the will of God receives only the dead letter into his mind, and his heart grows ever drier and harder.

The will and designs of God are the life of the soul no matter what the appearance under which the soul receives them or applies them to itself.

In whatever manner this divine will touches the mind, it nourishes the soul and continually enlarges it by giving it what is best for it at every moment. These happy effects are produced not by any particular event as such, but by God's design for each individual moment. What was best for the moment which has just passed, is so no longer because it is no longer the will of God; this now presents itself under other appearances and forms the duty of the present moment. It is this duty which, in whatever guise it may appear, is the most sanctifying for the soul.

If the duty of the present moment is to read, then reading will produce this mysterious fulfilment in the depths of the soul. If the divine will bids us turn from reading to the duty of contemplation, this duty develops the 'new man' in the depths of the heart, whereas to continue reading would be harmful and useless. If the divine will withdraws us from contemplation in order to hear confessions etc., even for a long time, this duty is the means of forming Jesus Christ in the depths of the heart, and all the sweetness of contemplation would only serve to drive him out.

From: *Self-Abandonment to Divine Providence* by Jean-Pierre de Caussade, translated from the Standard French Edition of *Father P. H. Ramière S.J.* by Algar Thorold

(Collins Fontana, 1971, pp. 38–9)

Saturday.

Holiness

JEAN-PIERRE DE CAUSSADE

It is the designs of God that are the fulfilment of all our moments. They manifest themselves in a thousand different ways which thus become our successive duties, and form, increase and perfect the 'new man' in us until we attain the full stature destined for us by divine wisdom. This mysterious growth in age of Jesus Christ in our hearts is the end and fulfilment produced by the designs of God; it is the fruit of his grace and his divine goodness.

This fruit, as we have said, is produced, fed and increased by the duties which are successively presented to us and are filled with the will of God. In performing these duties we are always sure of possessing the 'better part', for this holy will is itself the 'better part'. We have only to allow it freedom to work in us and abandon ourselves blindly to it in perfect confidence. It is infinitely wise, infinitely powerful, infinitely beneficent towards souls who place their hope in it utterly without reserve, who love and seek nothing but it alone, and who believe with unshakeable faith and confidence that what it does at each moment is the best, without looking elsewhere for something more or something less, and without pausing to consider the connection between God's designs and external things, for this is the mere seeking of self-love.

The will of God is the essential and real element and the power in all things; it is the will of God that adjusts and adapts them to the soul. Without it, all is nothingness, emptiness, lies and vanity, the mere letter without the spirit, empty husks and death. The will of God is the salvation, health and life of body and soul no matter what the external appearance of the thing to which it is applied. We must not therefore examine the suitability of things to mind and body in order to assess their value, for this is of little importance; it is the will of God which gives to things, whatever they may be, the power to form Jesus Christ in the depths of our hearts. We must not dictate to God's will nor set limits to its action, for it is all-powerful.

Whatever ideas the mind may choose to be filled with, whatever the feelings of the body; even if the mind be afflicted with distractions and worries, and the body with sickness and death, nevertheless the divine will is always for the present moment the life of the body and the soul, for in whatever state they are, both are ultimately sustained only by the divine will. Without it bread is poison; with it poison is a salutary remedy. Without it books do nothing but darken the mind, and with it darkness becomes light. It is everything that is good and true in all things. And in all things it gives us God, and God is the infinite being who takes the place of all things for the soul that possesses him.

From: *Self-Abandonment to Divine Providence* by Jean-Pierre de Caussade, translated from the Standard French Edition of *Father P. H. Ramière, S.J.* by Algar Thorold

(Collins Fontana, 1971, pp. 39–41)

LENT 1

The King and the Kingdom: Temptation

CHARLES WILLIAMS

The Gospel of St. Mark begins with a declaration: 'The beginning of the Gospel of Jesus Christ, the Son of God.' What the Son of God may be he does not explain, preferring to follow it up with a quotation from the old prophets which slides into an account of a certain John who came as the precursor of this Divine Hero. He has in St. Mark no other business, and this (though highly wrought to a fine passion of declamation and heraldry) is so in St. John. But in St. Luke there is something more. It is recorded that certain groups came to the Precursor – the common people, the tax-collectors, the soldiers. All these ask him for some kind of direction on conduct. St. Matthew adds the ecclesiastical leaders, but the Precursor offered them no more than invective. He answers the rest with instructions which amount very nearly to a gospel of temporal justice. All men are to share their goods freely and equally. The revenue officers are to make no personal profit out of their business. The soldiers are not to make their duties an excuse for outrage or violence; they (again) are to make no personal gain beyond their government pay. Share everything; neither by fraud nor by force let yourself be unfair to anyone; be content with your own proper pay. It is true he does not raise the question of the restoration of the dispossessed by force of arms; he is speaking of immediate duties as between individual and individual. 'He that has two coats let him give to him that hath none.' He prolongs the concern of the prophets with social injustice, without their denunciation of the proud. That had been declared, as a duty of the Imperial government, by the great poet dead forty-five years before: 'To impose the habit of peace, to be merciful to the down-trodden, and to overthrow the proud.'[1] There had been a similar note in the private song (again

---

[1] Pacisque imponere morem, Parcere subiectis et debellare superbos.

according to St. Luke) of the Mother of the coming Hero: 'the rich he hath sent empty away'.

At this moment the Divine Thing appears (it will be remembered that St. Matthew uses the neuter – 'that holy *thing*'; students of the Gospel may be excused for sometimes following the example, if only to remind ourselves of what the Evangelists actually said). In the rest of St. Mark's first chapter, the account of his coming is purely apocalyptic. Witness is borne out of heaven and on earth and from hell. He (since the masculine pronoun is also and more frequently used) begins his own activities. He calls disciples; he works miracles of healing; he controls spirits; he teaches with authority. What does he teach? What do the devils fear and the celestials declare and men wonder at? 'The time is fulfilled, and the Kingdom of God is at hand; repent ye and believe the gospel.'

From: *He Came Down From Heaven* by Charles Williams

(Heinemann, 1938, pp. 61–3)

Tuesday

The Ring and the Kingdom: Temptation

CHARLES WILLIAMS

Yes, but what gospel? What kind of Kingdom? The Precursor had said almost the same thing. In some expectation one turns the page . . . several pages. The works of healing continue swiftly, interspersed with the Divine Thing's comments on himself, and his reasons for existing. They are still not very clear. The old prophetic cry of 'pardon' returns. He has power to forgive sins – does he mean forget? He calls himself the 'Son of Man'; he is lord of ritual observances such as the keeping of the Sabbath; there exists some state of eternal sin and damnation. There is something – presumably the kingdom of heaven – which cannot be reconciled with old things; new, it must be fitted to the new.

Presently, in the parables, the description of the kingdom is continued. It is a state of being, but not a state of being without which one can get along very well. To lose it is to lose everything else. It is intensely dangerous, and yet easily neglected. It involves repentance and it involves 'faith' – whatever 'faith' may be. It is concerned with himself, for he attributes to himself the power and the glory. He says: 'I say unto thee, Arise'; 'it is I; be not afraid.' The Sermon on the Mount is full of his own decisions, just as it ramps with hell and destruction and hypocrites and being cast into the fire and trodden under foot and demands for perfection and for joy (not for resignation or endurance or forgiveness, not even a pseudo-joy) under intolerable treatment. Moses in old days had momentarily taken the power and the glory to himself, and had been shut out of the temporal promise. But the present Hero does it continuously, until (in the topmost note of that exalted arrogance) humility itself is vaunted, and the only virtue that cannot be aware of itself without losing its nature is declared by the Divine Thing to be its own nature: 'I am meek and lowly of heart.' This in the voice that says to the Syrophœnician woman when she begs help for her daughter: 'It is not meet to take the children's bread, and to cast it unto the dogs.' It is true her request is granted, in answer to her retort, something in the same manner as the Lord spoke to Job in answer to his.

From: *He Came Down From Heaven* by Charles Williams

(Heinemann, 1938, pp. 63–4)

Wednesday

The King and the Kingdom: Temptation

CHARLES WILLIAMS

About halfway through the book as we have it, there is a change. Up to Chapter viii it is possible to believe that, though the doctrine is anything but clear, the experience of the disciples is not unique. Figures are sometimes met who overwhelm, frighten, and delight those who come in contact with them; personality, and so forth – and what they say may easily sound obscure. But in Chapter viii there is a sudden concentration and even exposition. The Hero demands from his disciples a statement, not of their repentance or righteousness or belief in the I AM, which is what the old prophets clamoured for, but of their belief in himself, and he follows it up with a statement of his own. They say: 'Thou art the Christ.' No doubt when we have looked up annotated editions and Biblical dictionaries, we know what 'the Christ' means. It is 'the Anointed One.' But at the moment, there, it is a kind of incantation, the invocation of a ritual, antique, and magical title. Even if we look up the other Gospels and make it read: 'Thou art the Christ, the Son of the living God,' it does not much help. However inspired St. Peter may have been, it seems unlikely that he comprehended in a flash the whole complex business of Christian theology. What is the Son of God? The apostles and the devils agree; that is something. But on what do they agree?

The Divine Thing approves the salutation. It proceeds to define its destiny. It declares it is to suffer greatly, to be rejected by all the centres of jurisdiction to be seized and put to death, and after three days it is to rise again from the dead. Protests are abusively tossed aside. In all three gospels this definition of its immediate future is followed by a definition of its further nature and future; 'the Son of Man' is to be seen in the 'glory of His Father and with the holy angels,' that is, in the swift and geometrical glory seen by Isaiah and Ezekiel, the fire of the wheels and the flash of the living creatures, the terrible crystal and the prism of the covenant above, the pattern of heaven declared in heaven. The formula of the knowledge of this pattern on earth is disclosed; it is the loss of life for the saving of life, 'for my sake and the gospel's'. It is the denial of the self and the lifting of the cross.

From: *He Came Down From Heaven* by Charles Williams

(Heinemann, 1938, pp. 64–6)

Thursday

The King and the Kingdom: Temptation

CHARLES WILLIAMS

The denial of the self has come, as is natural, to mean in general the making of the self thoroughly uncomfortable. That (though it may be all that is possible) leaves the self still strongly existing. But the phrase is more intellectual than moral, or rather it is only moral because it is intellectual; it is a denial of the consciousness of the existence of the self at all. What had been the self is to become a single individual, neither less nor more than others; as it were, one of the living creatures that run about and compose the web of the glory. 'Do unto others as you would they should do unto you.' The contemplation demanded is not personal, of the self and of others – even in order that the self may be unselfish – but abstract and impartial. The life of the self is to be lost that the individual soul may be found, in the pattern of the words of the Son of Man. The kingdom is immediately at hand – 'Verily I say unto you, That there be some of them that stand here, which shall not taste of death, till they have seen the kingdom of God come with power'; again the words are historic and contemporary at once.

The declaration of the formula is followed by what is called the Transfiguration. Secluded among a few of his followers, the Divine Thing exhibits itself in a sudden brightness, in which, as if it receded into the eternal state of contemporaneousness, the ancient leaders of what had once been the inclusive-exclusive covenant of salvation are discerned to exchange speech with the new exclusive figure of inclusive beatitude. It is a vision which is to be kept a secret till the rising from the dead has been accomplished. But at least the kingdom has now been, to some extent, exhibited. Repentance is a preliminary to the denial of the self and the loss of the life, and the loss of the life for the saving of the life depends on that choosing of necessity by the Son of Man which will take him to his death and rising. 'He set his face to go up to Jerusalem.'

From: *He Came From Heaven* by Charles Williams

(Heinemann, 1938, pp. 66–7)

Friday

The King and the Kingdom: Temptation

CHARLES WILLIAMS

It is at some time during this period of the operation of the Christ that the problem of the Precursor reappears. Messengers from John arrive; 'art thou he that was to come?' After they have been dismissed, the Christ, turning to those that stood by (as it were to his mother and to his brethren), makes the astonishing declaration that 'among men born of women is none greater than John the Baptist, yet the least in the Kingdom of Heaven is greater than he.' The Church since then has implied that this can hardly be true in its literal sense, for the Precursor has been canonized (as it were, by acclamation) and been given a Feast to himself, a Primary Double of the First Class. Even so, even assuming that as a matter of fact the Precursor was and is one of the greatest in the kingdom of heaven, still the Christ must have had something in his mind. What, apart from the expectation of the Redeemer, was the gospel of the Precursor? It was something like complete equality and temporal justice, regarded as the duty of those who expect the kingdom. What has happened to that duty in the gospel of the Kingdom?

The new gospel does not care much about it. All John's doctrine is less than the least in the Kingdom. It cannot be bothered with telling people not to defraud and not to be violent and to share their superfluities. It tosses all that sort of thing on one side. Let the man who has two coats (said the Precursor) give one to the man who has none. But what if the man who has none, or for that matter the man who has three, wants to take one from the man who has two – what then? Grace of heaven! why, give him both. If a man has stolen the pearl bracelet, why, point out to him that he has missed the diamond-necklace! Be content with your wages, said the Precursor. The Holy Thing decorated that advice with a suggestion that it is iniquity to be displeased when others who have done about a tenth as much work are paid as much money: 'is thine eye evil because mine is good?' It is true that there is a reason – those who came in late had not been hired early. No one would accept that as a reason today – neither economist nor employer nor worker. But there is always a reason; the intellectual logic of the Prophets is carried on into the New Testament. Yet the separate and suitable reasons never quite account for the identical and indivisible command. The 'sweet reasonableness' of Christ is always there, but it is always in a dance and its dancing hall is from the topless heavens to the bottomless abyss. Its balance is wholly in itself; it is philosophical and unconditioned by temporalities – 'had, having, and in quest to have, extreme'.

From: *He Came Down From Heaven* by Charles Williams

(Heinemann, 1938, pp. 67–9)

Saturday

The King and the Kingdom: Temptation

CHARLES WILLIAMS

Half a hundred brief comments, flung out to the mob of men's hearts, make it impossible for a child of the kingdom, for a Christian, to talk of justice or injustice so far as he personally is concerned; they make it impossible for him to *complain* of the unfairness of anything. They do not, presumably, stop him noticing what has happened, but it can never be a matter of protest. Judgment and measurement are always discouraged. You may have them if you will, but there is a sinister note in the promise that they shall be measured back to you in the same manner: 'good measure, pressed down and running over shall men give into your bosoms'. If you must have law, have it, 'till thou hast paid the uttermost farthing'.

What then of all the great tradition, the freeing of slaves at the Exodus, the determination of the prophets, the long effort against the monstrous impiety of Cain? The answer is obvious; all that is assumed as a mere preliminary. The rich, while they remain rich, are practically incapable of salvation, at which all the Apostles were exceedingly astonished. Their astonishment is exceedingly funny to our vicariously generous minds. But if riches are not supposed to be confined to money, the astonishment becomes more general. There are many who feel that while God might damn Rothschild he could hardly damn Rembrandt. Are the riches of Catullus and Carnegie so unequal, though so different? Sooner or later nearly everyone is surprised at some kind of rich man being damned. The Divine Thing, for once, was tender to us; he restored a faint hope: 'with God all things are possible'. But the preliminary step is always assumed: 'sell all that thou hast and give it to the poor' – and then we will talk. Then we will talk of that other thing without which even giving to the poor is useless, the thing for which at another time the precious ointment was reserved from the poor, the thing that is necessary to correct and qualify even good deeds, the thing that is formulated in the words 'for my sake and the gospel's' or 'in my name'. Good deeds are not enough; even love is not enough unless it is love of a particular kind. Long afterwards St. Paul caught up the dreadful cry: 'though I bestow all my goods to feed the poor . . . and have not charity, it profiteth me nothing'. It is not surprising that Messias saw the possibility of an infinitely greater knowledge of evil existing through him than had been before: 'blessed is he whosoever shall not be offended at me'.

From: *He Came Down From Heaven* by Charles Williams

(Heinemann, 1938, pp. 69–71)

LENT 2

The King and the Kingdom: Conflict

CHARLES WILLIAMS

The Incarnation of the Kingdom has declared its destiny, the formula by which man may be unified with it, the preliminaries necessary to the spiritual initiation. The records of the Synoptics proceed to the awful and familiar tale: to the entry of the Divine Thing into Jerusalem, to its making of itself a substance of communication through the flesh, to its Passion. 'The Son of Man is betrayed into the hands of sinners.' In the ancient myth something of that kind happened to the good, the good in which the Adam had lived. But that good had not, in the myth, been imagined as a consciousness. The kingdom of heaven then had not been shown as affected by the sin of the Adam; only the Adam. The patience which had been proclaimed in the covenants had been the self-restraint of the Creator, but not – there – of the Victim. Another side of the aeonian process has issued slowly into knowledge; the operation of that in the Adam and in their descendants which had remained everlastingly related to the good.

The Gospel called 'of John' begins with that original. The Divine Thing is there identified with the knowledge of good which indefectibly exists in every man – indefectibly even though it should be experienced only as hell – 'the light which lighteth every man'. It is also that by which communication with the heaven of perfection is maintained, 'ascending and descending'. But this state of being which is called 'The kingdom of heaven' in the Synoptics is called in St. John 'eternal life'. There is no space here to work out singly the various definitions of itself which it provides in this Gospel. Briefly, it declares itself to be the union of heaven and earth (i. 51); the one absolutely necessary thing for escape from a state in which the contradiction of good is preferred (iii, 16, 36); it is the perfect satisfaction of desire (vi, 35; x, 27–8); it is judgment (v, 25–30; xii, 46–8); it is in perfect union with its Origin (x, 30, xiv, 11); it is universal and inclusive (xv. 5; xvii. 21); it restores the truth (v. 33; vii. 31–2; xviii. 37). Of these the last is perhaps the most related to the present argument. For by truth must be meant at least perfect knowledge (within the proper requisite degrees). 'Ye shall know the truth, and the truth shall make you free.' Right knowledge and freedom are to be one.

From: *He Came Down From Heaven* by Charles Williams

(Heinemann, 1938, pp. 71–2)

Tuesday

The King and the Kingdom: Conflict

CHARLES WILLIAMS

It is this 'truth' of which the Divine Hero speaks at the time of the Passion which he had prophesied – as necessity and as his free choice. Before one of the jurisdictions by which he is rejected and condemned he declares: 'To this end was I born, and for this cause came I into the world, that I should bear witness unto the truth. Everyone that is of the truth heareth my voice.' He formally claimed before another the ritual titles of Son of God and Son of Man, and his future descent 'in the clouds of heaven' and in the glory of heaven. But before then the earlier proclamation, 'the kingdom of heaven is at hand,' has changed. It has become concentrated; if the kingdom, then the moment of the arrival of the kingdom. The Gospels break into peremptory phrases: 'My time is at hand', 'this night', 'this hour'; an image of the hour absorbed into the Holy Thing is thrown up – 'this cup'; the hour arrives – 'behold, the Son of Man is betrayed into the hands of sinners'.

Around that moment the world of order and judgment, of Virgil and the Precursor, of Pharaoh and Cain, rushes up also. Its good and its evil are both concerned, for it cannot very well do other than it does do. The knowledge of good as evil has made the whole good evil to it; it has to reject the good in order to follow all that it can understand as good. When Caiaphas said that 'it was good that one man should die for the people', he laid down a principle which every government supports and must support. Nor, though Christ has denounced the government for its other sins, does he denounce either Caiaphas or Pilate for his own death. He answers the priest; he condescends to discussion with the Roman. Only to Herod he says nothing, for Herod desired neither the ecclesiastical nor the political good; he wanted only miracles to amuse him. The miracles of Christ are accidental, however efficient; the kingdom of heaven fulfils all earthly laws because that is its nature but it is concerned only with its own, and to try to use it for earth is to lose heaven and gain nothing for earth. It may be taken by violence but it cannot be compelled by violence; its Incarnation commanded that he should be awaited everywhere but his effectiveness demanded nowhere. Everything must be made ready and then he will do what he likes. This maxim, which is the condition of all prayer, has involved the Church in a metaphysic of prayer equivalent to 'Heads, I win; tails, you lose.'

From: *He Came Down From Heaven* by Charles Williams

(Heinemann, 1938, pp. 72–4)

Wednesday

The King and the Kingdom: Conflict

CHARLES WILLIAMS

The three jurisdictions acted according to all they could understand of good: Caiaphas upon all he could know of the religious law, Pilate of the Virgilian equity, Herod of personal desire. The Messias answered them in that first word of the Cross which entreated pardon for them precisely on the ground of their ignorance: 'forgive them, for they know not what they do'. The knowledge of good and evil which man had desired is offered as the excuse for their false knowledge of good. But the offer brings their false knowledge into consciousness, and will no longer like the prophets blot it out. The new way of pardon is to be different from the old, for the evil is still to be known. It is known, in what follows, by the Thing that has come down from Heaven. He experiences a complete and utter deprivation of all knowledge of the good. The Church has never defined the Atonement. It has contented itself with saying that the Person of the Kingdom there assumed into itself the utmost possible capacities of its own destruction and they could not destroy it. It separated itself from all good deliberately and (as it were) superfluously: 'thinkest thou I cannot now pray to the Father and he shall presently give me more than twelve legions of angels? But how then shall the scriptures be fulfilled, that thus it must be?' It could, it seems, still guiltlessly free itself, but it has made its own promise and will keep it. Its impotency is deliberate.

From: *He Came Down From Heaven* by Charles Williams

(Heinemann, 1938, p. 74)

Thursday

The King and the Kingdom: Conflict

CHARLES WILLIAMS

It denies its self; it loses its life to save it; it saves others because it cannot, by its decisions, save itself. It remains still exclusive and inclusive; it excludes all consent to the knowledge of evil, but it includes the whole knowledge of evil without its own consent. It is 'made sin', in St. Paul's phrase. The prophecy quoted concerning this paradox of redemption is 'A bone of him shall not be broken', and this is fulfilled; as if the frame of the universe remains entire, but its life is drawn out of it, as if the pattern of the glory remained exact but the glory itself were drawn away. The height of the process begins with the Agony in the Garden, which is often quoted for our encouragement; he shuddered and shrank. The shrinking is part of the necessity; he 'must' lose power; he 'must' know fear. He 'must' be like the Adam in the garden of the myth, only where they fled from their fear into the trees he goes among the trees to find his fear; he is secluded into terror. The process reaches its height, after from the cross he has still asserted the *pietas*, the exchanged human responsibility, of men: 'behold thy son, behold thy mother,' and after he has still declared the pure dogma of his nature, known now as hardly more than dogma: 'today thou shalt be with me in Paradise'. This is what he has chosen, and as his power leaves him he still chooses, to believe. He becomes, but for that belief, a state wholly abandoned.

From: *He Came Down From Heaven* by Charles Williams

(Heinemann, 1938, pp. 74–6)

Friday

The King and the Kingdom: Conflict

CHARLES WILLIAMS

Gibbon, in that superb as well as solemn sneer which is one of the classic pages of English prose as well as one of the supreme attacks on the whole history, may have been right. The whole earth may not have been darkened, nor even the whole land. Pliny and Seneca may have recorded no wonder because there was no wonder to record. The sun may have seemed to shine on Calvary as on many another more protracted agony. Or there may have been a local eclipse, or whatever other phenomenon the romantic pietists can invent to reconcile themselves to the other side. But that the life of the whole of mankind began to fail in that hour is not incredible; that the sun and all light, without as within, darkened before men's eyes, that the swoon of something more than death touched them, and its sweat stood on their foreheads to the farthest ends of the world. The Thing that was, and had always been, and must always be; the fundamental humanity of all men; the Thing that was man rather than a man, though certainly incarnated into the physical appearance of a man; the Thing that was Christ Jesus, knew all things in the deprivation of all goodness.

From: *He Came Down From Heaven* by Charles Williams

(Heinemann, 1938, p. 76)

Saturday

The King and the Kingdom: Conflict

CHARLES WILLIAMS

The darkness passed; men went on their affairs. He said: 'It is finished.' The Passion and the Resurrection have been necessarily divided in ritual and we think of them as separate events. So certainly they were, and yet not as separate as all that. They are two operations in one; they are the hour of the coming of the kingdom. A new knowledge arises. Men had determined to know good as evil; there could be but one perfect remedy for that – to know the evil of the past itself as good, and to be free from the necessity of the knowledge of evil in the future; to find right knowledge and perfect freedom together; to know all things as occasions of love. The Adam and their children had been involved in a state of contradiction within themselves. The law had done its best by imposing on that chaos of contradiction a kind of order by at least calling definite things good and definite things evil. The prophets had urged this method: repent, 'cease to do evil, learn to do well'. But even allowing that, in all times and places, it was possible to know what was good and what was evil, was it as easy as all that? Or what of Job who had done well and was overthrown? Or Ecclesiastes who had sought out righteousness and found it was all much the same vanity in the end? How could the single knowledge be restored? Or if the myth itself were false, how could the single knowledge be gained – the knowledge of perfection in all experience which man naturally desires and naturally believes and as naturally denies and contradicts?

The writing of the early masters of the new life, the life that was declared after the Resurrection, are full of an awful simplicity. The thing has happened; the kingdom is here. 'Fear not, little flock,' wrote one of them, 'it is your Father's good pleasure to give you the kingdom.' 'What shall deliver me', wrote another, 'from the body of this death? I thank God, through Jesus Christ our Lord.' This clarity of knowledge rides through the Epistles. All is most well; evil is 'pardoned' – it is known after another manner; in an interchange of love, as a means of love, therefore as a means of the good. *O felix culpa* – pardon is no longer an oblivion but an increased knowledge, a knowledge of all things in a perfection of joy.

From: *He Came Down From Heaven* by Charles Williams

(Heinemann, 1938, pp. 77–8)

LENT 3

Monday

The Work of Christ

Let me begin with a story which was reported in the Belgian papers some years ago.

Two passenger trains were coming in opposite directions at full speed. As they approached the station, it was found the levers would not work owing to the frost, and the points could not be set to clear the trains of each other. A catastrophe seemed to be inevitable; when a signalman threw himself flat between the rails, and with his hands held the tie rod in such a way that the points were properly set and kept; and he remained thus while the train thundered over him, in great danger of having his head carried away by the low-slung gear of the Westinghouse brake. When the train had passed, he quietly rose and returned to his work.

I offer you some reflections on this incident. It is the kind of incident that may be multiplied indefinitely. I offer you certain reflections, first, on some of its analogies with Christ's work, and secondly, on some of its differences.

1. This man, in a very true sense, died and rose again. His soul went through what he would have gone through if he had never risen from the track. He gave himself; and that is all a man can give at last. His deed had the moral value which it would have had if he had lost his life. He laid it down, but it did not please God to take it. Like Abraham's sacrifice of Isaac, it was complete and acceptable, even though not accepted. The man's rising from the ground – was it not really a resurrection from the dead? It was not simply a return to his post. He went back another man. He went back a heavenlier man. He had died and risen, just as if he had been called, and had gone, to God's presence – could he but remain there. There is a death and rising again possible to us all. If the death and resurrection of Jesus Christ do not end in producing that kind of thing amongst us, then it is not the power of God unto salvation. These moral deaths and resurrections are what make men of us. 'In deaths oft.' That is the first point.

2. The second point is this. Not one of the passengers in either of those trains knew until they read it what had been done for them, nor to whom they owed their lives. It is so with the whole world. Today it owes its existence, in a way it but poorly understands, to the death and resurrection of Jesus Christ. That is the permanent element in Christianity – the cross and resurrection of Jesus Christ. And yet it is nothing to all them that pass by . . . The success of Christ hides him. It is the death of Christ that is the chief condition of modern progress. It is not civilization that keeps civilization safe and progressive. It is that power which was in Jesus Christ and culminated in his death and resurrection. When people read the Bible, and get behind the Bible, and that principle comes home to them, it may sometimes be like the shock that those travellers would receive when they read in the newspaper of their risk and deliverance.

From: *The Work of Christ* by P. T. Forsyth

(Collins Fontana, 1965 pp. 42–4)

Tuesday

The Work of Christ

P. T. FORSYTH

Now I am coming on to the difference [between the sacrifice of the man who averted the train disaster and the sacrifice of Christ on the Cross]. This man died for people who would thrill with the sense of what they owed him as soon as they read about it. His act appeals to the instinct which is ready to spring to life in almost every breast. You felt the response at once when I told you the story. Some of you may have even felt it keenly. Do you ever feel as keenly about the devoted death of Christ? Perhaps you never have. You believed it, of course, but it never came home to you and gripped you as the stories of the kind I instance do. You see the difference between Christ's death and every case of human heroism. I am moving to answer that question I put a moment ago as to whether the development of the best in human nature would ever give us the work of Christ and the kingdom of God. I have been illustrating one of the finest things in human nature, and I am asking whether, if that were multiplied indefinitely, we should yet have the effect which is produced by the death of Christ, or which is still to be produced by it in God's purpose. No, there is a difference between Christ's death and every case of heroism. Christ's was a death on behalf of people within whom the power of responding had to be created. Everybody thrills to that story I told you, and to every similar story. The power of response is lying there in the human heart ready – it only needs to be touched. There is in human nature a battery charged with admiration for such things; you have only to put your knuckle to it and out comes the spark. But when we are dealing with the death of Christ we are in another position. Christ's was a death on behalf of people in whom the power of responding had to be created. We are all afraid of death, and rise to the man who delivers us from it. But we are not afraid of that worse thing than death from which Christ came to deliver us. Christ's death was not a case of heroism simply, it was a case of redemption. It acted upon dull and dead hearts. It was a death which had to evoke a feeling not only latent but paralysed, not only asleep but dead. What does Paul say? 'While we were yet without strength, Christ died for us' – without power, without feeling, as the full meaning is.

From: *The Work of Christ* by P. T. Forsyth

(Collins Fontana, 1965, pp. 44–5)

Wednesday

The Work of Christ

P. T. FORSYTH

What the work of Christ requires is the tribute not of our admiration or even gratitude, not of our impressions or our thrills, but of ourselves and our shame. Now we are coming to the crux of the matter – the tribute of our shame. That death had to make new men of us. It had to turn us not from potential friends to actual, but from enemies into friends. It had not merely to touch a spring of slumbering friendship. There was a new creation. . . . The love of God is not merely evoked within us, it is 'shed abroad in our hearts by the Holy Spirit which is given to us'. That is a very different thing from simply having the reservoir of natural feeling tapped. The death of Christ had to do with our sin and not with our sluggishness. It had to deal with our active hostility, and not simply with the passive dullness of our hearts. Our hostility – that is what the easy-going people cannot be brought to recognize. That is what the shallow optimists, who think we can now dispense with emphasis on the death of Christ, feel themselves able to do – to ignore the fact that the human heart is enmity against God, against a God who makes demands upon it; who goes so far as to make demands for the whole, the absolute obedience of self. Human nature put its back up against that. That is what Paul means when he speaks about human nature, the natural man . . . being enmity against God. Man will cling to the last rag of his self-respect. He does not part with that when he thrills, admires, sympathizes; but he does when he has to give up his whole self in the obedience of faith. How much self-respect do you think Paul had left in him when he went into Damascus? Christ, with the demand for saving obedience, arouses antagonism in the human heart And so will the church that is faithful to him. You hear people of the type I have been speaking about saying, If only the church had been true to Christ's message it would have done wonders for the world. If only Christ were preached and practised in all his simplicity to the world, how fast Christianity would spread. Would it? Do you really find that the deeper you get into Christ and the meaning of his demands Christianity spreads faster in your heart? Is it not very much the other way? When it comes to close quarters you have actually to be got down and broken that the old man may be pulverized and the new man created from the dust. Therefore when we hear people abusing the church and its history the first thing we have to say is, Yes, there is a great deal too much truth in what you say, but there is also a greater truth which you are not allowing for, and it is this. One reason why the church has been so slow in its progress in mankind and its effect on human history is because it has been so faithful to Christ, so faithful to his Cross. You have to subdue the most intractable, difficult, and slow thing in the world – man's self-will. You cannot expect rapid success if you truly preach the Cross whereupon Christ died, and which he surmounted not simply by leaving it behind but by rising again, and converting the very Cross into a power and glory.

Christ arouses antagonism in the human heart and heroism does not. Everybody welcomes a hero. The minority welcome Christ. We do resent his absolute command. We do resent parting completely with ourselves. We do resent Christ.

From: *The Work of Christ* by P. T. Forsyth

(Collins Fontana, 1965, pp. 47–9)

The Work of Christ

P. T. FORSYTH

I go back to the word I spoke about the tribute of our shame. The demand is unsparing, remorseless. It is not simply that you are called on by God for a certain due, a change, an amendment, but for the tribute of yourself and your shame. When you heard about that heroism of my story, when you thrilled to it, I wonder did you pat yourself on the back a little for being capable of thrilling to things so big, so fine? When you thrilled to that story you felt a certain satisfaction with yourself because there was as much of the God in you as allowed you to be capable of thrilling to such heroisms. You felt, If I am capable of thrilling to such things, I cannot be such a bad sort. But when you felt the meaning of Christ's death for you, did you ever pat yourself on the back? The nearer the Cross came to you, the deeper it entered into you, were you the more disposed to admire yourself? There is no harm in your feeling pleased with yourself because you were able to thrill to these human heroisms; but if the impression Christ makes upon you is to leave you more satisfied with yourself, more proud of yourself for being able to respond, he has to get a great deal nearer to you yet. You need to be – I will use a Scottish phrase which old ministers used to apply to a young minister when he had preached a 'thoughtful and interesting discourse' – you need to be well shaken over the mouth of the pit. The great deep classic cases of Christian experience bear testimony to that. Christ and his Cross came nearer and nearer, and we do not realize what we owe him until we realize that he has plucked us from the fearful pit, and the miry clay, and set us upon a rock of God's own founding. The meaning of Christ's death rouses our shame, self-contempt, and repentance. And we resent being made to feel ashamed of ourselves, we resent being made to repent. A great many people are afraid to come too near to anything that does that for them. That is a frequent reason for not going to church.

From: *The Work of Christ* by P. T. Forsyth

(Collins Fontana, 1965, pp. 49–50)

Friday

The Work of Christ

P. T. FORSYTH

You would have gone a long way to see this Belgian man [who saved the train]. You would have gazed upon him with something of reverence, certainly with admiration. You would have regarded him as one received back from the dead. You think, If all men were like that, the world would be heaven. Well, there are a great many more like that than we think, who daily imperil their life for their duty. But supposing every man and woman in the world were up to that pitch, and supposing you added them all together and took the total value of their moral herosim (if moral quantities were capable of being summed like that), would you then have the equivalent of the deed and death of Christ? No, indeed! If you took all the world, and made heroes of them all, and kept them heroic all their lives, instead of only in one act, still you would not get the value, the equivalent, of Christ's sacrifice. It is not the sum of all heroisms. It would be more true to say it is the source of all heroisms, the foundation of them all. It is the underground something that makes heroisms, not something that heroisms make up. When Christ did what he did, it was not human nature doing it, it was God doing it. That is the great, absolutely unique and glorious thing. It is God in Christ reconciling. It was not human nature offering its very best to God. It was God offering his very best to man. That is the grand difference between the church and civilization, even when civilization is religious. We must attend more to those great issues between our faith and our world. Our religion has been too much a thing done in a corner. We must adjust our religion to the great currents and movements of the world's history. And the great issue of the hour is the issue between the church and civilization. Their essential difference is this. Civilization at its best represents the most man can do with the world and with human nature; but the church, centred upon Christ, his Cross, and his work, represents the best that God can do upon them. The sacrifice of the Cross was not man in Christ pleasing God; it was God in Christ reconciling man, and in a certain sense, reconciling himself. My point at this moment is that the Cross of Christ was Christ reconciling man. It was not heroic man dying for a beloved and honoured God; it was God in some form dying for man. God dying for man. I am not afraid of that phrase; I cannot do without it. God dying for man; and for such men – hostile, malignantly hostile men. That is a puzzling phrase where we read in a gospel: 'Greater love hath no man than this, that a man lay down his life for his friends.' There is more love in the phrase of the epistle, that a man should lay down his life for his bitter enemies. It is not so heroic, so very divine, to die for your friends. Kindness between the nice people is not so very divine – fine and precious as it is. To die for enemies, that is the divine thing. Christ's was grace that died for such – for malignant enemies. There is more in God than love. There is all that we mean by his holy grace. Truly, 'God is love'. Yes, but the kind of love which you must interpret by the whole of the New Testament. When John said that, did he mean that God was simply the consummation of human affection? He knew that he was dealing with a holy, gracious God, a God who loved his enemies and redeemed them. Read with extreme care I John iv. 10.

From: *The Work of Christ* by P. T. Forsyth

(Collins Fontana, 1965, pp. 50–2)

Saturday

The Work of Christ

P. T. FORSYTH

Let me gather up the points of difference which I have been indicating.

First, that Belgian hero did not act from love so much as from duty. Secondly, he died only in one act, not in his whole life, dying daily. There have been men capable of acts of sacrifice like this hero; loose-living men who, after a heroism, were quite capable of returning to their looseness of life – heroes of the Bret Harte type. There have been many valiant, fearless things done on the battlefield by men who in the face of bullets never flinched, never turned a hair; and when they came home they could not stand against a breath of ridicule, they could not stand against a little temptation, and were soon wallowing in the mire. One act of sacrifice is not the same thing as a life gathered into one consummate sacrifice, whose value is that it has the whole personality put into it for ever.

Third, this man could not take the full measure of all that he was doing, and Christ could. Christ did not go to his death with his eyes shut. He died because he willed to die, having counted the cost with the greatest, deepest moral vision in the world.

Fourthly, the hero in the story had nothing to do with the moral condition of those whom he saved. The scoundrel and the saint in that train were both alike to him.

Again, he had no quarrel with those whom he saved. He had nothing to complain of. He had nothing from them to try his heroism. They were not his bitter enemies. His valour was not the heroism of forgiveness, where lies the wondrous majesty of God. His act was not an act of grace, which is the grand glory of the love of Christ. Christ died for people who not only did not know him, but who hated and despised him. He died, not for a trainful of people, but for the whole organic world of people. It was an infinite death, that of his, in its range and in its power. It was death for enemies more bitter than anything that man can feel against man, for such haters as only holiness can produce. Here is the singular thing: the greater the favour that is done to us, the more fiercely we resent it if it does not break us down and make us grateful. The greater the favour, if we do not respond in its own spirit, so much the more resentful and antagonistic it makes us. I have already said that we speak too often as though the effect of Christ's death upon human nature must be gratitude as soon as it is understood. It is not always gratitude. Unless it is received in the Holy Ghost, the effect may just be the other way. It is judgment. It is a death unto death.

From: *The Work of Christ* by P. T. Forsyth

(Collins Fontana, 1965, pp. 53–4)

LENT 4

Transfiguration

J. W. C. WAND

Many scholars have said that the one thing we can never do is to divine the mysteries of the inner thought of Jesus. Some have suggested that it is even impious to try. Others, accepting the inevitability of the attempt, have suggested that his basic thought throughout his ministry was of the coming Kingdom of God. Others have contended that, since the Messiah or Son of God was the agent by whom the Kingdom was to be ushered in, his more fundamental thought must always have been a filial consciousness, the steadfast belief that he was himself the chosen Servant, the Son of God, at least in the technical, messianic sense. Still others, not willing to go quite so far, have claimed that his fundamental thought was always of the actual presence of God and the need of constant and implicit obedience to him.

Of these thoughts the last is most likely to have been the ground of his normal thinking, the basis upon which conscious reflection built, the source from which ideas of essential rather than official sonship and of the Kingdom flowed. Jesus was surely the most *Gottbetrunken* man who ever lived, the most completely intoxicated with the thought of the ever-present power and companionship of God. If this was his basic consciousness, the thought of his own special vocation could never be far away. But we know that on at least one occasion, the agony in Gethsemane, he was in great doubt and distress. On another, the dread moment on the cross, the physical darkness coincided with the sense of spiritual dereliction, and the cry was forced from him, 'My God, my God, why didst thou forsake me?' If the foundation could thus be shaken, the superstructure must have required strengthening. It is possible to see in the Transfiguration a God-given reassurance for Jesus as to his place in the divine plan for his nation and for the world.

From: *Transfiguration* by J. W. C. Wand

(Faith Press, 1967, pp. 63–4)

G

Transfiguration

J. W. C. WAND

If it seems strange to think of Jesus as needing reassurance, we must remember that he was perfect man. We must not assume that as a result of the Incarnation any essential element of humanity had been lost. Even though the eternal Word of God expressed himself as fully as possible in and through Jesus of Narareth, he did it only in so far as it was possible for humanity to interpret the divine. The eternal Logos in becoming man did not remove any of the gifts or liabilities of human nature in order to let his divine character appear. What he did was to organize them, as individual traits must always be organized and combined, to make up a complete person: he revealed himself and his Father only in and through his humanity.

It follows that Jesus must have been subject to the psychological trials and temptations that afflict the ordinary human being. If he could experience the sense of dereliction on the cross, and the mental agony in the garden of Gethsemane, he must have felt the stresses of doubt, hesitation and frustration on many other occasions. What could have been more helpful in such circumstances than some token that he was acting in accordance with God's pre-ordained plan?

Such reassurance must undoubtedly have been given him on this occasion by the appearance, no less real if visionary, of Moses and Elias, representatives of the Law and the Prophets, within his inner consciousness expressing approval of what he was about to do. This would imply that the whole of God's ordained plan was behind the mission of Jesus. In accepting himself as the Christ and letting his disciples acclaim him as Messiah Jesus was not 'out on a limb'. What he was doing was in accord with the principles of his nation's religion and was upheld and confirmed by the greatest teachers of his people. It is difficult to think of anything that could give such complete reassurance to a lonely teacher.

As we shall see presently, the conversation with the Old Testament divines may have given Jesus reassurance not only as to his vocation in general but especially in regard to the passion that he must undergo in Jerusalem. Is it not precisely on this topic that he was heard conversing with them?

From: *Transfiguration* by J. W. C. Wand

(Faith Press, 1967, pp. 64–5)

Transfiguration

J. W. C. WAND

In pursuing this thought of a possible reassurance of Jesus it is not altogether irrelevant to examine more closely the actual nature of the Transfiguration: the metamorphosis was a change from what to what? There can be no doubt about the form *from* which he was transfigured: it was that of Jesus of Nazareth, the putative son of the carpenter and the present teacher and healer whom everybody knew. Before the Transfiguration, that is to say, he bore the appearance with which all his acquaintances were familiar.

It is not nearly so easy to say *to* what form he was transfigured. The process of the metamorphosis is described in considerable detail by the evangelists. Mark says that his garments became glistening with such a dazzling whiteness as no earthly bleaching could equal. Matthew adds that his face shone like the sun, and Luke agrees that the appearance of his face was altered to harmonize with the dazzling whiteness of the clothes. The 'form' then into which he appeared to be changed was a luminous whiteness of the face and clothes. It seems in other words to be an example of that splendour or 'glory' which was held to be characteristic of divinity.

No doubt it is that appearance which has given rise to the popular belief that in the Transfiguration it was Jesus' divinity that disclosed itself. It was a natural supposition that here for once the glory of deity was actually seen shining through the mask of humanity. But that is to misunderstand the situation. By the very terms of the Incarnation the divine nature could not so reveal itself. Whatever God did disclose of himself must be seen through the agency of the humanity and only the humanity.

This remains true even if we explain the event as something seen with the spiritual rather than with the physical sight. There is no evidence in the various versions of the narrative that the evangelists intended their readers to interpret the Transfiguration as a revelation of sheer divinity. What they did intend it to show was a confirmation of the Messianic office of Jesus. It was in such glory that the Messiah was expected to be seen: that was his 'image'. Certainly the Messiah was Son of man, a human being, but he belonged to the heavenly places. Trailing clouds of glory had he come from God who is our home. No doubt the Messiah's glory was a reflection of God's glory, but even as such it was a confirmation of his office and status.

This may not seem quite so bizarre an idea to us if we remember that St. Paul calls man in general the 'image and glory of God', because he reflects the character of God, in much the same way as woman, according to Paul, reflects the glory of man. If every man reveals something of the glory of God, it is obvious that the Messiah must show it in an especial degree. This connection can be seen already in Isaiah 4: 2, 'In that day the branch of the Lord shall be beauty and glory.' In the New Testament the idea of glory is strongly associated with the Son of Man, especially as he will appear in the clouds at the last day.[1] The Fourth Gospel has the idea that the glory seen in Christ was a resumption of 'the glory which I had with thee before the world was made'.[2]

We can conclude that, although the idea of glory was a much commoner conception than it is with us, it was nevertheless proper to deity and was associated in a special, though derivative, sense with the Messiah. The belief that the Old Testament worthies, Moses and Elijah, also appeared 'in glory' does not detract from this conclusion, but emphasizes that the whole episode occurred in an atmosphere that lifted it out of the ordinary, and was calculated to leave a deep and lasting impression on all who experienced it in any form, whether as witnesses or as the leading character in the transformation scene.

From: *Transfiguration* by J. W. C. Wand

(Faith Press, 1967, pp. 65–7)

Thursday

Transfiguration

J. W. C. WAND

There is one other feature in this general aspect of reassurance which we must not neglect. In the episode at Caesarea Philippi Peter's recognition of the Messiah had been quickly followed by the warning of their leader's imminent arrest and execution. That was something the disciples did not understand and were anxious to

[1] Matthew 24:30; Mark 8:38.
[2] John 17:5.

forget. We cannot doubt, however, that it remained very much in the mind of Jesus himself. He was fully aware of the inevitability of such an end, so long as he remained on his determined course. Previous would-be Messiahs had received no mercy at Roman hands, and even if Jesus' more pacifist rôle made him a less inimical figure to the Romans, his religious claims had already been rejected by the national leaders, and were certain to lead to deepening trouble. Jesus must surely have shrunk from the future he saw all too clearly. He had to bear the additional loneliness of one who is not understood even by his closest followers.

In such circumstances it is especially interesting that Luke describes the subject of the conversation between Jesus and the two Old Testament leaders as 'the exodus which he should accomplish at Jerusalem'. The unusual synonym for death seems to be chosen in order to give it a special dignity, and also to link it with the great historic event which had proved the foundation of Israel's national character. Jesus would die, but the result of his death would be a new deliverance and the inauguration of a new epoch for Israel. The narrator expects his readers to appreciate this situation as suggested by the term 'exodus,' and to understand the psychological reassurance it would give to one embarking on a dangerous and possibly fatal mission.

Summing up, we can can say that as far as Jesus himself was concerned it seems certain that the experience of the Transfiguration, even if it happened in his own inner consciousness, would be well calculated to give him strength and comfort in face of the trials that lay before him. It would confirm his belief that what he was doing was in close accord with the age-long purpose of God for Israel. The line he was taking was essentially that of the esoteric teaching of both Law and Prophets. In the end his Father would vindicate his own. The Messianic glory, which was visibly his for a moment today, would one day be recognized as settled, permanent and essential. The way of the cross was the path to glory. He would follow it to the end.

From: *Transfiguration* by J. W. C. Wand

(Faith Press, 1967, pp. 67–8)

Friday

Transfiguration

J. W. C. WAND

. . . With regard to the witnesses, their prevailing mood was one of wonder and perplexity. The extent of their confusion is shown by the way in which Peter mixes up the event with the feast of Tabernacles and suggests that the mount would be a good place on which to erect their festival booths. Nevertheless the fact that they were specially chosen out of the Apostolic band, and were privileged to be present when the event occurred, suggests that it had some special message for them. Even if they were not allowed to communicate the knowledge of it to others, it must have deepened their own understanding and strengthened their determination. It thus helped to build up at the heart of the apostolic band a nucleus of vital force which would serve to animate all the rest.

In any case the disciples shared in the hopes and fears of their Master. Those who were closest to him were naturally most fully aware of his feelings. The comfort he derived from the experience would also be shared by them.

Thus, as we have so often said, the incident would appeal to them most strongly as a firm corroboration of the profession already made by Peter at Caesarea Philippi. He had then declared Jesus to be the Messiah. That affirmation was now confirmed by the appearance of Jesus in Messianic glory and by the voice out of the cloud, 'This is my beloved Son.' Here for the moment they saw the Messiah as rabbinic teaching pictured him, no longer the carpenter of Nazareth or even the well-known teacher and healer, but the long-promised saviour of his people, in all the magnificence of a being who belonged as much to the other world as to this. Such a witness to the truth of Peter's bold affirmation must have brought relief and comfort indeed.

From: *Transfiguration* by J. W. C. Wand

(Faith Press, 1967, pp. 69–70)

Transfiguration

J. W. C. WAND

. . . The episode [of the Transfiguration] must have brought less welcome confirmation of Jesus' statement at Caesarea that he must come to a violent end. It is true that Luke is the only evangelist to tell us of the subject of the conversation between Jesus and the two Old Testament figures, and it is not clear whether he intends to suggest that the three disciples overheard or joined in the conversation. But the fact that the subject is recorded suggests that the three were told of it. That they are said to have been 'heavy with sleep' at the time need not involve any contradiction with this view, if we remember the dream-like atmosphere that hangs over Luke's narrative at this point. We imagine that the Master's announcement of his forthcoming passion must have weighed heavily on the minds of the disciples. Here then in this conversation with ancient heroes of the national faith was something which at least made it seem less outrageous. If the great personages of the past could discuss the Messiah's fate so dispassionately, it could not involve a complete thwarting of God's plans nor a complete destruction of their own hopes for the future.

In other words they would be encouraged to think of the dread possibility as in line with what they had read in their scriptures of a Suffering Messiah, especially in Isaiah 53. The discovery of the Dead Sea Scrolls with their references to a suffering 'Teacher of Righteousness' has led scholars to believe that the Song of the Suffering Servant may have been well known and much meditated by at least some of the several sects into which Judaism was divided.

The effect of the Transfiguration would be to impress this association of suffering with messiahship on the minds of the disciples. They were accustomed enough to the attempt to interpret current events as the expression of God's will: the whole history of their nation as described by the prophetic teachers had been subjected to this kind of rationalization. Things did not happen by chance or merely by human contrivance. All was under the direct command of God, and small events as well as great were due to the application of his authoritative power.

The difficulty about this method of reading history was that it required a skilled interpreter. It was only a specially gifted person who could pierce through the outward show of commonplace things and events to the inward and spiritual working of the divine will. Keble expresses the thought that any of us should be able to exercise this insight if only sin had not obscured our vision:

> Two worlds are ours: 'tis only sin
> Forbids us to descry
> The mystic heaven and earth within,
> Plain as the sea and sky.

It was, no doubt, this kind of insight that the Transfiguration achieved for the disciples. The somewhat ordinary and commonplace figure of a carpenter's son, which had become more and more clothed in mystery and majesty as their acquaintance with him developed, is now seen in a heroic rôle, in a guise that is more that of heaven than of earth. But he is seen in all the pathos as well as in all the majesty of the truly heroic figure. The combination is recognized as right and proper by the ancient worthies and is affirmed by the voice out of the cloud. The disciples need therefore feel no hesitation in giving their allegiance to Jesus. All was well and all would continue to be well if it was in line with God's will for his people.

From: *Transfiguration* by J. W. C. Wand

(Faith Press, 1967, pp. 70–2)

LENT 5

Word of Reconciliation

F. W. DILLISTONE

Of all Old Testament figures, with the possible exception of Moses, none is more clearly revealed in the depths of his personal struggles and anguish than is Jeremiah. Through the devotion of his companion and disciple, Baruch, oracles spoken by the prophet were committed to writing and to these were added accounts of events in his life-history. Though it is impossible to construct a biography in the modern sense of the term, events and utterances can be linked together to form a relatively connected whole. At the very least the poetic cries and ejaculations can be set within a context which makes them vivid and meaningful.

The dominant impression conveyed by the book is of a man of deeply sensitive nature who shrank from public life yet felt compelled to challenge the policies of rulers and the inclinations of his people in the name of God. In his own inner consciousness there was the intense struggle between the desire for withdrawal into obscurity and the compelling sense of responsibility to become engaged in political life: in his outer experience there was the agonizing tension between his ceaseless concern for his people and their welfare on the one side and his recognition of his duty to proclaim judgment and woe upon them on the other. At times the tension becomes almost unendurable and words break out from his despair which by a strange paradox are transfigured through the very act of speaking into an instrument of life and hope.

> Without healing is my sorrow
>   My heart upon me is faint
> For the breaking of my people am I broken
>   Seized by horror, I mourn
> O that my head were waters
>   And my eyes a fountain of tears
> That day and night I might weep
>   Over the slain of my people.[1]

[1] Jeremiah 8:18, 21; 9:1.

Again and again this extraordinary tension is revealed. Jeremiah's senses are strained to the limit on one side as he hears Yahweh's words of judgment, sees the earth made desolate, hears the sounds of battle, looks at the result of the invader's destructiveness: on the other side he makes the people's cry of distress his own, feels their misery, pleads for their deliverance, and so identifies himself with them that in a real sense he takes the judgment into his own inner being and absorbs it. He is *for* Yahweh and yet he is also *for* the objects of the divine judgment. His heart reaches breaking point and he cries a bitter cry of anguish. Yet even in this cry which holds together as it were the opposing poles of holiness and dereliction a promise of reconciliation can be discerned.

From: *The Christian Understanding of Atonement* by F. W. Dillistone

(James Nisbet, 1969, pp. 359–60)

Tuesday

Word of Reconciliation

F. W. DILLISTONE

This tension which is so characteristic of Jeremiah's experience is directly paralleled in many of the Psalms. Often indeed it is the Psalmist's own distress of body or mind which causes him to cry out in anguish.[1] At other times, however, he becomes the mouthpiece for his people's anguish.[2] As we read the Psalms we enter into the distresses of the total society as well as of the individual: persecution and oppression from envious outsiders, betrayal and treachery from trusted insiders. Here are human spirits deeply sensitive to the struggles and the tensions of life in the world and as they react to the extremes of physical and mental despair they become vicarious representatives of a universal humanity. They do not cloak their cries in sentimentality or unreality. They confront life at its most threatening and most intractable. But by a daring and seemingly impossible leap of faith they affirm and reaffirm the rule of Yahweh, His constant loving-kindness to His children and the final triumph of His Kingdom. He will save the soul of His servant, He will redeem Israel, He will turn the night of weeping into a morning bright with joy.

[1] Psalm 142.
[2] Psalm 129.

Probably no psalm approaches more nearly to the limits of human anguish and distress than does the 22nd. It matters little whether the poet is referring primarily to his own or to his people's suffering. He describes the scorn and derision of the bystanders, a company of evil-doers who pierce his hands and his feet and divide his garments amongst themselves. He exposes his own sense of utter weakness:

> I am poured out like water and all my bones
>   are out of joint:
> My heart is like wax, it is melted within
>   my breast;
> My strength is dried up like a potsherd
> And my tongue cleaves to my jaws.

Worst of all he tells of the bitterness of the feeling of having been forsaken by God:

> I cry by day but thou dost not answer and by night
>   but find no rest.
> 'He committed his cause to the Lord; let him deliver
>   him;
> let him rescue him, for he delights in him!'

Yet it is in the very expression of his despair and dereliction that he finds his salvation. He does not sink down in silence, he does not wrap himself round with his own hopelessness, he does not content himself with shouting defiance at his enemies. Rather he cries out and continues to cry out to the God Who delivered his fathers, the God Who preserved him from his mother's womb. In face of all that would deny faith, he refuses to abandon his hope that God will yet come to his aid.

> But thou, O Lord, be not far off!
> O thou my help hasten to my aid!

And in the cry is the resolution. When all human props have been removed, when the heart and the flesh have failed, God makes Himself known as man's strength and portion for ever.[1] In man's end is his beginning. In entering vicariously into the experience of total blackness the poet becomes the medium through whom the light of glory can be revealed.

From: *The Christian Understanding of Atonement* by F. W. Dillistone

(James Nisbet, 1968, pp. 360–1)

[1] Psalm 73.

Word of Reconciliation

F. W. DILLISTONE

In the Gospel-records, no sections are more significant for our enquiry about the interpretation of atonement than those which bear witness to sayings of Jesus in which the notes of tension and conflict become acute. Early Christians were constantly confronted by situations of stress and danger: any word which showed how Jesus reacted to such situations was utterly relevant to their own struggle. From the beginning they had confessed Jesus as Messiah and Lord. It is unlikely therefore that words suggestive of inner conflict would have been attributed to him unless there had been unusually strong evidence to support them.

Few sayings are more striking than those recorded in the account of the Temptations. Here we are presented with three vivid word-pictures of the struggle between traditional conceptions of Divine Sonship and the particular vocation which Jesus dedicated himself to fulfil. It was a struggle of peculiar intensity. Could not miracle, mystery and authority (in Dostoievsky's words) be used to save and heal mankind? And Jesus refused all three because the end-result would not have been a real salvation into a developing and expanding communion with God but rather the establishment of a perpetual childhood. Yet each time the conflict was resolved only in and through an agonized cry. 'Man doth not live by bread alone.' 'Thou shalt not put the Lord thy God to the test.' In such cries the conflict is transcended and the contraries momentarily reconciled.

From the initial conflict so graphically portrayed in the Temptation story the narratives move forward with constant references to Jesus' struggles – with his family, with his fellow-citizens in Nazareth, with scribes and Pharisees, with demonic powers; with unbelief, with misrepresentation, with envy, with impatience: and supremely the conflict between his deep concern and desire for the well-being of His own people and His recognition that their accepted way of life was bound to lead to disaster. Perhaps the key-passage revealing Jesus' own innermost tension is Luke 12:49–50.

> I came to cast fire on the earth;
>> would that it were already kindled.
> I have a baptism to be baptized with;
> How I am constrained until it is accomplished.

Such cries and ejaculations give us a glimpse of the tension under
which Jesus continually laboured. They are wrung from his lips at
moments when the conflict approaches the limits of endurance.
Earth's contradictions are resolved in a cry which pierces heaven.
The sinful resistance of the world is overcome in and through a
perfect confidence in and obedience to the Divine will. In His cry
is our hope and peace.

From: *The Christian Understanding of Atonement* by F. W. Dillistone

(James Nisbet, 1968, pp. 361–3)

Thursday

Word of Reconciliation

F. W. DILLISTONE

Within the Passion-stories we encounter words of peculiar
significance, throwing as they do light on the nature of Jesus' final
wrestling with treachery, failure and death . . .

The Words at the Last Supper: Few sayings in the world's literature
have been subjected to such intense scrutiny as have these words
attributed to Jesus. They appear in four New Testament narratives
and in no two of these are they in exactly the same form. Yet there is
enough material common to each to enable us to point with great
confidence to an original core which may indeed have gathered to
itself interpretative phrases in the course of its transmission. And
this original core is of the utmost significance. It consists of two
definitive phrases:

(a) This is my Body.

(b) This is my Blood of the Covenant.

Jesus has seen the growth of opposition without, the likelihood of
defections within the ranks of his own closest followers, the virtual
certainty that events would move to a crisis during the festival
season in Jerusalem. The whole atmosphere is full of memories of
another great crisis, the crisis in Egypt when after long struggles
and many uncertainties the hour of reckoning drew near. On that
occasion every family took a lamb, killed it, and roasted it for eating:
and at the same time took the blood, which had been separated from
the body, and smeared it on the framework of the door to preserve
the household from the destruction and death which were to be

abroad in the land that night. The atmosphere in Egypt and at every successive passover was redolent with death – the oppressor's cruelty, the succession of natural disasters which had befallen the land, the brooding sense of something still worse about to happen. Yet for the Hebrews there was also the promise of life through death, of the long-delayed deliverance becoming actual, of a new era about to begin in their national destiny. It was on such a night that Jesus, instead of taking the flesh of a lamb, took a loaf, broke it and said 'This is my Body': instead of taking a bowl of blood, took a cup of wine and said 'This is my Blood of the Covenant'. In face of the accepted certainty of his own death and what appeared to be the end of his own mission, He affirmed through act and word the triumph of God's purpose and the consequent salvation of the new Israel. Not through the flesh of a lamb but through the sharing in His own broken body. His followers would gain sustenance for their journey into freedom: not through the blood of a lamb but through sharing in His own outpoured blood His followers would be sealed within a new covenant under the assured protection of the God Whose mercies would never fail them.

No words could have been more daring, more expressive of a final trust in God and an ultimate concern for His own friends. Faced with death he leapt over death, out into the new era of the Spirit. The keynote of the Supper is the *new*. The old is at an end. The *new* has come. The new bread to sustain the new life: the new wine to establish the new covenant. In face of the crisis which outwardly spelt disaster and the end of all his hopes, Jesus dared cry out triumphantly: This broken bread is bringing life to all men: This cup is the assurance of the new order in which the prophecy will be completely fulfilled, 'I will be their God and they shall be my people.' In and through this acted parable Jesus becomes the cause of eternal salvation to all who follow in the steps of His faith and obedience.

From: *The Christian Understanding of Atonement* by F. W. Dillistone

(James Nisbet, 1968, pp. 363–4)

Friday

Word of Reconciliation

F. W. DILLISTONE

The Words of Gethsemane: The narrative describing the intense struggles in the Garden of Gethsemane has an extraordinarily dramatic quality. The triple sequence from the challenge to the three to stay awake to the second discovery of their stupefaction through sleep to the final acceptance of their complete insensitivity: the reiteration of the phrase 'the Hour' – the Hour of doom, the Hour of destiny: the Greek words translated into English as 'deep amazement and anxiety', suggestive of horror and shuddering and profound agitation: all these provide a setting for Jesus' words which serves to intensify the sense of inner conflict which they portray.

As far as the authenticity of the reported words is concerned there are slight differences in the three Synoptic accounts and there are verbal echoes of the Lord's Prayer which may have influenced the precise formulation. Yet the general character of the scene and of the words spoken is such that it is exceedingly difficult to imagine any motive for pure fabrication. A romancer would surely have depicted Jesus in an attitude of facing death with confidence and fearlessness and ready aceptance of the will of God. Instead there is the fearful encounter with horror and darkness issuing in the cry: My soul is weighed down with sorrow, even to the point of death. And whatever links there may be with the clauses of the Lord's Prayer, there is one outstanding image which seems to be the key to all, namely 'the cup'. Each evangelist reports the agonized plea that the cup might be removed. Matthew refers to it a second time – 'The cup' represents that from which Jesus shrinks back in horror and amazement. For the significance of this cup-symbol we naturally look to the Old Testament. It is true that in the Old Testament 'the cup' is used in two different senses. On the one hand the cup represents joy, salvation, new life, refreshment.

> What shall I render to the Lord
> For all his bounty to me?
> I will lift up the cup of salvation
>   and call on the name of the Lord.[1]

[1] Psalm 116:13.

On the other hand, and even more frequently, it represents suffering, punishment, dereliction, woe: it is a 'cup of wrath' and a 'bowl of staggering'.

> For not from the east or from the west and not from the wilderness comes lifting up; but it is God who executes judgment, putting down one and lifting up another. For in the hand of the Lord there is a cup, with foaming wine, well mixed, and he will pour a draught from it, and all the wicked of the earth, shall drain it down to the dregs.[1]

There has already been a reference to the cup in the incident recorded in Mark 10: 35–45. In that context the cup is certainly the symbol of tribulation and suffering. And now in Gethsemane it is psychologically understandable that an image which had been gathering associations in Jesus' mind should become overwhelmingly real and full of foreboding. The Cup. The Cup to be drained to the dregs. The cup containing the final judgment upon human sinfulness. Must He drink this Cup? Must He face this Hour? He wrestles and prays, He falls prostrate on the ground, He agonizes in a sweat of blood. Yet the final word that issues as a cry from the depths, as simultaneously the acceptance and the overcoming, is the utter paradox of two wills made into one:

> Nevertheless not what I will but
> may Thy will be done.

Here again it is in the cry itself that the promise of final reconciliation is contained.

From: *The Christian Understanding of Atonement* by F. W. Dillistone

(James Nisbet, 1968, pp. 364–5)

Saturday

Word of Reconciliation

F. W. DILLISTONE

The central Word from the Cross. The words spoken by Jesus while hanging on the Cross have brought encouragement and inspiration to His disciples and worshippers at all periods of history.

[1] Psalm 75:6–8.

The spirit of forgiveness towards His persecutors, of sympathy towards His fellow-sufferers in body and mind, of child-like trust in God through every kind of adversity – this quality of spirit breathes through the words which the Evangelists report and, whatever criticism may be applied to their exact formulation, that they represent the impression made by Jesus upon His devotees can hardly be doubted. There is, however, one other word, the only word to be reported by more than one evangelist, a word described as a loud cry or a great shout out of the darkness, the word in fact which in the view of Mark the earliest evangelist was the altogether memorable and representative cry of the crucified Messiah. In Mark's version the Aramaic form is given, in Matthew's the Hebraic. Obviously it is taken from Psalm 22 and we find ourselves confronted by this mysterious cry as the concentrated expression of Jesus' ultimate experience of suffering and rejection: My God, my God, why hast Thou forsaken me? . . .

When every effort has been made to examine the background of this cry and its appearance in this particular setting it seems impossible to resolve the mystery which surrounds these words logically or historically. One alternative is to regard them as a substantially correct record of this central moment in the experience of Jesus on the Cross. Darkness had enveloped him. Death is in sight. Spontaneously he cries out, using words which have burned themselves into his inner consciousness. The other alternative is to regard them as the interpretation of the cry of Jesus by the early Church: the Psalm is viewed as the record of a momentary eclipse of the Divine presence and approval being turned into a renewal of trust that God would vindicate His faithful servants.

Strong arguments can be advanced in favour of each of these alternatives. But whichever is adopted, reconciliation is only to be found in the sheer utterance of the word itself. Whether looked at from the point of view of Jesus Himself or from that of the early Church, the climax of death by crucifixion was terrible in the extreme. The darkness, the pain, the sense of desertion by all earthly friends, were symbolic of something deeper – that here the Divine reaction against every form of human sinfulness had come to its ultimate expression. Yet the One Who bears on His own spirit the crushing load of this Divine reaction, Who faces the threat of final annihilation, still cries 'My God, my God'. The question of how much of the rest of the psalm was uttered can never be resolved. But in the words *My God*, cried out in face of all that symbolized the withdrawal of the grace and favour of God, the crucial act of atonement is expressed. God through man reverses all that is contrary to God in man. From the human point of view the loud cry is the last word of dereliction. Within a Divine economy it is the word which opens gates of new life and begets an altogether new hope. In this one word the Atonement of the ages is effected. God has stood with man in the anguish of abandonment and by the utterance of one word has restored the joy of His presence to the afflicted.

From: *The Christian Understanding of Atonement* by F. W. Dillistone

(James Nisbet, 1968, pp. 365–7)

PALM SUNDAY

Monday before Easter

End and Beginning

ULRICH E. SIMON

The Church could interpret the death of Christ in terms of ancient ritual. Christ, the victim on the Cross, was seen as the high-priest from whom all sacrifice derives. Moreover, though killed once and for all, he was known to continue his priestly sacrifice eternally with God. Thus the tremendous themes of atonement were translated from temple ritual and annual observance to a celestial sanctuary where outside the limitations of man-made and temporal ceremonies he fulfils the whole cultic tradition. He who stood in need of no purification enters this sanctuary with his own blood to make restitution for the whole of mankind. The death of Jesus is therefore the very denial of an avoidable, though tragic, death, and his resurrection is more than the vindication of virtue. Rather the cosmic perfection depends upon his abiding work of sacrifice.

We can appropriate this pattern partly for the victims of Auschwitz not in the sense that they are now gods or that their work aspired to perfection. No such claim can be made for any man, Christian, Jew, or devoutly virtuous members of other cults. The claim is that all these, at the point of life-giving, enter into the supreme sacrifice by way of sharing analogy. As it was said that human rites before Christ prefigured his perfect consummation we now maintain that our holocausts are also deeply related thereto.

From: *A Theology of Auschwitz* by Ulrich E. Simon

(Gollancz, 1967, pp. 84–5)

Tuesday before Easter

End and Beginning

ULRICH E. SIMON

The complicated ritual of [the scapegoat in] Leviticus xvi summarizes not only Jewish but the whole human need to get rid of sin. Here survived an act by which the community solemnly and penitentially transferred its burden of guilt to the animal which was then taken to a cliff from which it was hurled to death, or to wander in the wilderness to take its load of sins to the home of the mystery of all evils, where it also died. Although not a few thinkers and pious leaders declared much of the institution of sacrifice to be of doubtful value, if not downright unnecessary and perverse, the core of the great need remained and demanded a sacrifice for sin.

The victims of the Nazi criminals were cast into this role of scapegoat. All the frustrations of the German people were seeking an outlet and found it in their own midst. The sins which were attributed to the Jews were precisely the sins which the nation knew itself to be guilty of. The Jews were accused of a shifty morality, of harbouring a corporate destructive intent, of a cowardly evasion of duty, of being aesthetically repellent. Looking now in cool detachment at the scene it is difficult to resist the generalizing judgment that these accusations were really self-accusations, now to be transferred to the victim. The passionate hatred, as has often been remarked, induced a strange identification between murderers and murdered, a blood tie, unconsciously sacrificial. To recall the scapegoat here is not a condonation of the venomous malice which enabled a whole people to offer another to die for its own sins. It is merely a citation of an important analogy which sets the incomprehensible within a framework which is psychologically not beyond our understanding today. But the psychological light is not redemptive, whereas the theological link may become so. It does not absolve the guilty of killing, but it accepts the place of the innocent in an act of universal identification. From the blood of Abel to the present day there runs a red thread of meaningful sacrifice through the history of men.

From: *A Theology of Auschwitz* by Ulrich E. Simon

(Gollancz, 1967, pp. 85–6)

End and Beginning

ULRICH E. SIMON

A further consequence of this identification focuses upon the resultant state of man. As St. Paul saw it, the removal of sin by God leads to a totally new evaluation of man. He is no longer the boastful fellow who requires self-justification and self-approval. Since death is seen in a new redemptive light of conquest it no longer proclaims defeat and shame. Now one of the worst consequences of a secular evaluation of Auschwitz has been, and still is, the apparent defeat of the innocent. There has been a feeling abroad that the shamefulness of their death is a stigma, not only to those who had a share in bringing it about, but also to the dead themselves. The sacrificial setting and our identification of the victims with Christ remove every stain of horror and obscure suspicions.

But these theological claims cannot get very far if they are mere fantasies spun by words. In this respect one must note not only the undoubtedly important psychological echo of our experience of the scapegoat, but also the experience of the Christian community. The death of Christ set forth as the perfect oblation was certainly not an esoteric absurdity but the heart of Christian existence from the start. It governed the Church's worship; although Eucharistic forms of worship varied from place to place they never failed to give the atoning death of Christ the central place in the liturgy. The living fellowship owed its all to him who after having been betrayed had taken bread and had anticipated his self-oblation by blessing, breaking, and sharing it. Similarly the cup of wine came to symbolize a share in his blood.

We do not know whether this meal was a Passover meal or not, but an intimate connection between the Lord's Supper and the Passover belongs to the earliest tradition. This adds a further insight into the meaning of Christ's death. If he dies in the manner of the Passover Lamb he sums up in his death the many traditions which the Passover retains to this day. Above all, it associates the death with liberation from Egyptian bondage, enabling every Israelite to say, as he must, 'I myself came out of Egypt.' The Passover background removes the barriers of space and time from Christ's death. With this background in mind the victim of Auschwitz may legitimately be set alongside the prototype of all suffering in the cause of righteousness. We may judge theologically that there is a great unity of suffering in the Sufferer who died for all men. The identification is irresistible.

From: *A Theology of Auschwitz* by Ulrich E. Simon

(Gollancz, 1967, pp. 87–8)

Maundy Thursday

End and Beginning

ULRICH E. SIMON

... The Passover connection permits us to take the ancient strand of the sacred dance, the ecstasy of the night of the spring equinox, and the blood shed to ward off and placate the demonic, and weave it into our theme of redemptive suffering. Christ died to save mankind from its pagan madness. The victims of Auschwitz died because pagan madness wished to extirpate the light and to rule the world in dark, ecstatic nihilism. The cause of passing over from darkness into light is theirs, and they have consecrated it afresh in the modern struggle against the destroying forces and their dark works.

The ritual of the bitter herbs and sweet food accentuates the ambiguity of Passover. It is terrible and delightful, the Cross and Auschwitz reveal the depth of the darkness to be crossed, but the meal of the unleavened bread also brings out the deathlessness and joy of the communion of the Passover. It is not only a feast of remembrance, but also a firm resolution to have done with darkness and despair. Though sacrificial, it is really a feast, and the Christian is bidden to celebrate the feast because 'Christ our Passover is sacrificed'. The casting out of the leaven symbolizes the decisive ethical step not to submit to natural fermentation and corruption. Thus also the Cross and Auschwitz are not meant to hand on to the future patterns of unending cruelty, but rather the ending of the torment. Just because they have endured to the end like sheep for the slaughter they plead for the abolition of the malice and wickedness, the old leaven of the old man.

Thus the Passover abolishes further killing and sets the mind free from blood-lust and grim fantasies of horror. Because the blood has been shed it cries out against the reiteration of the same. The re-enactment of history in the Passover does not inspire a philosophy of an eternal return, as if the thing remembered must recur. On the contrary it opens the vista to the future and leads the people of God to press on to the end. The prophetic apprehension of the Kingdom of God as the sole reality of life lies at the farther end of the Passover sacrifice. Thus even Auschwitz is set free from denoting only hell on earth. It demands the end of the old, and the making of the new, mankind.

We come to the dying Christ as we do to the dead of Auschwitz with a restrained *De Profundis* in our hearts. But we know we come to a place of transformation whose heart is an altar with an atoning sacrifice. The priestly understanding grows in its contemplation and adorns the terrible gibbet, the camp, the gas chambers, the towers, with praise and thanksgiving. The end must be the beginning.

From: *A Theology of Auschwitz* by Ulrich E. Simon

(Gollancz, 1967, pp. 88–9)

Good Friday

The Royal Way of the Holy Cross

THOMAS À KEMPIS

Unto many this seemeth a hard speech,' Deny thyself, take up thy cross, and follow Jesus.'

But much harder will it be to hear that last word, 'Depart from Me, ye cursed, into everlasting fire.'

For they who now willingly hear and follow the word of the cross, shall not then fear to hear the sentence of everlasting damnation.

This sign of the cross, shall be in the heaven, when the Lord shall come to judgment.

Then all the servants of the cross, who in their lifetime conformed themselves unto Christ, crucified, shall draw near unto Christ the judge with great confidence.

Why therefore fearest thou to take up the cross which leadeth thee to a kingdom?

In the cross is salvation, in the cross is life, in the cross is protection against our enemies, in the cross is infusion of heavenly sweetness, in the cross is strength of mind, in the cross joy of spirit, in the cross the height of virtue, in the cross the perfection of sanctity.

There is no salvation of the soul, nor hope of everlasting life, but in the cross.

Take up therefore thy cross and follow Jesus, and thou shalt go into life everlasting. He went before, bearing His cross and died for thee on the cross; that thou mayest also bear thy cross and desire to die on the cross with Him.

For if thou be dead with Him, thou shalt also live with Him. And if thou be His companion in punishment, thou shalt be partaker with Him also in glory.

From: *The Imitation of Christ* by Thomas à Kempis

(Suttaby & Co., pp. 86–7)

Easter Eve

The Royal Way of the Holy Cross

THOMAS À KEMPIS

Behold! in the cross all doth consist, and all lieth in our dying thereon; for there is no other way unto life, and unto true inward peace, but the way of the holy cross, and of daily mortification.

Go where thou wilt, seek whatsoever thou wilt, thou shalt not find a higher way above, nor a safer way below, than the way of the holy cross.

Dispose and order all things, according to thy will and judgment; yet thou shalt ever find, that of necessity thou must suffer somewhat, either willingly or against thy will, and so thou shalt ever find the cross.

For either thou shalt feel pain in thy body, or in thy soul thou shalt suffer tribulation.

Sometimes thou shalt be forsaken of God, sometimes thou shalt be troubled by thy neighbours; and, what is more, oftentimes thou shalt be wearisome to thyself.

Neither canst thou be delivered or eased by any remedy or comfort; for so long as it pleaseth God, thou must bear it.

For God will have thee learn to suffer tribulation without comfort; and that thou subject thyself wholly to Him, and by tribulation become more humble.

No man hath in his heart a sympathy with the passion of Christ, so much as he who hath suffered the like himself.

The cross therefore is always ready, and every where waits for thee.

Thou canst not escape it whithersoever thou runneth; for whereso-ever thou goeth, thou carriest thyself with thee, and shalt ever find thyself.

Both above and below, without and within, which way soever thou dost turn thee, every where thou shalt find the cross; and every where of necessity thou must hold fast patience, if thou wilt have inward peace, and enjoy an everlasting crown.

From: *The Imitation of Christ* by Thomas à Kempis

(Suttaby & Co., pp. 87–8)

EASTER DAY

Monday

The Resurrection of Christ

MICHAEL RAMSEY

The writer of this book remembers receiving something of a shock when it was first his privilege to attend the lectures of the late Sir Edwyn Hoskyns. The lecturer began with the declaration that as our subject was the Theology and Ethics of the New Testament we must begin with the passages about the Resurrection. It seemed to contradict all the obvious preconceptions. Was it not right to trace first the beginnings of the ministry of Jesus, the events of His life and the words of His teaching? Here, surely, the essence of the Gospel might be found, and as a finale the Resurrection comes so as to seal and confirm the message. No. The Resurrection is a true starting-place for the study of the making and the meaning of the New Testament.

We are tempted to believe that, although the Resurrection may be the climax of the Gospel, there is yet a Gospel that stands upon its own feet and may be understood and appreciated before we pass on to the Resurrection. The first disciples did not find it so. For them the Gospel without the Resurrection was not merely a Gospel without its final chapter: it was not a Gospel at all. Jesus Christ had, it is true, taught and done great things: but He did not allow the disciples to rest in these things: He led them on to paradox, perplexity and darkness; and there He left them. There too they would have remained, had He not been raised from death. But His Resurrection threw its own light backwards upon the death and the ministry that went before; it illuminated the paradoxes and disclosed the unity of His words and deeds. As Scott Holland said: 'In the Resurrection it was not only the Lord who was raised from the dead. His life on earth rose with him; it was lifted up into its real light.'

From: *The Resurrection of Christ* by A. M. Ramsey

(Collins Fontana, 1961, p. 9)

Tuesday

The Resurrection of Christ

MICHAEL RAMSEY

It is a desperate procedure to try and build a Christian Gospel upon the words of Jesus in Galilee apart from the climax of Calvary, Easter and Pentecost. If we do so we are professing to know Jesus better than the first disciples knew Him, and the Marcan record shows us how complete was their perplexity before the Resurrection gave them the key. Every oral tradition about Jesus was handed down, every written record of Him was made only by those who already acknowledged Him as Lord, risen from the dead.

It is therefore both historically and theologically necessary to 'begin with the Resurrection'. For from it, in direct order of historical fact, there came Christian preaching, Christian worship, Christian belief. Of the preaching much will be said in the pages that follow. As to the worship, the most stupendous change followed the Resurrection: Hebrew monotheists, without forsaking their monotheism, worshipped Jesus as Lord. As to the belief, there meets us throughout the Apostolic writings a close connection between the Resurrection and the Christian belief in God. The God of the Christians is essentially the God who raised Jesus Christ from the dead. In Paul's words they 'believe on him that raised Jesus our Lord from the dead'.[1] In Peter's words they are 'believers in God, which raised him from the dead and gave him glory; so that your faith and hope might be in God'.[2] Christian theism is Resurrection theism. Similarly Christian ethics are Resurrection ethics, defined and made possible by men being 'raised together with Christ'.[3] What is perhaps the earliest known Christian hymn contains the words: 'Awake, thou that sleepest, and arise from the dead, and Christ shall shine upon thee.'[4]

From: *The Resurrection of Christ* by A. M. Ramsey

(Collins Fontana, 1961, p. 10)

[1] Rom. iv:24.
[2] I Peter i:21.
[3] Col. iii:1.
[4] Eph. v:14.

Wednesday

The Resurrection of Christ

MICHAEL RAMSEY

The Gospel of God appears in Galilee: but in the end it is clear that Calvary and the Resurrection are its centre. For Jesus Christ came not only to preach a Gospel but to *be* a Gospel, and He is the Gospel of God in all that He did for the deliverance of mankind.

The Greek word 'evangelion', that lies behind the word 'gospel' in our English versions, is very rare; and its meaning in the New Testament is apparent only when we turn to the Old Testament, where the corresponding verb is specially used for God's coming intervention to deliver His people. The word tells of the good news that God is come, bringing (to use the Biblical words) salvation, righteousness, remission of sins, peace, mercy. 'O thou that tellest good tidings to Zion, get thee up into the high mountain; O thou that tellest good tidings to Jerusalem, lift up thy voice with strength; lift it up, be not afraid; say unto the cities of Judah, Behold your God! Behold, the Lord God will come as a mighty one, and his arm shall rule for him: behold his reward is with him, and his recompense before him'.[1] It is passages such as this that provide the background for the understanding of the words of the preaching of Jesus in Galilee: 'The time is fulfilled and the Kingdom of God is at hand; repent ye, and believe in the Gospel'.[2]

From: *The Resurrection of Christ* by A. M. Ramsey

(Collins Fontana, 1961, p. 11)

[1] Isa. xl:9–10; cf. lii:7, lxi:1.
[2] Mark i:14.

Thursday

The Resurrection of Christ

MICHAEL RAMSEY

The good news that Jesus proclaimed was the coming of the Reign of God. The reign had come. Both the teaching and the mighty works of the Messiah bore witness to it. The teaching unfolded the righteousness of the Kingdom, and summoned men and women to receive it. The mighty works asserted the claims of the Kingdom over the whole range of human life. The healing of the sick; the exorcism of devils; the restoration of the maimed, the deaf, the dumb, and the blind; the feeding of the hungry; the forgiveness of sinners; all these had their place among the works of the Kingdom. But though the Kingdom was indeed here in the midst of men, neither the teaching nor the mighty works could enable its coming in all its fullness. For the classic enemies – sin and death – could be dealt with only by a mightier blow, a blow which the death of the Messiah Himself alone could strike. And the righteousness of the Kingdom could not be perfected by a teaching and an example for men to follow; it involved a personal union of men with Christ Himself, a sharing in His own death and risen life. Thus He has a baptism to be baptized with, and He was straitened until it was accomplished. But when it was accomplished there was not only a Gospel in words preached by Jesus but a Gospel in deeds embodied in Jesus Himself, living, dying, conquering death. There is a hint at the identity between the Gospel of Jesus and the person of Jesus in the arresting words 'for my sake and the gospel's'.[1]

Thus it was that the Gospel preached by Jesus became merged into the Gospel that *is* Jesus. This is the Gospel which the Apostles preach. It is still the Gospel of God.[2] It is still the Gospel of the Kingdom[3]. But its content is Jesus. The striking phrase 'to gospel Jesus' appears.[4] They preach His life, death, Resurrection and gift of the Spirit; for all this constitutes the drama of the mighty acts of God who came to deliver and to reign.

From: *The Resurrection of Christ* by A. M. Ramsey

(Collins Fontana, 1961, pp. 11–12)

[1] Mark viii:35; x. 29.
[2] Rom. i:1; 2 Cor. iv:4.
[3] Acts, *passim*.
[4] Acts v:42; viii:35; xi:20.

The Resurrection of Christ

MICHAEL RAMSEY

We are able to form some picture of the preaching of the Apostles from the speeches recorded in the Acts and from the brief summaries of the basic Christian facts which we find in the Epistles. The speeches of Peter in Jerusalem[1] and in Caesarea[2] and of Paul at Antioch in Pisidia[3] disclose the common themes of the preaching. The same themes recur; and the evidence of Epistles confirms the presence of these themes in the earliest teaching of the Church. (1) The messianic age is come, 'The things which God foreshadowed by the mouth of all the prophets, He thus fulfilled.' (2) This has happened through the ministry, death, and Resurrection of the Messiah. He came as David's heir. His death was not a mere tragic defeat; it was a part of God's agelong purpose for the deliverance of mankind. It was foretold in the Scriptures. By the Resurrection God vindicated the Christ. (3) Jesus, exalted at God's right hand, is Lord. He shares in the sovereignty of God. (4) His sovereignty is attested by the outpouring of Holy Spirit upon the disciples. The gift comes from the exalted Jesus Himself. (5) The end is at hand, and Jesus will return as judge of the living and the dead. This is the drama wrought by God in the events in Jerusalem whereof the Apostles are witnesses. It implies the coming of the new age, the breaking into history of the powers of the world to come. It impels the Apostles to summon men to repent and to be baptized into the name of Jesus.

Such was the Gospel. With the accounts of the preaching in Acts we can compare the tradition which Paul says that he had received (presumably from Christians in Jerusalem):

> 'how that Christ died for our sins according to the scriptures; and that he was buried; and that he hath been raised on the third day according to the scriptures and that he appeared to Cephas; then to the twelve . . .'[4]

We can compare also the allusions to the content of the Gospel in a number of passages in the Epistles.[5] The Gospel was one. The same

[1] Acts ii:14–36; iii:12–36; iv. 8–12.
[2] Acts x:34–43.
[3] Acts xiii:16–41.
[4] 1 Cor. xv:3–5.
[5] Gal. iii:1; 1 Cor. i:23; Rom. viii:31–4.

framework of events underlies the primitive preaching in Jerusalem, the preaching of Paul, the final presentation of the Gospel in the four written Gospels. There were of course differences of emphasis ... But there was one Gospel. In it, amid whatever varieties, the Passion and the Resurrection had the pre-eminent place. And the whole story – ministry, Passion, Resurrection – was told not as a piece of biography but as the drama of God's mighty act as deliverer. It was not that the biographical interest in the Man Jesus came first, and a divine Gospel was subsequently deduced from it. It was that the events were from the first handed down as a divine Gospel, and only within the context of that Gospel did the biographical and human interest in Jesus survive and grow.

From: *The Resurrection of Christ* by A. M. Ramsey

(Collins Fontana, 1961, pp. 12–13)

Saturday

The Resurrection of Christ

MICHAEL RAMSEY

In the midst however of the Apostles' preoccupation with the Word of the Cross and with the glory of the Resurrection they did not lose sight of the earthly ministry of Jesus. Indeed their refusal to lose sight of it is impressive and significant. They knew Christ 'no longer after the flesh';[1] their immediate concern was with the contemporary Christ whom they worshipped; their message dwelt upon the absorbing and heart-rending episodes of a Crucified Messiah and a victory over death. But the words and deeds of the days of His flesh were not forgotten.

The Apostolic writers often give glimpses of the earthly ministry of Jesus. If Paul is concerned with the contemporary Christ, he recalls sayings of Jesus that have been handed down,[2] and he mentions His characteristics that have been remembered – His gentleness, His forbearance, His humility and His refusal to please Himself.[3] If the writer of Hebrews takes for his theme the heavenly priesthood of

[1] cf. 2 Cor. v:16.
[2] 1 Cor. vii:10; lx: 14.
[3] 2 Cor. x:1; Phil. ii:7; Rom. xv:2–3; cf. 1 Cor. xi:1.

Christ, he bids his readers contemplate the Man Jesus in His temptation, His prayers, His strong crying and tears, His godly fear, His endurance and faith. If John dwells upon the eternal Sonship, he insists also that Jesus sat by a well and was weary. The impress of the human life of Jesus rested upon the teachings of the Christians. They handed down His words and deeds, first in oral tradition and finally in written books.

But the earthly ministry was remembered, handed down and taught *never* as a self-contained biography, *always* as a part of the Gospel of God whose climax is the Passion and the Resurrection. The words and deeds of Jesus were narrated with the light of the Resurrection upon them. For the first Christians lived in a double perspective: the risen Jesus at the right hand of God and the Jesus of Galilee and Jerusalem. It is from this double perspective that all the Apostolic literature was written.

From: *The Resurrection of Christ* by A. M. Ramsey

(Collins Fontana, 1961, p. 14)

EASTER 1

Monday

The Resurrection of Christ

MICHAEL RAMSEY

The Gospels are works of an entirely novel and unique literary character. They are not biographies, for they pay little attention to the psychology of a hero and to many of those aspects of a life which are dear to a biographer. They are *Gospels*. They are written to tell of the events whereby the Reign of God came. The human story is told, as alone it survived to be told, in the frame of the Gospel of God. The Gospels reproduce the pattern of the preaching of the Apostles from the earliest days.

Finally there comes the *Fourth Gospel* bearing the name of John. Here the double perspective, that has been apparent at every stage of the Apostolic writings, is seen with a special and deliberate vividness.

For in this baffling and glorious book we find a blending of an emphasis upon the importance of historical fact with an emphasis upon those aspects of the truth in Jesus Christ that lie beyond the historical events. This blending of two strains puzzles the reader, and has caused the book to be regarded as a kind of problem-piece among the writings about Jesus Christ. Is the author, we ask, giving us good history, supplementing and correcting the history provided by the earlier Gospels? or is he deserting history and leading us into the realms of mystical interpretation? The problem has been baffling, for neither of these alternatives seem wholly to correspond with the author's purpose or wholly to explain all the characteristics of the book.

But when once we have perceived that the double perspective exists in all the Apostolic writings and in all the Apostolic teaching from the earliest days, then the Fourth Gospel appears in a less problematic light. For while it does indeed contain its own problems, its main problem is not a new one. It sums up the inevitable tension in Apostolic Christianity, and enables a truer understanding of that tension. John writes in order that his readers may believe that Jesus is the Christ the Son of God and believing may have life in His name.

H

With this end in view he will not allow his readers to ignore either of the two aspects of Christianity. (1) On the one hand he makes it clear that men in every age may be in touch with Jesus Christ, risen and glorified, and may by believing on Him and feeding on Him possess eternal life. 'He, the Paraclete, shall glorify me, for He shall take of mine and shall declare it unto you'. 'Blessed are they that have not seen and yet have believed.' The Incarnation was the prelude to the greater works that the disciples would do when Jesus had gone to the Father, and to the closer union between the disciples and Jesus made possible by His departure. Here and now men may dwell in Him, and He in them. (2) But at the same time John is at pains to shew that the contemporary Christ is known aright and that union with Him is possible, only if the Christians are in a constant relationship with the historical events of the Word-made-flesh. It is vital that the events really happened, events that men saw and heard and their hands handled. 'Back to history' is an avowed motive both in the Gospel and in the First Epistle of John.

From: *The Resurrection of Christ* by A. M. Ramsey

(Collins Fontana, 1961, pp. 16–17)

Tuesday

The Resurrection of Christ

MICHAEL RAMSEY

These two factors are essential to John's message. If at times he points his readers beyond history to the eternal significance of Jesus, he as often brings them to earth again with his sudden reminders of stark historical fact. But he will not let them rest in history; for the history cannot reveal God or be understood unless it points men beyond itself. Nor will he let them rest in an unhistorical mysticism, for the risen Christ, interpreted by the Paraclete, is known only by those who will believe and treasure the historical events in the flesh.

Thus John draws together the two facts which belong to Christianity from the beginning, the Jesus who lived and died in the flesh and the Jesus who is living, contemporary and life-giving. If he puzzles us by the tension between them neither the puzzle nor the tension are of his own making. The Fourth Gospel is what it is not only because of the special tendencies and insights of the writer, but because of the nature of Christianity. From the tension between history and that which is beyond history the Christian never escapes, and within that tension the strength of Christianity lies.

The ministry, the Passion, the Resurrection, the mission of the Paraclete – John presents these in a true unity. He does so by means of the theme of *Life* which runs through his Gospel. The teaching and the works of Jesus, meeting as they do a vast variety of human needs, are united by the single purpose of bringing the gift of Life in answer to the fact of Death, both the Death in the body and the Death of sin. Life and light are the divine answer to death and darkness. The Messiah comes that men may have life, and have it abundantly. His life-giving mission has its climax in His own death and Resurrection which enable the fullest release of life, through the Paraclete, for the disciples and for mankind. Thus John shews the unity of the mission of Christ by expounding it with the glory of the Resurrection upon it. The themes of the ministry in John are really the same in essence as those recorded in the Synoptists; but in John the light of Easter is allowed to shine backwards upon these themes, and the reader feels that this light is never absent from the story.

From: *The Resurrection of Christ* by A. M. Ramsey

(Collins Fontana, 1961, pp. 17–18)

Wednesday

The Resurrection of Christ

MICHAEL RAMSEY

There is yet another tension within the thought of the Apostolic Church; and this is the tension that is created by the contrast between the Crucifixion and the Resurrection. The preachers of the Gospel told their hearers of the humiliation of Jesus done to death between two criminals, and of the 'exceeding greatness' of the power of God when 'according to the working of the strength of his might'[1] He raised Jesus from the dead. 'He was crucified through weakness, yet he liveth through the power of God.'[2] We discover as we read the

[1] Eph. i: 19.
[2] 2 Cor. xiii: 4.

New Testament that the two events, seen first as opposites, are found increasingly to be like the two sides of a single coin. Here again it is John who finally shows us the perfect unity.

To the disciples the contrast between the Reign of God proclaimed by Jesus and the shameful death of the Messiah presented at first an unbearable paradox. But the Resurrection showed them that the Passion was a part of the divine counsel and a prelude to glory, both for their Master and for themselves. Finally, they came to see that the Passion was not only a necessary prelude, but itself a part of the glory. This truth peeps out at many points in the Apostolic writings, until it blazes into light in the Fourth Gospel.

In the primitive preaching of the Apostles there is only a linking of the death and the exaltation as two stages in the divine drama. Both had their place. Jesus is both Servant and Lord. The same linking appears in Peter's First Epistle; he who once had stumbled at the Messiah's choice of the Cross is now 'a witness of the sufferings of Christ who am also a partaker of the glory that shall be revealed'.[1] Paul however sees more than a linking of the two events; they are for him blended together. The risen Christ is for ever 'the Christ who has been crucified'. His theme is 'Christ Jesus that died, yea rather that was raised from the dead'.[2] Christ crucified is 'the power of God and the widom of God'.[3] To worship the risen Jesus is to accept the Cross in virtue of which He triumphed: to believe in the Crucified is to adhere to one who conquers and reigns. . . .

This blending of Passion and Resurrection was not a piece of picturesque dramatizing by the early Christians. It corresponded to their own discovery that to share in the sufferings of Christ was to know His triumph. They were 'always bearing about in the body the dying of Jesus that the life also of Jesus may be manifested in our body'.[4]

From: *The Resurrection of Christ* by A. M. Ramsey

(Collins Fontana, 1961, pp. 18–19)

---

[1] 1 Peter v:1.
[2] Rom. viii:34.
[3] 1 Cor. i:24.
[4] 2 Cor. iv:10.

Thursday

The Resurrection of Christ

MICHAEL RAMSEY

It is however in the narratives of the Passion in the Gospels that the drawing together to the two events is most significantly to be seen. In *Mark* the Passion is depicted as an austere and lonely scene: the Messiah dies in utter isolation, and the only word from the Cross is the cry 'My God, my God, why hast thou forsaken me?' Yet the scene is not one of pathos, or tragedy or defeat. The many references to the fulfilment of prophecy declare that here is no haphazard disaster, but a divine act of redemption. Its power shatters the barrier between Jew and Gentile, as is symbolized by the confession of the Roman centurion, 'Truly this was the Son of God.' Only the Resurrection could have so turned the darkness of Calvary into a light for the Gentiles. *Luke* goes further in drawing Cross and Resurrection together. He shews in the Passion the serenity and the mastery of love whereby the Son of Man reaches out in sympathy and tenderness to those around Him. It is they and not He whose need and plight are pitiable. The gloom of the scene as Mark depicted it is, in Luke, lightened by the love which is already conquering. More still, Luke hints at the connection between the Cross and the glory. It is he who in the story of the Transfiguration links that scene with the Passion by telling how Moses and Elijah appeared in glory and spake of the exodus that Jesus was to fulfil in Jerusalem.[1] It is he who records the words spoken on the way to Emmaus: 'Behoved it not the Christ to suffer these things and to enter into his glory?'[2].

From: *The Resurrection of Christ* by A. M. Ramsey

(Collins Fontana, 1961, pp. 19–20)

[1] Luke ix:31.
[2] Luke xxiv:26.

Friday

The Resurrection of Christ

MICHAEL RAMSEY

It is left to *John* to depict the unity in full measure, and to make the explicit equation of Crucifixion and Glory. He uses the word 'glory' not a few times in direct reference to the Passion; and his narrative of the Passion reflects this. In the garden the soldiers fall back, awe-struck at the majesty of Jesus. At the trial Pilate seeks to judge Jesus, but it is Jesus who is his judge. Master of the events, Jesus carries His own Cross to Calvary, freely lays down His own life, and cries 'It is finished', for the victory is His. On the Cross Jesus is King. The Crucifixion is not a defeat needing the Resurrection to reverse it, but a victory which the Resurrection quickly follows and seals. The 'glory' seen in the Cross is the eternal glory of the Father and the Son; for that eternal glory is the glory of self-giving love, and Calvary is its supreme revelation.

So it is that the centre of Apostolic Christianity is *Crucifixion-Resurrection:* not Crucifixion alone nor Resurrection alone, nor even Crucifixion as the prelude and Resurrection as the finale but the blending of the two in a way that is as real to the Gospel as it is defiant to the world. The theme is implicit in the mission of Jesus as the Servant of the Lord, and it becomes increasingly explicit until John says the final word. To say that this theme is the centre of the Gospel is not to belittle the life and words of Jesus that preceded it nor the work of the Paraclete that followed it. For Life-through-Death is the principle of Jesus' whole life; it is the inward essence of the life of the Christians; and it is the unveiling of the glory of the eternal God. So utterly new and foreign to the expectations of men was this doctrine, that it seems hard to doubt that only historical events could have created it.

From: *The Resurrection of Christ* by A. M. Ramsey

(Collins Fontana, 1961, pp. 20–1)

Saturday

The Resurrection of Christ

MICHAEL RAMSEY

While traditional Christianity insists upon distinguishing the revealed doctrine of Resurrection from a philosophical belief in the immortality of the soul, it regards the latter not as untrue and irrelevant so much as incomplete, distressingly dull and missing the gift of the Gospel. There are grounds, both philosophical and psychological and religious, for believing that the soul survives death; though the life of a soul without the body is a conception which it is difficult to imagine. It is *incomplete*; because the self is far more than the soul, and the self without bodily expression can hardly be the complete self. It is *dull*; because it implies the prolongation of man's finite existence for everlasting years. In contrast both with the incompleteness and the dullness of the immortality of the soul Christianity teaches a future state (not as of right but as of God's gift) wherein the soul is not unclothed but clothed upon a bodily expression, and wherein the finite human life is raised so as to share, without losing its finiteness, in the infinite life of Christ Himself.

The Christian Gospel was not first addressed to people who had *no* belief in a future state. Greeks were familiar with a philosophical doctrine of immortality. Jews believed in the resurrection of the body. Sometimes this was thought of as a resuscitation of human relics and a reconstruction of human existence after the fashion of the present life. Sometimes it was thought of as a transformation of dead bodies into an utterly new state of glory and spiritualization. But nowhere, either for Greek or for Jew, was belief in the future life vivid, immediate, central and triumphant. Nowhere did the belief combine a conscious nearness of the world to come with a moral exalting of life in this present world. This was what Christianity brought. Its doctrine was not a flight to another world that left this world behind, nor was it a longing for another world that would come when the history of this world was ended. It was the very near certainty of another world, with which the Christians were already linked and into which the life of this world would be raised up.

For the Christian belief about the future state centred in Jesus Christ. He had been seen and loved in this life; and He had been seen and loved also as one who had conquered death. He had become vividly known as the Lord both of the living and the dead; and the conviction of His people concerning the future life rested upon their conviction about Him in whose life they shared. It was an intense and triumphant conviction that where He was there also would His people be. It found utterance in ringing words. 'He hath brought life and immortality to light through the Gospel.' 'Fear not; I am the first and the last, and the living one; and I was dead, and behold I am alive for evermore, and I have the keys of death and of Hades.' 'Awake, thou that sleepest and arise from the dead, and Christ shall shine upon thee.'

From: *The Resurrection of Christ* by A. M. Ramsey

(Collins Fontana, 1961, pp. 102–3)

EASTER 2

The Church in History

LEON-JOSEPH SUENENS

At the present time, the church is like a ship exposed to every wind and battling through a sort of Bay of Biscay. One reason for this situation has nothing to do with the ship – it is caused by the condition of the sea. The church exists in and for the world and as such lies open to the influence of the unprecedented changes which the world is experiencing. But there is also another reason, which belongs to the condition of the ship itself. Ever since the Council, the church has been overhauling itself, not in some dry-dock but out in the open sea. The church itself looks like some great shipping port at capacity production: passengers and crew experience daily to what degree they share the same lot and how intimately life on board ship concerns us all.

This heightened awareness of a common concern is a new thing. The sense of the co-responsibility of all Christians has been awakened. We have a long way to go before all its consequences are apparent, but a beginning has been made which cannot but grow greater. At this moment the words of Victor Hugo are particularly applicable, 'Nothing is stronger than an idea whose hour has come.' Whether we like it or not, the church must adopt a new life style. . . .

No aspect of renewal stands alone. For example, if we wish to see a greater exercise of collegiality on the part of the highest authority of the church, then consistency demands that the image of the bishop within the local church or of the priest within each community be also re-thought in the same perspective. It is impossible to highlight the priesthood of the faithful without reconsidering the ministerial priesthood which, while always a part of the church's life, must be lived in a different way. The creation of permanent deacons and certain new responsibilities given to lay people automatically imply a greater flexibility in our traditional structures and a pluralism of ecclesiastical functions. Thus, everything exercises a mutual influence on everything else and everyone must rethink his relationships to everyone else. But that cannot happen overnight.

Such a rethinking of mutual relations supposes that we are able to distinguish clearly what is essential and what is secondary and can be discarded, in what we have inherited from the past. We Christians, used to accepting indiscriminately as one whole the pure gold of the gospel and the wrappings of human making, have not been trained to discern the difference. It is not easy to restore the interior of a gothic cathedral covered with baroque or modern plaster and to recover its original lines. To restore a cathedral like some Viollet le Duc requires more than momentary enthusiasm.

From: *The Future of the Christian Church* by Leon-Joseph Suenens and Arthur Michael Ramsey

(SCM Press, 1971, pp. 5–7)

Tuesday

The Church in History

LEON-JOSEPH SUENENS

A tree grows if it is pruned once in a while. When the excess growth is cut, the sap rises more abundantly in the main branches. But it takes a sure hand to prune without killing, and it takes a healthy optimism to have confidence in the power of Spring when one sees the pruned branches all around.

Today's renewal, so delicate to bring about, so burgeoning with life, is facing a great challenge: it is the very depth of the conversion demanded of us to be faithful to the gospel with all this entails. We are called to be faithful to what the world expects of us and this cannot be realized without pain, disappointments, and contradictions. Life is made up of tensions seeking a balance. The difficulties of the journey are the price we must pay to discover new horizons. The very depth of the work undertaken by the Holy Spirit within us, individually and collectively, requires time and patience.

As we wait for the continuity of the generations to be established, and for the Holy Spirit to triumph over the sin which is an obstacle to him in each one of us, it seems to me that it would be a service to the Christian of today, who is *en route* towards the twenty-first century to show that the church is a reality situated within history. The time in which we live becomes more understandable to us if we join it to yesterday and try to link it with tomorrow, just as in discovering the position of a ship we must calculate its latitude and longitude on the map. If we understand the relationship of the church to time in general, it will help us understand the church in relation to our time. We cannot but profit from viewing the church thus plunged within the very heart of history, and not like some abstract, unchangeable reality untouched by time. We have already suffered too much from a static view of the church defined juridically as a 'perfect society'.

Thanks be to God, we do not tend to look upon the church any more in juridical categories, but rather as a living thing animated by the presence and life of Christ which is making its way from Easter to the coming of the Lord. The church is a pilgrim walking through time and history, going from stage to stage along a way as yet incomplete. The history of the Exodus teaches us that God does not like to give to his people great supplies of provisions for the journey but rather to be with them and provide them with manna for the day. We had become accustomed to accumulating any number of constraining accessories and to building houses of stone and cement, rather than being happy with tents that can be folded and moved and allow us always to be ready to go on.

A church which has placed itself once again within history is more likely to awaken in its members a deeper sense of freedom and flexibility and an understanding of our obligation to remain faithful to the past, to the present, and to the future. This three-fold fidelity is at once the glory and the most radiant crown of the church.

From: *The Future of the Christian Church* by Leon-Joseph Suenens and Arthur Michael Ramsey

(SCM Press, 1971, pp. 7–8)

Wednesday

The Church and the Past

LEON-JOSEPH SUENENS

The church in all its being is rooted in the past. It must remain faithful to its beginning, to its principle of continuity, and to its tradition, if it does not want to deny its own reality. The church is nourished by that profound continuity which links it to its origin, as a tree lives by its roots. But it is important that the tree itself be not confused with those outgrowths which have sprung up at the foot of the tree during the course of time. Obviously it is not easy to distinguish that which pertains to authentic theology and dogma and that which results from sociological or cultural factors. A real theologian knows this better than anyone else and tries always to be aware of his own subjective attitude.

It is precisely an amazing ignorance of history, which one finds among conservatives, that makes conservatism so sure of itself and so closed to dialogue. Conservatives venture to 'dogmatize' well beyond the limits of dogma and to canonize opinions that are the products of a particular period of history. All this is rendered easier for them by the fact that such people lack any historical perspective.

History is not only 'the mistress of life'; it is also the guide to research. By the very fact that it can place a reality in context, making it relative to other factors and rendering conclusions more modest, circumspect, and balanced, it acts as a guideline along the road, indicating where to slow down and be careful. History teaches the art of perspective and proportion. How many arguments could be rescued from an impasse if one side or the other would agree to go back, to search out the beginnings, to investigate together complementary truths and hidden preconceptions! If I wish to really understand the meaning and importance of a past Council, then I must understand the context in which that Council occurred, the problems which it had to face, its *Sitz im Leben*, its fears, its preoccupations, and its areas of ignorance.

History is absolutely indispensable for the church in order to keep it truly faithful to its origins. But history also confers other riches on us by giving us in addition a good lesson in humility and confidence. We get a lesson in humility because history shows us vividly how we carry our treasures in earthen vessels. But we also learn confidence because we see how profoundly God is at work in the church through all its human inadequacy. We touch upon the principle already proposed by Gamaliel when, according to the Acts of the Apostles, he said to the tribunal which wished to condemn Peter and John, 'If this enterprise, this movement of theirs, is of human origin, it will break up of its own accord: but if it does in fact come from God you will not only be unable to destroy them, but you might find yourselves fighting against God.'[1] This apologetic argument is always valid.

From: *The Future of the Christian Church* by Leon-Joseph Suenens and Arthur Michael Ramsey

(SCM Press, 1971, pp. 8–9)

[1] Acts 5:39.

Thursday

The Church and the Past

LEON-JOSEPH SUENENS

Continuity with the past is a primary duty for the church. We could say that it is from there that it derives the sap of its life.

The remote origin of the church is found in the history of Israel. With the people of the ancient covenant, the church goes back through the course of centuries. The church never accepted a radical break with its Jewish past and it condemned Marcionism as a heresy when that movement proposed such a rupture. At Vatican II when the Fathers of the Council felt themselves obliged to make a declaration which was favourable to the Jews, their purpose was not only to render justice, but also to express the fidelity of the church to itself.

If the remote origin of the church is found within the ancient people of God, its direct source is found in those events that occurred twenty centuries ago: facts which are, at one and the same time, and in an indissoluble manner, both history and mystery. The church does not confuse history with historicism. She knows well enough that the whole reality from which she lives cannot be reduced to the dimensions and methods proper to the science of history. The very richness of the objective, original reality, transcends our neat compartments: the same reality is viewed under both the light of history and the light of faith.

However, the church opposes and will always oppose the attitude that sees the approach of faith and the approach of history as incompatible. It cannot admit that lack of continuity which modern liberal exegetes, before, with, and after Rudolf Bultmann, have attempted to establish between the Jesus of history and the Christ of faith. The decisive factor which gave rise to Christianity is the historical Jesus of the gospels and not the paschal faith of his disciples, even if these gospels themselves come to us from the post-Resurrection community. If we make of the paschal event a purely interior happening, which occurred within the souls of the disciples, touched off by a process that itself remains inexplicable, we fail to understand the very foundations of faith. It is good to see the reaction against such an 'interiorization' of the paschal reality growing ever stronger, even among Rudolf Bultmann's disciples, such as Wolfhart Pannenberg, and the proponents of the Theology of Hope, about which we will speak later.

From: *The Future of the Christian Church* by Leon-Joseph Suenens and Arthur Michael Ramsey

(SCM Press, 1971, pp. 9–10)

Friday

The Church and the Past

LEON-JOSEPH SUENENS

Christianity can never be reduced to a subjective projection, collective or individual, to an ideology or a dialectic. It is first and foremost an event, a person: Jesus Christ acknowledged as Lord. A Christian is not a philosopher who has opted for a certain explanation of the universe, but a man who has met in his own life Jesus of Nazareth, crucified on Good Friday and risen from the tomb. The cry of Claudel, 'Behold, all of a sudden you are Somebody', is the cry of faith for all generations, past and future. However, if the Christian is a man who derives his life from the past, who lives because of a unique event in the past, it is not as though he comes in contact with that past across a void of twenty centuries. The past comes to him because it is always living in the church. In saying to his disciples, 'Behold, I am with you always, even to the end of the world', the Lord intended to assure them of his presence in the church and to abolish, between himself and us, all that the past normally implies in distance and estrangement. In Christ, the past is overcome. Through him and in him, the church comes to us as the heir of a past which is living and radiant in its present reality.

The Christian of today moves towards his Lord, not only with his own personal faith, isolated and sometimes vacillating, but with the faith of the whole church, the faith of yesterday and that of today. He believes as the heir of the believers of yesterday. Just before receiving the Body of the Lord, the church puts upon our lips this great prayer, 'Lord, look not upon our sins, but upon the faith of your Church.' It is with this ecclesial faith that I come to meet the Son of God. I believe with the faith of the patriarchs and prophets; with the faith of Mary and the apostles and martyrs, the doctors, the confessors, the mystics, and the saints. It is the power of each poor Christian that he knows himself to be part of a great continuous whole, a link in a great chain welded to the Lord through those who have gone before us. It is always a great moment for me when, during an ordination liturgy, we sing the Litany of the Saints. It is good to feel oneself united with our forefathers in the faith, of whom we ask a mediating presence for the sake of the man to be ordained. This communion, which reaches out through the centuries and is joined to the glorious church, is a deep breath of fresh air for us. It is like some pause on the plateau of a mountain: there, before such a horizon, we breathe better.

From: *The Future of the Christian Church* by Leon-Joseph Suenens and Arthur Michael Ramsey

(SCM Press, 1971, pp. 10–11)

Saturday

The Church and the Past

LEON-JOSEPH SUENENS

In this chain that joins us to the past, there is a special link that commands our faith. We say in the Credo, 'I believe in the Apostolic Church', that is to say our faith derives from the privileged witness of the apostles. Built upon the Rock of Peter and the foundation of the Twelve, faith finds its anchor there and begins from this point, which is its source of transmission, reference, and fidelity.

The tradition that stands above all others as the peak of a mountain dominates the landscape and acts as a watershed is the tradition that rests upon the Word of God as lived and transmitted through the ministry of the Apostolic college. That which St. Paul wrote to Timothy, who was beginning his apostolic responsibility, remains valid for all times: 'Keep as your pattern the sound teaching you have heard from me, in the faith and love that are in Christ Jesus. You have been trusted to look after something precious; guard it with the help of the Holy Spirit who lives in us.'[1] These words apply to every Christian who is essentially one of the 'faithful'.

At a time when the ship is being battered we ought to offer to God and to his church a fidelity that is ever more pure and stable. Our fidelity ought to be purer because it relies no longer on the sociological underpinnings of a Christian culture that is disappearing, but upon God himself, who is experienced in our more personal con-

[1] 2 Tim, 1:13–14.

cerned and apostolic commitment. Our fidelity is more stable because we must go through and beyond the weakness of the church and know how to recognize and love its true face.

Despite the deep wrinkles on the face of his mother, an adult knows how to see in her look the eternal youth of a love that never grows old. When we were children we thought that our mother had the answer for everything. When we grew up we discovered her limitations; but this never diminished our love, it only made it more deeply real. As Christians who have grown up, we know that we owe to the church the very best that is in us. And that is sufficient reason why she remains for all of us, despite her 'wrinkles', our Mother, the Holy Church.

From: *The Future of the Christian Church* by Leon-Joseph Suenens and Arthur Michael Ramsey

(SCM Press, 1971, pp. 11–12)

EASTER 3

Monday

The Church and the Future

LEON-JOSEPH SUENENS

We would have a truncated image of the church if we considered
it only as turned towards the past. The church is pre-eminently a
reality of the present. If the salvation of the world is a fact accomplished once and for all by the Passion and Resurrection, redemption
goes on each day as it applies the fruits of this mystery to each
person. The past and the present are mutually interpenetrating: the
past is actualized by the present, which in turn flows out from the
past. Pascal once said, 'Christ is in agony through the centuries and
we must not sleep during this time.' The mystery of salvation is as
great as the centuries, and it is lived out before our very eyes. When
a priest holds up the consecrated Host before the faithful and says,
'This is the Lamb of God Who takes away the sins of the world',
he recalls to all that the paschal mystery is always being worked out.

The same can be said for the actuality of the gospel message. The
church lives from the past but it is completely oriented towards the
present, towards the opportune moment that the New Testament
calls the *kairos*. It offers God's message as Good News that keeps
its freshness and youth for each generation. Lacordaire once defined
a Christian in this magnificent phrase, 'A Christian is a man to whom
Jesus Christ has confided other men.' These men who have been
confided to us are not the men of yesterday; they are the people of
right now, our next door neighbours, our fellow workers, our fellow
students, all those whom we meet.

Devotion and respect in regard to the past have nothing in common with rigid lack of change or the respect properly accorded a
museum piece. The church must always draw from her treasure,
'the new and the old'. She must be actual, incarnate, and present in
the tangible reality of human life in all its dimensions. The Council
vividly recalled for us our duty to read and understand the signs of
the times. *Vox temporum vox Dei*, that motto is still true. Today,
God still speaks in and through events; we must believe in and bring

about the constant interplay between the living God and men of flesh and blood. Someone once asked Karl Barth, 'What do you do to prepare your Sunday sermon?' Barth answered, 'I take the Bible in one hand and the daily newspaper in the other.' To see events in their relationship to God is a part of the mediating mission of the church. It is a daily and difficult task, for new problems are continually arising.

The gospel is not an answer book. It offers 'Words of Life' that speak to the primal experiences of man. It is an unfailing spring of living water and that is why, in the church, the reading of its sacred pages is a constant duty.

From: *The Future of the Christian Church* by Leon-Joseph Suenens and Arthur Michael Ramsey

(SCM Press, 1971, pp. 13–14)

Tuesday

The Church and the Present

LEON-JOSEPH SUENENS

The church cannot afford to canonize the past. We must be on our guard against a certain kind of 'primitivism' about which I will be speaking later. This primitivism will consist in wishing to recreate some past age of the church as being the norm of its whole life. There is no golden age that ought to be restored. In this sense, we should have no nostalgia, even for the primitive church. We must not fool ourselves: the picture of the primitive Christian communities is far from idyllic and it contains diverging tendencies as different as Jewish and Hellenic cultures. A reading of the Acts of the Apostles shows us how free the Apostles were in adopting ways and means to suit their mission. Fidelity to tradition does not mean materially copying their efforts, but trying to do what they tried to do. . . .

If we should never yield to the temptation of primitivism we should be equally on our guard against the mirage of 'presentism', which is a sort of indiscriminate canonization of the present. This is the temptation that lies in wait for those who, in their enthusiasm to stress the church's obligation to be present to the world, either forget or minimize that which is always and irreducibly part of Christianity of any time.

The Constitution on the Church in the Modern World requires

that we read the signs of the times but it never intends to make the terms *Church* and *World* completely synonymous or to oblige us to change with every passing fashion of the day. Nor did the Council intend simply the translation of an eternal message into modern terms. Rather it offered an appeal to re-read the gospel in faith with the light of the Holy Spirit while living the experience of a man of today. What is asked of us is a re-reading with a view to a new hearing of that Word of God which is always living and actual. We must be free enough to understand today what the Spirit is saying to the churches. The church is not faithful to itself unless it is ready at every moment for the surprises of the Holy Spirit and the unexpectedness of God.

What men are waiting for from the church, whether they realize it or not, is that the church of today show them the gospel. Our contemporaries want to meet the Christ who is alive today; they want to see him with their eyes and touch him with their hands. Like those pilgrims who approached Philip one day, they say to us, 'We wish to see Jesus.' Our contemporaries want a meeting face to face with Christ. The challenge for us as Christians is that they demand to see Christ in each one of us; they want us to reflect Christ as clearly as a pane of glass transmits the rays of the sun. Whatever is opaque and besmirched in us disfigures the face of Christ in the church. What the unbeliever reproaches us with is not that we are Christians, but that we are not Christian enough: that is the tragedy. When Gandhi read the gospels, he was deeply moved and wanted to become a Christian, but the sight of the Christians around him stopped him and made him withdraw. Such is the great weight of our responsibility.

From: *The Future of the Christian Church* by Leon-Joseph Suenens and Arthur Michael Ramsey

(SCM Press, 1971, pp. 14–15)

Wednesday

The Church and the Present

LEON-JOSEPH SUENENS

Our vision of the church would not be complete unless we consider the church, again in that totality of its being, as turned and tending towards the future.

Modern man is to a surprising degree preoccupied with the future.

So profoundly influenced is he by this sense of the future, that he has made a science of prediction. Tomorrow and the day after tomorrow fascinate him.

At one time man sought to unlock the secret of the future by consulting the stars. Today, rather than force the door of the impenetrable, or seek to divine the future, man tries to create it, to invent it, to discover techniques to control his movement through time. Within the heart of the man of today, anguished and troubled as it may sometimes be, there is a great hope, which he is seeking to unleash.

Modern man is living by a temporal messianic hope; the church lives by a theological or God-centred hope. The church offers to men a hope that goes beyond anything the eyes of man have seen or human ears have heard; it is nothing else than that which God himself has prepared for those whom he loves.

Contemporary man and the church have found a meeting place: it is their common attention to the future. In his book, *The Principle of Hope*, the famous Marxist philosopher Ernst Bloch has written these words: 'Where there is hope, there is religion.' His formula may be ambiguous, but it has a valid meaning. It should not be surprising therefore that this same Ernst Bloch has enriched the thought of those theologians who have so strongly reaffirmed the eschatological aspect of the church: that aspect of '*en route* to the future'.

It is of the utmost importance that the false opposition between the church and the future be broken down. We can never accept the oft-repeated phrase, 'the church lives by its memories; the world by its hope'. It is absolutely essential that the gospel be presented to the world as a hope. This preoccupation of modern man is not completely new; Kant has already posed his three famous questions: 'What can I know?', 'What must I do?', 'What can I hope?'. His *Critique of Pure Reason*, his *Critique of Practical Reason*, and his *Critique of Aesthetic Judgment* are his attempts to answer this threefold question. The third question, 'What can I hope?' is found at the heart of modern philosophy with a new urgency, but it has also forced us to focus attention upon a dimension of Christianity that is all too frequently forgotten. Christianity is a religion turned towards the future, moving towards the *parousia*, towards the final meeting with the Lord.

From: *The Future of the Christian Church* by Leon-Joseph Suenens and Arthur Michael Ramsey

(SCM Press, 1971, pp. 16–17)

Thursday

The Church and the Future

LEON-JOSEPH SUENENS

In accepting openness to the future, the church will regain the
attention of youth who are preoccupied with the world to be created
and who are at once fascinated and awed by tomorrow. From now
on this world is, to a large degree, in our hands. Nature will never
again appear to man as an abstract fatality, as the rigid raw material
for his creativity, but rather as a supple medium, which he can use
at his discretion and include in his plans. Modern man is fascinated
by the world he must create, not by a ready-made world that he has
been forced to respect and oftentimes fear, a world that, even yesterday, seemed to dictate its laws to him while remaining hostile to him.
We are far from that time when Philip II of Spain, wishing to make
the Tagus river navigable, submitted his project to a commission.
The commission rejected the proposal, giving as its reason, 'If God
had wished that this river be navigable, he would have accomplished
it with a single word.' As a conclusion the commission said that, for
the future, 'it would be a rash trespass upon the rights of God if
human hands were to dare improve a work left unfinished by God
for reasons beyond our ken'. Our world is at the other extreme from
such an idea. We Christians must, as it were, form a meeting place
between the transcendence of God and the future of the world, without confusing God with some immanent earthly future as if God were
the term of some incredibly complex cosmic evolution.

Whatever shows the church as a community moving towards its
final destiny, towards God who will be 'all in all', towards the
glorified Christ, has a particular power of speaking to our time. We
ourselves must rediscover the God of the Bible; the God of Abraham,
Isaac, and Jacob; and not the God of the philosophers. We must free
ourselves from those aspects of Greek philosophy that viewed the
universe as a world enclosed upon itself, for ever destined to be a
cyclic whirlpool with no live movement towards the future. We must
rediscover the personal God of the Bible. He is not the God who
wishes to reveal to us first and foremost a series of theological propositions and theses, but the God of the promise which commits us to
the future, the God who reveals himself to us as a Love that is personal, spontaneous, unmerited, and irrevocable.

It is in this perspective that we can locate the church between the 'already' of Easter and the 'not yet' of the *parousia*. In the church, the past is always actual and the future is already present. In the church, tradition means perpetual renewal and evolution means continuity. In the church, there lives Christ who is 'the same yesterday, today, and forever'.

From: *The Future of the Christian Church* by Leon-Joseph Suenens and Arthur Michael Ramsey

(SCM Press, 1971, pp. 17–18)

Friday

The Church as Mission

LEON-JOSEPH SUENENS

The church is by essence missionary. We can also say that it is missionary by a very solemn command of the Lord. At the moment our Blessed Lord was leaving the earth he gave his apostles this solemn command: 'All authority in heaven and on earth has been given to me. Go, therefore, make disciples of all the nations; baptize them in the name of the Father and of the Son and of the Holy Spirit, and teach them to observe all the commands I gave you. And know that I am with you always; yes, to the end of time.'[1] I think that from time to time we have to read these sacred words as though we were listening to them for the first time. 'All *dynamis*, all power, all authority is given to *me*', and 'I will be with you'. We must connect these two statements of the Lord. All of us know what obstacles face us today, but we are to realize first of all, not the magnitude of the obstacles, but the fact that in Christ there is all power – and he is with us. We are often tempted to raise the same question the women did on the way to the Easter tomb: 'Who will remove the stone from the door of the tomb?' But the Lord is risen! He is here and his command is, 'Go, and bring the Gospel to every creature.'[2]

We are sent to everyone without exception. I remember a parish priest saying to me, 'But how can I go and visit twenty thousand parishioners? It is impossible.' I answered, 'Well, the command of the Lord is, "Go, and bring the gospel to every creature." The solution must be found; you have to find it. The Lord didn't say, and I,

[1] Matthew 28:18–20.
[2] Mark 16:15.

your Bishop, don't say to you, Go and visit those twenty thousand parishioners yourself, but still, you are responsible that they be visited and that the gospel be brought to them. This is your apostolic and pastoral duty. You must find ways of acting in full co-responsibility with all the Christians around you so that the gospel is brought to everyone in your parish.' We have to make these efforts and not allow our enthusiasm to ebb and flow with the tide of success. I remember having read the answer of a missionary in China who, before he was a priest, was a very successful layman. Someone said to him that it was a shame for him to have spent so many years as a missionary in China without any visible success. He answered, 'I am not here because of any past or future successes but to obey the command of the Master and bring the gospel to every creature.' That is, I think, an expression in faith of what our mission is: we go because the Lord said, 'Go', because Christ wishes to go, in and through us. He has told us to go and preach the gospel and, by that, he means all of the gospel; every page and every verse. Our duty is not satisfied when we have only sketched out the main lines of the gospel – no, we must make Christ present, for the gospel is Jesus; it is he whom we are meant to preach in all the reality, power, and attractive beauty of his being, so that all men hear within themselves the echo of the full implications of his call to holiness and union with the Father; we must go bearing this gospel to every creature to the end of the world.

From: *The Future of the Christian Church* by Leon-Joseph Suenens and Arthur Michael Ramsey

(SCM Press, 1971, pp. 52–4)

Saturday

The Church as Mission

LEON-JOSEPH SUENENS

. . . To those who preach the gospel today and feel at a loss as to what to say, I would consel: Don't be too impressed by the phenomenon of 'contemporary man'. He is not as completely unique as he sometimes likes to think he is. Allow yourself to experience the abiding problems of existence and to experience your faith in relation to those problems. There is something permanent in man and in mankind. Anyone, as long as he is truly man, cannot escape such questions as, 'Why am I here?', 'What is the meaning of life?', 'What is the meaning of suffering?', 'What is the meaning of Death?', 'What is tomorrow?' All these questions are there, living in every soul, and we must be convinced that when we are speaking and bringing the gospel we are answering an echo already existing in the people listening to us. Just a few days ago, I read these lines in Carl Jung's *Modern Man in Search of a Soul*: 'During the past thirty years people from all the civilized countries of the earth have consulted me. I have treated many hundreds of patients . . . among all my patients in the second half of life – that is over thirty-five – there has not been one whose problem in the last resort was not that of finding a religious outlook on life.' This is the finding of a psychiatrist speaking from vast experience and profound reflection. When we are free enough to experience our own problems in their depths as contemporary men, and know the healing power of the gospel in our own beings, we will not doubt its relevance for our brothers.

And so, just to end these reflections today, let us recall for our own encouragement, and that of the people for whom we are responsible, that the church is by her nature a mission to the man of today in obedience to the perennial command of the Lord: he will never fail to give us what we need to be faithful to him and to ourselves. I wish to add just one word: let us not forget that mission means redemption. Since the church is mission, and since the mission of the church is to continue the redeeming activity of the Lord, it is completely normal that it should know a Good Friday, that there should be suffering and even death. The mission we have to accomplish is not a sort of human propaganda; it is making present the redemption in all its reality and consequences: this means the suffering of the Cross in the power of the Resurrection. 'Wherever we go, we carry death with us in our body, the death that Jesus died, that in this body also life may reveal itself, the life that Jesus lives. For continually, while still alive, we are being surrendered into the hands of death, for Jesus' sake, so that the life of Jesus also may be revealed in this mortal body of ours.'[1]

From: *The Future of the Christian Church* by Leon-Joseph Suenens and Arthur Michael Ramsey

(SCM Press, 1971, pp. 62–3)

---

[1] 2 Cor. 4:10–11.

EASTER 4

Contemplating Now

MONICA FURLONG

The principle of non-activity, or 'waiting', comes so strangely to us in the West that often we can make no sense of it, and in our fear we are quick to dub it 'anti-life'. By conducting our discussions of the subject in a particular loaded way, e.g. should we feed the starving? we manage to convince ourselves that passivity is not only useless, but wicked, virtue then being defined in terms of works which can be immediately shown to produce some beneficial result. The special forms of suffering which we associate with some Eastern countries – for example, the corruption, starvation and disease of a city like Calcutta – are adduced by us to spring from the contemplative stance of Eastern religion with its disinterest in reform.

It may well be true that our own activist temperament, including the activist temperament of Western Christianity, has contributed very largely to a state of affairs in many Western countries in which virtually no one dies in the street, or of starvation. The soaring industrial prosperity which eventually (though slowly) lifted even the lowest-paid workers up to and above the bread line was clearly associated with a very positive belief in the virtue of work, a virtue which has commended itself to Protestantism more than to Catholicism.

To lift people from a condition of desperate want is no mean feat and it would be folly not to value this, not to value it as perhaps the supreme achievement of the West. Nevertheless we must go on from this point to ask whether most people do feel themselves rich in the more profound meanings of the word, and we are forced to recognize that, freed from the desperate preoccupation with hunger and employment, men and women have discovered new areas of indigence in their lives. The rapid increases in neurotic forms of illness, the rise in the suicide figures, the growing problem of addiction to drugs or alcohol, the random evidence of widespread sexual unhappiness, does not suggest that we live in a society in which there is very much joy and contentment. Nobody has learned more thoroughly than we have that man does not live by bread alone.

From: *Contemplating Now* by Monica Furlong

(Hodder & Stoughton, 1971, pp. 91–2)

Tuesday

Contemplating Now

MONICA FURLONG

'Man does not live by bread alone.' What does he live by then? Not by absence of bread, nor contempt for the faithful toil which produces it. It is too easy to turn a cherished belief on its head and insist that its opposite is true. But problems of great complexity are not solved in this way but by an unusual openness to contradictory elements in a situation, and a flexibility in dealing with them. Man's active side is one of the most precious gifts he has and the only way in which he could possibly have survived in a world that has often been cold and harsh; it is the side by which he controls his environment.

But it represents only half of him. If activity represents the side of man which controls his environment, then passivity, or what I have called 'contemplation', represents the side of him which recognizes that he is part of his environment, and at one with it. He is formed of the same matter as the life which surrounds him, and from the movement of conception the same current of life has flowed through him as flows through all else. He is deeply at one with all creation and at times can know this with the purest joy. This is his 'ancestry', his 'background', the source from which he comes and to which he must return. Man can only be happy, I suggest, if at fairly regular intervals in his life he renews his awareness of this ground in which he is rooted. 'Returning to one's roots is known as stillness', says Lao Tzu, and the alternative to such stillness may well be the frenetic busyness that does not know how to stop, or to sit still, or even to sleep. Robbed of his stillness man is driven to stimulants to keep him at work when his exhausted body can no longer continue, and tranquillizers to enforce the rest and relaxation which he has lost the trick of achieving for himself.

From: *Contemplating Now* by Monica Furlong

(Hodder & Stoughton, 1971, pp. 92–3)

Wednesday

Contemplating Now

MONICA FURLONG

What I believe we need is not a sudden Easternizing of ourselves, a wholesale selling out to gurus and fakirs, or even to contemplative prayer. The immediate need seems to be for something much more modest and down-to-earth, a simple recognition that we are *rhythmical* creatures, creatures who, obviously enough, need to follow bursts of strenuous activity with periods of rest and quietness; creatures who, less obviously (and this is where we touch upon deep fears), will have a natural tendency to follow periods of rest and quietness with periods of strenuous activity. The second is much more difficult to believe. When we made work into a virtue we made laziness into a sin, and as with all sins, we have a secret conviction that everyone (including ourselves) is dying to commit them. Ignoring our deep-felt *need* to work, and the rhythm which we can see at work in nature wherever we look, we think and talk continually as if laziness were our temptation. But is it? Is it still? Or is work, and the perfectionism which accompanies it, now the greater temptation?

If we are continually lashing ourselves to work at times when we do not feel like it, then we lose contact with, and confidence in, the natural voices within us which tell us to rest when we are tired, or to be active when we are energetic. If we overrule these voices often enough and for long enough, either by the strength of our will, or by the use of artificial aids such as drugs, then we forget how to listen even as they become more and more insistent, until often the first time that we hear them is when we are struck down by a disabling illness.

But it does not seem impossible that, just as we are learning a new respect for nature because of the desperate threat of pollution, so we may learn a new respect for the workings of our own exhausted and mismanaged bodies. We may learn to think again about the signals our over-civilized bodies put out – skin complaints, indigestion, constipation, allergies, insomnia – not in any hypochondriacal way but as signals of lives that have gone wrong. Perhaps we may come to see that if the word 'sin' still has meaning then these simple, everyday problems from which none of us is exempt, may help in sounding out the 'wrongness' of our lives.

From: *Contemplating Now* by Monica Furlong

(Hodder & Stoughton, 1971, pp. 93–4)

Contemplating Now

MONICA FURLONG

To live within a sense of rhythm means that, on a simple level at least, we must stay in touch with our physical needs, knowing, as a cat knows, the time to rest and the time to refrain from resting. Like the Zen archer we learn how to wait for 'It', the compelling purpose which signals the moment for action. Obviously our own tiredness or energy is not the only way in which we can know the working of 'It'. A hungry, crying baby, someone in need or distress or danger, a customer waiting to be served, a meal to be cooked, has an 'Itness' of its own that we cannot neglect. Yet there is a difference between performing such duties when we are in touch with our bodies from within, not driving them like unwilling slaves. If we can carry out even the most routine tasks recognizing that we and those for whom we perform them are alike caught up in the 'Itness' of things, then a new gracefulness, a new sense of relaxation, enters our work. It is as if action and contemplation have run together, making possible the healing kind of 'thereness' for which we have longed all our lives, and of which we have only caught tantalizing glimpses, usually from watching the movements of more primitive peoples.

Since we are not primitive people, however, then our awareness can extend from physical self-awareness to psychological awareness. We learn to know something about experience not just from within, e.g. the feeling in the arm when we would like to slap someone, the feeling we associate with hunger, thirst, sexual desire, sleep, or the urge to sneeze, but also from without. We can learn how to observe ourselves and others in such a way as to make intelligent deductions which go far beyond a simple awareness of our needs. This kind of deduction has taken man a very long way from his simple beginnings, making it possible for him to wield complex forms of power in technological, economic, political and psychological fields. Armed with this knowledge and the power that it gives, man becomes much more formidable, since his mistakes can occur on a much larger scale than before, and can be destructive of life – human, animal, or vegetable – on a scale that extends infinitely beyond the puny strength of the angry individual or the angry tribe.

From: *Contemplating Now* by Monica Furlong

(Hodder & Stoughton, 1971, pp. 97–8)

Friday

Contemplating Now

MONICA FURLONG

While he is still intoxicated by this power man does not care to be reminded of the primitive beginnings from which he is still in flight. He is scornful of human ways of living which do not start from the mastery of the intellect, and his repressed longings for the spontaneity, the sexual freedom and tribal closeness of primitive man, make him all the more eager to deny the side of his humanity which he has lost.

He is only likely to change when he has doubts – doubts about the inflation he senses within himself as he tries to live up to the power he has acquired, doubts about whether, in spite of all the effort and all the denial of powerful longings, he enjoys the happiness he longs for. There is then a strong likelihood of change, but in what direction? The unconscious, which plays so powerful a part in the life of primitive man, is again insisting that it be noticed since man is paying too heavy a price for his one-sidedness, his excessive consciousness.

This change which the unconscious forces upon him may take two courses. It may lead him upon a journey of self-awareness in which he rediscovers the power of the primitive man within him and learns to integrate him with the conscious self. This is the journey which, supremely, analysis is about, but which is also open to those who, for one reason or another, cannot manage that particular route. The arts, human relationships, religion, drugs, may all make essential contributions to such a journey, though such is the two-edged nature of all that is most important to us, that any of them may also serve as an escape from the journey. Those who embark upon this journey learn a new respect for much that conscious, technological man has learned to scorn – for the hinterland of dreams, images, symbols, rituals, myths by which traditionally man charted his journey, both individually and collectively. This kind of intimate relationship with all that leads us inward – the ability to move quite naturally within the inner territory – is of the essence of the contemplative experience.

But the other kind of change which the unconscious may produce is more alarming. The man who will not embark willingly upon his journey does not escape the force of the unconscious. By one method or another it may insist upon his notice – by illness, by depression, by anxiety, by obsessions, or by collective manifestations such as sadism, racialism and war. He finds himself *taken over* by forces which he does not understand and which lead him to a conclusion that he did not want. Our over-activity, which scorns the patient travelling of the contemplative, can lead us towards such a situation, puzzled why everything we attempt turns out badly however good our intentions.

From: *Contemplating Now* by Monica Furlong

(Hodder & Stoughton, 1971, pp. 96–8)

Saturday

Contemplating Now

MONICA FURLONG

Self-awareness means trying to live with all of ourselves, the dark, injured, and furtive parts as much as the strong and respectable ones. Only thus can we avoid the 'lost' bits of our personalities acting as a kind of fifth column which sabotages all our actions.

Just as important, the kind of rhythm and self-awareness that I have been talking about leads us towards a profound and satisfying sense of the meaningfulness of life, our own life and the life that flows around us. Because we are not exhausted, because we are prepared to try to keep in touch with ourselves, then we are free at last to discover, or rediscover (we knew about it as children) the breathtaking richness of life. 'A new feeling of self-forgiveness and self-acceptance begins to spread and circulate. . . . Shadow aspects of the personality continue to play their burdensome roles but now within a larger 'tale', the myth of oneself, just what one is which begins to feel as if that is how one is meant to be. My myth becomes my truth; my life symbolic and allegorical . . .' If we leave on one side the Jungian language in which Hillman speaks, we can still grasp the essence of his message. The journey inwards is what gives meaning to the life outside ourselves. Not in any static, dogmatic, once-for-all way either, but in a way that grows and develops and changes to meet different circumstances, different stages of development. Contemplation is not an optional extra – it is, as much as action, part of the very stuff of being human.

From: *Contemplating Now* by Monica Furlong

(Hodder & Stoughton, 1971, pp. 98–9)

EASTER 5

Monday

Prayer

JULIAN OF NORWICH

After this our Lord shewed concerning Prayer. In which Shewing I see two conditions in our Lord's signifying: one is rightfulness, another is sure trust.

But yet oftentimes our trust is not full: for we are not sure that God heareth us, as we think because of our unworthiness, and because we feel right nought, (for we are as barren and dry oftentimes after our prayers as we were afore); and this, in our feeling our folly, is cause of our weakness. For thus have I felt in myself.

And all this brought our Lord suddenly to my mind, and shewed these words, and said: *I am Ground of thy beseeching: first it is my will that thou have it; and after, I make thee to will it; and after, I make thee to beseech it and thou beseechest it. How should it then be that thou shouldst not have thy beseeching?*

Beseeching is a true, gracious, lasting will of the soul, oned and fastened into the will of our Lord by the sweet inward work of the Holy Ghost. Our Lord Himself, He is the first receiver of our prayer, as to my sight, and taketh it full thankfully and highly enjoying; and He sendeth it up above and setteth it in the Treasure, where it shall never perish. It is there afore God with all His Holy continually received, ever speeding [the help of] our needs; and when we shall receive our bliss it shall be given us for a degree of joy, with endless worshipful thanking from Him.

From: *Revelations of Divine Love* by Julian of Norwich

Tuesday

Prayer

JULIAN OF NORWICH

And also to prayer belongeth thanking. Thanking is a true inward knowing, with great reverence and lovely dread turning ourselves with all our mights unto the working that our good Lord stirreth us to, enjoying and thanking inwardly. And sometimes, for plenteousness it breaketh out with voice, and saith: *Good Lord, I thank Thee! Blessed mayst Thou be!* And sometime when the heart is dry and feeleth not, or else by temptation of our enemy, – then it is driven by reason and by grace to cry upon our Lord with voice, rehearsing His blessed Passion and His great Goodness; and the virtue of our Lord's word turneth into the soul and quickeneth the heart and entereth it by His grace into true working, and maketh it pray right blissfully. And truly to enjoy our Lord, it is a full blissful thanking in His sight.

From: *Revelations of Divine Love* by Julian of Norwich

Wednesday

Prayer

JULIAN OF NORWICH

For this is our Lord's will, that our prayer and our trust be both alike large. For if we trust not as much as we pray, we do not full worship to our Lord in our prayer, and also we tarry and pain our self. The cause is, as I believe, that we know not truly that our Lord is [the] Ground on whom our prayer springeth; and also that we know not that it is given us by the grace of His love. For if we knew this, it would make us to trust to have, of our Lord's gift, all that we desire. For I am sure that no man asketh mercy and grace with true meaning, but if mercy and grace be first given to him.

But sometimes it cometh to our mind that we have prayed long time, and yet we think to ourselves that we have not our asking. But herefor should we not be in heaviness. For I am sure, by our Lord's signifying, that either we abide a better time, or more grace, or a better gift. He willeth that we have true knowing in Himself that He is Being; and in this knowing He willeth that our understanding be grounded, with all our mights and all our intent and all our meaning; and in this ground He willeth that we take our place and our dwelling, and by the gracious light of Himself He willeth that we have understanding of the things that follow. The first is our noble and excellent making; the second, our precious and dearworthy again-buying; the third, all-thing that He hath made beneath us [He hath made] to serve us, and for our love keepeth it. Then signifieth He thus, as if He said: *Behold and see that I have done all this before thy prayers; and now thou art, and prayerst me.* And thus He signifieth that it belongeth to us to learn that the greatest deeds be [already] done, as Holy Church teacheth; and in the beholding of this, with thanking, we ought to pray for the deed that is now in doing: and that is, that He rule and guide us, to His worship, in this life, and bring us to His bliss. And therefor He hath done all.

From: *Revelations of Divine Love* by Julian of Norwich

Ascension Day

He Came Down From Heaven

CHARLES WILLIAMS

He rose; he manifested; he talked of 'the things pertaining to the kingdom'. He exhibited the actuality of his body, carrying the lovely and adorable matter, with which all souls were everlastingly conjoined, into his eternity. He left one great commandment – satisfy hunger: 'feed the lambs', 'feed the sheep'. Beyond the Petrine law he cast the Johannine – 'if I will that he tarry till I come . . .' but the coming may be from moment to moment and the tarrying from moment to moment. 'Jesus said not unto him, He shall not die; but, If I will that he tarry till I come, what is that to thee?' It is as if, from moment to moment, he withdrew and returned, swifter than lightning, known in one mode and another mode and always new. The new life might still be sequential (in the order of time) but every instant was united to the Origin, and complete and absolute in itself. 'Behold, I come quickly' – the coming and the going one, the going

I

and the coming one, and all is joy. 'It is not for you to know the times and the seasons . . . but you shall be witnesses to me . . . to the uttermost ends of the earth', through all the distances and all the operations of holy matter.

Then, as if it withdrew into the air within the air, and the air became a cloud about its passage, scattering promises of power, the Divine Thing parted and passed.

From: *He Came Down From Heaven* by Charles Williams

(Heinemann, 1938, pp. 81–2)

Friday

Prayer

JULIAN OF NORWICH

Prayer oneth the soul to God. For though the soul be ever like to God in kind and substance, restored by grace, it is often unlike in condition, by sin on man's part. Then is prayer a witness that the soul willeth as God willeth; and it comforteth the conscience and enableth man to grace. And thus He teacheth us to pray, and mightily to trust that we shall have it. For He beholdeth us in love and would make us partners of His good deed, and therefore He stirreth us to pray for that which it pleaseth him to do. For which prayer and good will, that we have of His gift, He will reward us and give us endless meed.

And this was shewed in this word: *And thou beseechest it.* In this word God shewed so great pleasance and so great content, as though He were much beholden to us for every good deed that we do (and yet it is *He* that doeth it) because that we beseech Him mightily to do all things that seem to Him good: as if He said: *What might then please me more than to beseech me, mightily, wisely, and earnestly, to do that thing that I shall do?*

And thus the soul by prayer accordeth to God.

From: *Revelations of Divine Love* by Julian of Norwich

Saturday

Prayer

JULIAN OF NORWICH

And then shall we, with His sweet grace, in our own meek continuant prayer come unto Him now in this life by many privy touchings of sweet spiritual sights and feeling, measured to us as our simpleness may bear it. And this is wrought and shall be, by the grace of the Holy Ghost, so long till we shall die in longing, for love. And then shall we all come into our Lord, our Self clearly knowing, and God fully having; and we shall endlessly be all had in God: Him verily seeing and fully feeling, Him spiritually hearing, and Him delectably in-breathing, and [of] Him sweetly drinking.

And then shall we see God face to face, homely and fully. The creature that is made shall see and endlessly behold God which is the Maker. For thus may no man see God and live after, that is to say, in this deadly life. But when He of His special grace will shew Himself here, He strengtheneth the creature above its self, and He measureth the Shewing, after His own will, as it is profitable for the time.

From: *Revelations of Divine Love* by Julian of Norwich

Monday

The Humanity of God

KARL BARTH

In *Jesus Christ*, as He is attested in Holy Scripture, we are not dealing with man in the abstract: not with the man who is able with his modicum of religion and religious morality to be sufficient unto himself without God and thus himself to be God. But neither are we dealing with *God* in the abstract: not with one who in His deity exists only separated from man, distant and strange and thus a non-human if not indeed an inhuman God. In Jesus Christ there is no isolation of man from God or of God from man. Rather, in Him we encounter the history, the dialogue, in which God and man meet together and are together, the reality of the covenant *mutually* contracted, preserved, and fulfilled by them. Jesus Christ is in His one Person, as true *God, man's* loyal partner, and as true *man, God's*. He is the Lord humbled for communion with man and likewise the Servant exalted to communion with God. He is the Word spoken from the loftiest, most luminous transcendence and likewise the Word heard in the deepest, darkest immanence. He is both, without their being confused but also without their being divided; He is wholly the one and wholly the other. Thus in this oneness Jesus Christ is the Mediator, the Reconciler, between God and man. Thus He comes forward to *man* on behalf of *God* calling for and awakening faith, love, and hope, and to *God* on behalf of *man*, representing man, making satisfaction and interceding. Thus He attests and guarantees to man God's free *grace* and at the same time attests and guarantees to God man's free *gratitude*. Thus He establishes in His Person the justice of God *vis-à-vis* man and also the justice of man before God. Thus He is in His Person the covenant in its fullness, the Kingdom of heaven which is at hand, in which God speaks and man hears, God gives and man receives, God commands and man obeys, God's glory shines in the heights and thence into the depths, and peace on earth comes to pass among men in whom He is well pleased. Moreover, exactly in this way Jesus Christ, as this Mediator and Reconciler between God and man, is also the *Revealer* of them both. We do not need to engage in a free-ranging investigation to seek out and construct who and what God truly is, and who and what man truly is, but only to read the truth about both where it resides, namely, in the fullness of their togetherness, their covenant which proclaims itself in Jesus Christ.

From: *The Humanity of God* by Karl Barth

(Collins Fontana, 1967, pp. 43–4)

Tuesday

The Humanity of God

KARL BARTH

Beyond doubt God's *deity* is the first and fundamental fact that strikes us when we look at the existence of Jesus Christ as attested in the Holy Scripture. And God's deity in Jesus Christ consists in the fact that God Himself in Him is the *subject* who speaks and acts with sovereignty. *He* is the free One in whom all freedom has its ground, its meaning, its prototype. *He* is the initiator, founder, preserver, and fulfiller of the covenant. *He* is the sovereign Lord of the amazing relationship in which He becomes and is not only different from man but also one with him. *He* is also the creator of him who is His partner. *He* it is through whose faithfulness the corresponding faithfulness of His partner is awakened and takes place. The old Reformed Christology worked that out especially clearly in its doctrine of the 'hypostatic union'; God is on the throne. In the existence of Jesus Christ, the fact that God speaks, gives, orders, comes absolutely first – that man hears, receives, obeys, can and must only follow this first act. In Jesus Christ man's freedom is wholly enclosed in the freedom of God. Without the condescension of God there would be no exaltation of man. As the Son of God and not otherwise, Jesus Christ is the Son of Man. This sequence is irreversible. God's independence, omnipotence, and eternity, God's holiness and justice and thus God's deity, in its original and proper form, is the power leading to this effective and visible sequence in the existence of Jesus Christ: superiority preceding subordination. Thus we have here no universal deity capable of being reached conceptually, but this concrete deity – real and recognizable in the *descent* grounded in that sequence and peculiar to the existence of Jesus Christ.

From: *The Humanity of God* by Karl Barth

(Collins Fontana, 1967, pp. 44–5)

Wednesday

The Humanity of God

KARL BARTH

. . . God's high freedom in Jesus Christ is His freedom for *love*. The divine capacity which operates and exhibits itself in that superiority and subordination is manifestly also God's capacity to bend downwards, to attach Himself to another and this other to Himself, to be together with him. This takes place in that irreversible sequence, but in it is completely real. In that sequence there arises and continues in Jesus Christ the highest communion of God with man. God's deity is thus no prison in which He can exist only in and for Himself. It is rather His freedom to be in and for Himself but also with and for us, to assert but also to sacrifice Himself, to be wholly exalted but also completely humble, not only almighty but also almighty mercy, not only Lord but also servant, not only judge but also Himself the judged, not only man's eternal king but also his brother in time. And all that without in the slightest forfeiting His deity! All that, rather, in the highest proof and proclamation of His deity! He who *does* and manifestly *can* do all that, He and no other is the living God. So constituted is His deity, the deity of the God of Abraham, Isaac, and Jacob. In Jesus Christ it is in this way operative and recognizable. If He is the Word of Truth, then the truth of *God* is exactly this and nothing else.

From: *The Humanity of God* by Karl Barth

(Collins Fontana, 1967, pp. 46–7)

Thursday

The Humanity of God

KARL BARTH

It is when we look at Jesus Christ that we know decisively that God's deity does not exclude, but includes His *humanity*. Would that Calvin had energetically pushed ahead on this point in his Christology, his doctrine of God, his teaching about predestination, and then logically also in his ethics! His Geneva would then not have become such a gloomy affair. His letters could then not have contained so much bitterness. It would then not be so easy to play a Heinrich Pestalozzi and, among his contemporaries, a Sebastian Castellio off against him. How could God's deity exclude His humanity, since it is God's freedom for love and thus His capacity to be not only in the heights but also in the depths, not only great but also small, not only in and for Himself but also with another distinct from Him, and to offer Himself to him? In His deity there is enough room for communion with man. Moreover God has and retains in His relation to this other one the unconditioned priority. It is His act. *His* is and remains the first and decisive Word, *His* the initiative, *His* the leadership. How could we see and say it otherwise when we look at Jesus Christ in whom we find man taken up into communion with God? No, God requires no exclusion of humanity, no non-humanity, not to speak of inhumanity, in order to be truly God. But we may and must, however, look further and recognize the fact that actually His deity *encloses humanity in itself*. This is not the fatal Lutheran doctrine of the two natures and their properties. On the contrary, the essential aim of this doctrine is not to be denied at this point but to be adopted. It would be the false deity of a false God if in His deity His humanity did not also immediately encounter us. Such false deities are by Jesus Christ once for all made a laughing stock. In Him the fact is once for all established that God does not exist without man.

From: *The Humanity of God* by Karl Barth

(Collins Fontana, 1967, pp. 46–7)

Friday

The Humanity of God

KARL BARTH

It is not as though God stands in need of another as His partner, and in particular of man, in order to be truly God. 'What is man, that thou art mindful of him, and the son of man that thou dost care for him?' Why should God not also be able, as eternal Love, to be sufficient unto Himself? In His life as Father, Son, and Holy Spirit, He would in truth be no lonesome, no egotistical God even without man, yes, even without the whole created universe. And He must more than ever be not *for* man; He *could* – one even thinks He *must* – be rather against him. But that is the mystery in which He meets us in the existence of Jesus Christ. He wants in His freedom actually not to be without man but *with* him and in the same freedom not against him for *for* him, and that apart from or even counter to what man deserves. He wants in fact to be man's partner, his almighty and compassionate Saviour. He chooses to give man the benefit of His power, which encompasses not only the high and the distant but also the deep and the near, in order to maintain communion with him in the realm guaranteed by His deity. He determines to love him, to be his God, his Lord, his compassionate Preserver and Saviour to eternal life, and to desire his praise and service.

From: *The Humanity of God* by Karl Barth

(Collins Fontana, 1967, pp. 47–8)

Saturday

The Humanity of God

KARL BARTH

In this divinely free volition and election, in this sovereign decision (the ancients said, in His decree), God is *human*. His free affirmation of man, His free concern for him, His free substitution for him – this is God's humanity. We recognize it exactly at the point where we also first recognize His deity. Is it not true that in Jesus Christ, as He is attested in the Holy Scripture, genuine deity includes in itself genuine humanity? There is the father who cares for his lost son, the king who does the same for his insolvent debtor, the Samaritan who takes pity on the one who fell among robbers and in his thoroughgoing act of compassion cares for him in a fashion as unexpected as it is liberal. And this is the act of compassion to which all these parables as parables of the Kingdom of heaven refer. The very One who speaks in these parables takes to His heart the weakness and the perversity, the helplessness and the misery of the human race surrounding Him. He does not despise men, but in an inconceivable manner esteems them highly just as they are, takes them into His heart and sets Himself in their place. He perceives that the superior will of God, to which He wholly subordinates Himself, requires that

He sacrifice Himself for the human race, and seeks His honour in doing this. In the mirror of this humanity of Jesus Christ the humanity of God enclosed in His deity reveals itself. Thus God is as He is. Thus He affirms man. Thus He is concerned about him. Thus He stands up for him. The God of Schleiermacher cannot show mercy. The God of Abraham, Isaac, and Jacob can and does. If Jesus Christ is the Word of Truth, the 'mirror of the fatherly heart of God', then Nietzsche's statement that man is something that must be overcome is an impudent lie. Then the truth of God is, as Titus 3:4 says, His loving-kindness and nothing else.

From: *The Humanity of God* by Karl Barth

(Collins Fontana, 1967, pp. 48–9)

WHITSUNDAY

Monday

The Holy Spirit and Inspiration

CHARLES GORE

Of the work of the Holy Spirit in the Church we may note four characteristics.

1. It is *social*. It treats man as a 'social being', who cannot realize himself in isolation. For no other reason than because grace is the restoration of nature, the true, the redeemed humanity, is presented to us as a society or Church. This is apparent with reference to either of the gifts which summarize the essence of the Church's life, grace, or truth. Sacraments are the ordained instruments of grace, and sacraments are in one of their aspects *social* ceremonies – of incorporation, or restoration, or bestowal of authority, or fraternal sharing of the bread of life. They presuppose a social organization. Those who have attempted to explain why there should be in the Church an apostolic succession of ministers, have seen the grounds of such appointment in the necessity for preserving in a catholic society, which lacks the natural links of race or language or common habitation, a visible and obligatory bond of association.

The same fact appears in reference to the truth, the knowledge of God and of the true nature and needs of man, which constitutes one main part of the Christian life. That too is no mere individual illumination. It is 'a rule of faith', an 'apostolic tradition', 'a pattern of sound words', embodied in Holy Scripture and perpetuated in a teaching Church, within the scope of which each individual is to be brought to have his mind and conscience fashioned by it, normally from earliest years. It would be going beyond the province of this essay to stop to prove that from the beginnings of the Christian life, a man was understood to become a Christian and receive the benefits of redemption, by no other means than incorporation into the Christian society.

From: *Lux Mundi* edited by Charles Gore

(John Murray, 1889, pp. 322–3)

Tuesday

The Holy Spirit and Inspiration

CHARLES GORE

. . . *The Spirit nourishes individuality.* The very idea of the Spirit's
gift is that of an intenser life. Intenser life is more individualized life,
for our life becomes richer and fuller only by the intensification of
personality and character. Thus Christianity has always trusted to
strongly marked character as the means by which religion is propa-
gated. It does not advance as an abstract doctrine, but by the subtle,
penetrating influences of personality. It is the illuminated man who
becomes a centre of illumination. 'As clear transparent bodies if a
ray of light fall on them become radiant themselves and diffuse their
splendour all around, so souls illuminated by the indwelling Spirit
are rendered spiritual themselves and impart their grace to others.'
Thus, from the first, Christianity has tended to intensify individual
life in a thousand ways, and has gloried in the varieties of disposition
and character which the full life of the Spirit develops. The Church
expects to see the same variety of life in herself as she witnesses in
Nature.

'One and the same rain', says St. Cyril of Jerusalem to his cate-
chumens, 'comes down upon all the world, yet it becomes white in
the lily, and red in the rose, and purple in the violets and pansies,
and different and various in all the several kinds; it is one thing in
the palm tree and another in the vine, and all in all things. In itself,
indeed, it is uniform and changes not, but by adapting itself to the
nature of each thing that receives it, it becomes what is appropriate to
each. Thus also the Holy Ghost, one and uniform and undivided in
Himself, distributes His grace to every man as He wills. He employs the
tongue of one man for wisdom; the soul of another He enlightens by
prophecy; to another He gives power to drive away devils; to another
He gives to interpret the Divine Scriptures; He invigorates one man's
self-command; He teaches another the way to give alms; another He
teaches to fast and train himself; another He trains for martyrdom;
diverse to different men, yet not diverse from Himself.'

Nor was this belief in the differences of the Spirit's work a mere
abstract theory. In fact the Church life of the early centuries did
present an aspect of great variety: not only in the dispositions of
individuals, for that will always be observable where human nature

is allowed to subsist, but in the types of life and thought cultivated in different parts of the Church. Early in the life of Christianity did something like the Roman type of Catholicism shew itself, but it shewed itself as one among several types of ecclesiasticism, easily distinguishable from what Alexandria or Africa or Antioch nourished and produced.

From: *Lux Mundi* edited by Charles Gore

(John Murray, 1889, pp. 323–4)

Wednesday

The Holy Spirit and Inspiration

CHARLES GORE

What is true in the life of religion as a whole is true in the department of the intellect. Here again the authority of the collective society, the 'rule of faith', is meant to nourish and quicken, not to crush, individuality. Each individual Christian owes the profoundest deference to the common tradition. Thus to 'keep the traditions' is at all times, and not least in Scripture, a common Christian exhortation. But this common tradition is not meant to be a merely external law. It is meant to pass by the ordinary processes of education into the individual consciousness, and there, because it represents truth, to impart freedom. Thus St. Paul speaks of the developed Christian, 'the man who is spiritual', as 'judging all things and himself judged of none'. And St. John makes the ground of Christian certainty to lie not in an external authority, but in a personal gift: 'ye have an unction from the Holy One and ye know all things'; 'ye need not that any one teach you'. There is then an individual 'inspiration', as well as an inspiration of the whole body, only this inspiration is not barely individual or separatist. As it proceeds out of the society, so it ends in it. It ends by making each person more individualized, more developed in personal characteristics, but for that very reason more conscious of his own incompleteness, more ready to recognize himself as only one member of the perfect Manhood.

From: *Lux Mundi* edited by Charles Gore

(John Murray, 1889, p. 324)

Thursday

The Holy Spirit and Inspiration

CHARLES GORE

3. Thirdly, the Spirit claims for His own, and *consecrates the whole of nature*. One Spirit was the original author of all that is; and all that exists is in its essence very good. It is only sin which has produced the appearance of antagonism between the Divine operation and human freedom, or between the spiritual and the material. Thus the humanity of Christ, which is the Spirit's perfect work, exhibits in its perfection how every faculty of human nature, spiritual and physical, is enriched and vitalized, not annihilated, by the closest conceivable interaction of the Divine Energy. This principle, as carried out in the Church, occupies a prominent place in the earliest theology; in part because Montanism, with its pagan idea of inspiration, as an ecstasy which deprived its subject of reason, gave the Church an opportunity of emphasizing that the fullest action of the Spirit, in the case of her inspired men, intensified and did not supersede their own thought, judgment, and individuality; still more because Gnostic dualism, turning every antithesis of nature and grace, of spirit and flesh, of natural and supernatural, into an antagonism, forced upon the Church the assertion of her own true and comprehensive Creed. That everything in Christianity is realized 'in flesh as in spirit' is the constantly reiterated cry of St. Ignatius, who of all men was most 'spiritual'. That the spiritual is not the immaterial, that we become spiritual not by any change or curtailment of nature, not by any depreciation or ignoring of the body, is the constantly asserted principle of St. Irenaeus. And the earliest writers in general emphasize the visible organization of the Church, and the institution of external sacraments, as negations of the false principle which would sunder nature from God, and repudiate the unity of the material and the spiritual which the Word had been made Flesh in order to reveal and to perpetuate.

From: *Lux Mundi* edited by Charles Gore

(John Murray, 1889, pp. 327–8)

Friday

The Holy Spirit and Inspiration

CHARLES GORE

It is because of this gradualness of the Spirit's method that it lays so great a strain on human patience. The spiritually-minded of all ages have tended to find the visible Church a very troubled and imperfect home. Most startling disclosures of the actual state of ecclesiastical disorder and moral collapse, may be gathered out of the Christian Fathers. Thus to found a 'pure Church' has been the instinct of impatient zeal since Tertullian's day. But the instinct has to be restrained, the visible Church has to be borne with, because it is the Spirit's purpose to provide a home for the training and improvement of the imperfect. 'Let both grow together unto the harvest.' 'A bruised reed will He not break, and smoking flax will He not quench.' The Church must have her terms of communion, moral and intellectual: this is essential to keep her fundamental principles intact, and to prevent her betraying her secret springs of strength and recovery. But short of this necessity she is tolerant. It is her note to be tolerant, morally and theologically. She is the mother, not the magistrate. No doubt her balanced duty is one difficult to fulfil. At times she has been puritanical, at others morally lax; at times doctrinally lax, at others rigid. But, however well or ill she has fulfilled the obligations laid on her, this is her ideal. She is the guardian, the depository of a great gift, a mighty presence, which in its essence is unchanging and perfect, but is realized very imperfectly in her experience and manifested life. This is what St. Thomas Aquinas means when he says 'that to believe in the Church is only possible if we mean by it to believe in the Spirit vivifying the Church'. The true self of the Church is the Holy Spirit, but a great deal in the Church at any date does not belong to her true self, and is obscuring the Spirit's mind. Thus the treasure is in earthen vessels, it is sometimes a light hid under a bushel; and the Church is the probation of faith, as well as its encouragement.

From: *Lux Mundi* edited by Charles Gore

(John Murray, 1889, pp. 331–2)

Saturday

The Holy Spirit and Inspiration

CHARLES GORE

It will not be out of place to conclude this review of the Spirit's method in the Church by calling attention to the emphasis which, from the first, Christians laid upon the fact that the animating principle both of their individual lives and of their society as a whole, was nothing less than the Holy Spirit Himself. To know Him was (as against all the philosophical schools, and in a sense in which the same could not be said even of the Divine Word) their peculiar privilege, to possess Him their summary characteristic. Under the old covenant, and in all the various avenues of approach to the Church, men could be the subjects of the Spirit's guidance and could be receiving gifts from Him; but the 'initiated' Christian, baptized and confirmed, possessed not merely His gifts, but Himself. He is in the Church, as the 'Vicar of Christ', in Whose presence Christ Himself is with them. He is the consecrator of every sacrament, and the substance of His own sacramental gifts. The services of ordained men indeed are required for the administration of sacraments, but as ministers simply of a Power higher than themselves, of a Personal Spirit Who indeed is invoked by their ministry, and pledges Himself to respond to their invocations, but never subjects Himself to their power. Therefore, the unworthiness of the minister diminishes in no way the efficacy of the sacrament, or the reality of the gift given, because the ministry of men neither creates the gift nor adds to or diminishes its force. He is the giver of the gift, and the gift He gives is the same to all. Only the meagreness of human faith and love restrains the largeness of His bounty and conditions the Thing received by the narrowness and variability of the faculty which receives it. According to our faith is it done to us, and where there is no faith and no love there the grace is equally, in St. Augustine's phrase, present and profitless.

From: *Lux Mundi* edited by Charles Gore

(John Murray, 1889, pp. 332–3)

TRINITY SUNDAY

Monday

Trinitarian Religion

The doctrine of the Trinity is the statement of the doctrine of God implied by the Christian life, and the Christian life was a new thing brought into the history of this world by Jesus Christ as He took His followers to share in His divine sonship and reproduced in them that way of life which had been His upon earth. Trinitarian theology is thus the interpretation of trinitarian religion. Religion and theology act and react upon each other. We do not really believe the creed, we only pay it lip-service, so long as it makes no difference to the way we worship and live. Conversely, the theology has no meaning for us unless it interprets our living religion.

If I am not mistaken the doctrine of the Trinity suffers more than other central doctrines of the Christian creed from not being thus closely related to the practice of the Christian religion. This need not be so. Dr. Albert Mansbridge, for example, in his autobiography *The Trodden Road*, has written:

'This is the Christian faith revealed to me by those who have borne witness to it, and responded to by me in the power of my own spirit. It is mysterious, but the doctrine of the Trinity in Unity of God meets the needs of human nature – God above, God incarnate, God inspiring. The whole being vibrates to its truth. Those who accept, or who are proceeding to the acceptance of its truth, are in the blessed company of all faithful people, and are immunized from capture by the spirits of evil – Satan and his angels – although they may be sore let and hindered, even injured, in their bodies and minds.'

That is well said. But how many Christians today, when trying to speak of the faith by which they live, would select the doctrine of the Trinity as that to whose truth their whole being vibrates? How many laymen would not rather regard it as an unintelligible metaphysical doctrine which orthodoxy requires them to profess, but which has no direct relevance to their life or their prayers? How many clergy, as Trinity Sunday draws near, groan within themselves at the thought that it will be their duty to try to expound this dry and abstract doctrine to congregations for whom they anticipate that it will have but little interest? It will indeed be of little interest so long as for the preacher it is a dry and abstract doctrine, so long as for the congregation the sermon is not an interpretation of the religion which its members are practising.

Our efforts to teach the doctrine will always, I am convinced, be futile so long as we try to teach it as an intellectual truth without having prepared the ground by teaching our hearers to live a trinitarian religion. Only when we are speaking to men and women who are living trinitarian lives shall we be able, by 'speaking to their condition', to kindle their interest in our exposition of the doctrine. Our first task, therefore, must be to consider how to teach trinitarian religion, how to initiate our congregations into the trinitarian way of life.

From: *The Doctrine of the Trinity* by Leonard Hodgson

(James Nisbet, 1960, pp. 176–7)

Tuesday

Trinitarian Religion

LEONARD HODGSON

What is needed in the first instance is not so much a matter of the intellect as of the imagination, practice in the maintaining of a certain attitude towards life. In my second lecture I referred to the experience of many a parish priest who has known members of his flock fall away to find their spiritual home in some sect which teaches them to live as those who are seeking to express the divine spark within them. Often, in such cases, they greet one with a new light in their eyes, as men and women who have found the religion that really grips and helps them. I then suggested that the reason of their falling away may be that they go to seek the help they need in the home of false theology because it has not been offered to them in the home of true.

This suggests the starting-point. We may begin by practising ourselves, and teaching and encouraging others to practise themselves, in living as men and women who have been adopted to share in Jesus Christ's relationship to the Father in Heaven and to the Father's world, in the Spirit. The formula for the Christian life is seeking, finding and doing the Father's will in the Father's world with the companionship of the Son by the guidance and strength of the Spirit. That is the meaning of our membership of the Church. This adoption was not of our own doing. It was the act of God, who reached out through His Church and baptized us into the fellowship. Just as in virtue of our physical birth many things are true of us of which we are quite unaware, and we grow in grasping what is already true of us by growing in the life which that birth has given us, so it is with our re-birth through water and the Spirit. The Church in its teaching can tell me about this act of God, about 'my Baptism; wherein I was made a member of Christ, the child of God, and an inheritor of the kingdom of heaven'. I have to make that truth my own by practising myself in living by it, until the lesson which was taught to my intellect takes possession of my whole being and becomes, as we might say, my second nature. I must cure myself of any tendency I may have to live as though I were myself the self-contained centre of my world, seeking to reconcile my earthly interests with my duty to the God who is a mysterious threeness in oneness above the skies. I must practise myself in substituting for this the attitude of one who is trying by the guidance of the Spirit to see the world as Christ sees it, that is, to see it as our heavenly Father's world, in which our Father's work is waiting to be found and done by those whose eyes are opened to find it.

From: *The Doctrine of the Trinity* by Leonard Hodgson

(James Nisbet, 1960, pp. 178–9)

Wednesday

Trinitarian Religion

LEONARD HODGSON

The best place to begin to practise [Trinitarian religion] is in our prayers. As we kneel to pray, we pause to recollect who we are and what we are doing. Moved by the Holy Spirit we are coming into the presence of our heavenly Father, brought in by the Lord Jesus whom we adore and worship as He takes us by the hand and presents us to our Father. We have turned aside out of the world. But as 'we offer ourselves, our souls and bodies', we bring with us all our worldly interests, for they are His interests – or should be. We offer our sins that they may be forgiven; we offer the interests He cannot share that He may wean us from them; we offer our thanks for the victories and ¹oys that He has given us, our petitions and intercessions for all those people, causes and things with which He wills us to be concerned. And as we rise to return to our life and work in the world, we look out in our mind's eye beyond the wall of the room or church where we may be, we look out into all the world around as those who are being sent forth, united with Christ and enlightened by the Spirit, in order that we may share God's joy in all that is good and true and beautiful, His grief at all that is ugly and base and sinful, His labour in overcoming the evil and building up the good.

There is nothing that sounds new in all this – and yet to many of us it may be something quite new if we are clearly and consciously realizing our distinct relationship to each person of the Blessed Trinity. We may sometimes address ourselves to the Spirit or to the Son as well as to the Father, for each is a He, none is an it. But we shall not be confusedly addressing ourselves sometimes to One and sometimes to Another without knowing when or why. We shall speak to the Spirit as to the Lord who moves and inspires us and unites us to the Son; we shall speak to the Son as to our Redeemer who has taken us to share in His sonship, in union with whom we are united to His Father and may address Him as our Father. We shall be entering into the meaning of that old English saying, 'God encompasseth us'.

From: *The Doctrine of the Trinity* by Leonard Hodgson

(James Nisbet, 1960, pp. 179–80)

Thursday

Trinitarian Religion

LEONARD HODGSON

It has been said, I forget (if I ever knew) by whom, that holding the true Christian doctrine of God is like walking along a razor's edge, carefully avoiding slipping off into the error of tritheism on the one side or into that of unitarianism on the other. This is a deplorable metaphor, suggesting as it does that orthodox Christianity is a matter of timidity and caution, forgetting that 'God hath not given us the spirit of fear; but of power, and of love, and of a sound mind'.

In the fourth lecture we remembered that in this world of space and time we have direct experience of ultimate unities only in their multiplicity; our experience of the multiplicity leads us to believe in the unity by an act of rational faith. It is one of the conditions of our life here on earth that in our religion God makes Himself known to us not directly in His unity, but in His several Persons. It is better that we should enrich our spiritual life by exploring to the full the possibilities of our threefold relationship to Him than that for fear of tritheism we should impoverish it and never enter fully into the heritage of our Christian revelation. The more progress we make as men who in their earthly thoughts and words and deeds acknowledge the Trinity, the more we shall find ourselves drawn on to worship the Unity.

Among other things, we need to remember a practical application of the fact that in the case of the Holy Spirit we speak of 'possession' rather than 'communion'. We need to remember that there is no inconsistency in believing both that it is often our duty to throw our whole self into what we are doing, and also to believe that in our doing of it we are guided and inspired by the Holy Spirit. Let me explain this by giving an instance of the kind of thing I mean. As I listen to sermons, I am impressed by the fact that over and over again preaching fails in effectiveness not because of defects in the preparation of the subject-matter, but because the preacher is not putting his whole self into the delivery of his message. One recognizes that the material is good, well and carefully thought out and put together. But it fails to catch fire and kindle answering sparks in the congregation because its utterance gives the impression of being the performance of a routine duty. It has been a great help to me personally to realize that what I have to pray for to the Holy Spirit, as I kneel before entering the pulpit, is that for the next twenty minutes or so I may be enabled to forget everything except this message and this congregation, and to put my whole self into bringing it home to them. Then, when I am in the pulpit, the time for prayer is past, the time for action has come. So too it is with all our activities. The gift of the Spirit for which we need to pray is the gift of concentration. The fruit of the Spirit is to be found in our power to bring our whole mind to bear upon the matter in hand.

From: *The Doctrine of the Trinity* by Leonard Hodgson

(James Nisbet, 1960, pp. 180–1)

Friday

Trinitarian Religion

LEONARD HODGSON

If in the ways I have indicated we exercise ourselves in the practice of trinitarian religion and in living trinitarian lives, and lead our congregation along these paths, then both we and they will be interested in the exploration and exposition of trinitarian theology, for it will be interpreting and illuminating the religion by which we live and the lives we are living. But if we try to think or speak of it except on the basis of such prayer and action both we and they will find it a jejune weaving of abstractions, for we shall be thinking and speaking of truths which, though they may be true, have no apparent relevance either to religion or to life.

A further point must be mentioned, a point of intellectual as well as practical interest, before we leave this subject. I have spoken of our sonship of the Father and our possession by the Spirit as privileges of the Christian consequent upon his adoption into membership of the body of Christ. How are these related to the universal fatherhood of God, and the activity of the Spirit inspiring the prophets of the Old Testament, the philosophers of Greece, and many another man and woman outside the borders of the Christian Church?

Here, as elsewhere, we have suffered too much from *a priori* methods of argument. If we follow the empirical method to which I have tried to be faithful in these lectures, our scrutiny of the New Testament evidence compels us to recognize that the coming of Jesus Christ did initiate a way of life among men which was the life of a community sharing His sonship and His mode of possession by the spirit. This was a new thing in history. To the evidence for it which was given in the second lecture I need now only add that when the author of the Fourth Gospel wrote 'The Holy Ghost was not yet given; because that Jesus was not yet glorified',[1] he was stating simply and straightforwardly a historical fact. The new life, the life in the Spirit, had not begun for any of the disciples before Pentecost, any more than St. Paul's new life in the Spirit had begun before he was made a new creature by his conversion on the road to Damascus and his baptism by Ananias. It was through the one Lord, the one

[1] John 7:39.

faith and the one baptism that Christians entered into their sonship of the one God and Father of us all.

From: *The Doctrine of the Trinity* by Leonard Hodgson

(James Nisbet, 1960, pp. 181–3)

Saturday

Religion

F. VON HÜGEL

Religion in proportion to its depth and self-knowledge, is never a means, is always an end, *the* end.

Religion, in proportion to its genuine religiousness, always affirms more and other than laws of the mind or impressions of the soul. It ever affirms Reality, a Reality, *the* Reality distinct from ourselves, the self-subsistent Spirit, God. It is, essentially, affirmation of Fact, of what *is*, what aboriginally, supremely *is*. It is, in this sense and degree, ontological, metaphysical: it is this, or it is nothing.

Religion presupposes, and reveals, man as inevitably moved by, and in travail with, this sense of, and thirst after truth, *the* truth, reality, *the* Reality. Man cannot renounce this sense and thirst as an illusion; the very dignity and passion that accompany or foster, at any time, his declaration of such illusion, ever imply such ontology – that there somehow exists a more than merely human truth and reality, and that man somehow really experiences it.

Religion requires the actuation of *all* man's faculties; it is in relation with *all* the other levels and ranges of man's experience. The sense of Beauty, the sense of Truth, the sense of Goodness – above all, the sense of the inadequacy of all our purely human expressions of them all, and yet that these senses are not vain or merely subjective and simply human: all these finally imply, all are necessary to, all are in relation with, the full and healthy life of religion.

From: *Essays and Addresses* (Second Series) by Baron Friedrich von Hügel

(J. M. Dent & Sons, Ltd., London, 1926, pp. 59–60)

TRINITY 1

Trinitarian Religion

LEONARD HODGSON

Although in this world we only meet the ultimate unities in their multiplicity, and God is revealed to us in His Persons severally, yet the divine unity is implied in this trinitarian revelation, and in it there is revealed to us the pattern for all true unity. As I said in my fourth lecture: 'The Christian doctrine of God . . . asserts that all the actual unities of our earthly experience, from the unity of the hydrogen atom to the unity of a work of art, of the human self, or of a human society, are imperfect instances of what unity truly is. . . . It is through the revelation of God in Christ that we find the unity of God to be of such a kind as to cast light upon all our lesser unities.' I want now to say something of the practical implications of this with regard to the unity of the human self, of political and international unity, and of the unity of the Church.

For this purpose, the essence of the doctrine of the Trinity is the doctrine that true unity is what I have called 'internally constitutive unity', that is to say, a unity which by the intensity of its unifying power unifies distinct elements in the whole. A unity can be deficient *as unity*, it can fail to exhibit perfection of unity, in either or both of two ways: either by failing to maintain its elements in their distinctness, or by failing in its power to unify them, or both.

Most of us know what it is to be torn in different directions by different elements in our personality; we know what the psalmist meant when he wrote 'With the pure thou shalt be pure, and with the froward thou shalt learn frowardness'. In the early morning, it may be, we kneel before God's altar, we are caught up to share in the worship of angels and archangels. We see the tawdriness of the world, the hatefulness of our sins. It is inconceivable that we should ever again be interested in anything except the service of the Lord. Later in the morning we are in the company of scholars, or engaged in scholarly work, and feel, in the words of Harnack, that 'if piety should suffer in the process, well, there was and is a stronger interest than that of piety – namely, that of truth'. The afternoon is occupied with administrative business, and as the fascination of it grips us we feel that the only life worth having would be one spent in ordering the affairs of men. A visit to an art gallery may bring out yet another self, and at tea we may meet a girl who makes us feel that all this world and the next would be well lost for love. As we relax among our friends after dinner, and vie with one another in telling tales and making remarks that will provoke laughter and appreciation, how dull and distant seems the heavenly worship of the early morning compared with the immediate reward of witty remarks, tinged though they may be with malice or impropriety. So, when the day is done, and we look back over it, and see this creature dragged hither and thither by this interest and that, we may well ask 'Which of these things is the real I? Am I really anyone at all?'

From: *The Doctrine of the Trinity* by Leonard Hodgson

(James Nisbet, 1960, pp. 183–4)

Tuesday

Trinitarian Religion

Practising psychologists know well that this problem of unifying the heterogeneous elements in a man's make-up is one of the central problems in human life. There are at least four false ways of dealing with it, ways which lead into their consulting rooms. There may be so complete a failure to unify that the result is the pathological state of divided personality. There may be a less complete and obvious failure, issuing in a sense of frustration at the apparent futility of life. There may be unification round a false or inadequate centre which produces in extreme forms monomaniacs, and in less degrees fanatics of various kinds. There may also be unification around the true centre achieved by suppressing or repressing elements which take their revenge in neurotic conditions.

But the true pattern of unity for men who are made in the image of God is one in which there is a place for all our different selves, so far as they are good selves, a unity in which each is to remain its own self in order that it may play its part in enriching the whole. The scholarly self with its passion for truth, the self which falls in love, the sociable self which enjoys good company, the self which is drawn by music, drama, painting or literature, all these and others, together with the self which aspires after the worship of heaven, have their value and their place.

We are, however, finite. Life is not long enough for each of us to give full expression to all his many selves. The love which is to unify them has therefore to take the form of recognizing the value of those which cannot be indulged. They are not to be suppressed or repressed as evil; they are to be offered in willing surrender to God because He wills us to give precedence to some other self as the centre of the particular work that he has for us to do on earth. The man who is called to be a scholar must curb his desire to engage in manifold practical activities. If for a while he has to go and be a soldier, he must put aside his civilian pursuits. If he is called to work in which marriage is impossible, he must be continent with a good grace. But he will only do any of these things with a good grace if he maintains a gracious attitude towards the selves he cannot satisfy, if he avoids the temptation to seal up the doors of his mind against the interests he cannot pursue and lets a love for them fertilize and enrich, without distracting, the self which is to be the centre of his life.

From: *The Doctrine of the Trinity* by Leonard Hodgson

(James Nisbet, 1960, pp. 184–5)

Wednesday

Trinitarian Religion

LEONARD HODGSON

This graciousness cannot be achieved by man except by the grace of God. Our natural pride makes us disinclined to acknowledge that we are finite beings who cannot foster all kinds of good; it inclines us to justify our self-limitation by holding that we have chosen what is better and renounced what is worse. So long as we are trusting in our own strength, our natural weakness requires us to buttress our self-denial by building up a sentiment of reprobation or scorn towards the interests we have renounced. Thus the achievement of a false unity in our own lives makes us incapable of taking a further step in graciousness, and appreciating the contributions which others can make to human life, just because they are different from our own. It may be that they are called to put in the centre selves which we have to put on one side. It may be that they can express selves which we do not seem to have in us at all, which may indeed even be uncongenial to our tastes.

For want of this graciousness we are a divided and distracted world. The business man despises the artist, and the artist returns the scorn with interest. The scientist thinks that the classic wastes his time among dead languages, the classic thinks that the scientist is blind and deaf to the higher ranges of human culture. White men, red men, yellow men and black men dislike one another for not being like themselves. Mutual appreciation between Jews and Gentiles, between Nordics and Latins, between Englishmen, Frenchmen, Germans, Slavs and Greeks, Turks and Bulgars, is hard to come by. Within Christ's Church protestants and catholics, Lutherans and Calvinists, Thomists, Barthians, liberals and modernists have this in common, that each wants to make the others as like to himself as possible and finds it difficult to join in worship otherwise.

It does not seem to be natural to men to appreciate other kinds of people because they are different, to want them to remain different while prospering equally. This well-spring of mutual antagonism in our hearts is the mark of the defacing of the image of God in us. The doctrine of the Trinity reminds us that though the capacity to love may not be in human nature as we have it, it is the essence of God's nature. What is Christianity, if it be not the message that God has entered into the history of this world for the purpose of restoring the image, of re-making our human nature after the pattern of the divine, of changing us beyond our capacity to change ourselves?

Thus the doctrine of the Trinity is directly relevant to all our endeavours to promote the peace and unity of mankind. For the unity of different types of churchmanship within the Church, for the unity of different groups and classes within a nation, for the unity of different nations within the commonwealth of mankind, we need to look to the pattern of unity which has been shown us in the Divine life through the revelation of God in Christ. We need to pray that the Church, by contemplating the unity of the divine Trinity, may find its own true unity and thus be able to lead the groups, classes, races and nations of mankind into that peace and unity which is God's will for them.

From: *The Doctrine of the Trinity* by Leonard Hodgson

(James Nisbet, 1960, pp. 185–7)

Trinitarian Religion

LEONARD HODGSON

When a Christian declares his belief in the resurrection of the body he is asserting, among other things, that in the life of the world to come each of us shall retain his individual personality, able to recognize and be recognized by his fellows. The connection between this belief and the doctrine of the Trinity was first brought home to me some fifteen years ago in conversation with an Indian philosopher. We were discussing the question of immortality, and he was maintaining the view that our destiny, if and when we shall ever be perfected, will be an absorption into the being of God in which we shall at last be rid of our individual self-consciousness. As the conversation proceeded, it became clear that this belief was implied by and deduced from his conception of the unity of God. Since for him the unity of God was the perfection of what I have earlier called the mathematical type of unity, a unity characterized by the absence of all internal distinctions, he had to believe that the incorporation of a man into that unity would involve the loss of his individual selfhood.

The conversation well illustrates a point that I made in my fourth lecture, that acceptance of the doctrine of the Trinity requires a revision of the idea of unity. The Indian's expectations with regard to the future life were not dictated by his religion but by his philosophy. Since the only reasonable form of theism is monotheism, he argued, and since unity is the complete absence of internal multiplicity, union with God must mean absorption into that undifferentiated unity. Given the premises, the conclusion must follow. The only way to dispute the conclusion was to attack the premises.

I have argued that scrutiny of the empirical evidence provided by the historical facts of the Christian revelation necessitates a revision of that idea of unity as applied to God. My present purpose is to exhibit the logical connection between the Christian doctrines of the Trinity and of immortality.

This connection is implied in the prayer ascribed to our Lord in St John 17, verses 20–24:

'That they may be one, even as we are one.' These words point to the connection between the two doctrines. It is as members of Christ, sharing in the immortality that is His by nature and ours by adoption and grace, that we look forward to life beyond the grave. Because for us the unity of God, which is the archetype and pattern of all true unity, is a life in which the divine love eternally unites and yet keeps distinct the Persons of the Trinity, therefore we, when we are taken up to share in that life, may hope each to be united with God, and with his fellows in God, in a life of love which shall preserve eternally our personal distinctness. Through countless ages, by means of our bodily life in space and time, God our Creator has been fashioning us into uniquely individualized personalities. This creation is no transient illusion, or mere appearance, as certain monistic and pantheistic theologies would have us think. God has given to this world such reality that He has Himself entered into its history, in order that He may fulfil His creative purpose by redeeming the souls that He is creating for union with Himself. And He Himself is such that that creative purpose can be fulfilled, as He takes those created souls to be one while remaining many in the unity of the Blessed Trinity.

From: *The Doctrine of the Trinity* by Leonard Hodgson

(James Nisbet, 1960, pp. 187–9)

Friday

Trinitarian Religion

LEONARD HODGSON

In his Gifford Lectures on *God and Personality* Dr. C. C. J. Webb argued that the idea of personality implies a plurality of persons. We cannot think of any life as truly personal unless it be a life of intercourse between persons. If, therefore, we are to think of God as unipersonal, we must think of Him as eternally related to some object of His personal attention. For this reason the idea of creation as the eternal object of God's personal love and care has always been congenial to unitarian theology. But the doctrine of creation, in orthodox Christianity, asserts that the created universe is not necessary to the being of God. It is entirely dependent upon God for its being, but God has no need of it in order to be entirely Himself in all the full richness of His Godhead.

The doctrine of the Trinity implies that in the eternal being of God, quite apart from creation, there exist all the elements necessary for a fully personal life. It enables us to believe that the life of God is essentially and eternally personal without denying the implications of the doctrine of creation. Taken together, the doctrines of the Trinity and of creation expressly forbid us to assert that this whole vast universe, let alone this world and the life of man upon it, are the centre of interest in the life of God. . . .

But this does not imply any diminution in our estimate of God's love and care for this world and for man. It is here that we must avoid being led astray by any confusion between physical and spiritual greatness. When we are dealing with the latter, inability to be fully cognizant of and concerned with details is a mark, not of greatness, but of the reverse. The fact that the general manager of a large railway company cannot be intimately concerned with the personal life of every least employee is due to his human finiteness and limitation, not to his greatness. God does not need this universe in order to be Himself. But, having created it, He knows its every detail, and gives to each that love and care which it needs in order that His purpose for it may be fulfilled. The gospel of His revelation of Himself in Christ is the proclamation of the depth of His love for us men. 'God so loved the world that He gave His only begotten Son.' 'What is man, that thou art mindful of him? . . . We see Jesus, who was made a little lower than the angels for the suffering of death, crowned with glory and honour; that he by the grace of God should taste death for every man. . . . For verily . . . he took on him the seed of Abraham.'[1]

The doctrine of the Trinity thus enables us to keep the right proportion in our faith, to acknowledge with humble gratitude God's infinite love for man and also to adore Him in the glory and perfection of His own being:

'For God has other Words for other worlds,
But for this world, the Word of God is Christ.'[2]

From: *The Doctrine of the Trinity* by Leonard Hodgson

(James Nisbet, 1960, pp. 190–1)

[1] John 3:16; Hebrews 2.
[2] H. E. Hamilton King: *The Sermon in the Hospital.*

Saturday

On God and Christian Prayer

F. VON HÜGEL

God is, indeed, not all unlike man. For how, if God were all unlike him, could man apprehend God, and love God, and try 'to be perfect even as our heavenly Father is perfect'? Yet God is also *other than man*. Other, because He, God, is a Reality, an Identity, a Consciousness, distinct from the reality, identity, consciousness of any of His creatures or of the sum-total of them. And God is other, because this His distinct Reality is, by its nature, so much higher and richer, not only in degree but in kind, than is the nature of man or of any other creature. 'Man is made in the image and likeness of God.' Yes, but we must not press this as an exhaustive norm, as though God were simply man writ large – man's better and best instincts and conditions on an immense scale. We shall doubtless be much nearer the facts if we think of God as the living Source and the always previous, always prevenient Realization, in degrees and ways for us ineffable, of our ideals and ever imperfect achievements – a Realization which must not be taken directly to contain concretely what our conditions and strivings contain ideally. I am deeply convinced that the truth, and hence the fascination of Religion, as really requires some such emphasis on the *unlikeness* of God as it requires emphasis upon the likeness. So, for instance, 'God is Love' is a central truth proclaimed by the New Testament and by all the saints of God. And so again, 'God careth for us' – that God is full of sympathy for all His creatures, and for man especially, Jesus Himself never ceases to proclaim and to illustrate. Yet we must beware not to press this further, so as to mean suffering in God. For suffering is an evil, and there exists no evil in God: the religious instinct spontaneously and unchangeably hungers after God as Pure Joy. With St. Bernard, in his classic lament on the death of his darling twin-brother Gerard, we will hold that there exists the deepest *compassio*, but no *passio* in God.

Yet our hearts long also (though less strongly, I believe) for downright fellow-suffering, when they suffer and when they are exhorted to suffer well. Such fellow-suffering (deeper than ever we ourselves could suffer, and in One Who shares with us the evil of suffering, but without any admixture of the far greater evil of sin) is supplied by the Humanity of Our Lord. The Humanity of Jesus Christ, we have already found, brings temptation as near to God as is compatible with Godhead. And now we find this same Humanity of Jesus brings suffering as near to God as is compatible with the same Godhead. Indeed, the sufferings are so great as to require, for their sustainment by His human nature, the presence and action of the Divine nature, of the Divine Person which has conjoined itself to, and which informs, this human nature.

Our prayer will profit greatly if we thus hold firmly and fervently this double truth: of the *Pure Joy of God* and of the *Deep Suffering of Jesus*. For we will thus neither diminish God to a man of but larger size than we little men are, nor will we dehumanize Jesus by ignoring the immense sufferings, as well as the storm and stress – the temptations – of His earthly life. The definition of the Council of Chalcedon, difficult as it may be to apply it in any great detail, will thus continue to enshrine for us, also as praying souls, an imperishable truth: Jesus Christ is both truly God and truly Man.

From: *Essays and Addresses* (Second Series) by Baron Friedrich von Hügel

(J. M. Dent & Sons, Ltd., London, 1926, pp. 222–3)

TRINITY 2

The Ladder of Perfection

W. HILTON

How Jesus is to be sought, desired and found

Seek then what you have lost, so that you may find it. I am convinced that anyone who could once have a little insight into the spiritual dignity and beauty which belong to the soul by nature, and which it may regain by grace, would loathe and despise all the joy, love, and beauty of the world as he would the stench of corruption. But for the frailty and essential needs of bodily nature, his sole desire night and day would be to long, lament, pray, and seek how he might regain it once more. Nevertheless, since you have not yet seen fully what it is, because the eyes of your soul are not opened, I know well one word in which is found all that you can seek, desire, and find, for in that word is all that you have lost. This word is Jesus. I do not mean this word Jesus as it might be painted on a wall, or written in a book, or spoken by the lips, or pictured inwardly by the workings of your mind, for in these ways a man without charity may find Him. I mean Jesus Christ the blessed One, God and Man, son of the Virgin Mary, whom this name expresses, and Who is all goodness, endless wisdom, love, and sweetness; your joy and your worship, your everlasting happiness, your God, your Lord, and your salvation.

If, then, you feel a great longing in your heart for Jesus – either by the remembrance of His Name Jesus, or of any other word, prayer, or deed – and if this longing is so strong that its force drives out of your heart all other thoughts and desires of the world and the flesh, then you are indeed seeking your Lord Jesus. And if, when you feel this desire for God, for Jesus – for it is all one – you are helped and strengthened by a supernatural might so strong that it is changed into love and affection, spiritual savour and sweetness and knowledge of truth, so that for the time your mind is set on no created thing, nor on any feeling or stirring of vainglory nor self-love nor any other evil affections (for these cannot appear at such a time) so that you are

enclosed in Jesus alone, resting in Him with the warmth of tender
love, then you have found something of Jesus.

From: *The Ladder of Perfection* by Walter Hilton

(Penguin Classics, 1957, pp. 56–7)

Tuesday

The Ladder of Perfection

W. HILTON

How profitable it is to have the desire for Jesus

I would rather feel in my heart a true and pure desire for my Lord
Jesus Christ, although I had very little spiritual knowledge of Him,
than perform all the bodily penances of all men living, or enjoy
visions and revelations of angels, hear sweet sounds, or experience
any other pleasurable outward sensations were they unaccompanied
by this desire. In short, all the joys of heaven and earth would have
no attraction for me unless I might also have this desire for Jesus.
I think that the prophet David felt this when he wrote: Lord, what
have I in heaven but Thee? And what can I desire on earth but Thee?[1]
As though he had said: Lord Jesus, what heavenly joy can satisfy
me, unless I desire Thee while I am on earth, and love Thee when I
come to heaven? Meaning, none indeed! Therefore, if you wish to
have any inward knowledge of Him, whether in body or soul, seek
nothing but an earnest desire for His grace and His merciful presence,
and recognize that your heart can find no satisfaction in anything
outside Him. This was David's desire, when he said: Lord, my soul
longed for the desire of Thy righteousness.[2] Therefore seek desire
by desire, as David did. And if in your prayers and meditations your
desire leads you to feel the inward presence of Jesus Christ in your
soul, hold firmly to it in your heart so that you do not lose it: then if
you should fall, you may soon find Him again.

Therefore seek Jesus whom you have lost. He wishes to be sought,
and longs to be found, for He Himself says: Every one who seeks
shall find.[3] The search is arduous, but the finding is full of joy.
Therefore if you wish to find Him, follow the counsel of the wise

[1] Quid enim mihi est in caelo? et a te quid volui super terram? Ps. lxxiii:23.
[2] Concupivit anima mea desiderare justificationes tuas in omni tempore. Ps.
cxix:20.
[3] Omnis qui quaerit, invenit. Matt. vii:8.

K

man, who said: If you seek wisdom – which is Jesus – like silver and gold, and dig deep for it, you shall find it.[1] You must dig deep in your heart, for He is hidden there, and you must cast out utterly all love and desire of earthly things, and all sorrows and fears with regard to them. In this way you shall find Jesus the true Wisdom.

From: *The Ladder of Perfection* by Walter Hilton

(Penguin Classics, 1957, pp. 58–9)

Wednesday

The Ladder of Perfection

W. HILTON

Where and how Jesus is to be sought and found

Be like the woman in the Gospel, of whom our Lord said: What woman is there who will not light a lamp, and turn her house upside down, and search until she finds it? Implying: none. And when she has found it, she calls her friends to her and says: Rejoice with me, for I have found the coin that I had lost.[2] This coin is Jesus, whom you have lost: if you wish to find Him, light the lamp of God's word. As David says: Lord, Thy word is a lamp to my feet.[3] By this lamp you will see where He is, and how you may find Him. You may light another lamp if you wish, which is your reason, for our Lord says: The light of your body is the eye.[4] Similarly it may be said that the lamp of the soul is the reason, by which the soul may come to see all spiritual things. With this lamp you will certainly find Jesus if you hold it up from underneath the measure. As our Lord says: No one lights a lamp in order to set it under a measure, but on a lampstand,[5] that is to say, your mind must not be engrossed in worldly activities, useless thoughts, and earthly desires, but must

[1] Si quaesieris quasi pecuniam sapientiam, et sicut thesauros effodieris illum: tunc intelliges timorem Domini, et scientiam Dei invenies. Prov. ii:4.

[2] Quae mulier habens drachmas decem, si perdiderit unam, nonne accendit lucernam, et everrit domum suam, et quaerit diligenter donec inveniat eam? Et cum invenerit, convocat amicos suos, cidens: Congratulamini mihi, quia inveni drachmam quam perdideram. Luke xv:8.

[3] Lucerna pedibus meis verbum tuum. Ps. cxix: 105.

[4] Lucerna corporis tui oculus tuus. Matt. vi:22.

[5] Nemo accendit lucernam et ponit eam sub modio, sed super candelabrum. Matt. v:15.

always aspire above all earthly things to the inward vision of Jesus Christ. If you do this, you will see all the dust, dirt, and small blemishes in your house, that is, all the worldly loves and fears within your soul. Yet not all, for as David says: Who may know all his sin?[1] Meaning, no one. Cast out all these sins from your heart, sweep your soul clean with the broom of the fear of God, wash it with your tears, and you shall find your coin, Jesus.

From: *The Ladder of Perfection* by Walter Hilton

(Penguin Classics, 1957, pp. 59–60)

Thursday

The Ladder of Perfection

W. HILTON

Where Jesus is lost, and through His mercy found again

See now the courtesy and mercy of Jesus. You have lost Him. But where? In your own house; that is, in your soul. If you had lost Him outside your own house – that is, if you had lost the power of reason through original sin – you would never have found Him again. But He left you your reason, and so He is within your soul, and will never be lost outside it. Nevertheless you are no nearer to Him until you have found Him. He is within you, although He is lost to you; but you are not in Him until you have found Him. In this, too, is His mercy, that He would suffer Himself to be lost only where He may be found. There is no need to travel to Rome or Jerusalem to search for Him: but turn your thoughts into your own soul where He is hidden, and seek Him there. For as the prophet says: Truly, Lord, Thou art a hidden God.[2] And Christ himself says in the Gospel: The kingdom of heaven is like a treasure hidden in a field, which when a man finds, for joy of it he goes and sells all that he has and buys that field.[3] Jesus is the treasure hidden in your soul. If you could find Him in your soul, and your soul in Him, I am sure that you would gladly give up the love of all earthly things in order to have Him. Jesus

---

[1] Delicta quis intelligit? Ps. xix, 12.

[2] Vere tu es deus absconditus. Isa. xlv:15.

[3] Simile est regnum caelorum thesauro abscondito in agro; quem qui invenit homo, pro gaudio illius vadit, et vendit universa quae habet, et emit agrum illum. Matt. xiii:44.

sleeps spiritually in your heart as he once slept bodily in the ship with His disciples. But they, fearing to perish, awoke Him, and He quickly saved them from the tempest. Therefore rouse Him as they did by prayer, and wake Him with the loud cry of your desire, and He will quickly rise and help you.

From: *The Ladder of Perfection* by Walter Hilton

(Penguin Classics, 1957, p. 61)

Friday

The Ladder of Perfection

W. HILTON

Prepare yourself, therefore, to be clothed with His likeness – that is, in humility and charity which are His livery – and then He will admit you to His friendship and show you His secrets. He Himself said to His disciples: Whoever loves Me shall be loved by My Father, and I will show Myself to him.[1] There is no virtue that you can acquire or work that you can do that will make you like our Lord without humility and charity, for these two are God's especial livery. This is clearly seen in the Gospel, where our Lord speaks of humility: Learn of Me, He says, not to go barefoot, or fast in the desert for forty days, or choose disciples, but learn from Me humility, for I am gentle and humble of heart.[2] And of charity He says: This is My commandment, that you love one another as I have loved you; for in this shall men know you for My disciples.[3] Not because you work miracles, or cast out devils, or preach and teach, but because each of you loves the other in charity. If you will be like Him, be humble and loving. And charity means that you must have a true love for your fellow-Christian.

From: *The Ladder of Perfection* by Walter Hilton

(Penguin Classics, 1957, p. 63)

---

[1] Qui diligit me diligetur a Patre meo, et manifestabo ei meipsum. John xiv: 21.

[2] Discite a me, quia mitis sum et humilis corde.

[3] Hoc est praeceptum meum; ut diligatis invicem sicut dilexi vos. Enim in hoc cognoscent homines qui discipuli mei estis, si dilectionem habueritis ad invicem. John xiii: 34.

Saturday

The Ladder of Perfection

W. HILTON

... When enabled to do so by special grace, the soul feels wonderful love and heavenly joy in the contemplation of [this] truth, for light and love are inseparable in a pure soul. For no love that springs from contemplation brings the soul so close to God as this does; it is the highest and most perfect knowledge of Jesus, God and man, that the light of grace can bring to a soul. Therefore the burning love kindled by this is greater than that kindled by any knowledge of created things, whether material or spiritual.

All this knowledge of God's creation and of God Himself, the Creator and Sustainer of the entire universe, which is infused into a soul by grace as I have mentioned, I call the fair words and communications of God to the soul chosen as His true spouse. He reveals mysteries and often offers rich gifts to it out of His treasury, and adorns the soul with them with great honour. She has no need to be ashamed when she appears before the face of God Her Spouse in the company of her fellows. All this loving and intimate conversation between God and the soul may be called a secret word, of which Holy Scripture says: A secret word is spoken to me, and my ear has caught the low murmur of His voice.[1] ... The inspiration of God is a secret word, for it is hidden from all who love the world, and revealed to those who love Him. It is by this means that a pure soul readily catches the sound of His murmured words, by which He reveals His truth. For each truth revealed by grace, and received with inward delight and joy, is a secret murmur of God in the ear of a pure soul.

From: *The Ladder of Perfection* by Walter Hilton

(Penguin Classics, 1957, pp. 251–2)

---

[1] Job iv:12.

St. Francis of Assisi

G. K. CHESTERTON

Francis of Assisi was slight in figure with that sort of slightness which, combined with so much vivacity, gives the impression of smallness. He was probably taller than he looked; middle-sized, his biographers say; he was certainly very active and, considering what he went through, must have been tolerably tough. He was of the brownish Southern colouring, with a dark beard thin and pointed such as appears in pictures under the hoods of elves; and his eyes glowed with the fire that fretted him night and day. There is something about the description of all he said and did which suggests that, even more than most Italians, he turned naturally to a passionate pantomime of gestures. If this was so it is equally certain that with him, even more than with most Italians, the gestures were all gestures of politeness or hospitality. And both these facts, the vivacity and the courtesy, are the outward signs of something that marks him out very distinctively from many who might appear to be more of his kind than they really are. It is truly said that Francis of Assisi was one of the founders of the medieval drama, and therefore of the modern drama. He was the very reverse of a theatrical person in the selfish sense; but for all that he was pre-eminently a dramatic person. This side of him can best be suggested by taking what is commonly regarded as a reposeful quality; what is commonly described as a love of nature. We are compelled to use the term; and it is entirely the wrong term.

St. Francis was not a lover of nature. Properly understood, a lover of nature was precisely what he was not. The phrase implies accepting the material universe as a vague environment, a sort of sentimental pantheism. In the romantic period of literature, in the age of Byron and Scott, it was easy enough to imagine that a hermit in the ruins of a chapel (preferably by moonlight) might find peace and a mild pleasure in the harmony of solemn forests and silent stars, while he pondered over some scroll or illuminated volume, about the liturgical nature of which the author was a little vague. In short, the hermit might love nature as a background. Now for St. Francis nothing was ever in the background. We might say that his mind had no background, except perhaps that divine darkness out of which the divine love had called up every coloured creature one by one. He saw everything as dramatic, distinct from its setting, not all of a piece like a picture but in action like a play. A bird went by him like an arrow; something with a story and a purpose, though it was a purpose of life and not a purpose of death. A bush could stop him like a brigand; and indeed he was as ready to welcome the brigand as the bush.

From: *St. Francis of Assisi* by G. K. Chesterton

(Hodder & Stoughton, pp. 97–9).

Tuesday

St. Francis of Assisi

G. K. CHESTERTON

We talk about a man who cannot see the wood for the trees. St. Francis was a man who did not want to see the wood for the trees. He wanted to see each tree as a separate and almost a sacred thing, being a child of God and therefore a brother or sister of man. But he did not want to stand against a piece of stage scenery used merely as a background and inscribed in a general fashion: 'Scene; a wood.' In this sense we might say that he was too dramatic for the drama. The scenery would have come to life in his comedies; the walls would really have spoken like Snout the Tinker and the trees would really have come walking to Dunsinane. Everything would have been in the foreground; and in that sense in the footlights. Everything would be in every sense a character. This is the quality in which, as a poet, he is the very opposite of a pantheist. He did not call nature his mother; he called a particular donkey his brother or a particular sparrow his sister. . . . St. Francis was a mystic, but he believed in mysticism and not in mystification. As a mystic he was the mortal enemy of all those mystics who melt away the edges of things and dissolve an entity into its environment. He was a mystic of the daylight and the darkness; but not a mystic of the twilight. He was the very contrary of that sort of oriental visionary who is only a mystic because he is too much of a sceptic to be a materialist. St. Francis was emphatically a realist, using the word realist in its much more real medieval sense. In this matter he really was akin to the best spirit of his age, which had just won its victory over the nominalism of the twelfth century. In this indeed there was something symbolic in the contemporary art and decoration of his period; as in the art of heraldry. The Franciscan birds and beasts were really rather like heraldic birds and beasts; not in the sense of being fabulous animals but in the sense of being treated as if they were facts, clear and positive and unaffected by the illusions of atmosphere and perspective. In that sense he did see a bird sable on a field azure or a sheep argent on a field vert. But the heraldry of humility was richer than the heraldry of pride; for it saw all these things that God had given as something more precious and unique than the blazonry that princes and peers had only given to themselves. Indeed out of the depths of that surrender it rose higher than the highest titles of the feudal age; than the laurel of Caesar or the Iron Crown of Lombardy. It is an example of extremes that meet, that the Little Poor Man, who had stripped himself of everything and named himself as nothing, took the same title that has been the wild vaunt of the vanity of the gorgeous Asiatic autocrat, and called himself the Brother of the Sun and Moon.

From: *St. Francis of Assisi* by G. K. Chesterton

(Hodder & Stoughton, pp. 99–101)

Wednesday

St. Francis of Assisi

G. K. CHESTERTON

This quality, of something outstanding and even startling in things as St. Francis saw them, is here important as illustrating a character in his own life. As he saw all things dramatically, so he himself was always dramatic. We have to assume throughout, needless to say, that he was a poet and can only be understood as a poet. But he had poetic privilege denied to most poets. In that respect indeed he might be called the one happy poet among all the unhappy poets of the world. He was a poet whose whole life was a poem. He was not so much a minstrel merely singing his own songs as a dramatist capable of acting the whole of his own play. The things he said were more imaginative than the things he wrote. The things he did were more imaginative than the things he said. His whole course through life was a series of scenes in which he had a sort of perpetual luck in bringing things to a beautiful crisis. To talk about the art of living has come to sound rather artificial than artistic. But St. Francis did in a definite sense make the very act of living an art, though it was an unpremeditated art. Many of his acts will seem grotesque and puzzling to a rationalistic taste. But they were always acts and not explanations; and they always meant what he meant them to mean. The amazing vividness with which he stamped himself on the memory and imagination of mankind is very largely due to the fact that he was seen again and again under such dramatic conditions. From the moment when he rent his robes and flung them at his father's feet to the moment when he stretched himself in death on the bare earth in the pattern of the cross, his life was made up of these unconscious attitudes and unhesitating gestures.

From: *St. Francis of Assisi* by G. K. Chesterton

(Hodder & Stoughton, pp. 101–2)

Thursday

St. Francis of Assisi

G. K. CHESTERTON

The popular instinct of St. Francis, and his perpetual preoccupation with the idea of brotherhood, will be entirely misunderstood if it is understoood in the sense of what is often called camaraderie; the back-slapping sort of brotherhood. Frequently from the enemies and too frequently from the friends of the democratic ideal, there has come a notion that this note is necessary to that ideal. It is assumed that equality means all men being equally uncivil, whereas it obviously ought to mean all men being equally civil. Such people have forgotten the very meaning and derivation of the word civility, if they do not see that to be uncivil is to be uncivic. But anyhow that was not the quality which Francis of Assisi encouraged; but an equality of the opposite kind; it was a camaraderie actually founded on courtesy.

Even in that fairy borderland of his mere fancies about flowers and animals and even inanimate things, he retained this permanent posture of a sort of deference. A friend of mine said that somebody was the sort of man who apologizes to the cat. St. Francis really would have apologized to the cat. When he was about to preach in a wood full of the chatter of birds, he said, with a gentle gesture 'Little sisters, if you have now had your say, it is time that I also should be heard.' And all the birds were silent; as I for one can very easily believe. In deference to my special design of making matters intelligible to average modernity, I have treated separately the subject of the miraculous powers that St. Francis certainly possessed. But even apart from any miraculous powers, men of that magnetic sort, with that intense interest in animals, often have an extraordinary power over them. St. Francis's power was always exercised with this elaborate politeness. Much of it was doubtless a sort of symbolic joke, a pious pantomime intended to convey the vital distinction in his divine mission, that he not only loved but reverenced God in all his creatures. In this sense he had the air not only of apologizing to the cat or to the birds, but of apologizing to a chair for sitting on it or to a table for sitting down at it. Anyone who had followed him through life merely to laugh at him, as a sort of lovable lunatic, might easily have had an impression as of a lunatic who bowed to every post or took off his hat to every tree. This was all a part of his instinct for imaginative gesture. He taught the world a large part of its lesson by a sort of divine dumb alphabet. But if there was this ceremonial element even in lighter or lesser matters, its significance became far more serious in the serious work of his life, which was an appeal to humanity, or rather to human beings.

From: *St. Francis of Assisi* by G. K. Chesterton

(Hodder & Stoughton, pp. 108–10)

Friday

St. Francis of Assisi

G. K. CHESTERTON

I have said that St. Francis deliberately did not see the wood for the trees. It is even more true that he deliberately did not see the mob for the men. What distinguishes this very genuine democrat from any mere demagogue is that he never either deceived or was

deceived by the illusion of mass-suggestion. Whatever his taste in
monsters, he never saw before him a many-headed beast. He only
saw the image of God multiplied but never monotonous. To him a
man was always a man and did not disappear in a dense crowd any
more than in a desert. He honoured all men; that is, he not only
loved but respected them all. What gave him his extraordinary
personal power was this; that from the Pope to the beggar, from
the sultan of Syria in his pavilion to the ragged robbers crawling
out of the wood, there was never a man who looked into those brown
burning eyes without being certain that Francis Bernardone was
really interested in *him*; in his own inner individual life from the
cradle to the grave; that he himself was being valued and taken
seriously, and not merely added to the spoils of some social policy
or the names in some clerical document. Now for this particular
moral and religious idea there is no external expression except
courtesy. Exhortation does not express it, for it is not mere abstract
enthusiasm; beneficence does not express it, for it is not mere pity. It
can only be conveyed by a certain grand manner which may be called
good manners. We may say if we like that St. Francis, in the bare
and barren simplicity if his life, had clung to one rag of luxury;
the manners of a court. But whereas in a court there is one king and
a hundred courtiers, in this story there was one courtier, moving
among a hundred kings. For he treated the whole mob of men as a
mob of kings. And this was really and truly the only attitude that
will appeal to that part of man to which he wished to appeal. It
cannot be done by giving gold or even bread; for it is a proverb that
any reveller may fling largesse in mere scorn. It cannot even be done
by giving time and attention; for any number of philanthropists and
benevolent bureaucrats do such work with a scorn far more cold and
horrible in their hearts. No plans or proposals or efficient rearrange-
ments will give back to a broken man his self-respect and sense of
speaking with an equal. One gesture will do it.

With that gesture Francis of Assisi moved among men.

From: *St. Francis of Assisi* by G. K. Chesterton

(Hodder & Stoughton, pp. 110–11)

Saturday

St. Francis of Assisi

G. K. CHESTERTON

... St. Francis must be imagined as moving thus swiftly through the world with a sort of impetuous politeness; almost like the movement of a man who stumbles on one knee half in haste and half in obeisance. The eager face under the brown hood was that of a man always going somewhere, as if he followed as well as watched the flight of the birds. And this sense of motion is indeed the meaning of the whole revolution that he made; for the work that has now to be described was of the nature of an earthquake or a volcano, an explosion that drove outwards with dynamic energy the forces stored up by ten centuries in the monastic fortress or arsenal and scattered all its riches recklessly to the ends of the earth. In a better sense than the antithesis commonly conveys, it is true to say that what St. Benedict had stored St. Francis scattered; but in the world of spiritual things what had been stored into the barns like grain was scattered over the world as seed. The servants of God who had been a beseiged garrison became a marching army; the ways of the world were filled as with thunder with the trampling of their feet and far ahead of that ever swelling host went a man singing; as simply he had sung that morning in the winter woods, where he walked alone.

There is undoubtedly a sense in which two is company and three is none; there is also another sense in which three is company and four is none. ... But there is yet another and a different sense in which four is company and three is none; if we use the word company in the vaguer sense of a crowd or a mass. With the fourth man enters the shadow of a mob; the group is no longer one of three individuals only conceived individually. That shadow of the fourth man fell across the little hermitage of the Portiuncula when a man named Egidio, apparently a poor workman, was invited by St. Francis to enter. He mingled without difficulty with the merchant and the canon who had already become the companions of Francis; but with his coming an invisible line was crossed; for it must have been felt by this time that the growth of that small group had become potentially infinite, or at least that its outline had become permanently indefinite. It may have been in the time of that transition that Francis had another of his dreams full of voices; but now the voices were a clamour of the tongues of all nations, Frenchmen and Italians and English and Spanish and Germans, telling of the glory of God each in his own tongue; a new Pentecost and a happier Babel.

From: *St. Francis of Assisi* by G. K. Chesterton

(Hodder & Stoughton, pp. 113–14)

Monday

St. Francis of Assisi

G. K. CHESTERTON

Before describing the first steps he took to regularize the growing group, it is well to have a rough grasp of what he conceived that group to be. He did not call his followers monks; and it is not clear, at this time at least, that he even thought of them as monks. He called them by a name which is generally rendered in English as the Friars Minor; but we shall be much closer to the atmosphere of his own mind if we render it almost literally as The Little Brothers. Presumably he was already resolved, indeed, that they should take the three vows of poverty, chastity and obedience which had always been the mark of a monk. But it would seem that he was not so much afraid of the idea of a monk as of the idea of an abbot. He was afraid that the great spiritual magistracies which had given even to their holiest possessors at least a sort of impersonal and corporate pride, would import an element of pomposity that would spoil his extremely and almost extravagantly simple version of the life of humility. But the supreme difference between his discipline and the discipline of the old monastic system was concerned, of course, with the idea that the monks were to become migratory and almost nomadic instead of stationary. They were to mingle with the world; and to this the more old-fashioned monk would naturally reply by asking how they were to mingle with the world without becoming entangled with the world. It was a much more real question than a loose religiosity is likely to realize; but St. Francis had his answer to it, of his own individual sort; and the interest of the problem is in that highly individual answer.

The good Bishop of Assisi expressed a sort of horror at the hard life which the Little Brothers lived at the Portiuncula, without comforts, without possessions, eating anything they could get and sleeping anyhow on the ground. St. Francis answered him with that curious and almost stunning shrewdness which the unworldly can wield like a club of stone. He said 'If we had any possessions, we should need weapons and laws to defend them.' That sentence is the clue to the whole policy that he pursued. It rested upon a real piece of logic; and about that he was never anything but logical. He was ready to own himself wrong about anything else; but he was quite certain he was right about this particular rule. He was only once seen angry; and that was when there was talk of an exception to the rule.

From: *St. Francis of Assisi* by G. K. Chesterton

(Hodder & Stoughton, pp. 114–15)

Tuesday

St. Francis of Assisi

G. K. CHESTERTON

One distinction between the old monks and the new friars counted especially in the matter of practicality and especially of promptitude. The old fraternities with their fixed habitations and enclosed existence had the limitations of ordinary householders. However simply they lived there must be a certain number of cells or a certain number of beds or at least a certain cubic space for a certain number of brothers; their numbers therefore depended on their land and building material. But since a man could become a Franciscan by merely promising to take his chance of eating berries in a lane or begging a crust from a kitchen, of sleeping under a hedge or sitting patiently on a doorstep, there was no economic reason why there should not be any number of such eccentric enthusiasts within any short period of time. It must also be remembered that the whole of this rapid development was full of a certain kind of democratic optimism that really was part of the personal character of St. Francis. His very asceticism was in one sense the height of optimism. He demanded a great deal of human nature not because he despised it but rather because he trusted it. He was expecting a very great deal from the extraordinary men who followed him; but he was also expecting a good deal from the ordinary men to whom he sent them. He asked the laity for food as confidently as he asked the fraternity for fasting. But he counted on the hospitality of humanity because he really did regard every house as the house of a friend. He really did love and honour ordinary men and ordinary things; indeed we may say that he only sent out the extraordinary men to encourage men to be ordinary.

From: *St. Francis of Assisi* by G. K. Chesterton

(Hodder & Stoughton, pp. 119–20)

Wednesday

St. Francis of Assisi

G. K. CHESTERTON

It was while the little knot of people at the Portiuncula was still small enough to gather in a small room that St. Francis resolved on his first important and even sensational stroke. It is said that there were only twelve Franciscans in the whole world when he decided to march, as it were, on Rome and found a Franciscan order. It would seem that this appeal to remote headquarters was not generally regarded as necessary; possibly something could have been done in a secondary way under the Bishop of Assisi and the local clergy. It would seem even more probable that people thought it somewhat unnecessary to trouble the supreme tribunal of Christendom about what a dozen chance men chose to call themselves. But Francis was obstinate and as it were blind on this point; and his brilliant blindness is exceedingly characteristic of him. A man satisfied with small things, or even in love with small things, he yet never felt quite as we do about the disproportion between small things and large. He never saw things to scale in our sense, but with a dizzy disproportion which makes the mind reel. Sometimes it seems merely out of drawing like a gaily coloured medieval map; and then again it seems to have escaped from everything like a short cut in the fourth dimension. He is said to have made a journey to interview the Emperor, throned among his armies under the eagle of the Holy Roman Empire, to intercede for the lives of certain little birds. He was quite capable of facing fifty emperors to intercede for one bird. He started out with two companions to convert the Mahommedan world. He started out with eleven companions to ask the Pope to make a new monastic world.

From: *St. Francis of Assisi* by G. K. Chesterton

(Hodder & Stoughton, pp. 121–2)

Thursday

St. Francis of Assisi

G. K. CHESTERTON

Innocent III, the great Pope, according to Bonaventura, was walking on the terrace of St. John Lateran, doubtless revolving the great political questions which troubled his reign, when there appeared abruptly before him a person in peasant costume whom he took to be some sort of shepherd. He appears to have got rid of the shepherd with all convenient speed; possibly he formed the opinion that the shepherd was mad. Anyhow he thought no more about it until, says the great Franciscan biographer, he dreamed that night a strange dream. He fancied that he saw the whole huge ancient temple of St. John Lateran, on whose high terraces he had walked so securely, leaning horribly and crooked against the sky as if all its domes and turrets were stooping before an earthquake. Then he looked again and saw that a human figure was holding it up like a living caryatid; and the figure was that of the ragged shepherd or peasant from whom he had turned away on the terrace. Whether this be a fact or a figure it is a very true figure of the abrupt simplicity with which Francis won the attention and the favour of Rome. His first friend seems to have been the Cardinal Giovanni di San Paolo who pleaded for the Franciscan idea before a conclave of Cardinals summoned for the purpose. It is interesting to note that the doubts thrown upon it seem to have been chiefly doubts about whether the rule was not too hard for humanity, for the Catholic Church is always on the watch against excessive asceticism and its evils. Probably they meant, especially when they said it was unduly hard, that it was unduly dangerous. For a certain element that can only be called danger is what marks the innovation as compared with older institutions of the kind. In one sense indeed the friar was almost the opposite of the monk. The value of the old monasticism had been that there was not only an ethical but an economic repose. Out of that repose had come the works for which the world will never be sufficiently grateful, the preservation of the classics, the beginning of the Gothic, the schemes of science and philosophies, the illuminated manuscripts and the coloured glass. The whole point of a monk was that his economic affairs were settled for good; he knew where he would get his supper, though it was a very plain supper. But the whole point of a friar was that he did not know where he would get his supper. There was always a possibility that he might get no supper. There was an element of what would be called romance, as of the gipsy or adventurer. But there was also an element of potential tragedy, as of the tramp or the casual labourer. So the Cardinals of the thirteenth century were filled with compassion, seeing a few men entering of their own free will that estate to which the poor of the twentieth century are daily driven by cold coercion and moved on by the police.

From: *St. Francis of Assisi* by G. K. Chesterton

(Hodder & Stoughton, pp. 122–4)

Friday

St. Francis of Assisi

G. K. CHESTERTON

Cardinal San Paolo seems to have argued more or less in this manner: it may be a hard life, but after all it is the life apparently described as ideal in the Gospel; make what compromises you think wise or humane about that ideal; but do not commit yourselves to saying that men shall *not* fulfil that ideal if they can. We shall see the importance of this argument when we come to the whole of that higher aspect of the life of St. Francis which may be called the Imitation of Christ. The upshot of the discussion was that the Pope gave his verbal approval to the project and promised a more definite endorsement, if the movement should grow to more considerable proportions. It is probably that Innocent, who was himself a man of no ordinary mentality, had very little doubt that it would do so; anyhow he was not left long in doubt before it did do so. The next passage in the history of the order is simply the story of more and more people flocking to its standard; and as has already been remarked, once it had begun to grow, it could in its nature grow much more quickly than any ordinary society requiring ordinary funds and public buildings. Even the return of the twelve pioneers from their papal audience seems to have been a sort of triumphal procession. In one place in particular, it is said, the whole population of a town, men, women and children, turned out, leaving their work and wealth and homes exactly as they stood and begging to be taken into the army of God on the spot. According to the story, it was on this occasion that St. Francis first foreshadowed his idea of the Third Order which enabled men to share in the movement without leaving the homes and habits of normal humanity. For the moment it is most important to regard this story as one example of the riot of conversion with which he was already filling all the roads of Italy. It was a world of wandering; friars perpetually coming and going in all the highways and byways, seeking to ensure that any man who met one of them by chance should have a spiritual adventure. The First Order of St. Francis had entered history.

From: *St. Francis of Assisi* by G. K. Chesterton

(Hodder & Stoughton, pp. 124–6)

Saturday

St. Francis of Assisi

G. K. CHESTERTON

The great saint was sane; and with the very sound of the word sanity, as at a deeper chord struck upon a harp, we come back to something that was indeed deeper than everything about him that seemed an almost elvish eccentricity. He was not a mere eccentric because he was always turning towards the centre and heart of the maze; he took the queerest and most zig-zag short cuts through the wood, but he was always going home. He was not only far too humble to be an heresi-arch, but he was far too human to desire to be an extremist, in the sense of an exile at the ends of the earth. The sense of humour which salts all the stories of his escapades alone prevented him from ever hardening into the solemnity of sectarian self-righteousness. He was by nature ready to admit that he was wrong; and if his followers had on some practical points to admit that he was wrong, they only admitted that he was wrong in order to prove that he was right. For it is they, his real followers, who have really proved that he was right and even in transcending some of his negations have triumphantly extended and interpreted his truth. The Franciscan order did not fossilize or break off short like something of which the true purpose has been frustrated by official tyranny or internal treason. It was this, the central and orthodox trunk of it, that afterwards bore fruit for the world. It counted among its sons Bonaventura the great mystic and

Bernardino the popular preacher, who filled Italy with the very beatific buffooneries of a Jongleur de Dieu. It counted Raymond Lully with his strange learning and his large and daring plans for the conversion of the world; a man intensely individual exactly as St. Francis was intensely individual. It counted Roger Bacon, the first naturalist whose experiments with light and water had all the luminous quaintness that belongs to the beginnings of natural history; and whom even the most material scientists have hailed as a father of science. It is not merely true that these were great men who did great work for the world; it is also true that they were a certain kind of men keeping the spirit and savour of a certain kind of men, that we can recognize in them a taste and tang of audacity and simplicity, and know them for the sons of St. Francis.

From: *St. Francis of Assisi* by G. K. Chesterton

(Hodder & Stoughton, pp. 180–2)

TRINITY 5

The Go-Between God

JOHN V. TAYLOR

'The church exists by mission as fire exists by burning.' It is not by chance that Emil Brunner chose that great biblical metaphor of the Spirit and his mission. Jewish teachers had taken the burning bush to be a symbol of the ideal Israel on fire with God's purpose and action in the world, yet unconsumed. The true church also exists by being the inexhaustible fuel of the Holy Spirit's mission in the world, and though this is a change of metaphor from the last sentence of the previous chapter, it really says the same thing. While they burn together the branches and twigs are the fire, yet they do not in themselves constitute the fire. The fire, rather, contains them, living around them in the interstices, and if a twig drops to the ground the fire that seemed to be in it soon vanishes. Only in their togetherness can Christians remain alight with the fire of the Spirit. That is the sole purpose of our visible fellowship – to be the fuel upon which the fire is kindled in the earth. The church must be shaped to carry out that purpose or it will be as frustrating as a badly laid fire. The question we have continually to put to the organization and structure of the church is this: does it bring Christian face to face with Christian in that communion which is the sphere of the Holy Spirit's presence?

Our theology would improve if we thought more of the church being given to the Spirit than of the Spirit being given to the church. For if we phrase it in the second way, although it is the New Testament way, we are in danger of perpetuating the irreverence of picturing God's spirit as a grant of superhuman power or guidance, like a fairy sword or magic mirror to equip us for our adventures. Unless all I have said so far is utterly mistaken, the promised power from on high is not of that kind at all. As I said in the last chapter, the primary effect of the pentecostal experience was to fuse the individuals of that company into a fellowship which in the same moment was caught up into the life of the risen Lord. In a new awareness of him and of one another they burst into praise, and the world came running for an explanation. In other words, the gift of the holy Spirit in the fellowship of the church first enables Christians to be, and only as a consequence of that sends them to do and to speak. It is enormously important to get this straight. Being, doing and speaking cannot in practice be disentangled, but if we put our primary emphasis on preaching or on serving we erect a functional barrier between ourselves and our fellow humans, casting ourselves in a different role from the rest of men. Hence the professional jealously of Christians, so often disconcerted when other humanitarians undertake the same service and other faiths propound the same truths.

From: *The Go-Between God* by John V. Taylor

(SCM Press, 1973, pp. 133–4)

Tuesday

The Go-Between God

JOHN V. TAYLOR

The Holy Spirit is given to enable 'the two or three gathered together' to embody Jesus Christ in the world. And what was his role and his relationship to the world? He came to be true Man, the last Adam, living the life of the new age in the midst of the world's life. His deliverance of men from various kinds of bondage, his existence for others, the laying down of his life, were not a task which he undertook but a function of the life of the new Man, just as breathing or eating is a function of physical life. What made his preaching of the Kingdom distinct from John's was that he not only promised but lived the Kingdom life. That is why he said that the least of those in the Kingdom was greater than John. And Kingdom life is not primarily religious but human. His parables make it clear that life in the Kingdom is the normal life that is open to manhood where man is found in his true relation to God as son – the abba-relationship. So the thirty years of hidden toil at Nazareth were to him not a mere passing of the time but were the very life of Man he had come to live. There he learned to say 'My Father has never yet ceased his work and I am working too', and by virtue of his absolute, glad obedience-in-co-operation Jesus as Man was able to be the vehicle of God's existence for others, as all men were potentially made to be. 'If it is by the finger of God that I drive out the devils, then be sure that the Kingdom of God has already come upon you' (Luke 11:20).

But the 'you' upon whom the Kingdom has come are not people in the church but people in the world. To say 'Jesus is Lord' pledges us to find the effects of his cross and resurrection in the world, not just in our inner lives, nor in the church.

As Bonhoeffer said:

> The space of the Church is not there in order to try to deprive the world of a piece of its territory, but precisely in order to prove to the world that it is still the world, the world which is loved by God and reconciled with Him. The Church has neither the wish nor the obligation to extend her space to cover the space of the world. She asks for no more space than she needs for the purpose of serving the world by bearing witness to Jesus Christ and to the reconciliation of the world with God through Him.

The way in which Jesus both declared the Kingdom and lived in the freedom of the Kingdom provides the model of what the church is created to be. The church is not the Kingdom but, through the Spirit indwelling their fellowship, Christians live the Kingdom life as men of the world.

The mission of the church, therefore, is to live the ordinary life of men in that extraordinary awareness of the other and self-sacrifice for the other which the Spirit gives. Christian activity will be very largely the same as the world's activity – earning a living, bringing up a family, making friends, having fun, celebrating occasions, farming, manufacturing, trading, building cities, healing sickness, alleviating distress, mourning, studying, exploring, making music, and so on. Christians will try to do these things to the glory of God, which is to say that they will try to perceive what God is up to in each of these manifold activites and will seek to do it with him by bearing responsibility for the selves of other men.

From: *The Go-Between God* by John V. Taylor

(SCM Press, 1973, pp. 134–5)

Wednesday

The Go-Between God

JOHN V. TAYLOR

While the life in the Spirit is essentially human and worldly, it is kept alive by the 'one-anotherness' that is given between those who are open to the truth of each other in the name of Christ. Some enthusiasts for a secular Christianity today would dismiss even a minimal gathering together of Christians as a relapse to the sort of religious fellowship Bonhoeffer contrasted with the true church. But this seems to me an exaggeration of his position. In the last but one of his letters to Eberhard Bethge, with whom he had shared all his explorations into 'religionless Christianity', he said: 'It is certain that in all this we are in a fellowship that sustains us.' The fellowship in Christ's name is necessary to sustain the *cantus firmus* beneath the flowing counterpoint of ordinary human life. The ideal shape of the church, therefore, is such as will provide this with the least possible withdrawal of Christians from life in the world. I shall return to this point a little later.

But beyond these two forms of responsibility which we might call natural response and fellowship response, Christians are also called to an evangelical response. By this I mean that Christians cannot avoid trying to make articulate the promise and invitation Jesus made articulate. They are caught up into the desire of the Spirit of God to make men profoundly aware of Jesus Christ, of what he is in himself and of what he makes available for the whole world, so that in him they may be confronted by the question and call of God, and make their free choice. This pointing to Christ can only be done by the Holy Spirit, but he may use both the words by which we tell of him and the style of life we live in him. The church makes Jesus visible by becoming, through the 'supply' of the Spirit of Jesus Christ, the obedient Son and the Suffering Servant, as he was.

We have already seen that the most characteristic forms of the action of the Spirit as Creator Redeemer are a constant pressure towards greater personhood, the creation of new occasions for choice, and the principle of self-surrender in responsibility for others. These must be the marks of any evangelism which is truly Christ's evangelism.

It must be deeply personal rather than propositional. We have already seen that the truth which converts is the truth of Jesus, not the truth about Jesus. How strange it is that people who have met the Truth should imagine that they are called to propound truths! How unlike Jesus himself, who would never violate the freedom or responsibility even of his enemies, are those who would win the world with a loud-hailer in one hand and a book of church statistics in the other. Christ-like evangelism consists in the passionate serving of the personhood of men in protest against all the depersonalizing pressures of the world. It consists also in that quality of faith in people as people, which can on occasion bring them to what is truly repentance more radically than any disparagement. To point to the cross is to point to one for whom people mattered supremely and whose very presence in silent suffering brought a hard-bitten non-commissioned officer to look twice at what seemed commonplace and rise to a more truly human personal response.

From: *The Go-Between God* by John V. Taylor

(SCM Press, 1973, pp. 135–7)

Thursday

The Go-Between God

JOHN V. TAYLOR

Josiah Pratt, the real architect of the Church Missionary Society, said right at the beginning, 'Put prayer first', and his words have been taken as the title for the annual directory for intercession which that society, like most others, makes available to its supporters. It is still a commonplace that prayer for the spread of the gospel and the coming of the Kingdom, with intercession for particular people in their particular needs, is the most important thing Christians can do for the furtherance of their mission. But one cannot, without sounding insufferably bland, repeat these pious injuctions as though nothing had happened to the spirit of man since the early nineteenth century. The experience of prayer will go dead for more and more of us unless we face the truth of ourselves in regard to two facts, one a constant condition of all humanity, the other a special condition of western man today. First: most Christians, like most men everywhere and in all ages, do not find that prayer comes naturally to them and, in fact, pray very little. Second: minds conditioned by scientific empiricism can no longer believe in a god who responds to prayer. This is not atheism; on the contrary, we find it is the very people who have the most profound sense of God's reality who find it most absurd to tell him what needs to be done or to ask him to interfere with the course of events, Their prayer, in consequence, is focused entirely on their personal communion with God-in-the-world or with God-in-themselves, and the link between such an exercise and the Christian mission is not very obvious.

Basically I agree with their position but I want to come at it in an entirely different way, a way that brings the lost dynamic back into prayer and frees it from our chronic reservations and scruples. For we are forced, as Leonard Hodgson has said, to the disconcerting realization 'that those who wrestle with God in prayer after the manner that we have renounced are growing in a richness and fullness of spiritual life beside which our efforts after self-culture appear intolerably thin and unsatisfying'. So we are driven to the conclusion, I believe, that the only way forward is to repudiate our contemporary 'flat-earthers' – the thinkers who reduce every vertical to a horizontal, all language to the literal meaning of words, all faith to an intention to behave in a certain way, all relation with God to a relation with men. Every conclusion I have reached in this study of the Holy Spirit falls to the ground if we will not reaffirm the 'beyondness' of the beyond-in-the-midst. I have tried to show that in every I-Thou experience an awareness of absolute otherness precedes any awareness of communion. I have concluded, echoing Bonhoeffer, that a true situation ethic can be grounded on nothing but response to the unmediated reality of God. I have argued that the only convincing authority is that which emanates from the intrinsic truth of, not from the objectified truth about, another being (which is the stuff of scientific investigation). And, above all, I have found the essential meaning of Jesus Christ in his continuous and direct intercourse with the Father. By all means let us find that Father in the here and now of our secular engagement, as I believe Jesus did, but at all costs let him be God. And this means testifying to an experience that is irreducible to any other terms. For, as Martin Buber taught, God is a primary term and there is no substitute for it. 'To put it bluntly', says David Jenkins, 'people believe in God because people believe in God, and if God does not keep people believing in himself, that will be the end of the matter.'

From: *The Go-Between God* by John V. Taylor

(SCM Press, 1973, pp. 223–4)

Friday

The Go-Between God

JOHN V. TAYLOR

Bishop John Robinson offered his testimony during the great *Honest to God* debate.

I do not pray to the ground of my being. I pray to God as Father. Prayer, for the Christian, is the opening of oneself to that utterly gracious personal reality which Jesus could only address as 'Abba, Father!' I have no interest whatever in a God conceived in some vaguely impersonal pantheistic terms. The only God who meets my need as a Christian is 'the God of Abraham, Isaac and Jacob', the God and Father of our Lord Jesus Christ.

Traditional religious instruction has so stressed the importance of prayer that we are prone to lose sight of the fact that Christian prayer was such a new experience for the church in New Testament times that it could properly be ranked as one of the signs of the new manhood of Jesus. The word 'pray' had to take on as much extra weight of meaning as the words 'love' or 'church'. The new experience of prayer was as unprecedented as the new experience of the Holy Spirit. Considering the richness of Jewish liturgy and family ritual, it is surprising to find a far more frequent use of the various words for prayer in the New Testament than in the Old, and this surely reflects a unique emphasis in the life of Jesus. Patriarchs, prophets and kings had from time to time acted as intercessors for the people, and Moses was the supreme example of this. Yet no figure in the Bible before the appearance of Christ seems to have depended upon the habit of communion with God as Jesus did. We tend to read back into the Old Testament and into the devotional patterns of other faiths those meanings which Jesus gave to the word 'prayer', and so conceal the fact that what was so characteristic of Jesus is almost unique amid the formal recitations which are the commonplace of religion everywhere else, including most of the churches. Other faiths have their mystics, but only in Jesus, I believe, can we find such spontaneous and personal communion with God combined with such passionate ethical concern for humanity. Both awareness of God and awareness of the world attain their zenith in him. Here we reach the holy of holies of the inner life of Jesus, momentarily unveiled by the spiritual insight of the fourth gospel, but implicit also in all the teaching about prayer which we find in the synoptic gospels.

> When you pray, go into a room by yourself, shut the door, and pray to your Father who is there in the secret place; and your Father who sees what is secret will reward you. In your prayers do not go babbling on like the heathen, who imagine that the more they say the more likely they are to be heard. Do not imitate them. Your Father knows what your needs are before you ask him. This is how you should pray . . . (Matt. 6:6–9)

And then for the first time, through the quiet tones of human speech, the sound-waves of this world were stirred by that eternal converse which is ever passing between the Father and the Son in the Being of God. And since the third person of the Trinity is himself that communion which flows between the Father and the Son, then the Spirit himself is the very breath of the prayer of Jesus. Immersed in the Go-Between Spirit he cried Abba! and knew himself as the Beloved Son. And pouring out that Spirit upon the openness-to-each-other of his friends he shared with them the right to use the same naively bold address: Abba!

From: *The Go-Between God* by John V. Taylor

(SCM Press, 1973, pp. 225–6)

Saturday

The Go-Between God

JOHN V. TAYLOR

The prayer of the first Christians was, therefore, simply a reflection of the living Christ in their midst. It was prayer 'in his name'; and by this we mean not that a formula was added at the end of every petition, but that in all their prayer they joined themselves to the prayer of Christ himself, and knew that it was his spirit which prayed in them. The best worship they could offer was simply his self-oblation in them. Praying in that Spirit, the Christian's prayer is immersed in the ocean of the Son's communion with the Father: 'In Holy Spirit praying, keep yourselves in the love of God' (Jude 21) 'Keep your watch with continous prayer and supplication, praying the whole time in the Spirit: with constant wakefulness and perseverance you will find opportunity to pray for all the Christian brethren' (Eph. 6:18, Wand translation). 'We do not even know how we ought to pray, but through our inarticulate groans the Spirit himself is pleading for us, and God who searches our inmost being knows what the Spirit means, because he pleads for God's own people in God's own way' (Rom. 8:26).

To live in prayer, therefore, is to live in the Spirit, and to live in the Spirit is to live in Christ. I am not saying that prayer is a means or a method which we have to use in order to have more of Christ in us or in order to be more fully possessed by the Spirit. I am saying something simpler and more fundamental: to live in Christ is to live in prayer. Prayer is not something you do; it is a style of living. It is living under the witness which the Spirit bears with our spirit that we are sons of God. Such a witness lays upon us the awful freedom of adult sonship. Prayer is our response to both the privilege and the responsibility whereby we cry Abba, Father! To engage in the mission of God, therefore, is to live this life of prayer; praying without ceasing, as St. Paul puts it, that is to say, sustaining a style of life that is focused upon God. This is indeed to engage in the mission of the Holy Spirit by being rather than by doing. To realize that the heart of mission is communion with God in the midst of the world's life will save us from the demented activism of these days.

> The end towards which we strive is not a material, external result, but the unfolding of a Person. A material result we may hope to produce or cause to be: the character, or nature, of the Person of Christ, though we may be agents of its manifestation, we cannot make. We cannot cause it to be ... We seek a revelation. A revelation is the unfolding of something that is, not the creation of something that is not.[1]

Revelation of that kind is, as we have seen, the métier of the Holy Spirit. When we say, then, that prayer is the very life-blood of mission we are not talking about one of several kinds of resources, like money and man-power and influence, which we muster to aid our enterprise; we are saying that the essential missionary activity is to live in prayer. John Venn, the father of the great Henry Venn, addressing the second Valedictory Meeting of the Church Missionary Society in the year 1806, gave this unexpected description of the character of a true missionary.

[1] Roland Allen, *Missionary Principles*, World Dominion Press, 1964.

He is one who, like Enoch, walks with God, and derives from constant communion with him a portion of the divine likeness.

From: *The Go-Between God* by John V. Taylor

(SCM Press, 1973, pp. 226–7)

TRINITY 6

The Go-Between God

JOHN V. TAYLOR

A true missionary is one who, like Enoch, walks with God, and derives from constant communion with him a portion of the divine likeness.

This is the real meaning of the approach to mission which has come to be known as 'Christian presence'. It is often confused with that method of approach to people of other faiths which is known as 'dialogue'. Christian presence and dialogue may often go hand in hand, it is true, but they are not the same. One of the purest examples of Christian presence which has ever been demonstrated is that of Père Charles de Foucauld, and of those who have followed in his steps, the Little Brothers and the Little Sisters of Jesus. Yet they have placed themselves under rule not to preach, nor to offer organized works, such as schools or hospitals, nor to employ any of the usual methods of evangelism. They believe they are simply called to live among the very poor of this world – on a house-boat amid the teeming refugees of Hong Kong, around a tiny courtyard high above the sacred waterfront of Benares, in a workman's shack on one of the sloping streets of Kabul, in an Eskimo hamlet in Alaska, a shanty suburb of Kampala, a labourers' settlement near Port Moresby, built on wooden piles above the sea like any other village of Papua. Unobtrusively they keep a routine of communal prayer and silent adoration, but every day they go out in their working clothes to do the same sort of job that their neighbours are doing and to offer them an unstinted friendship in the doing of it. A few years ago one Brother was working with a Muslim shoemaker; a Little Sister had found employment as a housemaid among the households of coloured servants in Washington, and another was employed with 300 other immigrant workers in a handkerchief factory in Sydney. Here again a Brother is working as a mason for a local firm of contractors in the Punjab. Out of sight, out of mind of the church as a whole, way below the poverty line, scattered in their twos and threes across the face of the earth, they do not work for their neighbours, they work with them. Their role is that of prayer and of a silent, hidden presence of love. Such extreme renunciation of all the normal activities of mission would suggest either a lack of concern or a policy of despair, were it not for Charles de Foucauld's ardent passion for evangelism. 'I wish to cry the gospel by my whole life', he said; and again, 'For the spreading of the gospel I am ready to go to the ends of the earth and I am likewise ready to live until the Day of Judgement.' To live thus totally towards God for the sake of the world is a profoundly missionary and, indeed, redemptive way. But only faith can perceive this. In her great book on worship, Evelyn Underhill wrote:

> Worship is therefore in the deepest sense creative and redemptive. Keeping us in constant remembrance of the Unchanging and the Holy, it cleanses us of subjectivism, releases us from 'use and wont' and makes us realists . . . Each separate soul thus transfigured by the spirit of selfless adoration advances that transfiguration of the whole universe which is the coming of the Kingdom of God.

From: *The Go-Between God* by John V. Taylor

(SCM Press, 1973, pp. 227–9)

Tuesday

The Go-Between God

JOHN V. TAYLOR

Worship is therefore in the deepest sense creative and redemptive. Keeping us in constant remembrance of the Unchanging and the Holy, it cleanses us of subjectivism, releases us from 'use and wont' and makes us realists . . . Each separate soul thus transfigured by the spirit of selfless adoration advances that transfiguration of the whole universe which is the coming of the Kingdom of God.[1]

To an activist church engaged in struggle and protest and development, that must seem like an escape into a dream unless one remembers that what a man is towards God he is also towards his neighbour. To worship silently and to communicate the gospel silently, as

[1] Evelyn Underhill, *Worship*, James Nisbet, 1936.

the Little Brothers and Sisters do, is some guarantee of their skill in silent communication in all other areas of human concern. The link between these two has been beautifully described by Ivan Illich in a meditation introducing an hour of silent prayer at a course he initiated to prepare ministers, teachers and social workers for the Spanish-speaking ghettos of New York. He began with the discovery by linguistic experts that more is relayed from person to person through the pauses and hesitations of speech than through its words. 'It takes more time and effort and delicacy to learn the silence of a people than to learn its sounds.' Then he developed an analogy between our city priest with men and our silence with God. 'The silence of a city priest on a bus listening to the report of the sickness of a goat is a gift, truly the fruit of a missionary form of long training in patience . . . In the prayer of silent listening, and nowhere else, can the Christian acquire the habit of this first silence from which the Word can be born in a foreign culture.' But all too often, says Illich, the missionary grows impatient, failing to see what a gift his enforced silence is. 'The man who forgets the analogy of the silence of God and the silence of others and does not seek its growth in prayer, is a man who tries basically to rape the culture into which he is sent. . . . As long as he sees himself as 'missioner' he will know that he is frustrated, that he was sent but got nowhere; that he is away from home but has never landed anywhere; that he left his home and never reached another. He continues to preach and is ever more aware that he is not understood.' Only the very brave, says Illich, dare then to go back to the helpless silence of being learners and listeners – 'the holding of hands of the lovers' – from which deep communication may grow. 'Perhaps it is the one way of being together with others and with the Lord in which we have no more foreign accent.'[1]

The simple truth that our manner of communication with God moulds the manner of our communication with people throws an entirely new light upon the connection between prayer and mission. Yet it follows quite logically from the fact we noted in the first chapter, that awareness is multi-directional, and we cannot be opened towards God without being opened also towards the ticking of the clock and towards all the joy and pain of the world.

That is why we can affirm, as I believe the New Testament does, that every kind of prayer is summed up and included in the basic communion with God which the cry Abba! epitomizes. It is not difficult to see how this is the case with the three types of prayer – thanksgiving, prayer for guidance, and intercession – which can be

---

[1] Ivan D. Illich, *Celebration of Awareness,* Calder & Boyars, 1971.

L

distinguished in the New Testament, apart from the direct, loving regard of the prayer of communion.

From: *The Go-Between God* by John V. Taylor

(SCM Press, 1973, pp. 228–30)

Wednesday

The Go-Between God

JOHN V. TAYLOR

There are two kinds of prayer associated with these two aspects of God which I prefer to call the prayer of stillness and the prayer of movement. The classical distinction between contemplation and meditation is no longer obvious from their dictionary definitions, and has been further confused by popular teachers of 'transcendental meditation'. The difference does not lie in subject-matter but in the way in which one looks at it. It is not that in the prayer of movement we choose to dwell upon passages in the Bible or incidents in the life of Christ or the needs of the world, while in the prayer of stillness we seek the vision of God in a direct exposure to the uncreated light. The difference is much simpler than that. In the prayer of movement our mind moves from thought to thought and from image to image as it does most of the time when we are 'thinking' either about God or tonight's dinner, an article in the newspaper or a chapter in the Bible, the Christians in the Sudan or the pack in the Welsh rugby team. But in the prayer of stillness the mind stands still and looks, takes in what is standing before it and gives itself, but does not move from thought to thought.

I can make this clearer, perhaps, by recalling the distinction I have drawn several times between the truth about someone or something and the truth of someone or something. In the prayer of movement we try to open ourselves to more of the truth about Jesus by dwelling on part of the gospel; or to open ourselves to more of the truth about the Sudanese church by reading a letter and using our imaginations with compassion. In the prayer of stillness we try to hold ourselves open to the impact of the truth of Jesus not in a succession of bits and pieces, but as one whole person; or, aided by such knowledge as we already have about the Sudan, we try to hold ourselves still before the truth of those Christians 'because they are there', open to their reality without thinking any new thoughts about them.

The real difficulty of the prayer of movement is that the words we are given to think with, and the images we are given to picture with, strike us as stale, incredible or emptied of meaning because they reflect a mentality and a situation we left behind many centuries ago. No culture can survive on its old masters alone, and no church can continue to live on 'incomparable liturgies' from the past. New versions of the Bible, contemporary styles of prayer and song, formulations of the faith that speak today, symbols that convey old meanings with the shock of fresh discovery, personal devotion and corporate worship that turn drama and dance, fantasy and play to account and allow more scope to our physical nature and our interpersonal dynamics – none of these can generate the awareness of the living Lord which the Holy Spirit alone can give, but they can at least throw the doors open and allow the Spirit entry.

But all that we have so far learned about that Spirit suggests that our greater need is for a recovery of the prayer of stillness. It can best be understood in terms of presence, We have already seen what the practice of Christian presence means in the lives of the Little Brothers and Sisters of Jesus. It is the direct giving of self without any auxiliary or token giving of words or work. We are back at the scene of the annunciation once more.

> These neither speak nor movement make,
> But stare into their deepening trance
> As if their gaze would never break.

I would offer two reasons for thinking that most of us in the western churches, and not those only who are temperamentally so inclined, need to re-learn the prayer of stillness. The first is that we are all becoming the prisoners of our activism. We speak with the tongues of men and of angels in a dozen different committees; our gift of prophecy and knowledge defeats the politicians at their own game; our faith removes mountains of discrimination; our goods feed the hungry millions, our bodies are burned up in evangelistic zeal. Yet we lack charity, the only quality which makes contagious Christians, from whom others may catch the love of God. And charity comes by adoration.

From: *The Go-Between God* by John V. Taylor

(SCM Press, 1973, pp. 236–8)

Thursday

The Go-Between God

JOHN V. TAYLOR

Both because of our activism and our mistrust of words and symbols, we would do well to find the way to God in the prayer of stillness. That is certainly the direction in which the younger generation of the western world feels it needs to be pointed. But it is a way of prayer for which we are peculiarly disqualified. For so long we have worshipped the process of analytical argument and played down every other way to knowledge that our amalgam of brain and body has almost grown incapable of any form of thought except 'one damn thing after another'. We have lost the simple power of attention by which our mind can stand still at one point, doing nothing but taking in what is there. This is the skill which Father Slade's community at Anchorhold, and the Fellowship of Meditation at Guildford, are undertaking to teach again. They have quickly realized that the unceasing movement of our conscious minds, combined with the strain and noise in which most of us now exist, have strung us up to such a pitch of muscular tension that we need some technique, such as Yoga or the T'ai Chiih Chuan, to relax the body enough for the mind to allow itself to rest and stand still.

The next step is to enter into an awareness of some other creature. Father Slade finds it most helpful to focus a loving attention upon some simple object, rich in associations, such as a lit candle, a flower, a glass of water or wine. It is a deliberate attempt to experience the same quality of encounter and mutuality which comes unbidden to each of us from time to time; and if, as I have suggested, it is the Spirit of God who gives us those unlooked-for annunciations, it is he alone who can give the living awareness we seek deliberately in this prayer of stillness. When the current of communion is there between oneself and the candle flame or the water, so that one is aware with every sense of the otherness of it, the truth of it, then one tries, with the minimum of thinking about it, to see it as a symbol or embodiment of Christ – the Light, the Living Water – so that one's awareness is of him and it is he who confronts and beckons. The next stage is to shut off the external, visible object in order to bring its presence, its reality which is the presence and reality of Christ, into the heart and concentrate one's whole being upon him there in stillness.

And finally the mental image of the symbol should be quietly removed, leaving in its place a space, at the very heart of one's heart, which is filled with Christ.

Because of the difficulty and possible dangers or re-learning these skills of the mind and soul those who undertake to teach them usually do so in groups. This in itself is a protection against any neo-quietism which would be merely egocentric. It also helps to overcome the resistance of those who find it impossible to make any commitments except corporate ones. It is easy to see how closely this development accords with the recovery of the eucharist in an increasingly corporate form as the main, and in many cases the only, act of worship and prayer in which Christians of the younger generation can find vivid significance. They know intuitively that the Spirit is always the Go-Between, the fire amid the branches of the burning bush, the giver of Christ's presence to the two or three gathered together.

From: *The Go-Between God* by John V. Taylor

(SCM Press, 1973, pp. 239–40)

Friday

The Go-Between God

JOHN V. TAYLOR

It may come as a surprise to many seekers to learn that the prayer of stillness can be a shared, corporate experience, and that it can be directed towards any other than the pure Being of God. It is enormously important, I believe, to dissociate this direct, wordless prayer from the rarefied mysticism to which we think only the saints can aspire. The prayer of stillness is that which most naturally deepens our communion with the Father and reproduces in us the abba-relationship that Jesus knew. But the same manner of praying can make Jesus himself more real to us; it is a form of intercession also whereby other people are held in our loving regard and sympathy. It can make us more profoundly aware of the crying needs of mankind and the mysterious bond between ourselves and the physical world.

This richness should make it impossible for us to disregard the many who can find their God only by the same gradual progression as the disciples, first knowing Jesus as a man who draws them humanly and commands their allegiance as no other being has ever done, who becomes the point of reference by which they set their standards and make their decisions, into whose presence they want to bring their perplexity and pain, whom in fact they begin to treat as God long before they have formulated theologically their convictions about him. If this was legitimate for the fishermen of Galilee – or, rather, if it was illegitimate yet neccessary, for them – may it not be permitted to secular man to treat the man Jesus as his God even before he can admit that there is any meaning in the word 'divine'?

It does not matter whether the Christ who fills our vision is the historical Jesus, or the living Saviour, or the Christ of the Body and the Blood, or the Logos and Lord of the universe, or the master and meaning of history, or the Christ in my neighbour and in his poor. These are only aspects of his being. In whatever aspect it is most real to us, what matters is that we adore him. For, loving him whom we think we know, we are drawn to that Lord Jesus who transcends our knowing. But all too often we have lost him amid our enthusiasms. What dominates our mind is not the figure of Jesus of Nazareth but our New Testament studies, not the living Saviour but the doctrines of salvation, not Christ in the neighbour but the civil rights movement.

This is not a plea for pietism but for adoration. The Jesus of history, whensoever we discern him, is not a topic of debate but a master and brother to be loved and followed. Christ in his poor is neither a case nor a cause, but a mystery before whom we bow even while we serve. Whatever way of knowing him is valid for us – and it may be simply as the one whose 'give ye them to eat' sends us into the fight for a new world order – we must be in love with him, not with ourselves or our schemes. We must find time to let our minds dwell on him. The beauty of holiness in the midst of this revolutionary world belongs to those who set the Lord always before their eyes. *Venite adoremus*!

From: *The Go-Between God* by John V. Taylor

(SCM Press, 1973, pp. 240–2)

Saturday

The Go-Between God

JOHN V. TAYLOR

When the prayer of stillness takes the form of intercession, it consists quite simply in allowing the Holy Spirit to make other people present to us and us aware of them. We should try to focus our stilled minds upon them in the same way as Father Slade teaches us to focus our stilled minds upon a candle. Such prayer will probably not feel like a religious act at all. Some years ago I received a letter from a missionary in a rather desolate area of Nigeria. She wrote both from a sense of shame at the ineffectualness of the intercession, and also to share a basic query. 'Let me give an example,' she said. 'There were five boys weighing on my mind at the end of last term as I knew their fees for this year were just hopelessly inadequate. They were pretty constantly in my mind, yet I do not recall that I formulated any prayer for them. However, within a month four of them had adequate financial assistance. A week later came a Christmas gift from my sister and her husband for any student needing help; so that was the fifth! I quite simply regard this as miraculous – the result of God's concern – and I do not see that formal intercession would have made any difference one way or the other.' When someone whose life is simply and sacrificially dedicated to God has any fellow man 'pretty constantly in mind' to the extent that the feeling of concern leads to responsible action, that, surely is the whole of intercession, For a timeless moment it makes one totally present with the other person or persons across the intervening distances, without words and in a manner that goes beyond thought. It is simply a matter of 'being there for them' in a concentration upon the other which obliterates all awareness of self and yet is not strung up but totally relaxed. In that stillness which lies beyond thought we are to let the presence of that other person impinge upon our spirit across the distance, with all his rich reality and all his need and burden. His presence matters more than our own.

So is it also when the other on whom our silent regard is concentrated is once again God Himself. For in this prayer of awareness we swing from intercession to worship and back again, we alternate between communion with fellow men and with God, the image of the symbol merges into the image of Christ, without any break in the stillness. This is the gift of the Spirit, the beloved Go-Between, the opener of eyes and giver of life.

A colleague has recently described to me an occasion when a West Indian woman in a London flat was told of her husband's death in a street accident. The shock of grief stunned her like a blow, she sank into a corner of the sofa and sat there rigid and unhearing. For a long time her terrible tranced look continued to embarrass the family, friends and officials who came and went. Then the schoolteacher of one of her children, an Englishwoman, called and, seeing how things were, went and sat beside her. Without a word she threw an arm around the tight shoulders, clasping them with her full strength. The white cheek was thrust hard against the brown. Then as the unrelenting pain seeped through to her the newcomer's tears began to flow, falling on their two hands linked in the woman's lap. For a long time that is all that was happening. And then at last the West Indian woman started to sob. Still not a word was spoken and after a little while the visitor got up and went, leaving her contribution to help the family meet its immediate needs.

That is the embrace of God, his kiss of life. That is the embrace of his mission, and of our intercession. And the Holy Spirit is the force in the straining muscles of an arm, the film of sweat between pressed cheeks, the mingled wetness on the backs of clasped hands. He is as close and as unobtrusive as that, and as irresistibly strong.

From: *The Go-Between God* by John V. Taylor

(SCM Press, 1973, pp. 242–3)

TRINITY 7

Courage

R. E. C. BROWNE

Courage cannot be explained with reference solely to itself. A courageous man is one who has courage to do something, to be something. That is, he believes that there is more to be done with life than prolong it. It is said that a man must have the courage of his convictions, but he can have no courage unless he has convictions.

The NT in general, and the Sermon on the Mount in particular, makes it clear that the courageous man's first victory is a conquest over anxiety. Anxiety can be described under these headings: (1) *Material* – Fear of increased prices, inflation, unemployment, changes in trade, nationally and internationally, illness, infirmity. These might be summarized as a general, though vague, feeling of political and economic insecurity. (2) *Spiritual* – Fear of loss of freedom and power to keep one's identity. Fear of being a hypocrite or incapable of significant action. Fear of being inadequate in personal relationships especially in the family. (3) *Religious* – Fear of the failure and disappearance of the church on account of the small number of practising members. Fear through a reluctance to think and live in the light of the fact that Christians walk by faith and not by sight and therefore cannot answer all the questions men may ask. Christians do not claim that only Christians can be courageous but that a man, or woman, requires courage to be a Christian in any century – whether in facing violence, torture and death or enduring the constant battle to be fought out against anxiety.

It is brave to accept dangers oneself but it is even braver to allow and even exhort others to be courageous in their particular spheres of living – for example, a bishop ordaining clergy, parents encouraging their sons and daughters to leave home and take full responsibility for themselves, friend helping friend to make a decision where one should be made no matter at what cost.

Christians learn that courage is a necessity rather than a virtue through their frequent meditation on the passion and triumph of our Lord. In every generation orthodox doctrine and individual piety are most clearly expressed in the compassion and courage of church members. Where there is no courage, compassion dwindles and where compassion is absent courage tends to become arrogant self-display.

From: *A Dictionary of Christian Ethics*, edited by John Macquarrie

(SCM Press, 1967)

Tuesday

Childlikeness

R. E. C. BROWNE

Childlikeness and childishness are both terms in common use and need to be distinguished from one another. Childishness is used often to describe the habitually self-centred adult. This self-centredness can be seen in self-display, in making excessive demands on others for attention, affection and praise; it is seen in the man who considers everything he does to be of the utmost importance and judges every event and person in terms of benefit to himself. No one finds it easy to free himself (and his associates) from all traces of childishness. Many would wish to make the Pauline words their own: 'When I was a child, I spoke like a child, I thought like a child, I reasoned like a child; when I became a man I put away childish ways.'

After our Lord's example we take the image of a little child to symbolize the innocence, gaiety and trustfulness which should be found in a Christian life. The child has no ulterior motives: he does not want to be popular with all or accepted by some important power group. Childlikeness in an adult appears as foolishness to many when they see the cost of its generosity and truthfulness.

Childlikeness in an adult is known in a man who does not set out to turn events and persons to his own advantage; that is, he lives with an innocence associated with little children. The innocence of a child is largely due to ignorance and lack of experience; the innocence of an adult is maintained in spite of his knowledge of men and affairs and the ways to act for personal advantage. There is no such thing as a little child who is habitually innocent and admirable but there is much innocence seen in these four characteristics of childhood – trust, spontaneity, curiosity, growth. The childlike innocency of mature men and women is noted in these same characteristics. For example – philosophers go on trusting that human thinking is significant despite seemingly contradictory evidence; artists delight and enrich us with their spontaneous discoveries; scientists allow their love of truth to carry them into dark uncharted territory, theologians are ready to adjust their system of thought on account of growth in knowledge of the physical universe and on account of the changes in human behaviour brought about by the present urban civilization.

Churchmen are to protect the innocence (the childlikeness) of the Church. They must avoid giving by word and deed even the appearance that the Church has an ulterior motive in the interest taken in individuals and institutions. Childishness in church life is usually seen in either false church centredness (i.e. when people are more concerned in preserving the institution than in the church's worship and mission) or in a false member-centredness (when the riches of corporate life are in danger through looking at church life from the individual member's point of view). Childlikeness is expressed in joyful worship and the ready acceptance of the church's mission in the wicked world which God loves.

From: *A Dictionary of Christian Ethics*, edited by John Macquarrie

(SCM Press, 1967)

Wednesday

Jealousy

R. E. C. BROWNE

The second of the Ten Commandments describes God as being a jealous God; this is, not tolerating people who find satisfaction in relationship with any being other than himself. Christian revelation has broken up this primitive conception of God as jealous and vengeful.

People do not decide to behave jealously, they drift into such behaviour with little or no conscious knowledge of what is happening until they find themselves imprisoned. The detection of jealousy is usually difficult because it is often born of the warmth of a generous love – thus parents in their protective love for their children will try to limit their companionships, thereby robbing them of their human birthright of independence and ability to develop freely. Jealousy in an engaged couple is a sign of danger, in marriage a sign of disaster because jealousy breeds suspicion, distrust and deception.

Churchmen, in the name of the Church, are often jealous of social institutions because of the amount of time given by church members to them and the place and power they hold in society. To alter St. Paul's words, the institutions that be are ordained of God, to be accepted, loved and criticized but never to be ignored, destroyed or regarded as permanent.

There is no simple cure for jealousy, no sure way of stopping it at its first sign. Its absence is a tribute to a loving disposition which feeds and is fed by a regard for the individuality of each person and a sense of responsibility for his, or her, full human development which requires a width of relationship far beyond a limited companionship. The masters of spirituality continually remind us, century by century, of the beauty of ordinate affection where people share a love of God, which is greater than their love for one another.

From: *A Dictionary of Christian Ethics*, edited by John Macquarrie

(SCM Press, 1967)

Thursday

Temperance

R. E. C. BROWNE

A man is to be temperate in all things – even in the practice of the virtues and specially in the practice of temperance. Temperance does not lie in not doing too much of anything, but in a general sobriety of living in which a person is controlling what can be controlled and does not attempt to control what cannot be controlled.

Intemperance is evident in one who thinks too much, too quickly, about too many subjects. Temperance is quietness of mind in which concentration makes for profound lucid thinking. The intemperate talk too much to too many people, taking too many into their confidence. Temperance is a readiness to pay attention to what others have to say and only talking about subjects appropriate to the occasion and relationship. The intemperate are too grateful, too sympathetic, too prone to give advice. Temperance is grateful and sympathetic in proportion to the occasion for gratitude or sympathy.

To be intemperate is to have too much travelling on account of too many appointments, committees, obligations, commitments and responsibilities. The temperate man knows that a man's life, and usefulness, does not consist in the abundance of his activities; he knows also that the attempt to do too many pieces of work, at the same time, has almost the same result as if no such attempt were made. Temperance entails a ruthless selection of activities on the part of the artists, scientists, philosophers, social workers, pastors and all other serious people.

Some take to talking and work in the way others take to alcohol and other drugs as a means of dulling the edges of their fears and keeping themselves from becoming too aware of what is happening to them, within them and through them. All forms of intemperance contain a neurotic element and arise from causes best described as spiritual.

Institutions, societies and the Church itself, through officials, need to be watchful in case the over-willing (the intemperate) be given more work than they can do. In particular the Church is to preserve temperance through maintaining the balance of urgency and tranquillity in all authentic Christian living. In the table of the seven virtues, temperance is placed before fortitude – perhaps to suggest that only the temperate can be brave and that temperance requires bravery. Christian Scripture says: 'Let your moderation be known unto all men'. This is, let your temperance be known because the truth can only be spoken and done by temperate men.

From: *A Dictionary of Christian Ethics*, edited by John Macquarrie

(SCM Press, 1967)

Friday

Humility

R. E. C. BROWNE

Humility is not self-abnegation; it is self-affirmation made possible by the calling and power of Christians to be the light of the world and the salt of the earth. This work cannot be done by the habitually self-centred even if they are concerned with fulfilling a wish to be humble. The humble man loses his self-centredness by his habitual attempts to proclaim the gospel with his whole being. In essence, humility is exposing oneself by a wholehearted attempt to express deep feelings and beliefs in a manner neither uncontrolled nor self-conscious. This is what the apostle means when he says '. . . we have the mind of Christ' (1 Cor. 2.16).

One of the most familiar Christian images of humility is found in Phil. 2: 'Have this mind among yourselves, which you have in Christ Jesus, who, though he was in the form of God, did not count equality with God a thing to be grasped, but emptied himself, taking the form of a servant, being born in the likeness of men. And being found in human form he humbled himself and became obedient unto death, even death on a cross.'

In the medieval attempt to describe the good life by use of the table of the seven virtues humility is omitted. The omission may presuppose either that the practice of the seven virtues makes for humility or that only the humble man could practise them. In the second half of the twentieth century people tend to explain the good life in terms of human relationships and would think of humility in that context. The humble would be described as neither boastful nor domineering, not given to self-display, always prepared to do well what he can do well and, as occasion demands, to attempt what he cannot do well. If an official of an institution he will think more of the work pertaining to his office than of his own importance as an official.

No man can make himself humble by acts of will; continued attempts to do so produce a condition which is not humility. Others cannot make him humble though they may humiliate him, and yet humiliation is part of the raw material out of which humility is so mysteriously made. There is no single activity which could be called being humble; it is rather a quality which flavours what a man does. Humility is given to men obliquely; it is, as it were, a by-product of the Christian style of living. This style is made through the consistent attempt to love God, neighbour and self in thought, word and deed – aware that each individual is at the same time first, a creature limited in knowledge and power; secondly, a being made in the image of God, capable of a relationship with God; thirdly, a sinner in constant need of repentance.

From: *A Dictionary of Christian Ethics*, edited by John Macquarrie

(SCM Press, 1967)

Saturday

Covetousness

R. E. C. BROWNE

The last of the Ten Commandments is the only one of them that deals directly with sins of thought as distinct from sins of word and overt deeds. It is concerned with covetousness: 'You shall not covet your neighbour's house; you shall not covet your neighbour's wife, or his manservant, or his maidservant, or his ox, or his ass, or anything that is your neighbour's'. Covetousness is a dynamic state which is liable to explode into violent action but more often it stimulates plans to get the things so much desired. That is the course of covetousness in strong men. Covetousness in timid people shows itself in resentment, discontent, irritability and a readiness to belittle the possessor of the coveted thing or things.

Covetousness is in complete contradiction of the Christian doctrine of man and his possessions. Our Lord says: 'Take heed, and beware of all covetousness; for a man's life does not consist in the abundance of his possessions.'

Covetousness could be called an obsession: St. Paul spoke of it as idolatry because he thought of it as a thing-centred religion with an interior pattern of wishes, thoughts and characteristic behaviour forms.

From: *A Dictionary of Christian Ethics*, edited by John Macquarrie

(SCM Press, 1967)

TRINITY 8

The Pilgrim's Progress

JOHN BUNYAN

Then I saw in my dream, that on the morrow he got up to go forward; but they desired him to stay till the next day also; and then, said they, we will, if the day be clear, show you the Delectable Mountains, which, they said, would yet further add to his comfort, because they were nearer the desired haven than the place where at present he was; so he consented and stayed. When the morning was up, they had him to the top of the house, and bade him look south; so he did: and behold, at a great distance, he saw a most pleasant mountainous country, beautified with woods, vineyards, fruits of all sorts, flowers also, with springs and fountains, very delectable to behold.[1] Then he asked the name of the country. They said it was Immanuel's Land; and it is as common, said they, as this hill is, to and for all the pilgrims. And when thou comest there from hence, said they, thou mayest see to the gate of the Celestial City, as the shepherds that live there will make appear.

Now he bethought himself of setting forward, and they were willing he should. But first, said they, let us go again into the armoury. So they did; and when they came there, they harnessed him from head to foot with what was of proof, lest, perhaps, he should meet with assaults in the way. He being, therefore, thus accoutred, walketh out with his friends to the gate, and there he asked the porter if he saw any pilgrims pass by. Then the porter answered, Yes.

Christian. Pray, did you know him? said he.

Porter. I asked him his name, and he told me it was Faithful.

Christian. Oh, said Christian, I know him; he is my townsman, my near neighbour; he comes from the place where I was born. How far do you think he may be before?

Porter. He is got by this time below the hill.

Christian. Well, said Christian, good Porter, the Lord be with

[1] Isaiah 33:16–17.

thee, and add to all thy blessings much increase, for the kindness that thou hast showed to me.

Then he began to go forward; but Discretion, Piety, Charity, and Prudence would accompany him down to the foot of the hill. So they went on together, reiterating their former discourses, till they came to go down the hill. Then said Christian, As it was difficult coming up, so, so far as I can see, it is dangerous going down. Yes, said Prudence, so it is, for it is a hard matter for a man to go down into the Valley of Humiliation, as thou art now, and to catch no slip by the way; therefore, said they, are we come out to accompany thee down the hill. So he began to go down, but very warily; yet he caught a slip or two.

From: *The Pilgrim's Progress* by John Bunyan

(Dent, 1937, pp. 63–4)

Tuesday

The Pilgrim's Progress

JOHN BUNYAN

Then I saw in my dream that these good companions, when Christian was gone to the bottom of the hill, gave him a loaf of bread, a bottle of wine, and a cluster of raisins; and then he went on his way.

But now, in this Valley of Humiliation, poor Christian was hard put to it; for he had gone but a little way; before he espied a foul fiend coming over the field to meet him; his name is Apollyon. Then did Christian begin to be afraid, and to cast in his mind whether to go back or to stand his ground. But he considered again that he had no armour for his back; and therefore thought that to turn the back to him might give him the greater advantage with ease to pierce him with his darts. Therefore he resolved to venture and stand his ground; for, thought he, had I no more in mine eye than the saving of my life, it would be the best way to stand.

So he went on, and Apollyon met him. Now the monster was hideous to behold; he was clothed with scales, like a fish (and they are his pride), he had wings like a dragon, feet like a bear, and out of his belly came fire and smoke, and his mouth was as the mouth of a lion. When he was come up to Christian, he beheld him with a disdainful countenance, and thus began to question with him.

Apollyon. Whence come you? and whither are you bound?

Christian. I am come from the City of Destruction, which is the place of all evil, and am going to the City of Zion.

Apollyon. By this I perceive thou art one of my subjects, for all that country is mine, and I am the prince and god of it. How is it, then, that thou hast run away from the king? Were it not that I hope thou mayest do me more service, I would strike thee now, at one blow, to the ground.

Christian. I was born, indeed, in your dominions, but your service was hard, and your wages such as a man could not live on, 'for the wages of sin *is* death';[1] therefore, when I was come to years, I did as other considerate persons do, look out, if, perhaps, I might mend myself.

Apollyon. There is no prince that will thus lightly lose his subjects, neither will I as yet lose thee; but since thou complainest of thy service and wages, be content to go back: what our country will afford, I do here promise to give thee.

Christian. But I have let myself to another, even to the King of princes; and how can I, with fairness, go back with thee?

From: *The Pilgrim's Progress* by John Bunyan

(Dent, 1937, pp. 65–6)

Wednesday

The Pilgrim's Progress

JOHN BUNYAN

Apollyon. Thou hast done in this, according to the proverb, 'changed a bad for a worse'; but it is ordinary for those that have professed themselves his servants, after a while to give him the slip, and return again to me. Do thou so too, and all shall be well.

Christian. I have given him my faith, and sworn my allegiance to him; how, then, can I go back from this, and not be hanged as a traitor?

Apollyon. Thou didst the same to me, and yet I am willing to pass by all, if now thou wilt yet turn again and go back.

Christian. What I promised thee was in my nonage; and, besides, I

[1] Romans 6:23.

count the Prince under whose banner now I stand is able to absolve me; yea, and to pardon also what I did as to my compliance with thee; and besides, O thou destroying Apollyon! to speak truth, I like his service, his wages, his servants, his government, his company and country, better than thine; and, therefore, leave off to persuade me further; I am his servant, and I will follow him.

Apollyon. Consider, again, when thou art in cool blood, what thou art like to meet with in the way that thou goest. Thou knowest that, for the most part, his servants come to an ill end, because they are transgressors against me and my ways. How many of them have been put to shameful deaths; and, besides, thou countest his service better than mine, whereas he never came yet from the place where he is to deliver any that served him out of their hands; but as for me, how many times, as all the world very well knows, have I delivered, either by power, or fraud, those that have faithfully served me, from him and his, though taken by them; and so I will deliver thee.

Christian. His forbearing at present to deliver them is on purpose to try their love, whether they will cleave to him to the end; and as for the ill end thou sayest they come to, that is most glorious in their account; for, for present deliverance, they do not much expect it, for they stay for their glory, and then they shall have it, when their Prince comes in his and the glory of the angels.

From: *The Pilgrim's Progress* by John Bunyan

(Dent, 1937, pp. 66–7)

Thursday

The Pilgrim's Progress

JOHN BUNYAN

Apollyon. Thou hast already been unfaithful in thy service to him; and how dost thou think to receive wages of him?

Christian. Wherein, O Apollyon! have I been unfaithful to him?

Apollyon. Thou didst faint at first setting out, when thou wast almost choked in the Gulf of Despond; thou didst attempt wrong ways to be rid of thy burden, whereas thou shouldest have stayed till thy Prince had taken it off; thou didst sinfully sleep and lose thy choice thing; thou wast, also, almost persuaded to go back, at the sight of the lions; and when thou talkest of thy journey, and of what thou hast heard and seen, thou art inwardly desirous of vain-glory in all that thou sayest or doest.

Christian. All this is true, and much more which thou hast left out; but the Prince whom I serve and honour is merciful, and ready to forgive; but, besides, these infirmities possessed me in thy country, for there I sucked them in; and I have groaned under them, been sorry for them, and have obtained pardon of my Prince.

Apollyon. Then Apollyon broke out into a grievous rage, saying, I am an enemy to this Prince; I hate his person, his laws, and people; I am come out on purpose to withstand thee.

Christian. Apollyon, beware what you do; for I am in the king's highway, the way of holiness; therefore take heed to yourself.

Apollyon. Then Apollyon straddled quite over the whole breadth of the way, and said, I am void of fear in this matter: prepare thyself to die; for I swear by my infernal den, that thou shalt go no further; here will I spill thy soul.

From: *The Pilgrim's Progress* by John Bunyan

(Dent, 1937, pp. 67–8)

Friday

The Pilgrim's Progress

JOHN BUNYAN

And with that he threw a flaming dart at his breast; but Christian had a shield in his hand, with which he caught it, and so prevented the danger of that.

Then did Christian draw, for he saw it was time to bestir him: and Apollyon as fast made at him throwing darts as thick as hail; by the which, notwithstanding all that Christian could do to avoid it, Apollyon wounded him in his head, his hand, and foot. This made Christian give a little back; Apollyon, therefore, followed his work amain, and Christian again took courage, and resisted as manfully as he could, This sore combat lasted for above half a day, even till Christian was almost quite spent; for you must know that Christian, by reason of his wounds, must needs grow weaker and weaker.

Then Apollyon, espying his opportunity, began to gather up close to Christian, and wrestling with him gave him a dreadful fall; and with that Christian's sword flew out of his hand. Then said

Apollyon, I am sure of thee now. And with that he had almost pressed him to death, so that Christian began to despair of life: but as God would have it, while Apollyon was fetching of his last blow, thereby to make a full end of this good man, Christian nimbly stretched out his hand for his sword, and caught it, saying, 'Rejoice not against me, O mine enemy: when I fall I shall arise';[1] and with that gave him a deadly thrust, which made him give back, as one that had received his mortal wound. Christian perceiving that, made at him again, saying, 'Nay, in all these things we are more than conquerors through him that loved us'.[2] And with that Apollyon spread forth his dragon's wings, and sped him away, that Christian for a season saw him no more.[3]

From: *The Pilgrim's Progress* by John Bunyan

(Dent, 1937, pp. 68–9)

Saturday

The Pilgrim's Progress

JOHN BUNYAN

In this combat no man can imagine, unless he had seen and heard as I did, what yelling and hideous roaring Apollyon made all the time of the fight – he spake like a dragon; and, on the other side, what sighs and groans burst from Christian's heart. I never saw him all the while give so much as one pleasant look, till he perceived he had wounded Apollyon with his two-edged sword; then, indeed, he did smile, and look upward; but it was the dreadfullest sight that ever I saw.

> A more unequal match can hardly be, –
> *Christian* must fight an angel; but you see,
> The Valiant man by handling Sword and Shield,
> Doth make him though a Dragon, quit the field.

So when the battle was over, Christian said, 'I will here give thanks to him that delivered me out of the mouth of the lion, to him that

[1] Micah 7:8.
[2] Romans 8:37.
[3] James 4:7.

did help me against Apollyon.' And so he did, saying –

> 'Great Beelzebub, the captain of this fiend,
> Designed my ruin; therefore to this end
> He sent him harnessed out: and he with rage
> That hellish was, did fiercely me engage.
> But blessed Michael helped me, and I,
> By dint of sword, did quickly make him fly.
> Therefore to him let me give lasting praise,
> And thank and bless his holy name always.'

Then there came to him a hand, with some of the leaves of the tree of life, the which Christian took, and applied to the wounds that he had received in the battle, and was healed immediately. He also sat down in that place to eat bread, and to drink of the bottle that was given him a little before; so, being refreshed, he addressed himself to his journey, with his sword drawn in his hand; for he said, I know not but some other enemy may be at hand. But he met with no other affront from Apollyon quite through this valley.

From: *The Pilgrim's Progress* by John Bunyan

(Dent, 1937, pp. 70–1)

Monday

Government of the Tongue

JOSEPH BUTLER

If any man among you seem to be religious and bridleth not his tongue, but deceiveth his own heart, this man's religion is vain. (James 1:26)

There is such a thing as a disposition to be talking for its own sake; from which persons often say anything, good or bad, of others, merely as a subject of discourse, according to the particular temper they themselves happen to be in, and to pass away the present time. There is likewise to be observed in persons such a strong and eager desire of engaging attention to what they say, that they will speak good or evil, truth or otherwise, merely as one or the other seems to be most hearkened to. . . .

This unrestrained volubility and wantonness of speech is the occasion of numberless evils and vexations in life. It begets resentment in him who is the subject of it; sows the seeds of strife and dissension amongst others; and inflames little disgusts and offences, which if let alone would wear away of themselves: it is often of as bad effect upon the good name of others, as deep envy or malice; and, to say the least of it in this respect, it destroys and perverts a certain equity of the utmost importance to society to be observed; namely, that praise and dispraise, a good or bad character, should always be bestowed according to desert. The tongue used in such a licentious manner is like a sword in the hand of a madman; it is employed at random, it can scarce possibly do any good, and for the most part does a world of mischief; and implies not only great folly and a trifling spirit, but great viciousness of mind, great indifference to truth and falsity, and to the reputation, welfare, and good of others. So much reason is there for what St. James says of the tongue, 'It is a fire, a world of iniquity, it defileth the whole body, setteth on fire the course of nature, and is itself set on fire of hell.' (Jas. 3.6.) This is the faculty or disposition which we are required to keep a guard upon: these are the vices and follies it runs into, when not kept under due restraint.

From: *Butler's Fifteen Sermons* by Joseph Butler

(S.P.C.K., 1970, pp. 42–3)

Tuesday

Government of the Tongue

JOSEPH BUTLER

The due and proper use of any natural faculty or power, is to be judged of by the end and design for which it was given us. The chief purpose, for which the faculty of speech was given to man, is plainly that we might communicate our thoughts to each other, in order to carry on the affairs of the world; for business, and for our improvement in knowledge and learning. But the good Author of our nature designed us not only necessaries, but likewise enjoyment and satisfaction, in that being He hath graciously given, and in that condition of life He hath placed us in. There are secondary uses of our faculties: they administer to delight, as well as to necessity: and as they are equally adapted to both, there is no doubt but He intended them for our gratification, as well as for the support and continuance of our being. The secondary use of speech is to please and be entertaining to each other in conversation. This is in every respect allowable and right: it unites men closer in alliances and friendships; gives us a fellow-feeling of the prosperity and unhappiness of each other; and is in several respects serviceable to virtue, and to promote good behaviour in the world. And provided there be not too much time spent in it, if it were considered only in the way of gratification and delight; men must have strange notions of God and of religion, to think that He can be offended with it, or that it is any way inconsistent with the strictest virtue. But the truth is, such sort of conversation, though it has no particular good tendency, yet it has a general good one: it is social and friendly, and tends to promote humanity, good-nature, and civility.

As the end and use, so likewise the abuse of speech, relates to the one or other of these: either to business, or to conversation. As to the former; deceit in the management of business and affairs does not properly belong to the subject now before us: though one may just mention that multitude, that endless number of words, with which business is perplexed; when a much fewer would, as it should seem, better serve the purpose: but this must be left to those who understand the matter. The government of the tongue, considered as a subject of itself, relates chiefly to conversation; to that kind of discourse which usually fills up the time spent in friendly meetings, and visits of civility. And the danger is, lest persons entertain themselves and others at the expense of their wisdom and their virtue, and to the injury or offence of their neighbour. If they will observe and keep clear of these, they may be as free, and easy, and unreserved, as they can desire.

From: *Butler's Fifteen Sermons* by Joseph Butler

(S.P.C.K., 1970, pp. 43–4)

Wednesday

Government of the Tongue

JOSEPH BUTLER

The Wise Man observes, that 'there is a time to speak, and a time to keep silence'. One meets with people in the world, who seem never to have made the last of these observations. And yet these great talkers do not at all speak from their having anything to say, as every sentence shews, but only from their inclination to be talking. Their conversation is merely an exercise of the tongue: no other human faculty has any share in it. It is strange these persons can help reflecting, that unless they have in truth a superior capacity, and are in an extraordinary manner furnished for conversation; if they are entertaining, it is at their own expense. Is it possible, that it should never come into people's thoughts to suspect, whether or not it be to their advantage to shew so very much of themselves? 'O that you would altogether hold your peace, and it should be your wisdom.'[1] But one would think it should be obvious to everyone, that when they are in company with their superiors of any kind, in years, knowledge, and experience; when proper and useful subjects are discoursed of, which they cannot bear a part in; that these are

[1] Job 13:5.

times for silence: when they should learn to hear, and be attentive; at least in their turn. It is indeed a very unhappy way these people are in: they in a manner cut themselves out from all advantage of conversation, except that of being entertained with their own talk: their business in coming into company not being at all to be informed, to hear, to learn; but to display themselves; or rather to exert their faculty, and talk without any design at all. And if we consider conversation as an entertainment, as somewhat to unbend the mind; as a diversion from the cares, the business, and the sorrows of life; it is of the very nature of it, that the discourse be mutual. This, I say, is implied in the very notion of what we distinguish by conversation, or being in company. Attention to the continued discourse of one alone grows more painful often, than the cares and business we come to be diverted from. He therefore who imposes this upon us is guilty of a double offence; arbitrarily enjoining silence upon all the rest, and likewise obliging them to this painful attention.

From: *Butler's Fifteen Sermons* by Joseph Butler

(S.P.C.K., 1970, pp. 44–5)

Thursday

Government of the Tongue

JOSEPH BUTLER

The last thing is, the government of the tongue as relating to discourse of the affairs of others, and giving of characters. These are in a manner the same: and one can scarce call it an indifferent subject, because discourse upon it almost perpetually runs into somewhat criminal.

And first of all, it were very much to be wished that this did not take up so great a part of conversation; because it is indeed a subject of a dangerous nature. Let anyone consider the various interests, competitions, and little misunderstandings which arise amongst men; and he will soon see, that he is not unprejudiced and unpartial, that he is not, as I may speak, neutral enough, to trust himself with talking of the character and concerns of his neighbour, in a free, careless, and unreserved manner. There is perpetually, and often it is not attended to, a rivalship amongst people of one kind or another, in respect to wit, beauty, learning, fortune; and that one thing will insensibly influence them to speak to the disadvantage of others, even where there is no formal malice or ill design. Since therefore it is so hard to enter into this subject without offending, the first thing to be observed is, that people should learn to decline it; to get over that strong inclination most have to be talking of the concerns and behaviour of their neighbour.

From: *Butler's Fifteen Sermons* by Joseph Butler

(S.P.C.K., 1970, p. 46)

Friday

Government of the Tongue

JOSEPH BUTLER

Since it is impossible that this subject [of other people] should be wholly excluded [from] conversation; and since it is necessary that the characters of men should be known: the next thing is, that it is a matter of importance what is said; and therefore, that we should be religiously scrupulous and exact to say nothing, either good or bad, but what is true. I put it thus, because it is in reality of as great importance to the good of society, that the characters of bad men should be known, as that the characters of good men should. People, who are given to scandal and detraction, may indeed make an ill use of this observation; but truths, which are of service towards regulating our conduct, are not to be disowned, or even concealed, because a bad use may be made of them. This however would be effectually prevented, if these two things were attended to. First, that, though it is equally of bad consequence to society, that men should have either good or ill characters which they do not deserve; yet, when you say somewhat good of a man which he does not deserve there is no wrong done him in particular; whereas, when you say evil of a man which he does not deserve, here is a direct formal injury, a real piece of injustice done him. This therefore makes a wide difference; and gives us, in point of virtue, much greater latitude in speaking well than ill of others. Secondly, a good man is friendly to his fellow-creatures, and a lover of mankind; and so will upon every occasion, and often without any, say all the good he can

about everybody; but, so far as he is a good man, will never be
disposed to speak evil of any, unless there be some other reason for it,
besides barely that it is true. If he be charged with having given an
ill character, he will scarce think it a sufficient justification of himself
to say it was a true one, unless he can also give some further
account how he came to do so: a just indignation against particular
instances of villainy, where they are great and scandalous; or to
prevent an innocent man from being deceived and betrayed, when
he has great trust and confidence in one who does not deserve it.
Justice must be done to every part of a subject when we are considering it. If there be a man, who bears a fair character in the world,
whom yet we know to be without faith or honesty, to be really an ill
man; it must be allowed in general, that we shall do a piece of service
to society, by letting such an one's true character be known. This
is no more than what we have an instance of in our Saviour Himself;
though He was mild and gentle beyond example. However, no words
can express too strongly the caution which should be used in such
a case as this.

Upon the whole matter: If people would observe the obvious
occasions of silence, if they would subdue the inclination to tale-
bearing, and that eager desire to engage attention, which is an original
disease in some minds; they would be in little danger of offending with
their tongue; and would, in a moral and religious sense, have due
government over it.

From: *Butler's Fifteen Sermons* by Joseph Butler

(S.P.C.K., 1970, pp. 46–7)

Saturday

Bury Me in My Boots

SALLY TRENCH

I was coming home very late one night from the country, feeling
weary and looking forward to a warm bed. Against a background
noise of chamber music intermingled with the groans and sneezings
of the engines, I passed the ticket office into the main hall. 'Oh, I
beg your pardon!' I swung round to see who I had bumped into.
She was an old lady, so wrapped up in moth-eaten scarves that her

face was hardly visible. She wore a dress down to her ankles and a man's sweater, three times too big for her. She had no stockings, but a pair of disintegrating slippers covered part of her feet. She stood hunched over her brown paper parcels; I do not think she had noticed the impact as I had collided with her, not to mention my apology. I walked on. I noticed scruffy men bedded down under newspapers on the benches, others slouched dejectedly in the corners. They were all dirty and unshaven, a few of the lucky ones had overcoats to protect them against the winter nights, the rest just sat shivering. How easy it was to walk past. How easy it was to sympathize from a distance. How easy it was to pass by on the other side of the road like the Levite in the New Testament.

I stopped and turned back. I parked myself in the middle of a bench between two of the scruffiest men. All at once my Good Samaritan intentions left me and I became nervous. The men had not batted an eyelid. I could smell the alcohol. I fumbled in my pockets for cigarettes and, as I lit one, the two men seemed to wake up. One lurched sideways and leaned against me. I was really frightened. 'Go' any to spare?' he slurred. I lit one and handed it to him and repeated the gesture for the bloke on my other side. The man was becoming heavy. If I edged away he might take offence, so I did the only thing possible. I took him by the shoulders and straightened him.

'Want any help, Missy?' A large West Indian, with his hands on his hips, a hat pushed to one side, and a most amiable grin on his round face, swayed before me. 'You don't belong here, Missy, not a high-class filly like you,' he reprimanded gently.

'I'm not a permanent, just passing through,' I said hastily.

'Just visiting. You're too pretty to be amongst us dirty drunks. You're not one of us. Go home.'

'I will. I just thought they might like a cigarette. What will happen to them? Will they go home?' He threw back his head and laughed.

'Home? Man they got no home. This is their bedroom for tonight.' He bent down to me. 'Now you go home yourself, Missy, and don't you worry about us. Go home and thank the good Lord you got a home to go to.'

The background music had stopped, the engines were bedded down and the station porters were calling out their final farewells. The vast station, an active terminus during the day, was silent save for the periodical cooing of a sleepless pigeon. The homeless, neglected and unwanted shivered under their newspapers. I shoved the packet of cigarettes into the West Indian's hands and did as I was told. I left the cold and hungry dossers to the night. But when I lay in my warm bed with my dog at my feet and a glass of hot chocolate in my hand, I did thank the kind Lord for having blessed me with a family and a home.

From: *Bury Me in My Boots* by Sally Trench

(Hodder & Stoughton, 1969, pp. 19–20)

TRINITY 10

Bury Me in My Boots

SALLY TRENCH

It was as cold and silent as the other night. Underneath the newspapers were the same grey debauched faces. I lowered my haversack
and poured out the coffee. Someone had woken up, another was
stirring. I handed them the hot cups. Along the line of benches, the
bodies shifted and haggard faces appeared. I refilled the cups and
passed them down the line. I placed cigarettes between icy-mauve
lips and poured out more hot coffee for grabbing hands. When I
ran dry, I went over to the hot drinks machine and bought more
and rationed it to half a cup per man. Cigarettes were being divided
also.

The big clock struck two, and as it did so a general move took
place. Dossers staggered to their feet, their eyes still closed, and
wandered off; they were still asleep as they walked into the telephone
booths or down the station where they could not be seen. Some, on
hearing the move, automatically rolled off the benches, still snoring,
picked themselves up and sauntered behind closed bookstalls where
they stood up asleep, hanging on to the bars or the grill. At first I was
nonplussed, but I soon discovered the reason for it. In the distance
I saw the blue uniform. Quickly I collected up my pieces and hid
myself in the shadows of the arches. I had a front-stall view! There
were two of them, and between them they woke every man up.
They were polite until the man proved obstreperous or difficult,
then they just hauled him to his feet and shoved him towards the
exit. Some they escorted off the premises, others they dragged away
roughly. The more respectable-looking citizens they asked to see
their tickets, for there were a few who were staying the night to
catch the first trains at dawn. If they failed to produce a ticket, they
were removed too. I was to learn later that this was a regular two-
hourly feature throughout the night. Part of the routine for the law-
boys, but a purely symbolic gesture, for they later stood by and
watched the same faces reappear and did not bother to move them on

till two hours later. I retreated to my bike, passing sleeping men still on their feet, but the general drift back to the benches had begun.

My routine with the dossers on Waterloo Station became a regular shift. I learnt to sleep till two, be at the station by three and home by four. Even my nerves were becoming nerveless! . . . The lads at the station became as accustomed to the whiff of hot coffee in their sleep, as they did to the two-hourly move-on.

From: *Bury Me in My Boots* by Sally Trench

(Hodder & Stoughton, 1969, pp. 21–2)

Tuesday

Bury Me in My Boots

SALLY TRENCH

It was by the hand of fate that I was walking up Ladbroke Grove, an indigent area of London, one evening when I came across a down-and-out sprawled in the gutter. He was groaning quietly as if in pain. People just walked past as if they had not seen him. I knelt down beside him and turned him on to his back. I could not see his face for dirt. 'What's the trouble?'

'They hit me.'

'Who?'

'Them blokes.' I could see no one apart from the occasional passer-by.

'Where do you live?'

'Golborne.'

'Where's that?'

'Up that road there.'

'Do you think you can stand? Have a bash and I'll help you back.'

Together we stumbled to our feet, hanging on to each other, and with his arm round my neck we began to walk leisurely back – to Golborne. Crammed tightly in the middle of a row of shops, just off the Portobello Road, behind a vegetable and fruit stall, was the Golborne Centre, We pushed open the unlatched front door and walked in. I was staggered, we were standing in a church. It was a large drab room with a pulpit at one end looking down on rows of shabby chairs and cigarette ends and up at a false roof stretching across to hide what was once a circular gallery. My companion led me to the spiral staircase. It was an ancient one, of wrought iron, just wide enough for one man to ascend at a time. We climbed into the gallery. It was packed with two-tier bunks and narrow steel lockers. I clung to a bunk looking down at the false roof which, though safe enough, had a precarious feel to it. I helped the old man on to his bed and he lay there huddled in equally old blankets. I descended the spiral staircase even more gingerly than I had climbed it and went in search of someone.

From: *Bury Me in My Boots* by Sally Trench

(Hodder & Stoughton, 1969, pp. 27–8)

Wednesday

Bury Me in My Boots

SALLY TRENCH

I found a tiny kitchen with two old gas stoves in it but no people. It was partitioned off from the church, and from it I could hear talking in the next partitioned room. As I entered, the smell of tobacco was overpowering and visibility very poor. I was in a fair-sized room, filthy and bleak, but warm. Crippled tables and chairs stood around on which were hunched vagrants, delinquents, ex-convicts and inadequates. A battered television set at the other end was the only other piece of furniture. No one looked up as I made my way through dog-ends and dinner scraps on the bare wooden floor. I sat myself beside a young man with shoulder-length hair. His features were sharp and his eyes cold and narrow; a dangerous friend to make, I thought.

'Hello. Like a cigarette?' I gave him a friendly smile. His eyes narrowed to almost closing; from his pocket he pulled some loose tobacco and began to roll his own. I put mine away. He watched me suspiciously.

'I brought back one of your chaps,' I explained. He continued rolling his cigarette, watching me like a hawk.

'I took him upstairs to his bunk.' Pause. 'I hope that's all right?' He put the cigarette between his lips and slowly went through his pockets, never taking his eyes off me. He produced a lighter and flicked it alight. Instead of lighting his cigarette, he enlarged the flame. I felt his shifty eyes burning behind that flame. I sat, cold with

M

fear, wondering what his next move was going to be. Suddenly he stuck the lighter under my nose. I threw my head back to avoid the heat, and with clenched fists banged his arm on to the table. It was an automatic reaction. Fear gripped me for his face was red with rage. He spat the cigarette out and rolled his eyes and laughed.

'You're not f . . . bad,' he commented.

'Thank you,' I said dryly, not sharing the joke. 'You're not bad at making friends yourself.' I found myself saying this angrily before I could check myself. He glanced at me and burst into more laughter.

'You should have seen your face; right green you were.'

'Now that we're talking, who's in charge here?' I enquired.

'Depends 'ow you look on it, don't it? No one's in charge of me.'

'Well, who runs the place then?'

'The Guv.' Patience was never my virtue.

'And who's the Guv?'

'Peake, the Right Reverend Peake.'

'Where would I find him?'

'Gone 'ome.'

'Well, who's in charge while he's away?' He grinned at me and I noticed his front teeth were missing.

'Dunno.'

The door swung open and a tall grey-bearded man entered. He saw me and came over. 'Can I help you?'

'Well, actually I just brought back one of your lads. I found him in Ladbroke Grove. Apparently, there was a fight.'

'That was good of you. Thanks. Would you like to come into the office?' I rose to follow him.

'Thank you for nothin'. Good-bye.' The young man I had been talking to threw back his chair and pushed in front of me and out of the door in a temper. Greybeard turned to me: 'Don't take any notice of Bob, he's got a temperature like a yo-yo!'

From: *Bury Me in My Boots* by Sally Trench

(Hodder & Stoughton, 1969, pp. 28–9)

Thursday

Bury Me in My Boots

SALLY TRENCH

In the office I learned from Dave (he told me his name later) that the Reverend Peake, a Nonconformist minister, had turned his church into a doss-house some years previously, and could now sleep anything up to fifty men. He offered them the draughty protection of his church and three square meals a day; it was not a lot, but a castle compared with the Embankment or the gutter. At first the minister slept them in the gallery among the pews, and they used to hang their washing across the church and over the pulpit; by their very presence, three-quarters of his congregation, who considered that this was carrying practical Christianity to unreasonable lengths, refused to come to his services. But the project grew, and the pews made way for bunks and lockers. After many visits to Golborne, I realized that outwardly it seemed to offer considerably less than many of the more orthodox establishments in the way of material comfort, and wondered why so many sought refuge at the Centre. For two reasons perhaps. One a practical consideration. In the centres set up by the local authorities, the homeless man had to present himself early in the evening if he was to be fortunate enough to secure himself a bed for the night. In the morning he was expected to help with the cleaning and other essential chores, and then he was told to leave. He has nowhere to go during the day and so just waits till five or six o'clock in the evening, when he will again be queuing at the same centre, or, having wandered too far from it, will be in search of a warm spot where he can sleep out the night. However, at Golborne, such a man was taken in and could stay indefinitely, leave when he liked and could consider himself a resident free to come and go in a small community. The other reason lay in the minister himself. His aim was to rekindle in each of his men some sense of their own dignity and importance. It was the individual, warm concern for the residents' well-being which raised Golborne high above any of the other centres for dossers.

From: *Bury Me in My Boots* by Sally Trench

(Hodder & Stoughton, 1969, pp. 29–30)

Friday

Bury Me in My Boots

SALLY TRENCH

My relationship with the lads took some months to establish. Some of them clearly looked upon me as a rather amusing curiosity and teased me incessantly about the way I spoke. This worried me at first and I thought it might prove a difficult barrier to cross, but I felt it was better than putting on a phoney accent which they might distrust. The more intelligent were perceptive enough to realize that I did not quite fit, and were highly suspicious. My presence, though, made no difference to the way they behaved. The language was well punctuated with the usual swear words and adjectives and as often as not, someone came out with a string of abuse just to see how I would react.

Having made a casual acquaintance with the boys, my problem became how to transform this superficial and fleeting relationship into one of greater depth and permanency without becoming too intimate. Gaining their acceptance was always the first step, but gaining their trust proved a very difficult second! Throughout my visits I concentrated on keeping the atmosphere personal and in-formal. On the whole the response was relaxed, but occasionally I met abruptness and suspicion and a generally inflexible attitude; with this type it was not easy to communicate friendship.

One of these was Bob. Having been accepted by him as a regular visitor, I began to encourage him to talk factually about himself, especially about his home and family, to establish a relaxed and informal atmosphere. He was the eldest of five from a poor working-class family. His mother was a semi-invalid and his father also suffered from poor health. He was a strict authoritarian and Bob had resented the restrictions put on him. Whilst at school, when he was not playing truant, he produced inadequate work and lacked any kind of concentration. With another boy he became a peripheral member of a large and quite notorious group of youths involved in anti-social activities. He left school at fifteen and found a factory job. He found this both unpleasant and boring, and was eventually sacked. By now he had developed an ugly temper which he enjoyed losing; fighting was a regular outlet for his emotions. A couple of youth clubs were unable to cope with him and his own friends were transient. He worked up considerable hostility against any kind of authority. At sixteen he walked out of home never to return and roamed around England obtaining the odd job on a fairground or on a building site. The rest of his time he spent in coffee bars or pubs. He resented anyone who had money, and his own philosophy was that money was the be-all and end-all of everything, with the implication that with remuneration one can do anything, everything. His attitude towards sex lacked respect: sexual intercourse was regarded as a matter of course at the first opportunity in any relationship. Later I was to discover that he had a wife somewhere and three children, though he swore only one was his. Since he left home he had been in and out of prison for pilfering and violence; when I met him he had just been discharged, having completed a four-year sentence for knifing a policeman, His attitude towards prison was particularly light-hearted, in fact he claimed to enjoy being 'inside', and it was a kindness on society's part to return him to prison, since the strain of living outside was so painful and intense.

From: *Bury Me in My Boots* by Sally Trench

(Hodder & Stoughton, 1969, pp. 31–2)

Saturday

Bury Me in My Boots

SALLY TRENCH

I was to encounter many like Bob later. It became quite clear to me that repeated punishment was having less and less effect on the ex-convict and was serving almost the exact opposite purpose to that presumably intended, for it was neither deterring nor reforming him. It seemed to me axiomatic that the more often a man offended and went back to prison, the more clearly he was showing a need for care and understanding. Prison only covered behavioural or person-ality maladjustments with a layer of 'institutional neurosis', officially described as 'prisonization'. Prison conditioned these men so that they were almost totally incapable of living outside. Was this because we set them standards that they were incapable of attaining and then followed it up by punishing them? Or was it that because their disabilities did not manifest themselves in physical symptoms or in any recognizable forms, they drew no understanding or acceptance? I did not know the cause and I was equally unsure of the answers.

I persisted with my relationship with Bob despite the obvious suspicion and hostility. He refused to meet me in Golborne and so we met in a café in the Portobello Road at a prearranged time. This refusal was a self-recognition of his disreputable environment. Often he never turned up, or when he did, his behaviour was rude and insulting. I felt he was trying me and waiting to hear the familiar threat, 'I'm not going to have anything more to do with you', but on these occasions I managed to hold my tongue and ignore him, which as often as not infuriated him more. Patience and perseverance over many months eventually proved their worth, though failure and success were relative concepts and I spent little time in considering them. When we did not meet in the coffee bar, we met in the pub where he would boast about how much drink he could take.

It took many meetings before he began to ask me for my help and advice. At first I was very cautious with my answers – I put out feelers. I tried not to dictate or deprive him of the right to self-determination, because I felt this would not help him to come to terms with himself or to develop a sense of responsibility towards his own affairs. When he consulted me about his problems I made no attempt to provide a ready-made solution or to pass moral judgment on the rights or wrongs of the situation. I tried to show him the involvements of his problems and the consequences of any action he might be contemplating. With Bob, I learnt that asking the right question was more important than knowing the right answer and more useful than any lecturing and moralizing.

From: *Bury Me in My Boots* by Sally Trench

(Hodder & Stoughton, 1969, pp. 33–4)

Bury Me in My Boots

SALLY TRENCH

The first visible breakthrough came ten months after he left prison and five months after our first meeting at Golborne. I was sitting in Johnny's Café waiting for Bob; a couple of Teds were on the next table taking the micky out of me by referring to my 'posh' clothes and 'upper class' smell when Bob came in looking rather sheepish. He was smartly dressed and for the first time, shaved. But what took my breath away was the haircut. No longer did he look a troglodyte but a well-groomed young man. I wished that he had some false teeth, because the ugly gap when he smiled rather spoilt the effect.

'Bob, what a vast improvement!' I encouraged.

'I could take you anywhere now, couldn't I?'

'Indeed you could. To the best hotel.'

'Yeah – Sal, I want to get a job.'

'Good. Anything in mind?' I wanted to sound pleased but not enthusiastic, in case I frightened him off the idea.

'Well, I 'ad a job in a baker's once. I've got a mate who's said 'e'll fix me up workin' beside 'im in a bakery.'

'Sounds admirable. Looking as you do, you'd get any job you applied for, but that sounds a splendid idea.' I wanted to ask when he was thinking of starting, but I refrained. I was glad I had.

'My mate thinks 'e can get me in on Monday. You think that's all right? And when I get a bit of lolly I'll take you out.'

'That would be lovely. I'll look forward to that. Meanwhile here's a packet of cigarettes.' It gave him the opening he wanted.

'Er . . . Sal, could you lend me a quid to see me over?'

'Okay, as long as it doesn't all go on drink.' I knew it would, but it did not worry me. I had given him a small amount previous to this and it had been lavishly spent in the pub, but I felt that our relationship was not established enough to refuse him his demand without an almighty scene and a final break-up.

Bob took the job in the bakery, and twice a week I met him after work, in the pub. Initially, the mere fact of having a job boosted his ego, not to mention the wages. Expansively, he insisted on taking me out for meals, and often we went to the cinema. Once or twice I brought along a girl-friend so that he would become accustomed to having females around him without having to think of going to bed with them. On our outings, he was always the gentleman, well-mannered and protective, yet he was still very moody and very quick-tempered. Drink was still his downfall and he was always ready to take on anyone who was prepared to fight. If someone refused to fight him he went into tantrums like a spoilt child, though next morning when he had sobered up, he would have forgotten all about it.

From: *Bury Me in My Boots* by Sally Trench

(Hodder & Stoughton, 1969, pp. 34–5)

Tuesday

Bury Me in My Boots

SALLY TRENCH

The second barrier was broken three months after Bob had taken his bakery job.

'Sal, will yer 'elp me?'

'If I can. What's the trouble?'

'I want to go home and see my old lady again.' This took the wind out of my sails.

'Splendid! But why do you want my help?'

'Well, I don't think my old man'll have me in the house, having not been in touch in the last five years like, and I was wonderin' if you could go and see them first?'

'Why not go together one day?' . . .

'Would you do that then?'

'Of course. Where do they live?' . . .

I was at the bus stop on Thursday as agreed. Together, we travelled to West Byfleet. Alone we crossed a canal bridge towards a row of council houses. We stopped outside one of them. Bob's confidence deserted him. 'You go and face the old man first,' he urged.

Leaving him at the front gate, I walked up the path not knowing quite what to expect. Having tapped on the front door with no result, I edged it open. I was standing in a minute kitchen.

'Come in, dear, what can I do for you? I'm through here.'

I looked into the adjoining room and saw a vast figure bulging over a chair; despite her size, her face was haggard and lined, a face that had tasted poverty and suffering.

'I'm sorry to disturb you, my name's Sally. You must be Mrs. H. Could I talk to you for a minute?' I noticed another figure in the corner. He was long and lanky like Bob but his features were softer; his eyes were tired and his expression was one of weary resignation. He greeted me suspiciously.

'I'll be quite frank with you,' I began. 'I've come down about your son, Bob. I've been seeing a lot of him lately and he's doing very well for himself. He's in a good job now.' There was no reaction.

'I thought 'e was in prison,' his father said eventually.

'No, he's been out nearly a year now and is really making a go of it.'

'Believe that when I see it!'

'As a matter of fact you can. Bob's outside.' . . .

'He's spent four years paying his debts,' I went on hastily, 'he's squared it up, now he's wanting to square it up with you. Give him that chance. He is your son.'

'Let me see the boy, Dad. It's been a long time,' Mrs. H. burst out.

He stared at her astonished. 'Since when did you concern yourself about your eldest?' She began to cry. I sat like a stuffed rabbit feeling utterly helpless while they argued. Words were useless when fighting bitterness.

'Let me see 'im. You don't have to,' Mrs. H. wept.

'Stop your crying.' He sat puffing his pipe; only the monotonous tick of the clock broke the silence. 'Well, since he's here, he'd better come in,' he said gruffly.

Outside, Bob was like an excited child, hopping from one foot to the other.

'Come on,' I said, 'they're waiting for you.' He followed behind as I led him into the drawing-room. His father got to his feet and they faced each other like a couple of angry bulls. Mrs. H. broke it.

'Hello, son.'

'Hello, Ma.' Silence and then Bob put out his hand to his father.

'Hello, Dad. Sorry I haven't written.' His father made no move to reciprocate the gesture. I saw Bob's ears go red, and his eyes began to narrow. His mother caught her breath, and I bit my lip. They were both too big for me to hold from fighting. Then the man took the pipe from his lips and laid it down on the mantelpiece. Grudgingly he extended his hand. I breathed again. 'You'll stay to lunch, won't you?' he said.

From: *Bury Me in My Boots* by Sally Trench

(Hodder & Stoughton, 1969, pp. 35–7)

Wednesday

Bury Me in My Boots

SALLY TRENCH

[Sally Trench went amongst drug-addicts in a bar in London.]

When I first rolled up in my denim jeans and polo neck sweater beneath a matching denim shirt, with long straight hair hanging limply over my shoulders plus the traditional 'eye-concealing' fringe, I was no different from numerous other females there – or males! What with both sexes wearing elaborate rings and bracelets it only provided further complications in discriminating one from the other, though as often as not the men wore ear-rings in the form of crucifixes whilst the girls just had gold rings.

At first conversation was non-existent, and for over two weeks I spent every evening there without a word passing my lips, whilst conspicuous glances passed among them. Yet it was obvious that I was receiving the same treatment that every unknown face was given: a greeting of hostility in case I might be a social worker or some kind of religious preacher who might attempt to 'guide' or 'help' them. I discovered they were averse to any kind of patronizing and equally reluctant to committing themselves to friendship. I found that as long as I was undemanding, they were prepared to give me a chance and talk to me. At the same time, having skirted various cafés and their dingy havens, I realized that fear of launching out into an unknown relationship or of rebuffal played a predominant part in their hostility. For months I patronized the addicts' hideouts and was given the cold shoulder; if I spoke without having been spoken to first they turned their backs and walked away. It was made perfectly clear that I was not one of them. When I passed a group of youths talking they would fall silent until I was well out of ear-shot. If one of them was trying to con a drink out of someone, they never tried me. I was out on a limb and was made to feel so. This Coventry applied by all the youngsters was very hurtful, and often when I was out of sight I would burst into tears and pray for the guts and perseverance to return the following evening. It was not easy and I dreaded the slow, uncommunicative passing of time.

From: *Bury Me in My Boots* by Sally Trench

(Hodder & Stoughton, 1969, pp. 62–3)

Thursday

Bury Me in My Boots

SALLY TRENCH

Quite suddenly it came to me that the simple failure of people to make contact with one another was often the cause of such human problems. What a paradox! We can bounce messages off the moon and send space probes to Mars, yet we are finding it more difficult as each day passes to communicate with the minds and hearts of those we love. Love is the climate in which all living things flourish. This language of love is designed to crack the shell of isolation by effective channels of communication. It is a universal language that is sadly neglected. Love is like gratitude, not much good unless you can show it. No doubt these addicts had relations who nominally loved them, but for these lone wolves it must be a tender understanding and a personal care, not just verbal concern. They needed compassion, not condemnation.

I was able to give compassion, not pity, and because of this giving it became a reciprocal action. They loved me in return. They began to love me so much that they asked me to fix them. At first I refused because I did not want to be part of it. I did not want to be involved. But I was involved and I was part of it. I was identified as one of them. So gritting my teeth so that I should not be sick, I began to give fixes. I had been fixing Stuart, a registered addict, for some weeks with ten grains, when it occurred to me that I might try cutting it down without him knowing. Over a period of three months I had cut him down to five grains without him noticing. I hoped there would be a time that I would be just injecting water into him. But as I learnt to deal with these drug addicts and look after them, I arrived at the opinion that a true addict is unable to come off without hospitalization. Many a time a youth has wept his heart out on my shoulder because he is unable to give it up without a drug to take its place. Yet the majority who are fortunate enough to receive hospitalization return straight to drugs on their release. Therefore there are two actions necessary to help the addicts and control addiction. The addicted must receive medical aid, and the source must be stopped. Until the peddlers are exterminated; drug addiction will be on the up-and-up not only amongst the young, but amongst all ages and classes. I don't blame the young for their idiocy, I blame the hard, calculating peddler who provides the ammunition for them to destroy themselves with – and they do.

From: *Bury Me in My Boots* by Sally Trench

(Hodder & Stoughton, 1969. pp. 68–9)

Friday

Bury Me in My Boots

SALLY TRENCH

Darkness had fallen and the steady rain had changed to a mere drizzle. Black shadows frowned over the deserted streets as tattered clouds were driven in scattered formation across the sky. My clothes hung coldly to my back. I walked faster across the slumbering City. The chill wind was freezing my face and numbing my fingers. I passed an old nightwatchman, sitting solemnly in his canvas box, staring at the glow of the brazier and the line of red lights that surrounded the road works. I called a cheerful greeting as I passed, which he acknowledged with a grunt. I crossed the vast empty bus terminus, my steps amplified in the eerie silence. Deserted buses stood in neat rows, their windows glazed and reflective. I continued down drenched streets where rivulets scuttled down steps and whirlpools gushed round gratings. Past grey uniform buildings and a graveyard where the rain pattered mournfully upon the tombs – upon the just and unjust alike. Everywhere was filled with the raw night air, damp, dark and cold.

I came to a junction and turned left, leaving the Whitechapel Road behind me. I wondered if they would be here. The wet breeze blew my hair over my face in a kind of mockery. I was nearly there. Just past these abandoned derelict buildings, carcasses of 'home', and beyond that creeping wall. The stillness spread like a blanket into the distance. I approached the ramp as softly as I could, and advanced from behind the sodden wall. There was a dull red glow of a wood fire. Beside it cowered figures with hands outstretched to meet the grateful warmth. With limbs huddled together and heads bowed, they bent over the fitful light. In the smouldering embers these stricken figures sat the nights out, amongst the ashes and dust and debris of the bomb-site. The figures neither spoke nor turned to look at me. Quietly I moved across to one of the stooping figures who clasped a bottle; gently I unlocked his fingers and the glass smashed to pieces as it hit the ground, echoing across the night. The stooping figure rocked forward and I grabbed him as he was about to fall into the embers. His clothes were soaked. Little by little, with an intense effort, he lifted his head and looked at me. His eyes were red and glazed.

'Hello, Benghazi! It's all right, it's only me. How are you?'

He stared expressionlessly at my face. His lips began to move, but no sound came from them in reply. I dug into my pockets and produced a packet of squashed cigarettes. I lit one for him and placed it between his swollen lips. I looked around to see how many of the regulars were here tonight. I counted eleven heads in all, that was including the three prostrate bodies lying over by the wall. I recognized seven faces by name. Some had lived on this bomb-site for seventeen years, some were newcomers. Others who had once lived here had passed away, their guts and stomach burnt dry by methylated spirits or eau-de-cologne. Some just died of exposure; a few, so drunk, fell into the fire and were burnt to death, and the occasional one was killed by some angry drunkard. They lived animals' lives with a law of their own. How I longed for a lighter room, bright fires and cheerful faces, the music of happy voices, words of love and welcome and warm hearts. It was a night to be home, asleep by a warm hearth.

From: *Bury Me in My Boots* by Sally Trench

(Hodder & Stoughton, 1969, pp. 70–1)

Saturday

Bury Me in My Boots

SALLY TRENCH

I glanced across at the heaped bodies of Canada, Hank, Steela Horse, Jock and Paddy. Their faces, concealed behind knotted stubble and stale old grime, were muffled under flea-ridden overcoats. Benghazi suddenly rocked forward again and I put out a supportive hand. He seemed to pull himself to consciousness as he felt my grip and smiled at me in recognition, revealing a few discoloured fangs scattered around in his mouth. He gave me his hand in friendship. It was rough and very dirty, his gritty fingernails were jagged and yellow. He was unwholesome and animal-like. Each night I met him he seemed to grow weaker and more feeble and care-worn. The mask of death that I had seen so many times before, was about to claim another victim.

Canada turned over and stretched out for a bottle beside him. . . .

Jock stumbled to his feet and bent over Steela Horse. He kicked him awake. 'Horse! Horse! Canada wants some jake.' There was a muffled grunt of agreement; Jock took the bottle that he was clasping tightly to his chest, and handed it to the tottering Canada. 'Sit down b'fore yer fall down,' Jock cried and pushed him over. He crashed on top of Benghazi and the two of them rolled in the mud, grappling for the bottle.

Meanwhile Paddy was whimpering by the almost dead fire. I was about to get up and see what the matter was when Jock put a restraining hand on me. 'Ye canna do anythin' for 'im, Sal. 'E won't last the night out, I don't think.' I looked at the writhing body, the haggard face looking mauve in the spark-light of the embers. The eyes were sunken and black and the open mouth gasping for breath. Bile dribbled down his chin. I had seen it all before. I closed my eyes and prayed. I forced myself to my feet and went and knelt beside him. I took his ice-cold languid hand and rubbed it. For a second he opened his puffed eyes and gave me a glassy stare. I smiled caringly at him. I knew there was nothing I could do, I knew that he was beyond medical help. I smiled again and grasped his hand. As long as he knows he's not alone, that someone cares, that was all I wanted to transmit to him in my smile. It was so little and cost me nothing, and yet could mean the whole world to a dying man.

A few hours later, everyone had drifted back to sleep. The fire and Paddy had died together. I looked around at his mates; many of them would be joining him soon, and they did not care. They had nothing left in life to live for.

From: *Bury Me in My Boots* by Sally Trench

(Hodder & Stoughton, 1969, pp. 72–3)

TRINITY 12

The Church in Czechoslovakia

BROTHER ANDREW

After the service I introduced myself to the preacher. When I mentioned that I had come from Holland chiefly to meet with Christians in his country, he seemed overwhelmed.

'I had heard,' he said, 'that Czechoslovakia was going to begin opening its borders. I didn't believe it. We've been' – he looked around – 'almost imprisoned since the war. You must come and talk with me.'

Together we went to his apartment. It was only later that I learned how dangerous a thing for him this was in the Czechoslovakia of 1955. He told me that the Government was trying to get a total grip of the Church. It was the Government that selected theological students – choosing only candidates who favoured the regime. In addition, every two months a minister had to renew his licence. A friend had recently had his renewal application denied – no explanation. Each sermon had to be written out ahead of time and approved by the authorities. Each church had to list its leaders with the State. That same week in Brno five brethren were on trial because their church did not permit the naming of leaders.

It was time for the second service at the church.

'Would you come and speak to us?' he asked suddenly.

'Is that possible? Can I really preach here?'

'No. I did not say "preach". One must be careful with words. As a foreigner you can't preach, but you can bring us "greetings" from Holland. And,' my friend smiled, 'if you wanted to, you could bring us "greetings" from the Lord.'

My interpreter was a young medical student named Antonin. First I brought greetings from Holland and the West. That took a couple of minutes. And then for half an hour I brought greetings to the congregation 'from Jesus Christ'. It worked so well that Antonin suggested we try the device again in another church. All in all, that day I preached four times and visited five churches. Each was memorable in its own way, but the last one most of all. . . .

We travelled across Prague until we came to a small out-of-the-way Moravian church. I was astonished at the number of people there, especially young people. There must have been forty persons between the ages of eighteen and twenty-five. I spoke my greetings and then answered questions. Could Christians in Holland get good jobs? Did anyone report you to the Government when you went to church? Could you attend church and still get into a good university?

'You see,' Antonin told me, 'it's unpatriotic to be a Christian in Czechoslovakia these days. Some of these people have been blackballed at work. Many have missed out on education. And that' – he took a small box from the hands of a young man who stood beside him – 'is why they want you to have this.'

The young man was speaking to me very earnestly in Czech.

'Take this to Holland with you,' Antonin translated, 'and when people ask you about it, tell them about us and remind them that we are part of the Body, too, and that we are in pain.'

I took the box and opened it. Inside was a silver lapel ornament in the shape of a tiny cup. I had seen several of the young people wearing them and had wondered what they were.

Antonin was pinning it to my jacket. 'This is the symbol of the Church in Czechoslovakia. We call it the Cup of Suffering.'

From: *God's Smuggler* by Brother Andrew

(Hodder & Stoughton, 1970, pp. 86–8)

Tuesday

A Monastery in Thessaly

PETER HAMMOND

The convent of St. Stephen, built on the site of a hermitage founded in 1312, lies on the farther side of a chasm spanned by a drawbridge. In order to gain access to most of the monasteries, however, it was necessary to be hoisted in a net lowered from the gate-house of the monastery (commonly situated some 150 feet above the farthest point to which the traveller could attain by his own unaided efforts), or to clamber up ladders somewhat imperfectly secured by long

wooden pegs to the face of the precipice. Travellers' accounts abound
in references to the perils of either means of ascent: to frayed ropes
which were replaced only after a catastophe had actually occurred,
and to the horrors of ladders hung perpendicularly upon the face of
the cliff, below which, as Curzon relates: 'the precipice went sheer
down to so tremendous a depth, that my head turned when I surveyed
the distant valley over which I was hanging in the air like a fly on a
wall.'

Of all the monasteries now inhabited St. Stephen had, it seemed
evident, sustained far the greatest calamities as the result of war.
Sacked first by the Italians and later by the Communists, it was a
mere shell of a building, its unglazed windows affording little protection – as we learned by bitter experience – against wind or snow.
Its former guest-rooms were crammed with wrecked furniture and
empty ammunition boxes, while the eikons in the smaller of the two
churches (the chapel dedicated to St. Stephen) had been wantonly
defaced.

The *Igoumenos* [Abbot] of St. Stephen's was the Deacon Anthimos,
who came to the Meteora between the wars from the great Athonite
house of Vatopedi – 'a good house and garden . . . snakes very big
and long in it', notes Dr. Covel. There were also living at St. Stephen
three simple monks – lay-brothers, as they would be called in the
west – Ephrem, who has been a monk for twenty years, Eusebius,
who was formerly a policeman, and Cyril. Whilst we were staying
at the monastery there arrived from Trikkala a certain Papa Iannis,
an octogenarian with three married daughters. He had obtained
his bishop's permission to come and share the life of the monks
(there being no other priest in the community). Finally there was
Basil, a layman of sixty-five, who, after spending his boyhood in
America, had returned to his native Thessaly to serve more than one
monastery as a resourceful factotum; and there were the inevitable
stylite cats. The *Igoumenos* was plainly a sick man – it was little
wonder, considering what he had been through during the last few
years and the rigours of the life at St. Stephen's – and the morning
we left the monastery there was not a monk capable of getting to his
place in church for [the midnight office and Lauds.][1]

Life at the Meteora today is hard indeed, and under such conditions as prevail it is hardly astonishing that the liturgical life of the
monasteries should exhibit but little of the dignity and splendour
which one rightly looks for in a large and well-ordered community.
We were none the less deeply impressed by the efforts which are

[1] *Mesonyktikon* and *orthros*.

made to maintain the regular course of the *opus Dei*. Night after night, while Kalambaka sleeps, the few remaining ascetics of the Thebaid of Staghi gather in the dimly-lighted chapels among the high rocks to perform what for the monk must always be his primary liturgy; morning by morning as the sun touches the heights of Pindos with new fire and the flickering candles grow pale in the first light of dawn, the great trinitarian doxology banishes the shades of night and unites heaven and earth, angels and archangels, sinful men and those whose warfare is accomplished, in a single bond of adoration:

> Glory to God in the highest,
> And on earth peace, goodwill towards men.
> > We praise Thee,
> > We bless Thee,
> > We worship Thee,
> > We glorify Thee,
> We give thanks to Thee for Thy great glory.
> > O Lord King,
> > O God of Heaven,
> > Father Almighty;
> O Lord, Only-begotten Son, Jesus Christ,
> And O Holy Spirit.

From: *The Waters of Marah* by Peter Hammond

(Rockliff, 1956, pp. 77–8)

Wednesday

Margaret

J. D. ROSS

'You mean I'm going to die?'

'Yes . . . I mean you're going to die.'

In the five minutes which followed Margaret went through several rigidly defined phases, and, I implicitly believe, received that intangible, dismissed by so many as myth, the Holy Spirit.

First was knowledge, the Truth, as she realized what I had said, and what it meant with all its implications. At her Confirmation eighteen months before she had received the gift of Ghostly Strength, which, dormant ever since but always there, now blossomed with terrific force. The Spirit of Truth flooded her whole being; she assessed, cut through all the secondary issues of self-pity or self-desire, saw clearly the greater will, and by the grace which was hers, obeyed. . . .

That was her supreme moment, her test, when of her own free will she could either reject what I had said, break down completely into panic or hysteria (which I knew she would not, knowing her worth), or try to put up a brave front of the 'So what the hell' attitude. Or she could do just what she did – take her sentence in all its material meaning in terms of earthly values, and translate it into those which her Creator wished her to.

She was tested to the maximum, confronted by death itself, and turned without question or hesitation to God. And He never forsook her.

The assimilation of knowledge was followed by a short period during which she clung to me and wept unrestrainedly – from relief. Between tears she said that for weeks the feeling of something being kept from her had grown; she had never found any of us anything but natural and cheerful in our attitude, but we had overlooked the strength of the ties between us, and she felt instinctively, in each one of us, something she could not understand and which had started vague fears of her own. . . .

Now she knew the truth and there would be no more deceit, no more undercurrent of tension, she could relax and be perfectly happy with us. And if she had to die. . . .

'I'm not afraid of dying . . . I believe you know that. It will be so much more difficult for all of you.'

Yes, she was very relieved, because she knew now where she stood, and what she could do about it. I let her weep for some time, only soothing her, then dried her tears and saw with wonder the third stage she had come to, which lasted to the very end. In the weeks to come every person who saw Margaret remarked on the transformation she had undergone, for it was nothing less than that. Her acceptance of the facts from the start, without question or bitterness, was alone a quality which uplifted and strengthened those about her. I repeat, acceptance. Once I heard someone say: 'How wonderful for her to be so resigned.' The speaker was hopelessly lost in their estimation of the situation. Resignation implies putting up with that which cannot be altered, stoically, bravely even, but quite definitely only submitting to something one would rather do without! Margaret accepted in the fullest sense of the word. She looked all the facts squarely in the face, and with peace and joy embraced what she had to do. In the many conversations I was to have with her it became ever more clear that she was streets ahead of us in the comprehension of what suffering and dying, as the acceptance of God's will, meant.

Tranquillity, a sense of humour that never deserted her, and a quality that was more than radiance were hers. They shone in her eyes and face as I sat with her now – five minutes from being told she must die.

From: *Margaret* by James Davidson Ross

(Hodder & Stoughton, 1970, pp. 58–60)

Thursday

Let My People Go

ALBERT LUTHULI

The arrested men were quartered in two large cells, but we could meet during the day. We redistributed the population of these cells and assigned a chaplain to each – we were fortunate in having among us two Anglican priests, Fathers Gawe and Calata. It was necessary to have one in each cell since, although their new congregations were relatively small, we spent most of the twenty-four hours locked in. It was necessary to lock each priest in with his parish.

We shook down very quickly. Obviously, there was no temptation towards idleness. It is extraordinarily difficult in so large a country as South Africa for resistance leaders to meet together, especially since many of us do not belong to the travelling classes. Yet here we all were, met together, and with time on our hands. What distance, other occupations, lack of funds, the police interference had made difficult – frequent meetings – the Government had now insisted on. We could at last confer *sine die*, at any level we liked. Delegates from the remotest areas were never farther than one cell away.

But to prevent too great an absorption with resistance affairs, we saw to it that there was relief. We organized debates, indoor games, lecturers, regular worship both Muslim and Christian – and, of course, music. According to Prison Regulations we were supposed to fall silent at 8 p.m. Dr. Naicker and I usually insisted on silence somewhere between 10 and 11 p.m. The guards seemed to recognize tacitly that this regulation was better honoured in the breach than in the observance.

We were heartened by the news that the Bishop of Johannesburg and other good citizens were arranging our defence against the charges. Never low in morale, the arrested men were immeasurably encouraged by this, by visits of defence lawyers, and by the evidence that reached us of the generosity of a host of Johannesburg people. Among other visitors such as the Bishop and the Revd. Canon A. Blaxall, I was delighted to see Dominie du Toit, the man who had led our Christian Council delegation to India almost twenty years before. Such a visit takes more courage than is readily understood.

On the day when we were taken to the Magistrate's Court in closed vans to be formally charged, we had some hint of the stir which the arrests had created. We were carefully insulated, but the evidence that the crowds were not far away was obvious. Even so, this was nothing compared in size with what was to come. . . .

On our last Sunday in the cells Father Calata led our devotions. It was a most moving service, a real spiritual preparation for what lay ahead, which made its mark even on the non-Christians and atheists among us. Afterwards we all stood around in a great circle and sang some of our freedom songs. I led the prisoners in our pledging ourselves to solidarity in the cause of liberation – it proved a touching little impromptu ceremony about which were both formality and dedication. There was no doubt about it, we had not languished in gaol, our morale was very high.

From: *Let My People Go* by Albert Luthuli

(Collins Fontana, 1971, pp. 147–9)

Friday

My Image

R. WURMBRAND

Dear brothers and sisters,

The examining officer was in a good mood today. You could sense it from the very beginning. There would be no beating. He just wanted to amuse himself with some pleasant conversation.

He asked me, 'Do you believe that God created man in his own image?' I answered, 'I certainly do.' 'Do you believe that you are in the image of God?' 'Of course.'

Then he took a mirror out of his pocket and handed it to me. 'Look into the glass. See how ugly you are. You have dark circles under your eyes. You are all skin and bones. Your whole appearance is haggard, like a madman. If you are in the image of God, God must be as ugly as you are. Why should you worship him?'

I had already seen myself in a mirror once since I had been in jail, and I knew that I was terribly ugly, I who had been considered a handsome man. I had been horrified to see myself in such shape. Now, my ugliness was being made into a theological problem.

Happily, Christians do not have to think beforehand what to answer. The words are given to them.

I said, 'Yes, my God has an ugly face like me. In Hebrew there is no such word as "face". You can only say "faces" – *panim*. The word has no singular. There is a deep meaning in this, because no man has only one face. He shows one countenance when he speaks to a superior, another when he bullies an inferior, one when he is grieved, another when he hears good news. Our God also has many faces. One is a face of complete serenity, the serenity of a Being who has foreordained everything and can see from the beginning the happy end of the tortuous road, He has a face radiant with joy, sharing the pleasure of all who rejoice, even that of a little girl who has been given a new doll. But he has also another image, one of even worse suffering and ugliness than mine. We saw this face on Golgotha. His hair was disordered, his brow was disfigured by wounds. Spittle and blood mingled on his face. He had dark circles under his eyes. He had no form nor comeliness. This, too, is one of the faces of the Godhead. Christ is not ashamed to call me his brother.'

I hope the Communist officer may have understood at least something of what I told him.

From: *If Prison Walls Could Speak* by Richard Wurmbrand

(Hodder & Stoughton, 1972, pp. 24–5)

Saturday

The Remnant of My Faith

R. WURMBRAND

Dear brothers and sisters,
A faith which can be destroyed by suffering is not faith.

I have read many stories of men who experienced great sorrows, but who believed to the end; stories of martyrs, and of missionary heroes. Bishop Hannington of Uganda must have preached to the cannibals about a faith which endures through every suffering. Then they took him away to be eaten. On the way to the place where they cut his body into pieces, he repeated to himself all the time, 'Love your enemies; pray for them which despitefully use you.' When his sons took his place as missionaries and converted the bishop's murderers, they were told the story. So he must have kept his faith unaltered to the end. A man will continue to hold his true creed even in the face of death. You give up only what you imagined you believed.

Today I have had a time of quiet to think about what I have really retained of the creed I used to hold. . . .

Certainly I believe that God is the maker of heaven and earth. I could not explain the existence of the universe otherwise. This is called theism. But really it is unimportant to me how this universe came to be. God made it. Fine. Reason is satisfied with this. But what about the rest?

My reason categorically refuses to believe that God is love. Your interrogators tie you to a chair. Your head has been shaved, and at intervals of one minute, tup-tup-tup, a drop of water falls on you, always in the same spot. And this happens in a world ruled by the God of love! Luther called reason a beast because it gave him arguments against the faith. But I treat it as a beast when it puts forward arguments to convince me that belief is the right thing. Reason tells me fairy tales: that I have free will and that I, and others, have chosen to sin. Hence all sorrows! Suffering is the unavoidable outcome of sin. (Something unavoidable in the universe of an almighty God! It makes me laugh!) But why then do babies suffer? What have they done to deserve it? . . .

The whole story of a God of love is madness. It is madness that God should love, not only the good people, but also those who use the Chinese drip torture and make jokes while you suffer. And how can he love the dictator who sits quietly in his office and never touches anybody himself, but orders these things to happen? Equally mad is the story of redemption by the blood of Christ. My reason rejects it. And if I don't keep my reason, the purpose of the Communists will have been attained. I shall begin to yell, and to bang on the door. I shall be put in a strait jacket. I shall end up in an asylum. . . .

There is a foolishness in God, and a corresponding foolishness in the saints. My reason stops short at theism. But Einstein demanded that we relinquish convictions which we have held for so long that they have become synonymous with common sense. I will give up common sense in religion, too. If Einstein consigned to the flames the classic laws of physics, we must do the same with the classic notion of love. God loves in a sense of this word which is different from our use of it. And, as for me, my foolish love will not stop where my reason stops. God loved us without any deserving on our part. I will love him, and believe in him and in his plan of redemption, without any reasonable cause, simply because it pleases him.

And having once given up reason I will go all the way with madness. I will love my torturers, too, though to do so is sheer folly. And when you, Jesus, come to take us to yourself, I will make it difficult for you. I will refuse to go with you. I will keep my arms firmly around the worst of hangmen, and I will say to you, 'I go to heaven only if he comes too.' You will have to yield.

From: *If Prison Walls Could Speak* by Richard Wurmbrand

(Hodder & Stoughton, 1972, pp. 45–9)

TRINITY 13

Monday

St. Vincent de Paul

ABBÉ HUVELIN

I should like to say a few words to you today about . . . St. Vincent de Paul. I had an idea of devoting several conferences to him, but I have been restrained by a scruple that may seem strange in a priest. It is this: he is, in a way, too good, too holy. Pascal translated a phrase of Tacitus thus: 'Too much kindness is annoying.' Well, no matter what the audience may be, too much holiness . . . *irritates* is, perhaps, rather too strong a word, but *tires* may perhaps do. He is a little bit too rich, too unceasing, too overflowing in good works. Each of us has our own individuality, each of us lives by a breath from on high, and I should be afraid of wearying your attention, because I do not know how to set him forth sufficiently well.

We shall come back to his good works on some other occasion. Today I should like to give you an idea of the man, and his work.

If a stranger arrived in Paris about 1650 or 1652, in the time of the Fronde, he would have found the name of M. Vincent on every lip. Everything spoke of him. If you left Paris by the gate of St. Denis, you would find yourself opposite the Priory of St. Lazare, where M. Vincent's missionaries were being trained. And then, if you went along by the chapel you would find yourself in front of the house of the Sisters of Charity. On the left bank of the river, near the Church of St. Nicholas du Chardonnet, was the house in which Mademoiselle le Gras had received the first sisters, and not very far away was the Collège des Bons Enfants, where the work of the missionaries had begun.

At the General Infirmary, where the Ladies of Charity had begun to visit the sick, only M. Vincent was spoken of.

Still further off stood a huge building, the General Hospital, called La Salpêtrière, where tramps and old people up to the number of four thousand were received.

If you left Paris by the gate opposite to that of St. Denis – Bicêtre

– once more everything spoke of M. Vincent.

A sower of works of charity. What a sower of good works! Living works, deep-rooted works that will last! Something like the grain of mustard-seed, which, after having barely been sown, shoots up into a great tree, and how many are sheltered beneath those spreading branches, all living by virtue of the same sap – the spirit of charity! Very little remains today of the Paris of those times, but you may still find M. Vincent's works in the seminaries, in the Sisters of Charity, in the Vincentians, in the hospitals. He is no less great today; in matter of fact he is greater in the nineteenth century than he was in the seventeenth.

If I wished to get to know M. Vincent just a little I should try and get an introduction to one of the meetings of the Ladies of Charity over which he often presided. He held a general meeting only once a year and then he gave an address; but he often presided over district meetings, in spite of all his occupations, and then he used to make a little speech. If you came looking for genius, that something which shone in the eyes of Bossuet, that flowed from his lips in living and impetuous words, you would be a little bit disappointed. M. Vincent did not belong to that school. His countenance was a trifle inexpressive, but people loved to listen to him: the sweetness of his words penetrated the hearts of his hearers; it did not force them open, it flowed in drop by drop; you felt as if you were listening to God himself.

From: *Some Spiritual Guides of the Seventeenth Century* by Abbé Huvelin

(Burns Oates & Washbourne Ltd., London, 1927, pp. 109–11)

Tuesday

St. Vincent de Paul

ABBÉ HUVELIN

St. Vincent's mission was revealed to him late in life. He was born in 1576. Consider the training he went through! God guides very, very slowly those whom He calls on to produce great results. If St. Vincent went rather slowly to work on whatever he took up, it was because he knew God proceeds slowly and surely. He was destined to relieve all sorts of material and spiritual misery, and God let him have an experience of them all.

He was ordained priest in 1600, in his twenty-fourth year. On a sea voyage from Marseilles to Cette (I am leaving out a great deal that is very well known) he was captured by pirates and taken to Barbary. He there converted the master to whom he had been sold, and God let him see the wretched lot of Christian slaves sold into bondage on the coast of Africa. This fact would never have been known if he had not written a letter at the time to one of his friends. When he heard, later on, that the letter was in existence he wanted, at any cost, to get it back and destroy it. It was only preserved by a pious ruse of the Vincentians. We may easily see from that fact alone how humble St. Vincent really was.

He was chaplain for a short time to Queen Margaret; he was also entrusted with a mission from Cardinal d'Ossat to Henry IV. And at length he went to the De Gondis. This was a noble family in which the bishopric of Paris seemed to be hereditary. St. Vincent became a tutor of his brother's children; one of his pupils (it must have been a great trial to him) was the famous Cardinal de Retz, who was as sarcastic as St. Vincent was charitable: he had marvellous skill in etching a portrait, an incredible malice in making faults stand out in relief. St. Vincent did not teach him how to do that.

After his wife's death M. de Gondi became an Oratorian Father. Madame de Gondi was an admirable woman, but, at times, she must have been a little bit trying to St. Vincent; she was devoured with scruples. . . .

There are some scruples which are based on an unconquerable obstinacy, on a spirit of resistance, pushed to the uttermost extreme. Other scruples – such as Madame de Gondi's – arise from fear of offending God, even in trifles, and such a fear terrorizes a soul that desires to belong wholly to God. She needed St. Vincent; he alone could soothe her. In her he revered a really beautiful soul, beloved by God. God kept him at her side for a long time in order to let him see what the heart of a woman is capable of, its happy ideas and generous initiatives. Madame de Gondi had extremely happy suggestions to make about the works she undertook, in spite of the uneasiness and torment of her mind. She taught St. Vincent the infinite resources of a Christian soul, and so, later on, he was never mistrustful of the zeal of the Ladies of Charity, he was never afraid lest their resources should fail; he knew the joy of giving. Once that bait has been nibbled at, there is no longer any possibility of rejecting the happiness of self-sacrifice.

And that's the reason why God's providence kept him with the Gondis for such a length of time.

From: *Some Spiritual Guides of the Seventeenth Century* by Abbé Huvelin

(Burns Oates & Washbourne Ltd., London, 1927, pp. 123–6)

Wednesday

St. Vincent de Paul

ABBÉ HUVELIN

M. de Gondi was General of the galleys. These were vessels, built on the model of the ancient triremes, that sailed the Mediterranean. The Kings of France were rather proud of the speed of these vessels. They were big ships . . . where poor convicts in red jackets manned the oars; a ship propelled by human arms travelled two leagues an hour. The galley slaves were the most unfortunate wretches in the world. There were about four thousand of them when Colbert was minister; they were scarcely human. In Louis XIV's time justice was administered harshly. As experience showed that it was a difficult task to train rowers, and as their labours at first were worthless, Colbert demanded that the two first years at the galleys should not be regarded as part of the sentence. Besides the convicts there was a motley crowd of men abandoned by heaven and earth; there were Turks among them remarkable for their strength. 'As strong as a Turk.' Surely it was on the galleys that they earned the right to that appellation.

St. Vincent went amongst them, like St. Peter Claver amongst the negroes. He knew there was something to be hoped for from these wretched men. . . . In the purple rags that covered the convict's shoulders he recognized not only our Lord's mantle, but his Blood clothing them with the infinite resources of his grace. St. Vincent bent over these poor men *ut sciant gentes quia homines sunt.*

At the De Gondis' he also learnt the extent of the ignorance and neglect of the peasantry. Country folk today, the country folk around Paris, are not so much ignorant as selfish; they adore the earth, not in the shape of a statue, but in the plot of ground they have manured, from which they expect their crops, and that is the reason why both the love of God and of their neighbour has perished in them.

St. Vincent saw this sad state of affairs, but it would not be correct to attribute exclusively to him the beginning of their evangelization. There was a Jesuit who, from 1625 to 1640, had devoted himself to the work with admirable zeal and charity; this was St. Francis Regis, the apostle of the Vivarais; he began his mission in Protestant countries, and kept on giving missions for fifteen years. In Brittany Fathers Le Noblets and Maunoir had permeated the hearts of the peasantry around Vannes with the Christian spirit. But these were isolated attempts. St. Vincent's merit lay in organizing the work by establishing a congregation with the object of preaching the Gospel to the poor.

From: *Some Spiritual Guides of the Seventeenth Century* by Abbé Huvelin

(Burns Oates & Washbourne Ltd., London, 1927, pp. 126–8)

Thursday

St. Vincent de Paul

ABBÉ HUVELIN

St. Vincent de Paul was also interested in foreign missions. His heart was so large that it embraced any place where a victory might be won for Christ. And so he thought of such distant mission fields as Barbary, where he had suffered; Madagascar; the Levant, where the greatness of France was bound up with Catholic interests; and the Vincentians were sent on missions to Greece, to the Archipelago, and to Syria.

But his efforts were not confined to missions organized by himself. . . . At the corner of the Rue des Bernardins and the Quay, quite close to St. Nicholas du Chardonnet, Madame de Miramion had begun a number of good works. . . . She almost rivalled Mademoiselle le Gras. She had established a work-room, an asylum for penitents, etc. All that emanated from St. Vincent de Paul. Sunbeams cannot be counted, nor can the sunbeams radiating from the hearts of saints into which our Lord has shed a little of his own sunshine be counted.

To perform works of charity in those days was not merely a fashion, it was a necessity, and it was not only women such as Madame de Miramion who performed them, but women like the

Princess Palatine. . . . She established a home for old men, and spent not only her superfluous wealth on it, but even money she badly needed for herself.

Take a name still less devout, or, if you prefer, a more characteristic one – take Madame de Montespan; she, too, threw herself into doing good. She was a little bit annoying, buzzing around, one of those people who want to do everything themselves. She had a home for young girls, called after St. Joseph; she ruled them and busied herself about getting them married. When one of her girls refused an offer that she herself approved of, she wrote, with a spelling as lofty as her style, of 'those sort of scum that nothing can be made of'. If I had been one of her young girls I would have cleared off at the first glimpse of her.

When we do a good turn to our neighbour, and keep on doing it, charity is developed by repeated acts, and as there are not two kinds of charity, one of God and another of one's neighbour, we cannot devote ourselves to the service of the poor without seeing God hidden behind their features. Madame de Montespan came to that; she arrived at the love of God, at a love for penance. She cleverly concealed her mortifications, which were severe, and under fine linen wore a hair shirt to macerate her flesh.

I mention these two names, the Princess Palatine and Madame de Montespan, because they are not looked on as exactly devout. Very well, then, St. Vincent was the centre of all that charitable movement.

From: *Some Spiritual Guides of the Seventeenth Century* by Abbé Huvelin

(Burns Oates & Washbourne Ltd., London, 1927, pp. 128–31)

Friday

St. Vincent de Paul

ABBÉ HUVELIN

What was the motive that animated St. Vincent de Paul? Was it philanthropy? An infinite compassion for human misery? Compassion does not suffice to effect what he did.

There is a sort of compassion that is almost physical; it may exist in persons who are anything but tender; they cannot bear the sight of a cat that has been hurt, or a dog with a sore paw; they will say to you: 'Take it away!' Such compassion was to be met with even amongst the pagans. But if it be separated from charity it perishes quickly. . . .

St. Vincent de Paul was moved by something higher [than pagan charity]: the love of God, charity, the charity that does not love one's neighbour for his own sake, but for the sake of God. That is, God is loved in our neighbour; consequently he is always loved, no matter who our neighbour may chance to be. That is the new commandment given by our Lord. Charity is a gift of God's: *Caritas diffusa est in cordibus vestris per Spiritum sanctum* [Charity is spread abroad in your hearts through the Holy Spirit]. Charity is the love whereby God loves his creatures; it is the love he has poured forth into men's hearts; it is a love that is his very own, descending from him to take up whatever place it may find in our hearts; it is a divine feeling that reveals to man his fellow-men, not merely as creatures of God, but as redeemed by Jesus Christ. The spirit of charity is not merely a love that inclines us to good; it is a love of predilection, causing us to desire the welfare of those we love, in accordance with the petition set out in the *Pater Noster*, 'Hallowed be thy name', by men whom thou didst create to bless thee, men who know and bless thee so seldom! 'Thy Kingdom come' on this poor earth so arid and so barren.

That is the spirit our Lord desired for His Apostles, when, after having given them Himself at the Last Supper, He said: '*Mandatum novum do vobis* [A new commandment I give unto you]. I pour forth into your hearts what is in my own.'

Hence the Apostle can say, *Hoc sentite in vobis, quod et in Christo* [Let this mind be in you which was also in Christ], because this commandment is to be the sign whereby Christ's disciples may be known; the sign of their union with Him is that they love one another.

What is charity in a priest? When a priest holds our Lord in his hands he is gripped by the great idea of the moral union of the body and its Head, of Jesus Christ and His members. When he sees in the sufferings of these members the same sufferings that our Lord willed to undergo, he experiences a more intimate, a more penetrating obligation to practise charity, and the most cutting reproach it is possible to make to Christian souls is *sine corde fuerunt* [they were without heart]. They were heartless, because they did not see God in their neighbour.

And that is the reason for the blend of an element of severity and close union with God that you may notice in St. Vincent's life, which was so utterly devoted to his neighbour, for he felt the need, both for himself and his followers, of being reinvigorated at the source and fountain-head of all charity.

From: *Some Spiritual Guides of the Seventeenth Century* by Abbé Huvelin

(Burns Oates & Washbourne Ltd., London, 1927, pp. 131–3)

Saturday

St. Vincent de Paul

ABBÉ HUVELIN

The ladies found fault with [St. Vincent de Paul]; he did not go fast enough. They were all ardour, all fire and flame. Once the flame of good deeds was kindled in their generous hearts they wanted to spread it; but raging zeal runs a risk of going headlong, and M. Vincent worked slowly. He sowed. If he saw the tender shoot pushing up he lavished all his care on what had taken root, and then, *little* by *little*, just in proportion as the works fulfilled the conditions he had laid down, he gave them a fixed shape, and made use of time to aid him – that is to say, he acted as God's providence does in establishing things. And so they thought him slow: 'He is so kind, he is charity itself; but isn't he slow?'

The saint replied by speaking of the ark that Noah took a hundred years to build. He also spoke of the hidden life of our Lord, that lasted thirty years in Nazareth, before he began his public life, which lasted for only three years. You feel that he wanted to build the exterior on the interior. You feel, even in the case of the Daughters of Charity, whom he sent out in all directions to comfort the poor, that he wanted, first of all, to establish a spirit of prayer; energy in doing good would develop of itself. What he wanted was to see after the interior, to unite the soul to God, to make it strike root, to grow in the life of the spirit; after that he could be certain of external success, which would not be the result of haste, or infatuation, but just the work of charity, as he conceived it – that is to say, of the love of God blossoming out into the love of the neighbour.

That is M. Vincent's character: just precisely that apparent slowness. He reproached the ladies – in a phrase that was often on his lips – for *outstripping Providence*. He wanted to follow Providence.

They were always telling him that he was not moving fast enough, and yet you see all that he has done. No man ever did more. And yet he went step by step, and he forced the impatient to keep pace with him, and he kept pace with the providence of God; it was the pace of a man who wished to establish his works on the foundation of the love of God, on that inner life which is just as necessary for a support as for a foundation.

His words were moving, and they were very simple; *simplicity*, *humility*, was the watchword of his sermons. They are not sermons, if you like, but just a flow of words – words closely connected together, because there is a spirit in them that makes them live. St. Paul speaks of charity as the bond of perfection. Well, charity is like a golden chain on which pearls and precious stones are strung; the chain linking them together makes a beautiful necklace of them, and it is such a golden chain – the very spirit of charity – that binds together all M. Vincent's natural and supernatural faculties. His eloquence, extremely simple, is alive with the spirit of charity. It is the spirit of charity that gives it its unity.

From: *Some Spiritual Guides of the Seventeenth Century* by Abbé Huvelin

(Burns Oates & Washbourne Ltd., London, 1927, pp. 111–13)

TRINITY 14

The Family

F. W. DILLISTONE

The fabric of human relationships in God's original plan was designed to reveal an overall pattern of growth through mutual interdependence. Within a continuing rhythm of give-and-take, lives would flow together, thereby enriching and fulfilling one another. God and man, man and man, would be linked together within a total organismic structure of developing personal relationships. But self-asserting and self-inturning have disrupted this harmonious rhythm. How can free circulation be restored? How can an unimpeded flow of life be renewed?

In any organismic structure the condition variously described as stale, anaemic, diseased can be changed only by means of some fresh introduction of life-giving energies. But to do this is a supremely difficult operation. Separated elements must come together and be held together; weak elements stimulated and encouraged to reflow together. Moreover this must be done without causing damage to the delicate fabric of interconnections which constitutes the total life-process.

It is the claim of the New Testament that into the situation where man had withdrawn from free relationship with God, God Himself entered in a new way. This initiative had nothing of the nature of a forced entry. As a child, through lowly doors, in a process of deepening identification, dissolving barriers of suspicion and mistrust, ultimately from within this humanity making the perfect self-offering and reopening the channel through which life could again freely flow. 'God was in Christ reconciling the world to Himself' – drawing it away from its isolation and separation, shaming its proud self-assertiveness and renewing the condition of flowing together in which all can find their true relation to one another by virtue of the enjoyment of an unhindered relationship with God in Christ.

We are no longer in the realm of wide-ranging cosmic reconciliation: we have drawn inwards from the customs and laws of clans and tribes: we are now in the more intimate and familiar territory of the human family, an institution as ancient and as universal as any known to man. In this context human relationships can be natural, spontaneous, uninhibited: on the other hand they can be tense, unnatural, hurtful. The structure of the family has passed through many variations in the course of human development and yet no single institution has been more durable. It is probably under a more severe strain today than at any time in human history and yet it retains an extraordinary hold upon the emotional and imaginative life of mankind.

From: *The Christian Understanding of Atonement* by F. W. Dillistone

(James Nisbet, 1968, pp. 216–17)

Tuesday

The Family

F. W. DILLISTONE

Let us look at some of the basic elements of a family structure. First and foremost there is the relationship of mother and child. The woman conceives a child within her own body but at birth it is separated from its complete physical dependence upon her. Yet almost immediately the new-born babe is reunited with the mother in the process of lactation, sucking in nourishment from the body out of which it was taken. Further there is obviously a flow of blood in the child's body and this blood must be the same as that of the mother. In other words mother and child still in a sense form a single organism. Even though separated in so far as each now occupies a particular position in space, they constitute parts of a single whole which lives and grows within a constant mutual relationship.

But although mother and child together constitute the primal unit there are many other elements in the total family. There is the home and the hearth, the small-holding surrounding the home and the domestic animals – all are included in the family complex. Far more important there are the other children of the mother, and the man who has been bound to her by the marriage-tie. Family structures have varied at different times and places with the mother's sister sometimes occupying a privileged position as her occasional substitute, with the brother sometimes occupying a special role as protector of the children. But whatever structures of this kind may have existed, still the man who has a special marital relation to the woman, whether or not his part in the conception of children is recognized, is regarded as bearing major responsibility for the protection and nurture of wife and children alike. He by reason of his superior strength and his exemption from many of the child-rearing duties easily assumed a position of authority within the household. But it is still authority within *the total living organism*. The primary emotional ties are between the children and the mother. The child grows towards maturity as it maintains its proper place within the total family complex.

From: *The Christian Understanding of Atonement* by F. W. Dillistone

(James Nisbet, 1968, pp. 217–18)

Wednesday

The Family

F. W. DILLISTONE

The organic character of family life is subjected to strains and even shocks through the crisis of weaning and the still greater stresses of initiation. But the effect has not normally been to disrupt the family pattern entirely but to re-establish it on a more mature basis. The son does not cease to be a son after initiation though he is less dependent emotionally on the mother. The totality of life is maintained and any breaches or misdemeanours are still *within the family*. Where there is disorder or default the combined resources of the total organism flow in, as it were, to restore health and sanity. Every member finds fulfilment as he occupies his assigned place and performs his proper function within the whole.

Nowhere in the literature of the ancient world are family relationships more vividly and more attractively described than in the Scriptures of the Old Testament. The stories of the patriarchs, the judges and the kings all in their own way reveal the conception of the family as it was held in Israel. This conception, Pedersen affirms, is of 'an organism which grows and spreads in the shoots which it is constantly sending forth'. The symbol of the plant or the tree naturally suggests itself and the ancients themselves already made use of it. When we speak of genealogical trees, the symbol, properly speaking, can only be applied with certain limitations. We are thinking of the individual as owing his existence to the preceding generation; but he emancipates himself more and more, until as a grown-up man he has his point of gravity entirely in himself. In the eyes of the Israelites, however, the symbol is fully applicable; indeed it is rather more than a symbol, for tree and human species are two entirely analogous forms of life. Just as the branch not only owes its existence to the trunk and the root, but constantly sucks its nourishment from it, in the same manner the individual holds his life only in connection with his family. It is that which is expressed by the sons bearing the name of the father.

From: *The Christian Understanding of Atonement* by F. W. Dillistone

(James Nisbet, 1968, pp. 218–19)

Thursday

The Family

F. W. DILLISTONE

[It is interesting to note] the place that Abraham, the forefather of Israel, occupies not only in Genesis but in the prophets and the New Testament writings: the dramatic relationship between Abraham, Sarah and Isaac and later between Isaac, Rebekah and their two sons: the significance of the stories of Joseph and his brothers: the tensions and struggles within the family of David. In the total picture the mother remains in the background but is never merely a cipher: her influence upon her sons and especially upon a favourite son is obviously great. But the major interest in the stories concerns the relationship between the father and the son. Ideally the blessing of the father is transmitted to the son, the achievements of the son redound to the glory of the father. The father sees the continuity of his own life in the son: the son rejoices if he is able to enhance the dignity and fame of his father's house. The father is the centre of authority but there is little thought of exercising this for his own individual satisfaction. He is the head in whom the whole family coheres and when the time comes his honour descends easily and naturally to the son whom he loves.

This is the ideal. But even in Israel there were defections from this state of harmonious growth. We recall the struggle between Esau and Jacob, the jealousies and intrigues amongst Jacob's sons, the conflicts between Moses and his kinsfolk, above all, perhaps, the cruelties and the treacheries of the sons of David. These aberrations could not be dealt with by external penalties for they were offences *within the family*, breaches within the total life of the organism. They were unnatural and perverse. Moses when he views the defection of his brother Aaron and the apostasy of his people is torn between his sense that righteous judgment must fall and his conviction that being himself part of the total life of God's family he must share the judgment and disgrace. David, when he learns of his son's treachery and above all of Absalom's rebellion, moves hesitantly and uncertainly. The offence cannot be condoned and yet it is an offence *within the family*: all are in a certain sense implicated. How can harmony be restored without doing irreparable harm to the offender? How can he, at one and the same moment, be *against* Absalom and yet also *for* Absalom? Intermediaries try to bring the king and Absalom together but there seems to be no way of overcoming the tension at the very heart of the family's life. Absalom is determined to usurp the highest place of authority and nothing can save him from his doom.

From: *The Christian Understanding of Atonement* by F. W. Dillistone

(James Nisbet, 1968, pp. 219–20)

Friday

The Family

F. W. DILLISTONE

As has often been remarked, the Old Testament uses direct family images to describe the relationship between God and His people only sparingly. Yet the strong assumption is certainly present that it was God Who had called Abraham and his seed, that God's own purpose was bound up with, even incarnated in, this one family, and that its behaviour brought honour or shame, as the case might be, to God's cause in the world. When Israel was unfaithful no third party could intervene. The only hope was that from within Israel itself a man here, a man there, might arise to detach himself temporarily from his nation's perfidy and to reaffirm as it were from God's side the abiding principles of truth and loyalty. In and through the prophets God recalled His people, His family, to the fundamental prin-

ciples of their own authentic existence. In and through the prophets
God expressed His own suffering caused by the faithlessness of His
people. At the same time the prophets, by their own identification
with the people, experienced in their own lives the suffering and
distress which estrangement from God was bound to involve.

The family tension, the prophet's involvement, the suffering of
God, the distress of the child, the restoration to organic wholeness
all come to dramatic expression in the concluding chapters of the
book of the prophet Hosea and illustrate the use of family imagery
to describe the relations between God and man.

> When Israel was a child, I loved him and out of Egypt
>   I called my son.
> It was I who taught Ephraim to walk,
> I took them up in my arms, but they did not know
>   that I healed them.
> How can I give you up, O Ephraim?
> How can I hand you over, O Israel?
> My heart recoils within me, my compassion grows
>   warm and tender.
> I will heal their faithlessness;
> I will love them freely.

All these are the words of the prophet himself. Now he is speaking
indignantly, now he is speaking compassionately: now he is speaking
in the name of God, now in the name of the people: now in terms of
ultimate judgment, now of final reconciliation. He remains always
within and a part of the total organic family of God and His people.
Through the initiative of God in moving him to speak, the prophet
takes his own initiative and opens a way of redemption and restoration. Though the children have forsaken the father's house and
turned towards idols, the prophet brings a new revelation of the
father's heart of love and invites them to return to their true health
and their true home.

But the pattern which appears 'at sundry times and in divers
manners' in the Old Testament comes to full expression through the
New Testament revelation of Him who is the perfect son within the
Divine family. No title of Jesus of Nazareth expresses a greater depth
of meaning than the simple name 'Son'. He is 'the beloved Son', the
'only-begotten Son', the Son of His love, the Son of God. No reference to the Divine activity is more significant than that which states
with complete simplicity that God sent His Son into the world. This
is pre-eminently the imagery used in the Johannine writings though

none is more characteristic of the New Testament as a whole. The children of men are seen as unfaithful children: the Son is seen as the bearer of a new initiative who will turn the hearts of the children to their true Father and bring them home to God.

From: *The Christian Understanding of Atonement* by F. W. Dillistone

(James Nisbet, 1968, pp. 220–1)

Saturday

The Family

F. W. DILLISTONE

This appeal to family relationships raises one difficult question. It has often been asked whether the New Testament teaches that God is the Father of all men and that all begin, as it were, with the status of children within the divine family: or whether it teaches that all begin as strangers and foreigners in relation to the Divine fatherland and can only gain a new standing through God's creative act and their own willed response. At the risk of seeming illogical I am bound to affirm not only that both conceptions are to be found in the New Testament but that each is valid within its own framework of reference. Even in the Hebrew social structure made familiar to us by the Old Testament the practice of 'adoption' was allowed though in point of fact few instances are to be found. But the very circumstances of the Gentile mission in early Christianity made it necessary to employ this kind of imagery if the already existing body of doctrine and devotion relating to the Divine Fatherhood and Jesus' new revelation of the nature of sonship was to become meaningful. In differing contexts there are differing emphases. But the basic relationship of father to son is common to all.

So far as the New Testament records are concerned the first body of imagery is derived from the unshakable conviction that God had called and chosen Abraham to be the father of God's family on earth, a family through which all the peoples of the earth would receive blessing. With this conviction there existed innumerable questionings about who, at any precise period, constituted the true children of Abraham. All who were circumcised? All who kept the law? All who were of pure physical descent? All who abjured idolatry in any shape or form? All who shared Abraham's faith? The possibilities were almost limitless. Yet in Jewish minds the conviction held fast that the family of God existed in the world. It might only constitute a minority or a remnant but still its marks could be recognized. It was an organism continuous in its life from the past: it was God's flock: it was God's vineyard: it was God's family.

Within such a framework of thought and imagination it was natural to conceive of God's new and climactic initiative in terms of seeking out the lost sheep of the house of Israel, of cleansing and restoring the life of the vineyard, of gathering the children as a hen gathers her chickens under her wings, of bringing back the prodigal to his true inheritance. One writer insists that the Saviour who came into the world had to concern himself with the descendants of Abraham.[1] He had to share their flesh and blood, he had to be made like them in every respect so that he might act on their behalf in the things pertaining to their true life and destiny in God. Considerable attention is paid to the genealogy of Jesus of Nazareth in the New Testament writings: he is Son of David, he is Son of Abraham, he is of the tribe of Judah, he is a true Israelite – all of these titles indicating that He could rightly claim to be the brother of those He had come to save, that so far as flesh and blood were concerned He shared the lot of the family of God and was in every way qualified both to be the bearer of the fresh initiative from the Divine side and to act on behalf of the maimed and disordered family on the human side.

From: *The Christian Understanding of Atonement* by F. W. Dillistone

(James Nisbet, 1968, pp. 221–2)

---

[1] Hebrews 2:16.

Monday

The Secular City

HARVEY COX

No one rules by divine right in secular society. In presecular society, everyone does. Just as nature is perceived by tribal man both as a part of his family and as the locus of religious energy, so the political power structure is accepted as an extension of familial authority and as the unequivocal will of the gods. The identification of the political with the religious order, whether in a primitive tribe where the chief is also the sorcerer, or in the Roman Empire where the emperor is both political ruler and pontifex maximus, betrays the same sacral legitimation of political power.

A 'pure' sacral-political identification is difficult to find. All societies begin early to differentiate roles and responsibilities; whether this separation of powers can be carried through to a successful conclusion depends entirely on whether the basic symbol system of the culture allows for such differentiation.

Needless to say, significant political and social change is almost impossible in societies in which the ruling regime is directly legitimated by religious symbols, in which the ruler is believed to be divine or a direct expression of the divine intention. Political change depends on a previous desacralization of politics. The process is closely related to the disenchantment of nature. Since nature always repeats itself, while history never does, the emergence of history rather than nature as the locus of God's action opens a whole new world of possibilities for political and social change.

From: *The Secular City* by Harvey Cox

(SCM Press, 1966, p. 25)

Tuesday

The Secular City

HARVEY COX

In tracing the desacralization of politics to its biblical roots, the Exodus must be the focal point of study. For the Hebrews Yahweh had spoken decisively not in a natural phenomenon, such as a thunderclap or an earthquake, but through a historical event, the deliverance from Egypt. It is particularly significant that this was an event of social change, a massive act of what we might today call 'civil disobedience'. It was an act of insurrection against a duly constituted monarch, a pharaoh whose relationship to the sun-god Ra constituted his claim to political sovereignty. There had no doubt been similar escapes before, but the Exodus of the Hebrews became more than a minor event which happened to an unimportant people. It became the central event around which the Hebrews organized their whole perception of reality. As such, it symbolized the deliverance of man out of a sacral-political order and into history and social change, out of religiously legitimated monarchs and into a world where political leadership would be based on power gained by the capacity to accomplish specific social objectives.

The Exodus delivered the Jews from Egypt, yet there was a persistent temptation to return to sacral politics, especially during the period of the monarchy. But the prophetic bands always stood in the way, preventing such a relapse. Since the prophets always had a source of authority separate from the royal favour, the priest-king was never really possible again. The Exodus had made it forever impossible to accept without reservation the sanctions of any monarch. Yahweh could always stage a new Exodus, or work through history to bring down a monarch with delusions of grandeur. No royal house was ever afterward unquestionably secure on its throne.

From: *The Secular City* by Harvey Cox

(SCM Press, 1966, pp. 25–6)

The Secular City

HARVEY COX

The contest between pope and emperor in the Middle Ages is a parable of the futility of any attempt to return to simple sacral politics once the secularization process has begun. The emperor would have liked to be the religious as well as the political sovereign of the West – wistful longings for a 'Holy Roman Empire' headed by a monarch with sacral functions indicate this desire. Similarly, many of the popes would have liked to wield the sword of empire as well as the Keys of Saint Peter – theological efforts to subsume the temporal under the spiritual realm testify to this incessant hankering. Neither side won. The pope finally lost his temporal power along with the Papal States and the emperor lost everything when the Empire itself dissolved. Since then the spiritual and moral authority of the pope has increased. At the same time, political leaders in the West have by and large accepted the fact that they can make only provisional and limited demands on their citizens. When a political leader makes religious or totalitarian claims, when a Hitler or a Stalin tries once again to assert himself as the pure expression of the *Zeitgeist* or the dialectic, free men recognize this as an affront to their deepest convictions about politics. Our political consciences have all been secularized.

From: *The Secular City* by Harvey Cox

(SCM Press, 1966, pp. 26–7)

Thursday

The Secular City

HARVEY COX

The tension between Judaeo-Christian religion and political absolutism has been a recognized element in the tradition of Western political philosophy since Augustine. In fact, conflict between church and state is really possible only on ground prepared by the biblical faiths. There is no conflict if a faith is anti-political, as were the mystery cults, or if it merges imperceptibly with the political system, as did the imperial religion of Rome. The mystery cults turned their backs on 'this world' and thus gave the political regime an open field to fashion whatever tyrannies it chose. The imperial cult simply identified the establishment with the will of the gods. Only with the Christian church did a real tension become possible, a tension for which Saint Augustine spelled out the basis. Augustine said that the state has its own good, but that this good is not the highest or truest good. The state is an order, but is good order only insofar as man is a sinner. It has no contribution to make to the salvation of man. To grant the state a *provisional* worth strikes a harder blow at tyranny than a total devaluation of the state, which allows the church to withdraw into an enclave.

The early years of the Christian church present a particularly good example of how this desacralization of politics worked out in practice. It was accomplished not by a wholesale rejection of political authority but by a conditional acceptance. The first Christians were willing to pray for the emperor but not to burn incense on his altar. The difference between these two acts is crucial. To pray for the emperor is to grant him the right to exercise authority in a particular, restricted realm, a realm defined not by him but by the one who is praying. To refuse to put incense on his altar is to deny him any sacral-religious authority. The early Christians thus made a telling contribution to the desacralization of politics and were in this sense relentless and consistent secularizers.

In Dietrich Bonhoeffer's term, the early Christians exhibited a kind of 'holy worldliness'. They rejected the cults of Cybele, Isis, and Mithra because these mystery religions were escapist and the Christians did not wish to abandon a world God had made and to which their Lord, they believed, would soon return in visible triumph. But they also rejected the cult of the emperor because, although worldly, it was not holy enough. It did not cohere with the sharp chasm between the Holy One and the political system which they confessed when they called Jesus the only true *Kyrios*. It did not conform to the desacralized politics which had begun with the Exodus and continued to call into question all religio-political systems. Holding the tension between holiness and worldliness, the Christians thus constituted a threat to the Roman imperial tyranny which resulted in an endless series of persecutions, but finally toppled it.

From: *The Secular City* by Harvey Cox

(SCM Press, 1966, pp. 27–8)

Friday

The Secular City

HARVEY COX

The conversion of Constantine presented the early Christians a new test. Some theologians tried to rewrite Christianity into an imperial ideology – and almost succeeded for a time. But their attempt to resacralize politics never eliminated the tension between God and the regime which the biblical faith had planted in the consciousness of man. From now on, no political system could ever safely claim a direct and undisputed sacral legitimation, and no sovereign could infringe on that aspect of his subjects' lives which pointed them to an authority beyond him. Indeed, the tension between Christian faith and political authority was so pointed that it has continued to bother Western political thinkers in every generation. Niccolò Macchiavelli (1469–1529), the Renaissance philosopher and statesman, argued that it was impossible to build a strong state among Christians since the Christian religion elicited universalistic feelings that subverted the required nationalism. Marsilius of Padua (died ca 1342) contended in his *Defensor Pactis* that it was extremely difficult even to have a state where the church puts forward its customary claims. How can a state defend its citizens, he wanted to know, when there is one group within its borders which claims a kind of supranational loyalty and will grant only conditional allegiance to the earthly monarch? This line of thought came to a very consistent position in the French philosopher Pierre Bayle (1647–1706), who moved even further in seeking to deal with the same tension. He believed not only that a state of atheists was possible, but also that it was probably even desirable, since an atheistic state would not be tempted to force one particular world-view or metaphysic on any of its citizens. Bayle failed to foresee the rise of a fanatical political atheism just around the corner, a secularistic religion which would prove just as oppressive as the theistic religions of the past. It is worth noting here that Ludwig Feuerbach (1804–72), whose work greatly influenced Karl Marx, dedicated his first book to Bayle. Marx himself resolved the tension by suggesting that eventually both religion and the state would disappear. His prediction is not likely to be fulfilled, but it does illustrate the fact that no political thinker can avoid dealing in

some way with the inherent limitation of politics that is built into
Western culture through the desacralization of political power. . . .

From: *The Secular City* by Harvey Cox

(SCM Press, 1966, pp. 28–9)

Saturday

The Secular City

HARVEY COX

Sacral politics have not been completely abolished. Secularization
is a process, not a state of affairs. In Spain a quasi-sacral state still
obtains, as it does in such small Asian countries as Nepal. Furthermore, the danger of a relapse into a neosacral politics is always
present. National Socialism in Germany and Fascism in Italy represented relapses of catastrophic proportions; the Stalinist cult of personality was another. There are indications that the regime of Kwame
Nkrumah in Ghana may represent a kind of neotribal politics. But
the secularizing counter-forces are nearly omnipresent today and will
eventually swing into movement. Communism itself, though it still
has semi-religious characteristics, may eventually strengthen the
tendency toward the desacralization of politics. Communist social
theory, as already mentioned, since it teaches that the state apparatus
merely expresses the will of the ruling elite, envisages the eventual
withering away of the state in the classless society. However im-
probable this may appear in reality, it does deprive a regime of the
kind of ultimate legitimation available in sacral societies. It strength-
ens the recent Marxist contention that the cult of Stalin, rather than
being an expression of the essence of communism, in reality marked
a grave departure from it. In any case, the presence today of the
desacralizing currents of the biblical faith and of the movements
deriving from it suggests that in the urbanized technological world
of tomorrow, no significant reversal of the trend toward secularization can be expected.

From: *The Secular City* by Harvey Cox

(SCM Press, 1966, pp. 29–30)

TRINITY 16

Journal of a Soul

POPE JOHN

[January 1903. After a year in the army, Angelo Roncalli is back at Rome as a seminarian.]

I have seen the first dawn of a new year. I welcome it in the name of the Lord and I consecrate it to the loving Heart of Christ, that for me it may be a year really full of good works, my year of salvation, the year in which I shall at last make myself holy. Jesus, I am yours once more and for ever.

Tomorrow, the first Friday of the month and of this new year, is especially consecrated to the Sacred Heart: it shall be a day of quite extraordinary fervour and love.

Just recently, since I finished the Spiritual Exercises, I have felt a very urgent need to strengthen my resolves and to set before my soul, already beginning to sink into lethargy, some noble examples – in a word, to begin again from the beginning.

Much against my will, I must again confess my ineffectualness. I am a poor sinner, a disloyal and useless servant, I am up to my eyebrows in pride: I am scatterbrained, unmannerly, and worthless. My Jesus, mercy!

The new year has begun: let it be a new life too. I think of to-morrow's holy communion as of an event of the greatest importance: I will make my communion tomorrow as if I had just finished the Spiritual Exercises. I recall the feelings of that day, its promises and resolutions, and in particular I reflect on that aspect of myself in which I feel most weak, as is proved by the disappointing experience of the last few days.

My guiding principles remain the same: humility in everything, especially in my speech, union with God (the most important thing, of which I feel an even greater need today) and the will of God, and not my own, in all I do. I must mind my own business, think of myself and the pursuit of the devout life, without undue agitation. Intense, tranquil and recollected study now; at all times and in all things great peace and sweetness in my heart.

From: *Journal of a Soul* by Pope John XXIII

(Geoffrey Chapman, 1965, p. 103)

Tuesday

Journal of a Soul

POPE JOHN

After ten years of priesthood: 1904 – 10 August, 1914

Groppino, 10 August, 1914.
  Today my heart is full of a sense of joyful contentment and at the same time full of shame.
  I have received from God so many ordinary and special graces during these ten years! In the sacraments, received and administered, and in the many and varied duties of my ministry, in words and works, in public and in private, in prayer, in study, amidst the little difficulties and disappointments, successes and failures – my experience growing richer and stronger every day, in my contacts with my Superiors, with the clergy and with people of all ages and all social conditions. The Lord has indeed been faithful to the promise he made me on the day of my ordination in Rome, in the church of Santa Maria in Monte Santo, when he said to me: 'No longer do I call you a servant . . . but a friend.' Jesus has been a real friend to me, allowing me to share in all the sacred intimacies of his Heart. When I think of all that he knows about me and has seen in me, I should be lacking in sincerity if I did not admit to feeling a great satisfaction in my soul. In the field which I sowed, and in which I have worked, there are in fact a few ears of corn, enough perhaps to make up a small sheaf. I bless you, Lord, for this, because it is all due to your love.
  But for my own part, I can only feel ashamed that I have not done more, that I have reaped so little. I have been like barren waste ground. With all the grace I have received, or even with much less, so many others would already be holy. I have had so many good impulses which have not yet borne fruit. My Lord, I acknowledge my failings, my total worthlessness; be generous in forgiveness and mercy. . . .

But my dominant thought, in my joy at having accomplished ten years as a priest, is this: I do not belong to myself, or to others; I belong to my Lord, for life and death. The dignity of the priesthood, the ten years full of graces which he has heaped upon me, such a poor, humble creature – all this convinces me that I must crush the self and devote all my energies to nothing else but work for the kingdom of Jesus in the minds and hearts of men, as I do in my own simple way, even in obscurity; but from this time forth it must be done with a greater intensity of purpose, thoughts and deeds.

From: *Journal of a Soul* by Pope John XXIII

(Geoffrey Chapman, 1965, pp. 183–4)

Wednesday

Journal of a Soul

POPE JOHN

My own natural disposition, my experience and my present circumstances all indicate calm peaceful work for me, far removed from the field of battle, rather than controversial action, polemics and conflict. Ah well, if this is the case I will not try to save my soul by defacing an original painting, which has its own merits, in order to become an unsuccessful copy of someone else whose character is entirely different from mine. But this peaceful disposition does not mean pampering my self-love, seeking my own comfort, or mere acquiescence in thoughts, principles and attitudes. The habitual smile must know how to conceal the inner conflict with selfishness, which is sometimes tremendous, and when need arises show the victory of the soul over the temptations of the senses or of pride, so that my better side may always be shown to God and my neighbour.

I have now been a priest for ten years; what will my life be in the future? That remains hidden from me. It may be that but a short time remains before I am called to render my final account. O Lord Jesus, come to take me now. If I am to wait for some, perhaps many, years, then I hope they will be years of intense labour, upborne by holy obedience, with a great purpose running through everything, but never a thought straying beyond the bounds of obedience. Preoccupations about the future, which arise from self-love, delay the work of God in us and hinder his purposes, without ever furthering our material interests. I need to be very watchful about this, every day, because I foresee that with the passing of years, and perhaps in the near future, I shall have many struggles with my pride. Let whoever will pass before me and go on ahead; I stay here where Providence has placed me, with no anxieties, leaving the way clear for others.

I mean to preserve my peace of mind, which is my liberty. So I shall always remember those four things which Thomas à Kempis[1] says bring great peace and true freedom:

(1) Seek to do another's will, rather than your own.
(2) Choose always to have less rather than more.
(3) Always take the lowest place, so as to be inferior to everyone.
(4) Always desire and pray that the will of God may be wholly fulfilled in you.

With these resolves, O Lord, today once more I offer you the precious chalice of my soul, hallowed by your anointing. Fill it with your strength which made the apostles, martyrs and confessors; make use of me in something good, noble and great, for you, for your Church, for the souls of men. I live only, I wish to live only for this.

From: *Journal of a Soul* by Pope John XXIII

(Geoffrey Chapman, 1965, pp. 184–5)

Thursday

Journal of a Soul

POPE JOHN

Retreat, 27 November – 2 December, 1926
Rome, Monastery of St. Paul

(1) I have been a Bishop for twenty months. As I clearly foresaw, my ministry has brought me many trials. But, and this is strange, these are not caused by the Bulgarians for whom I work but by the central organs of ecclesiastical administration. This is a form of mortification and humiliation that I did not expect and which hurts me deeply. 'Lord, you know all.'[2]

[1] Book III, chap. 23.
[2] John 21:17.

(2) I must, I will accustom myself to bearing this cross with more patience, calm and inner peace than I have so far shown. I shall be particularly careful in what I say to anyone about this. Every time I speak my mind about it I take away from the merit of my patience. 'Set a guard over my mouth, O Lord.'[1] I shall make this silence, which must be, according to the teaching of St. Francis de Sales, meek and without bitterness, an object of my self-examinations.

(3) The time I give to active work must be in proportion to what I give to the work of God, that is to prayer. I need more fervent and continual prayer to give character to my life. So I must give more time to meditation, and stay longer in the Lord's company, sometimes reading or saying my prayers aloud or just keeping silent. I hope the Holy Father will grant me the boon of reserving the Blessed Sacrament in my home in Sofia. The company of Jesus will be my light, my comfort and my joy.

(4) I must take great care to show charity in my conversation. Even with trustworthy and venerable people I must be very chary about mentioning things which refer to the most delicate part of my ministry and concern the good name of others, especially if these are invested with authority and dignity. Even when I feel the need to confide in someone, in hours of solitude and loneliness, silence and meekness will make suffering for the love of God more productive of good.

(5) The brief experience of these months as Bishop convinces me that for me, in this life, there is nothing better than bearing my cross, as Jesus sets it on my shoulders and on my heart. I must think of myself as the man bearing the cross, and love the cross that God sends me without thinking of any other. All that is not to the honour of God, the service of the Church and the welfare of souls is extraneous to me, and of no importance.

From: *Journal of a Soul* by Pope John XXIII

(Geoffrey Chapman, 1965, pp. 208–9)

---

[1] Psalm 140 (141):3.

Journal of a Soul

POPE JOHN

Ideas for a good apostolate

[13 August, 1961]
Everyone must be treated with respect, prudence and evangelical simplicity.

It is commonly believed and considered fitting that even the everyday language of the Pope should be full of mystery and awe. But the example of Jesus is more closely followed in the most appealing simplicity, not dissociated from the God-given prudence of wise and holy men. Wise-acres may show disrespect, if not scorn, for the simple man. But those wise-acres are of no account; even if their opinions and conduct inflict some humiliations, no notice should be taken of them at all: in the end everything ends in their defeat and confusion. The 'simple, upright, God-fearing man' is always the worthiest and the strongest. Naturally he must always be sustained by a wise and gracious prudence. He is a simple man who is not ashamed to profess the Gospel, even in the face of men who consider it to be nothing but weakness and childish nonsense, and to profess it entirely, on all occasions, and in the presence of all; he does not let himself be deceived or prejudiced by his fellows, nor does he lose his peace of mind, however they may treat him.

The prudent man is he who knows how to keep silent about that part of the truth that it would be inopportune to declare, provided that this silence does not affect the truth he utters by gainsaying it; the man who knows how to achieve his own good purpose, choosing the most effective means of willing and doing; who, in all circumstances, can foresee and measure the difficulties set before him, and knows how to choose the middle way which presents fewer difficulties and dangers; the man who, having chosen a good, or even a great and noble objective, never loses sight of it but manages to overcome all obstacles and see it through to the end. Such a man in every question distinguishes the substance from the accidentals; he does not allow himself to be hampered by the latter, but concentrates and directs all his energies to a successful conclusion; he looks to God alone, in whom he trusts, and this trust is the foundation of all he does. Even if he does not succeed, in all or in part, he knows he has done well, by referring everything to the will and greater glory of God.

Simplicity contains nothing contrary to prudence, and the converse also is true. Simplicity is love: prudence is thought. Love prays: the intelligence keeps watch. . . .

From: *Journal of a Soul* by Pope John XXIII

(Geoffrey Chapman, 1965, pp. 309–10)

Saturday

Journal of a Soul

POPE JOHN

[15 September, 1962]

My retreat, with only Father Ciappi and Mgr. Cavagna to see me, in immediate and personal preparation for the Council, today comes to an end, although I have not been able to use it, as I wished, solely and entirely for the purpose I had set myself.

But it set a good example; it prevented me from being distracted by any exterior matters, business, literature or anything else. It was a more intense effort to find union with the Lord, in prayers, thoughts, and a calm and determined will. It leaves me with an increased fervour in my heart for all that concerns the substance of my ministry and my apostolic mandate. Lord Jesus, supply what I lack. 'Lord you know all; you know that I love you.'

*Summary of graces bestowed on a man
who thinks poorly of himself . . .*

First grace. To have accepted with simplicity the honour and the burden of the pontificate, with the joy of being able to say that I did nothing to obtain it, absolutely nothing; indeed I was most careful and conscientious to avoid anything that might direct attention to myself. As the voting in Conclave wavered to and fro, I rejoiced when I saw the chances of my being elected diminishing and the likelihood of others, in my opinion truly most worthy and venerable persons, being chosen.

Second grace. To have been able to accept as simple and capable of being immediately put into effect certain ideas which were not in the least complex in themselves, indeed perfectly simple, but far-reaching in their effects and full of responsibilities for the future. I was immediately successful in this, which goes to show that one must accept the good inspirations that come from the Lord, simply and confidently.

Without any forethought, I put forward, in one of my first talks with my Secretary of State on 20 January, 1959, the idea of an Ecumenical Council, a Diocesan Synod and the revision of the Code of Canon Law, all this being quite contrary to any previous supposition or idea of my own on this subject.

I was the first to be surprised at my proposal, which was entirely my own idea.

And indeed, after this everything seemed to turn out so naturally in its immediate and continued development.

After three years of preparation, certainly laborious but also joyful and serene, we are now on the slopes of the sacred mountain.

May the Lord give us strength to bring everything to a successful conclusion!

From: *Journal of a Soul* by Pope John XXIII

(Geoffrey Chapman, 1965, pp. 325–6)

TRINITY 17

Monday

Society of St. John the Evangelist

PETER F. ANSON

Standing a few yards back from the Iffley Road, Oxford, along which in these times there is a ceaseless stream of traffic by day and by night, is a simple but dignified church, built of bathstone ashlar now weathered to cream colour; its long unbroken roof line ending with a low square tower. . . .

Beyond the east end of the church will be found a rather confused group of buildings, solid and simple, but with nothing particularly striking about their architecture. A queer-looking lofty red-brick house with a chapel at the top adjoins them and is obviously of earlier date. It is said that Father Benson regarded aesthetic taste as something not far removed from the lust of the eye and that he once described the Mission House, with sardonic humour, as the ugliest building in Oxford. Behind all these buildings is a garden, into which protrudes a Gothic Revival chapel – the Lady Chapel or House Chapel. . . . Here is the spiritual heart of the Society of St. John the Evangelist. It is used for the recitation of their choir offices with the exception of Evensong, which is sung daily in the conventual church. By tradition the cells of the Community are their usual places for meditation and private prayer.

Thus in a rather drab and uninteresting suburb of Oxford, beyond Magdalen Bridge, has been located for nearly a century the Mother House of the second religious community of men to be founded in the Church of England. It can claim to be the first to survive and prosper.

Since Joseph Leycester Lyne had established his Benedictine Brotherhood at Claydon Rectory, Suffolk, in the spring of 1863, other people had been considering the foundation of a less bizarre sort of community for men. That same year, on July 22, the feast of St. Mary Magdalene, Mr. Keble preached a sermon at Wantage in which he pleaded for the formation of Christian Brotherhoods as well as Sisterhoods. In the autumn of 1864 two articles, written by the Reverend Simeon Wilberforce O'Neill, a curate at Wantage, were published in *The Ecclesiastic*. They advocated the establishment of missionary brotherhoods. A third article appeared early in 1865. Mr. O'Neill informed his readers that, 'seeing, therefore, that the need of religious houses for men is so great for the perfection of our Church and her success in propagating the Gospel, it has been resolved to form a monastic body of clergy and laymen under the spiritual direction of a most able guide. The rule of life will not be too lax to be efficient, nor yet so severe as to be burdensome. Its spirit must be the same as that which of old inspired the rules of so many great Orders, but its form must be adapted to the present time. The aim and object of this Society will be mission work both at home and abroad, but it will be free to undertake any other Christian work not directly missionary which may present itself, provided that by so doing its first object be not interfered with. Any person who feels called by God to give himself to this work may have further particulars by applying to the writer of this paper.'

From: *The Call of the Cloister* by Peter F. Anson

(S.P.C.K., 1964, pp. 72–3)

Tuesday

Society of St. John the Evangelist

PETER F. ANSON

The first to apply was a young layman, George Lane-Fox. In spite of having been Captain of the Boats at Eton and a somewhat worldly undergraduate at Christ Church, he wanted to become a lay brother in this community. One of his friends was the Hon. Charles Wood, the future Lord Halifax. He also wished to enter as a lay brother. The ever-impetuous Lane-Fox then rushed off to Monte Cassino, to study monastic life at its source. On his return from Italy he found that things were moving.

A young American Episcopalian clergyman, named Charles Grafton, had arrived in England. He and his spiritual director, the Reverend Oliver S. Prescott, had already been trying to live a quasi-monastic life. Dr. Pusey advised Mr. Grafton to get in touch with Mr. O'Neill. He also presided over a meeting held at All Saints,

Margaret Street, when the proposed foundation was discussed. In February 1865 a second meeting was arranged in the clergy house of St. Mary's, Crown Street, Soho. It was presided over by the Reverend R. Tuke, a curate at this church, who hoped to join the Community. Those present included Bishop Forbes of Brechin, the Reverend R. M. Benson, the Reverend C. C. Grafton, Mr. Charles Wood, and Mr. George Lane-Fox. In after years Lord Halifax recalled that 'before the close of the meeting Mr. Benson and Mr. Grafton definitely expressed the desire to give themselves to such a life. The Bishop of Brechin seemed to share their wishes, but was doubtful how far his circumstances would prevent their realization.'

Meanwhile Dr. Pusey, having been informed of the meeting, recommended action before words. He was 'conscious that a Victorian bishop would generally say "Don't", if he were asked, but might look the other way if confronted with a *fait accompli*'. Another meeting was held in London, this time at the House of Charity, Soho, at which Dr. Pusey, the Reverend T. T. Carter, and the Reverend S. W. O'Neill were present. Bishop Forbes stated that, having taken the advice of his doctor and friends, he regretted that he could not consider being one of the founders of the proposed community. The Reverend R. M. Benson agreed to direct the new venture. Until then he had taken little or no direct part in the negotiations for establishing a brotherhood.

From: *The Call of the Cloister* by Peter F. Anson

(S.P.C.K., 1964, pp. 73–6)

Wednesday

Society of St. John the Evangelist

PETER F. ANSON

Richard Meux Benson was born in 1824. At Christ Church, Oxford, he graduated with Honours in 1847, and was Kennicott Hebrew Scholar. He was ordained deacon the following year and priest in 1849, and, after serving a curacy at Surbiton, was appointed in 1850 Vicar of Cowley, Oxford. Ten years later he built an iron church, dedicated to St. John the Evangelist, to serve the needs of the western part of the large parish. To quote from the late Prebendary

H. F. B. Mackay, Benson was 'an embodiment of the devotion, reserve, austerity and self-effacement of the Tractarians'. He lived at Cowley 'unobserved, in prayer and labour among the poor. He felt a call to missionary work, and set his heart on India.' He had already drawn up a scheme to found a Collegiate Society in the North-West Province, where priests and laymen would live on a common fund, some staying at home to keep up the life of prayer, while others went out two and two on evangelistic tours. All his plans were made, but Bishop Wilberforce begged him to remain among the poor in a suburb of Oxford. This – as Prebendary Mackay points out – 'was the great act of renunciation of Benson's life. When he gave up India for Cowley St. John, he gave to God all he was and cared for, and by so doing found a point of entrance for the Religious Life into the modern Church of England.'

It had been decided that the first 'monastery' of the infant community should be in Mr. Benson's little house in Magdalen Terrace. The time had now come to inform Dr. Wilberforce, Bishop of Oxford, of the foundation which was to be made in his diocese. Benson wrote to him towards the end of July 1865 describing the spirit and work of the Community. He said that they would be a 'Congregation of Priests and laymen, giving up the world, living by simple rule and devoting ourselves to prayer, study and mission work'. He stressed that the members would strive to be 'not only loyal to the Church of England, but also careful to act in harmony with her ecclesiastical system'. They would not intrude themselves into any diocese against the will of the bishop. The programme of apostolic action was clearly defined and comprehensive:

'(1) Missions for a week or fortnight in any parish in London or the country where the incumbent may invite us. (2) More settled mission work in London, where we intend to have a house which will be the centre of the various agencies, educational and controversial, by which to get hold of boys and young men. (3) A house in Oxford for scholars, who wish to live by rule, while getting a University education; for students in theology; for clergy who wish to retire for a time of study. (4) A chapel in London where we may chiefly address the educated classes upon the dangers of the fashions and scepticism of the present day. (5) Foreign Missions. (6) Retreats. . . .

Bishop Wilberforce's reply was brief but favourable. He wrote: 'I like the idea of your *College* very much indeed'; adding that he would be glad to discuss certain details with Mr. Benson. Objections were raised as to a 'distinctive dress or badge', the taking of vows by members, and the bishop insisted that 'all questions of ritual should be decided absolutely' by himself, and that no office should be introduced without his previous sanction. After the exchange of several letters Bishop Wilberforce gave the Community his blessing, even if he might not agree absolutely with all details of its rule, etc.

From: *The Call of the Cloister* by Peter F. Anson

(S.P.C.K., 1964, pp. 76–7)

Thursday

Society of St. John the Evangelist

PETER F. ANSON

The Missionary Brotherhood came into being very quietly and with no publicity in August 1865, when Mr. Benson and Mr. Grafton began to live together under rule in that little house near the Iron Church off the Iffley Road. Soon after they were joined by Mr. Prescott. Bishop Wilberforce gave these clergymen preachers' licences in the diocese of Oxford, thus showing his confidence in the experiment. Charles Wood and George Lane-Fox – both still hoping to become lay brothers – followed during the autumn. Mr. Tuke intended to join the Brotherhood when he was able to give up his curacy in Soho, but he changed his mind at the last moment. Lord Halifax recalled in after-years Lane-Fox wearing 'an Inverness cape, ringing the bell for Lauds at six o'clock in the morning of a cold winter's day, in the iron church . . . which was as cold in winter as it was hot in summer'. The rest of the offices were generally recited in a tiny oratory, according to *The Day Hours of the Church of England*. Benson told Charles Wood that it was his duty to go back to the world; that his vocation lay elsewhere. As to the volatile and eccentric George Lane-Fox, he had begun to have grave doubts about the catholicity of the Church of England. He yearned for something more 'monastic' than the austere and simple life of this little Brotherhood.

During the autumn of 1865 Grafton and O'Neill went to London to give spiritual help to the victims of the cholera epidemic. Here they worked in Bethnal Green in company with Dr. Pusey. Charles Wood acted as secretary of a temporary hospital. Benson could not join them because of his parochial duties.

On the feast of St. John the Evangelist, 27 December 1866, Benson, Grafton, and O'Neill made their religious professions; promising to live in celibacy, poverty, and obedience as Mission Priests of St. John the Evangelist until their life's end. Not long after this the Community moved to another house in Iffley Road where they remained until 1868 when the Mission House in Marston Street was ready for occupation. This enabled the Society to receive clergymen and laymen for retreats; a work which had been indicated from the first as one of its undertakings.

A Rule had to be drawn up. Benson consulted Bishop Forbes, and after digesting Holstenius' *Codex Regularum Monasticarum*, the founder compiled a Rule of his own. Inspired indirectly by some of the older monastic Rules, the one evolved by Fr. Benson was indeed modern a hundred years ago. There is no wonder that the manner of life of this Society of Mission Priests was approved by Bishop Wilberforce, since here was the realization of the scheme he had envisaged in his letter to Fr. Ignatius, i.e. 'a college of clergymen'.

From: *The Call of the Cloister* by Peter F. Anson

(S.P.C.K., 1964, pp. 77–9)

Friday

Society of St. John the Evangelist

PETER F. ANSON

The object of the Society of St. John the Evangelist was, 'to seek that sanctification to which God in His Mercy calls us, and in so doing to seek, as far as God may permit, to be instrumental in bringing others to be partakers of the same sanctification'. Fr. Benson was not interested in the romantic and picturesque externals of the Religious Life. . . . The ideal he set before his brethren was to cultivate the spark of the religious life within themselves till it became a flame. Then it would make itself felt. . . . Those who came to test their vocations at the Mission House were expected to perform cheerfully whatever duties were assigned to them, to be prepared for every kind of humiliation that might break down pride and self-will, and being trained to live in poverty and simplicity with no other end in view but to promote the glory of God. Neither was there much to compensate for this austerity, for there was little or no glamour about the services in that ugly iron church in which the Community assembled every morning for a simple Eucharist celebrated according to the rite of the Book of Common Prayer, without any liturgical enrichments or interpolations. As to the bare, bleak chapel perched on the roof of the Mission House, with its dull-red painted deal fittings, where the *Day Hours of the Church of England* were recited with a minimum of ceremonial, and much time spent in mental prayer, there was nothing attractive about that either.

The chapel has been described romantically as 'an embodiment in brick and wood of poverty and detachment, like St. Damiano and the Carceri, but planted in an ugly English midland suburb with none of the Italian charm'.

The driving force, the leader and the father of this community, was Fr. Benson himself, 'who had no form or comeliness apart from the tranquil shining spirit which shone through his dim short-sighted eyes, and in the strong, benevolent lines of his mouth. A little shrivelled, bent, thin, wiry, ascetic figure, full of energy, often looking as though he were concealing physical suffering – but at fitting times brimming over with laughter and humour, a shabby faded cassock, a neck-cloth renewed not very often, stockingless feet thrust into old shoes, the cassock girded very tightly – that is the figure people remember; a harsh, rather hesitating voice, no power of popular preaching, nothing to attract you short of the highest characteristics of all.'

From: *The Call of the Cloister* by Peter F. Anson

(S.P.C.K., 1964, pp. 79–81)

Saturday

Society of St. John the Evangelist

PETER F. ANSON

Fr. Benson died on 14 January 1915, having lived to see his Society spread over three continents. One of his sons – Fr. Burton, later Bishop of Nassau – who was in close touch with the founder during his last years – summed up his personality as: 'a heart of steel towards self, a heart of flesh towards man, a heart of flame towards God'. He recalls how at the age of eighty-four, seven years before he died, Fr. Benson always kept a 'black fast' on Friday, and ate nothing from

Maundy Thursday till Easter morning. 'He never spoke of pain or complained of blindness, or mentioned his arthritis. He was an old war-horse, venerated from afar. From his lips, from his whole being poured forth words of love of God as radiant and mellowing as the noonday sunshine.' Bishop Burton tells us that the founder's last Masses were 'terrifying to serve, for he was lame and blind'. . . .

Cut into the wooden panelling behind the stalls of the community chapel in the mother house at Cowley are the names of the brethren who have gone before with the sign of faith and who sleep the sleep of peace – what memories they revive to those of an older generation! There were giants in the earth in those days. The founder himself whose many books help to keep alive his spirit though he passed to his eternal rest in 1915 . . . Fr. Hollings, who lived more in the next world than in this and whose name is revered in many a Sisterhood; Fr. Congreve, the gentle preacher and author of so many books which formed the basis of the spiritual life of countless members of the Church of England half a century ago; Fr. Elwin, who wrote fascinating reminiscences of India; Fr. Longridge, the giver of innumerable retreats and the exponent of the 'Spiritual Exercises' of St. Ignatius Loyola; Fr. Puller, that doughty fighter, who attacked marriage with a deceased wife's sister, defended Anglican Orders and Fasting Communion, and even set out to prove that many of the primitive saints had shown scant respect to Popes; Fr. Waggett, always something of an *enfant terrible*, endowed with a brain and a wit that raised him far above most of his contemporaries; Fr. Callaway, who has left us so many memories of his missionary labours in South Africa, where he was a member of a small community, the Society of St. Cuthbert, which was absorbed in S.S.J.E. early this century; Fr. Trenholme, the historian and liturgist; and Fr. Cary, who was both an authority on the more technical side of the Religious Life, and a devoted student of the great Spanish mystics. None of these Cowley Fathers ever sought the limelight: their aim was to be hidden and to efface themselves. Some managed to achieve this, others became famous, but one and all never forgot those lessons they learned from Fr. Benson when they were novices: 'We do not come into our Community primarily to convert others, but rather with the desire, first of all, to be converted ourselves. Then, if by God's grace we are converted to Him, He may use us in missionary work, or in any other way that He pleases. . . .'

From: *The Call of the Cloister* by Peter F. Anson

(S.P.C.K., 1964, pp. 82–4)

Monday

The Cloud of Unknowing

CLIFTON WOLTERS

Just as the meditations of those who seek to live the contemplative life come without warning, so, too, do their prayers. I am thinking of their private prayers, of course, not those laid down by Holy Church. For true contemplatives could not value such prayers more, and so they use them, in the form and according to the rules laid down by the holy Fathers before us. But their own personal prayers rise spontaneously to God, without bidding or premeditation, before-hand or during their prayer.

If they are in words, as they seldom are, then they are very few words; the fewer the better. If it is a little word of one syllable, I think it is better than if it is of two, and more in accordance with the work of the Spirit. For a contemplative should always live at the highest, topmost peak spiritually.

We can illustrate this by looking at nature. A man or woman, suddenly frightened by fire, or death, or what you will, is suddenly in his extremity of spirit driven hastily and by necessity to cry or pray for help. And how does he do it! Not, surely, with a spate of words; not even in a single word of two syllables! Why? He thinks it wastes too much time to declare his urgent need and his agitation. So he bursts out in his terror with one little word, and that of a single syllable: 'Fire!' it may be, or 'Help!'.

Just as this little word stirs and pierces the ears of the hearers more quickly, so too does a little word of one syllable, when it is not merely spoken or thought, but expresses also the intention in the depth of our spirit. Which is the same as the 'height' of our spirit, for in these matters height, depth, length, and breadth all mean the same. And it pierces the ears of Almighty God more quickly than any long psalm churned out unthinkingly. That is why it is written 'Short prayer penetrates heaven'.

From: *The Cloud of Unknowing* by Clifton Wolters

(Penguin, 1971, pp. 96–7)

Tuesday

The Cloud of Unknowing

CLIFTON WOLTERS

We must pray in the height, depth, length, and breadth of our spirits. Not in many words, but in a little word of one syllable. What shall this word be? Surely such a word as is suited to the nature of prayer itself. And what word is that? First let us see what prayer is in itself, and then we shall know more clearly what word will best suit its nature.

In itself prayer is nothing else than a devout setting of our will in the direction of God in order to get good, and remove evil. Since all evil is summed up in sin, considered casually or essentially, when we pray with intention for the removing of evil, we should neither say, think, nor mean any more than this little word 'sin'. And if we pray with intention for the acquiring of goodness, let us pray, in word or thought or desire, no other word than 'God'. For in God is all good, for he is its beginning and its being. Do not be surprised then that I set these words before all others. If I could find any shorter words which would sum up fully the thought of good or evil as these words do, or if I had been led by God to take some other words, then I would have used those and left these. And that is my advice for you too.

But don't study these words, for you will never achieve your object so, or come to contemplation; it is never attained by study, but only by grace. Take no other words for your prayer, despite all I have said, than those that God leads you to use. Yet if God does lead you to these, my advice is not to let them go, that is, if you are using words at all in your prayer: not otherwise. They are very short words. But though shortness of prayer is greatly to be recommended here, it does not mean that the frequency of prayer is to be lessened. For as I have said, it is prayed in the length of one's spirit, so that it never stops until such time as it has fully attained what it longs for. We can turn to our terrified man or woman for an example. They never stop crying their little words, 'Help!' or 'Fire!' till such time as they have got all the help they need in their trouble.

From: *The Cloud of Unknowing* by Clifton Wolters

(Penguin, 1971, pp. 98–9)

O

The Cloud of Unknowing

CLIFTON WOLTERS

In the same way you should fill your spirit with the inner meaning of the single word 'sin', without analysing what kind it is, venial or mortal, or pride, anger, envy, avarice, sloth, gluttony, or lust. What does it matter to contemplatives what sort of a sin it is, or how great? For when they are engaged in contemplation, they think all sins are great in themselves, when the smallest sin separates them from God, and prevents spiritual peace.

Feel sin in its totality – as a lump – without specifying any particular part, and that all of it is you. And then cry ceaselessly in your spirit this one thing: Sin! Help! this spiritual cry is better learned from God by experience than from any man by word. It is best when it is entirely spiritual, unpremeditated and unuttered. On occasion perhaps the over-full heart will burst out into words, because body and soul alike are filled with sorrow, and the burden of sin.

In the same way too you should use this little word 'God'. Fill your spirit with its inner meaning, without considering any one of his works in particular, for example, whether it is good, better, or best of all, or whether it is physical or spiritual, or whether it is a virtue wrought in a man's soul by grace, and in this last case without classifying it as humility or charity, patience or abstinence, hope, faith, self-control, chastity, or voluntary poverty.

What does all this matter to contemplatives? For in God they find and experience every virtue. In him is everything: he made it and he maintains it. They know that if they have God they have all good, and so they covet no good thing in particular, but only good God. Do the same, as far as you can by grace, and mean God wholeheartedly, and the whole of Him. So that nothing works in your mind or will, but God alone.

And because all the while you live this wretched life you have to experience in some sort this filthy and nauseating lump of sin, part and parcel of yourself, you must constantly revert to these two words in turn, 'sin' and 'God'. With the knowledge that if you had God you would not have sin, and if you had not sin, then you would have God!

From: *The Cloud of Unknowing* by Clifton Wolters

(Penguin, 1971, pp. 99–100)

The Cloud of Unknowing

CLIFTON WOLTERS

If you are to ask me what discretion you should exercise in this work, my answer is 'None whatever'! In everything else you do, you have to use your own discretion, as, for example, in the matter of food and drink and sleep and keeping warm or cool, the time you spend in praying or reading, your conversations with your fellow Christians. In all these you have to use discretion, so that they are not too much or too little. But in this work, cast discretion to the wind! I want you never to give this work up all the while you live.

I am not saying that you will always come to it fresh, for that cannot be. Sometimes illness or some other upset of body or soul, or natural necessity will prove a real hindrance, and often prevent you from contemplating. But you should always be at this work, both 'on duty' and 'off', in intention if not in reality. For the love of God beware of illness as much as you can, so that as far as possible your self is not the cause of any weakness. I tell you the truth when I say that this work demands great serenity, an integrated and pure disposition, in soul and in body.

So for the love of God control your body and soul alike with great care, and keep as fit as you can. Should illness come in spite of everything, have patience and wait humbly for God's mercy. That is all that is asked. For I tell the truth when I say that patience in sickness and other kinds of tribulation often pleases God far more than any pleasant devotion you might show in health.

You will ask me, perhaps, how you are to control yourself with due care in the matter of food and drink and sleep and so on. My answer is brief: 'Take what comes!' Do this thing without ceasing and without care day by day, and you will know well enough, with a real discretion, when to begin and when to stop in everything else. I cannot believe that a soul who goes on in this work with complete abandon, day and night, will make mistakes in mundane matters. If he does, he is, I think, the type who always will get things wrong.

Therefore, if I am able to give a vital and wholehearted attention to this spiritual activity within my soul, I can then view my eating and drinking, my sleep and conversation and so on with comparative indifference. I would rather acquire a right discretion in these matters by such indifference, than by giving them my close attention, and

O*

weighing carefully all their pros and cons. Indeed, I could never bring it about in such a way, for all I might do or say. Let men say what they will: experience teaches. Therefore lift your heart up with this blind upsurge of love, and consider now 'sin', and now 'God'. God you want to have; sin you want to lose. You lack God: you know all about sin. Good God help you now, for it is now that you have need of him.

From: *The Cloud of Unknowing* by Clifton Wolters

(Penguin, 1971, pp. 101–2)

Friday

The Cloud of Unknowing

CLIFTON WOLTERS

See to it that there is nothing at work in your mind or will but only God. Try to suppress all knowledge and feeling of anything less than God, and trample it down deep under the cloud of forgetting. You must understand that in this business you are to forget not only all other things than yourself (and their doings – and your own!) but to forget also yourself, and even the things you have done for the sake of God. For it is the way of the perfect lover not only to love what he loves more than himself, but also in some sort to hate himself for the sake of what he loves.

So you are to do with yourself. You must loathe and tire of all that goes on in your mind and your will unless it is God. For otherwise surely whatever it is is between you and God. No wonder you loathe and hate thinking about yourself when you always feel your sin to be a filthy and nauseating lump – you do not particularize – between you and God, and that that lump is yourself. For you are to think of it as being identified with yourself: inseparable from you.

So crush all knowledge and experience of all forms of created things, and of yourself above all. For it is on your own self-knowledge and experience that the knowledge and experience of everything else depend. Alongside this self-regard everything else is quickly forgotten. For if you will take the trouble to test it, you will find that when all other things and activities have been forgotten (even your own) there still remains between you and God the stark awareness of your own existence. And this awareness, too, must go, before you experience contemplation in its perfection.

From: *The Cloud of Unknowing* by Clifton Wolters

(Penguin, 1971, pp. 102–3)

Saturday

The Cloud of Unknowing

CLIFTON WOLTERS

You will ask me next how to destroy this stark awareness of your own existence. For you are thinking that if it were destroyed all other difficulties would vanish too. And you would be right. All the same my answer must be that without God's very special and freely given grace, and your own complete and willing readiness to receive it, this stark awareness of yourself cannot possibly be destroyed. And this readiness is nothing else than a strong, deep sorrow of spirit.

But in this sorrow you need to exercise discretion: you must beware of imposing undue strain on your body or soul at this time. Rather, sit quite still, mute as if asleep, absorbed and sunk in sorrow. This is true sorrow, perfect sorrow, and all will go well if you can achieve sorrow to this degree. Everyone has something to sorrow over, but none more than he who knows and feels that he is. All other sorrow in comparison with this is a travesty of the real thing. For he experiences true sorrow, who knows and feels not only what he is, but that he is. Let him who has never felt this sorrow be sorry indeed, for he does not yet know what perfect sorrow is. Such sorrow, when we have it, cleanses the soul not only of sin, but also of the suffering its sin has deserved. And it makes the soul ready to receive that joy which is such that it takes from a man all awareness of his own existence.

From: *The Cloud of Unknowing* by Clifton Wolters

(Penguin, 1971, pp. 103–4)

Monday

The Pilgrim's Progress

JOHN BUNYAN

Now, while they lay here, and waited for the good hour, there was a noise in the town that there was a post come from the Celestial City, with matter of great importance to one Christiana, the wife of Christian the pilgrim. So inquiry was made for her, and the house was found out where she was: so the post presented her with a letter, the contents whereof were, 'Hail, good woman! I bring thee tidings that the Master calleth for thee, and expecteth that thou shouldst stand in his presence, in clothes of immortality, within these ten days.'

When he had read this letter to her, he gave her therewith a sure token that he was a true messenger, and was come to bid her make haste to be gone. The token was an arrow with a point sharpened with love, let easily into her heart, which by degrees wrought so effectually with her, that at the time appointed she must be gone.

When Christiana saw that her time had come, and that she was the first of this company that was to go over, she called for Mr. Great-heart her guide, and told him how matters were. So he told her he was heartily glad of the news, and could have been glad had the post come for him. Then she bid that he should give advice how all things should be prepared for her journey. So he told her, saying, Thus and thus it must be; and we that survive will accompany you to the river side.

Then she called for her children, and gave them her blessing and told them, that she yet read with comfort the mark that was set in their foreheads, and was glad to see them with her there, and that they had kept their garments so white. Lastly, she bequeathed to the poor that little she had, and commanded her sons and her daughters to be ready against the messenger should come for them.

When she had spoken these words to her guide and to her children, she called for Mr. Valiant-for-truth, and said unto him, Sir, you have in all places showed yourself true-hearted; 'be faithful unto death', and my King will give you 'a crown of life'. I would also entreat you to have an eye to my children; and if at any time you see them faint, speak comfortably to them. For my daughters, my sons' wives, they have been faithful, and a fulfilling of the promise upon them will be their end. . . .

Then came in that good man Mr. Ready-to-halt to see her. So she said to him, Thy travel hither has been with difficulty; but that will make thy rest the sweeter. But watch and be ready; for at an hour when you think not, the messenger may come.

From: *The Pilgrim's Progress* by John Bunyan

(Dent, pp. 368–70)

Tuesday

The Pilgrim's Progress

JOHN BUNYAN

In process of time there came a post to the town again, and his business was with Mr. Ready-to-halt. So he inquired him out, and said to him, I am come to thee in the name of him whom thou hast loved and followed, though upon crutches; and my message is to tell thee, that he expects thee at his table to sup with him, in his kingdom, the next day after Easter; wherefore prepare thyself for this journey.

Then he also gave him a token that he was a true messenger, saying, I have broken thy golden bowl, and loosed thy silver cord.[1]

After this, Mr. Ready-to-halt called for his fellow-pilgrims, and told them, saying, I am sent for, and God shall surely visit you also. So he desired Mr. Valiant to make his will; and because he had nothing to bequeath to them that should survive him but his crutches and his good wishes, therefore thus he said, These crutches I bequeath to my son that shall tread in my steps, with a hundred warm wishes that he may prove better than I have done.

Then he thanked Mr. Great-heart for his conduct and kindness, and so addressed himself to his journey. When he came at the brink of the river, he said, Now I shall have no more need of these crutches, since yonder are chariots and horses for me to ride on. The last words he was heard to say was, Welcome life! So he went his way.

From: *The Pilgrim's Progress* by John Bunyan

(Dent, pp. 371–2)

[1] Eccles. xii:6.

The Pilgrim's Progress

JOHN BUNYAN

When days had many of them passed away, Mr. Despondency was sent for; for a post was come, and brought this message to him: Trembling man, these are to summon thee to be ready with thy King by the next Lord's day, to shout for joy for thy deliverance from all thy doubtings.

And said the messenger, that my message is true, take this for a proof; so he gave him the grasshopper to be a burden unto him.[1] Now, Mr. Despondency's daughter, whose name was Much-afraid, said, when she heard what was done, that she would go with her father. Then Mr. Despondency said to his friends, Myself and my daughter, you know what we have been, and how troublesome we have behaved ourselves in every company. My will and my daughter's is, that our desponds and slavish fears be by no man ever received, from the day of our departure, for ever; for I know that after my death they will offer themselves to others. For, to be plain with you, they are ghosts the which we entertained when we first began to be pilgrims and could never shake them off after; and they will walk about and seek entertainment of the pilgrims; but, for our sakes, shut ye the doors upon them.

When the time was come for them to depart, they went to the brink of the river. The last words of Mr. Despondency were, Farewell night, welcome day. His daughter went through the river singing, but none could understand what she said.

From: *The Pilgrim's Progress* by John Bunyan

(Dent, pp. 372–3)

Thursday

The Pilgrim's Progress

JOHN BUNYAN

Then it came to pass, a while after, that there was a post in the town that inquired for Mr. Honest. So he came to his house where he was, and delivered to his hand these lines: Thou art commanded

[1] Eccles. xii:5.

to be ready against this day seven-night, to present thyself before thy Lord, at his Father's house. And for a token that my message is true, 'All thy daughters of music shall be brought low'.[1] Then Mr. Honest called for his friends, and said unto them, I die, but shall make no will. As for my honesty, it shall go with me; let him that comes after be told of this. When the day that he was to be gone was come, he addressed himself to go over the river. Now the river at that time overflowed the banks in some places; but Mr. Honest in his lifetime had spoken to one Good-conscience to meet him there, the which he also did, and lent him his hand, and so helped him over. The last words of Mr. Honest were, Grace reigns. So he left the world.

After this it was noised abroad, that Mr. Valiant-for-truth was taken with a summons by the same post as the other; and had this for a token that the summons was true, 'That his pitcher was broken at the fountain'.[2] When he understood it, he called for his friends, and told them of it. Then, said he, I am going to my Father's; and though with great difficulty I am got hither, yet now I do not repent me of all the trouble I have been at to arrive where I am. My sword I give to him that shall succeed me in my pilgrimage, and my courage and skill to him that can get it. My marks and scars I carry with me, to be a witness for me, that I have fought his battles who now will be my rewarder. When the day that he must go hence was come, many accompanied him to the river side, into which as he went he said, 'Death, where is thy sting?' And as he went down deeper, he said, 'Grave, where is thy victory?' So he passed over, and all the trumpets sounded for him on the other side.

From: *The Pilgrim's Progress* by John Bunyan

(Dent, pp. 374–5)

Friday

The Pilgrim's Progress

JOHN BUNYAN

Then there came forth a summons for Mr. Stand-fast – this Mr. Stand-fast was he that the rest of the pilgrims found upon his knees in the Enchanted Ground – for the post brought it him open in his

[1] Eccles. xii. 4.
[2] Eccles. xii:6.

hands. The contents whereof were, that he must prepare for a change of life, for his Master was not willing that he should be so far from him any longer. At this Mr. Stand-fast was put into a muse. Nay, said the messenger, you need not doubt the truth of my message, for here is a token of the truth thereof: 'Thy wheel is broken at the cistern.'[1] Then he called unto him Mr. Great-heart, who was their guide, and said unto him, Sir, although it was not my hap to be much in your good company in the days of my pilgrimage; yet, since the time I knew you, you have been profitable to me. When I came from home, I left behind me a wife and five small children; let me entreat you, at your return (for I know that you will go and return to your Master's house, in hopes that you may yet be a conductor to more of the holy pilgrims), that you send to my family, and let them be acquainted with all that hath or shall happen unto me. Tell them, moreover, of my happy arrival to this place, and of the present [and] late blessed condition that I am in. Tell them also of Christian, and Christiana his wife, and how she and her children came after her husband. Tell them also of what a happy end she made, and whither she has gone. I have little or nothing to send to my family, except it be prayers and tears for them; of which it will suffice if thou acquaint them, if per-adventure they may prevail.

When Mr. Stand-fast had thus set things in order, and the time being come for him to haste him away, he also went down to the river. Now there was a great calm at that time in the river; wherefore Mr. Stand-fast, when he was about half-way in, stood awhile, and talked to his companions that had waited upon him thither; and he said, This river has been a terror to many; yea, the thoughts of it also have often frightened me. Now, methinks, I stand easy, my foot is fixed upon that upon which the feet of the priests that bare the ark of the covenant stood, while Israel went over this Jordan.[2] The waters, indeed, are to the palate bitter, and to the stomach cold; yet the thoughts of what I am going to, and of the conduct that waits for me on the other side, doth lie as a glowing coal at my heart.

From: *The Pilgrim's Progress* by John Bunyan

(Dent, pp. 375–6)

---

[1] Eccles. xii: 6.
[2] Jos. iii:17.

Saturday

The Pilgrim's Progress

JOHN BUNYAN

I see myself now at the end of my journey, my toilsome days are ended. I am going now to see that head that was crowned with thorns, and that face that was spit upon for me.

I have formerly lived by hearsay and faith; but now I go where I shall live by sight, and shall be with him in whose company I delight myself.

I have loved to hear my Lord spoken of; and wherever I have seen the print of his shoe in the earth, there I have coveted to set my foot too.

His name has been to me as a civet-box; yea, sweeter than all perfumes. His voice to me has been most sweet, and his countenance I have more desired than they have most desired the light of the sun. His word I did use to gather for my food, and for antidotes against my faintings. 'He has held me, and hath kept me from mine iniquities; yea, my steps hath he strengthened in his way.'

Now, while he was thus in discourse, his countenance changed, his strong man bowed under him; and after he had said, Take me, for I come unto thee, he ceased to be seen of them.

But glorious it was to see how the open region was filled with horses and chariots, with trumpeters and pipers, with singers and players on stringed instruments, to welcome the pilgrims as they went up, and followed one another in at the beautiful gate of the city.

As for Christian's children, the four boys that Christiana brought with her, with their wives and children, I did not stay where I was till they were gone over. Also, since I came away, I heard one say that they were yet alive, and so would be for the increase of the CHURCH in that place where they were, for a time.

Shall it be my lot to go that way again, I may give those that desire it an account of what I here am silent about. Meantime, I bid my reader,

ADIEU.

From: *The Pilgrim's Progress* by John Bunyan

(Dent, pp. 377–8)

Sorrow of the World

FRANCIS PAGET

Cassian, whose long life nearly covers the latter half of the fourth century and the former half of the fifth, may be placed first in the first group of those who have written concerning . . . accidie. Trained during his early years in a monastery at Bethlehem, he had spent a long time among the hermits of the Thebaid, before he turned to his great work of planting in the far West the monasticism of the East, founding his two communities at Marseilles, and writing his twelve books. One book is entitled *De Spiritu Acediæ*; and in the first chapter of that book he gives a provisional and somewhat scanty indication of its subject. 'Acedia' may be called a weariness or distress of heart; it is akin to sadness; the homeless and solitary hermits, those who live in the desert, are especially assailed by it, and monks find it most troublesome about twelve o'clock; so that some of the aged have held it to be 'the sickness that destroyeth in the noonday', the 'dæmonium meridianum' of the ninety-first psalm. But the most striking part of all that Cassian has to say about accidie is the description in the second chapter of a monk who is suffering from a bad attack of the malady. When the poor fellow is beset by it, he says, it makes him detest the place where he is, and loathe his cell; and he has a poor and scornful opinion of his brethren, near and far, and thinks that they are neglectful and unspiritual. It makes him sluggish and inert for every task; he cannot sit still, nor give his mind to reading; he thinks despondently how little progress he has made where he is, how little good he gains or does – he, who might so well direct and help others and who, where he is, has nobody to teach and nobody to edify. He dwells much on the excellence of other and distant monasteries; he thinks how profitable and healthy life is there; how delightful the brethren are, and how spiritually they talk. On the contrary, where he is, all seems harsh and untoward; there is no refreshment for his soul to be got from his brethren, and none for his body from the thankless land. At last he thinks he really cannot be saved if he stops where he is; and then, about eleven or twelve o'clock, he feels as tired as if he had walked miles, and as hungry as if he had fasted for two or three days. He goes out and looks this way and that, and sighs to think that there is no one coming to visit him; he saunters to and fro, and wonders why the sun is setting so slowly; and so, with his mind full of stupid bewilderment and shameful gloom, he grows slack and void of all spiritual energy, and thinks that nothing will do him any good save to go and call on somebody, or else to betake himself to the solace of sleep. Whereupon his malady suggests to him that there are certain persons whom he clearly ought to visit, certain kind inquiries that he ought to make, a religious lady upon whom he ought to call, and to whom he may be able to render some service; and that it will be far better to do this than to sit profitless in his cell.

From: *The Spirit of Discipline* by Francis Paget

(Longmans, 1906, pp. 7–10)

Tuesday

Sorrow of the World

FRANCIS PAGET

. . . Of far deeper interest, of surer and wider value, is the treatment of acedia by St. Thomas Aquinas. The very place which it holds in the scheme of his great work reveals at once its true character, the secret of its harmfulness, its essential antagonism to the Christian life, and the means of resisting and conquering it. – 'The fruit of the Spirit', wrote St. Paul to the Galatians, 'is love, joy, peace.' And so Aquinas has been speaking of love, joy, peace, and pity, as the first effects upon the inner life of that *caritas* which is the form, the root, the mother, of all virtues. *Caritas*, that true friendship of man with God; that all-embracing gift which is the fulfilling of the Law; that 'one inward principle of life', as it has been called, 'adequate in its fullness to meet and embrace the range of duties which externally confront it'; – *caritas*, which is in fact nothing else but 'the energy and the representative of the Spirit in our hearts', expands and asserts itself, and makes its power to be known by its fruits of love, joy, peace, and pity in the character of man. Mark, then, how joy springs out at once as the unfailing token of the Holy Spirit's presence, the first sign that He is having His Own way with a man's heart. The joy of the Lord, the joy that is strength, the joy that no man taketh from us, the joy wherewith we joy before God, the abundant joy of faith and hope and love and praise, – this it is that gathers like a radiant, fostering, cheering air around the soul that yields itself to the grace of God, to do His holy, loving Will. – But, over against that joy, different as winter from summer, as night from day, aye, even as death from life, looms the dreary, joyless, thankless, fruitless gloom of sullenness, the sour sorrow of the world, the sin of accidie; the wanton, wilful self-distressing that numbs all love and zeal for good; that sickly, morbid weariness in which the soul abhors all manner of meat, and is even hard at death's door; that woeful lovelessness in which all upward longing fails out of the heart and will – the sin that is opposed to the joy of love. So St. Thomas speaks of accidie, and so he brings it near, surely, to the conscience of many men in every age.

From: *The Spirit of Discipline* by Francis Paget

(Longmans, 1906, pp. 57–9)

Wednesday

Sorrow of the World

FRANCIS PAGET

. . . There is a particular way in which the sin of accidie gathers power and opportunity out of the conditions of the present day. The moral influence of any form of unbelief which is largely talked about, reaches far beyond the range of its intellectual appeal; it is felt more widely than it is understood; in many cases it gets at the springs of action without passing through the mind. And this is likely to come about with especial readiness when the prevalent type of unbelief makes little demand for precise knowledge or positive statement, and easily enters into alliance with the general inclination of human nature. The practical effect of agnosticism is favoured by these advantages, and it mixes readily with that pervading atmosphere of life which tells for so much more in the whole course of things than any definite assertion or any formal argument. Hooker noticed long ago that trait of human faultiness which is always ready to befriend suggestions such as those of agnosticism. 'The search of knowledge is a thing painful, and the painfulness of knowledge is that which

maketh the will so hardly inclinable thereunto. The root hereof,
Divine malediction; whereby the instruments being weakened where-
withal the soul (especially in reasoning) doth work, it preferreth rest
in ignorance before wearisome labour to know.' It is very easy to
translate into the sphere of action that renunciation of sustained and
venturesome and exacting effort which in the sphere of thought is
sometimes called agnosticism; and so translated it finds many tendencies prepared to help its wide diffusion. If 'the search of knowledge is a thing painful', the attainment of holiness does not come
quickly or naturally to men as they now are; and it is not strange
that while many are denying that it is possible to know God, many
more are renouncing the attempt to grow like Him.

From: *The Spirit of Discipline* by Francis Paget

(Longmans, 1906, pp. 42–4)

Thursday

Sorrow of the World

FRANCIS PAGET

It occurs to one at once that this misery of accidie lies on the
border-line between the physical and the spiritual life; that if there
is something to be said of it as a sin, there is also something to be
said of it as an ailment. It is a truth that was recognized long ago
both by Cassian and by St. Thomas Aquinas, who expressly discusses
and dismisses this objection against regarding accidie as a sin at all.
Undoubtedly physical conditions of temperament and constitution,
of weakness, illness, harassing, weariness, overwork, may give at
times to such a mood of mind and heart a strange power against us;
at times the forces for resistance may seem frail and few. It is a truth
which should make us endlessly charitable, endlessly forbearing and
considerate and uncritical towards others; but surely it is a truth that
we had better be shy of using for ourselves. . . . Surely it has been the
secret of some of the highest, noblest lives that have helped the world,
that men have refused to make allowances for themselves; refused to
limit their aspiration and effort by the disadvantages with which they
started; refused to take the easy tasks which their hindrances might
seem to justify, or to draw premature boundaries for the power of
their will. As there are some men to whom the things that should

have been for their wealth are, indeed, an occasion of falling, so are
there others to whom the things that might have been for their
hindrance are an occasion of rising; 'who going through the vale of
misery use it for a well, and the pools are filled with water'. – And
'they shall go from strength to strength' – in all things more than
conquerors through Him Who loveth them; wresting out of the very
difficulties of life a more acceptable and glorious sacrifice to lift to
Him; welcoming and sanctifying the very hindrances that beset them
as the conditions of that part which they, perhaps, alone can bear in
the perfecting of His saints, in the edifying of the body of Christ.
And in that day when every man's work shall be made manifest, it
may be found, perhaps, that none have done Him better service than
some of those who, all through this life, have been His ambassadors.
in bonds.

From: *The Spirit of Discipline* by Francis Paget

(Longmans, 1906, pp. 60–3)

Friday

Sorrow of the World

FRANCIS PAGET

Lastly, then, brethren, let me speak very simply of [two] ways in
which we may, God helping us, extend and reinforce the power of our
will to shut out and drive away this wasteful gloom, if ever it begins
to gather round us; [two] ways of doing battle against this sin of
accidie.

In the first place, it will surely be a help, a help we all may gain, to
see more, to think more, to remember and to understand more, of
the real, plain, stubborn sufferings that others have to bear; to
acquaint ourselves afresh with the real hardships of life, the trials,
and anxieties, and privations and patience of the poor – the unfanci-
ful facts of pain. For 'blessed is he that considereth the poor and
needy; the Lord shall deliver him in the time of trouble'. It is one part
of the manifold privilege of a parish priest's life that day by day he
has to go among scenes which almost perforce may startle him out of
any selfish, wilful sadness. . . .

From: *The Spirit of Discipline* by Francis Paget

(Longmans, 1906, p. 63)

Saturday

Sorrow of the World

FRANCIS PAGET

But there is yet one way, above all other ways, I think, in which we ought to be ever gaining fresh strength and freedom of soul to rise above such moods of gloom and discontent; one means by which we should be ever growing in the steadiness and quiet intensity of the joy of love. It is the serious and resolute consideration of that astounding work of our redemption which the Love of God has wrought at so immense a cost. It is strange indeed – it would be inconceivable if it were not so very common – that a man can look back to Calvary and still be sullen; that he can believe that all that agony was the agony of God the Son, willingly chosen for the Love of sinful men, and still be thankless and despondent. Strange that he should be sullen still, when he believes that that eternal and unwearied Love is waiting, even during the hours of his gloom and hardness – waiting, watching at his dull, silent heart, longing for the change to come; longing just for that turn of the will which may let in again the glad tide of light and joy and health. Strange that any one should be able to think what a little while we have in which to do what little good we may on earth, before the work is all sealed up and put aside for judgment, and yet take God's great trust of life, and wilfully bid the heaven be dark at noon, and wrap himself in an untimely night wherein no man can work. Strange, most strange, that any one should believe that this world is indeed the place where he may begin to train his soul by grace for an everlasting life of love and praise and joy, prepared for him in sheer mercy by Almighty God, and still be sullen. Ah! surely, it can only be that we forget these things; that they are not settled deep enough in our hearts; that in the haste of life we do not think of them, or let them tell upon us. For otherwise we could hardly let our hearts sink down in any wilful, wanton gloom, or lower our eyes from that glory of the western sky which should ever brighten our faces as we press towards God; that glory which our Blessed Lord was crucified to win for us; that glory whither the high grace of God the Holy Ghost has been sent forth to lead us.

From: *The Spirit of Discipline* by Francis Paget

(Longmans, 1906, pp. 67–8)

SAINTS' DAYS AND HOLY DAYS

The Circumcision of Christ, or the Naming of Jesus – January 1

Mater Christi

MOTHER ST. PAUL

After one week of peace and joy, Mary is called on to suffer with, and on account of, her Son. The Law of God is clear. 'On the eighth day, the infant shall be circumcised.'[1] And there is no doubt in the minds of Mary and Joseph, that, though the Holy Child has no need of the rite which probably cleansed away original sin, He must nevertheless submit to it, as being part of His Father's law, every jot and tittle of which He has come to fulfil. So JESUS, of His own free will, classes Himself with sinners, and offers to God the firstfruits of that Blood which He will shed for them on Calvary.

The Circumcision of her Son means much to Mary; she sees Him suffer; she hears His cry of pain; she sees the Blood flow; and she understands that to be the Mother of God means being the Mater Dolorosa; and now she has fresh matter for her Meditations. Her Son is to be the Victim for sin, and she unites her sacrifice to His.

The rite of Circumcision was to the Jew a sign of the Covenant that God had made with his nation – it marked him out as one of God's own people; it was a mark of his dependence on God, and also of his slavery to sin till God set him free.

'True Circumcision is that of the heart,' St. Paul tells us, 'in the spirit, not in the letter; whose praise is not of men, but of God.'[2] By assisting with Mary at the Circumcision of her Son, I mean that I want to understand something of this circumcision of the heart – understand, that is, that God has made a covenant with me, that I belong to Him, and am dependent on Him; I mean that I am ready with the knife of mortification to cut away all that prevents me from being a good servant, ready to 'resist unto blood', if need be, but, at any rate, ready to make myself a victim with Jesus, as Mary did, willing to suffer anything which He calls upon me to suffer.

From: *Mater Christi*

(Longmans, 1937, pp. 49–50)

[1] Lev. xii:3.   [2] Rom. ii:29.

The Conversion of St. Paul – January 25

St. Paul

W. R. INGE

Among all the great men of antiquity there is none, with the exception of Cicero, whom we may know so intimately as Saul of Tarsus. The main facts of his career have been recorded by a contemporary, who was probably his friend and travelling companion. A collection of letters, addressed to the little religious communities which he founded, reveals the character of the writer no less than the nature of his work. Alone among the first preachers of Christianity, he stands before us as a living man. . . . We know very little in reality of Peter and James and John, of Apollos and Barnabas. And of our divine Master no biography can ever be written.

With St. Paul it is quite different. He is a saint without a luminous halo. His personal characteristics are too distinct and too human to make idealisation easy. For this reason he has never been the object of popular devotion. Shadowy figures like St. Joseph and St. Anne have been divinised and surrounded with picturesque legends; but St. Paul has been spared the honour or the ignominy of being coaxed and wheedled by the piety of paganised Christianity. No tender fairy-tales are attached to his cult; he remains for us what he was in the flesh. It is even possible to feel an active dislike for him. Lagarde . . . abuses him as a politician might vilify an opponent. 'It is monstrous' (says he) 'that men of any historical training should attach any importance to this Paul. This outsider was a Pharisee from top to toe even after he became a Christian' – and much more to the same effect. Nietzsche describes him as 'one of the most ambitious men, whose superstition was only equalled by his cunning. A much tortured much to be pitied man, an exceedingly unpleasant person both to himself and to others. . . .' These outbursts of personal animosity, so strange in modern critics dealing with a personage of ancient history, show how vividly his figure stands out from the canvas. There are very few historical characters who are alive enough to be hated. . . .

There is something transitional about all St. Paul's teaching. We cannot take him out of his historical setting, as so many of his commentators in the nineteenth century tried to do. This is only another way of saying that he was, to use his own expression, a wise master-builder, not a detached thinker, an arm-chair philosopher. To the historian, there must always be something astounding in the magnitude of the task which he set himself, and in his enormous success. The future history of the civilised world for two thousand years, perhaps for all time, was determined by his missionary journeys and hurried writings. It is impossible to guess what would have become of Christianity if he had never lived; we cannot even be sure that the religion of Europe would be called by the name of Christ. This stupendous achievement seems to have been due to an almost unique practical insight into the essential factors of a very difficult and complex situation. We watch him, with breathless interest, steering the vessel which carried the Christian Church and its fortunes through a narrow channel full of sunken rocks and shoals. With unerring instinct he avoids them all, and brings the ship, not into smooth water, but into the open sea, out of that perilous strait. And so far was his masterly policy from mere opportunism, that his correspondence has been 'Holy Scripture' for fifty generations of Christians, and there has been, on one side at least, a return to St. Paul. Protestants have always felt their affinity with this institutionalist, mystics with this disciplinarian. The reason, put shortly, is that St. Paul understood what most Christians never realise, namely, that the Gospel of Christ is not *a* religion, but religion itself, in its most universal and deepest significance.

From: *Outspoken Essays* by W. R. Inge

(Longmans, 1919, pages 205–6, & 229)

The Presentation of Christ in the Temple, or the Purification of St. Mary the Virgin – February 2

Mater Christi

MOTHER ST. PAUL

It is the fortieth day after the birth of her Son, the day when it is Mary's turn to keep the legal observances, and so to identify herself in all things with her Son. There is no need for her to be purified, before she is allowed to enter God's Temple; neither is there any need for her to present her First-born in the Temple and pay the ransom money for Him, for His Name is Saviour and He is Himself the Ransom for His people. There is no *need*; but Mary gladly does both, that she may enter more closely into the spirit of her Son, Who had undergone the rite of circumcision.

How many unnecessary humiliations and unpleasant duties do I undertake just for the sake of identifying myself with Jesus and Mary, and sharing their spirit?

We may imagine the Holy Family quietly setting out for their two hours' walk to the Temple, attracting no more notice than was usually attached to an event so common. Passing remarks were probably made as to its being the first time she was out; as to the disparity in their age; as to their poverty, for Joseph was carrying two doves, the offering of the poor, to be offered by Mary for her Purification.

Ah, how little the world *sees*! Extraordinary things are going on, though they are hidden, as is ever God's wont, under things most ordinary. Mary, the purest of creatures, the Virgin of virgins, the Queen of Heaven, of Angels and of men, is bearing in her arms the Lord of glory, who is on His way to visit His Temple for the first time, and thus to fill it with a greater glory than ever Solomon's Temple had possessed. Angels are worshipping and adoring at every step of that journey, and presently they will throw open wide the gate of the Temple to let the King of Glory in. And the humble and silent Joseph is playing a part which no Jew before or since has ever played; for though the verdict of the world is that he is too poor to afford to take a lamb, in reality he is too rich to need one, for is he not bringing to the Temple the Lamb of God – an offering which no one has ever been rich enough to make before? Let us try to see things and judge them from God's point of view – not from the world's.

From *Mater Christi*

(Longmans, 1937, pp. 52–3)

St. Matthias the Apostle – February 24

Against Hypocrisy

CHARLES GORE

There is nothing against which our Lord warns us so terribly as against hypocrisy. The discernment of Frenchmen and Germans has detected, or fancies it has detected, that Englishmen are specially liable to be hypocrites, to profess what they do not practise, to care for the outward appearance of morality and religion while they neglect their inward essence. Whether this be specially true of us or no, it behoves us to look to ourselves. In literature, in journalism, in the pulpits, in political life, there are so many 'prophets', so many professors, so many remedy-mongers. They speak fair words, and brilliant success often seems to attend them. 'Have we not prophesied in thy name,' they cry, 'and in thy name cast out devils, and in thy name done many wonderful works?' But not all the fair-seeming words, not all the brilliant, even miraculous successes can compensate for the absence of personal character. That is the one thing to which our Lord looks. He warns us that not the most brilliant results can avail anything if we lack that inner character which is like Christ's.

This is a tremendous warning for days of wide and somewhat vague philanthropy, of restless activity, of nervous anxiety for successes and results, for days such as our own day. It is a tremendous warning for days of journalism, when everyone is tempted to advertise himself or allow himself to be advertised, when everything is dragged prematurely into publicity, and even those who are working for Christ are apt to be morbidly anxious to produce results which can be tabulated in parish magazines or even proclaimed in newspapers. We need to remember that all these results in Christ's eyes will not bear looking at, except so far as they are the product of inward Christian character, a character which He can recognize as His own. For He cannot accept anything, whatever its orthodox profession, in which He does not trace the lineaments of His own character.

From: *The Sermon on the Mount*

(John Murray, 1897, pp. 177–9)

The Annunciation of the Blessed Virgin Mary – March 25

Mater Christi

MOTHER ST. PAUL

The Lord is with thee. These words were often said of or to those to whom God was about to entrust some special work. He was 'with Joseph' while he was in Potiphar's prison, preparing him for the great work of serving the nation during the famine.[1] 'I will be with thee,' God said to Moses at the burning bush, when He told him that it was he who was to bring the children of Israel out of Egypt.[2] And to Joshua, who had to bring the chosen people into the promised land, He said: 'As I have been with Moses, so I will be with thee. Fear not, and be not dismayed: because the Lord thy God is with thee in all things whatsoever thou shalt go to.'[3] 'The Lord is with thee, O most valiant of men.' This was the message the angel brought to Gideon at the threshing floor, for he was to leave his wheat and go to deliver God's people from idolatry and from their enemies.[4]

And now when Mary is being singled out for the greatest work that was ever entrusted to any child of Adam – that of being the Mother of Him Who was to save not one nation only, but the whole world, God sends an Archangel and bids him to say to her: *The Lord is with thee*. God was with Mary always; but now all three Persons of the Blessed Trinity are to be with her in a very special way to enable her to co-operate with God's designs for her. But the message goes further: 'Blessed art thou among women'. Gabriel tells her that God's message to her is that she is blessed, and more blessed than other women! It is praise indeed, and praise from God Himself. But God can trust Mary with praise. She is full of humility, for she is full of grace; and God knows that she will look at things from His point of view – not from her own.

I may get some consolation from these words for myself. God sometimes gives me work to do for Him. How blessed I am to be picked out and chosen by Him! And I may be quite sure that He is *with me* for it. It is His own work, and He will look after it Himself; but He needs an instrument. The workman is never far from his tools,

[1] Gen. xxxix:21.
[2] Ex. iii:12.
[3] Jos. i:5–9.
[4] Jud. vi:12.

unless he has thrown them on one side as useless. 'The Lord is with thee.' If I see to it that I am an instrument fit and ready for His service, I need have no other anxiety. He will use me when He wants me; the responsibility of the work will be all His, and He will be with me, doing His works by means of me.

From: *Mater Christi*

(Longmans, 1937, pp. 21–3)

St. Mark the Evangelist – April 25

'For they were afraid'

R. H. LIGHTFOOT

I desire to suggest . . . that it may be exceptionally difficult for the present generation to sympathize with St. Mark's insistence on fear and amazement as the first and inevitably and, up to a point, right result of revelation. One of the most obvious and disturbing phenomena in the religious life of Christendom during the last seventy or eighty years has been the disappearance of the awe or dread or holy fear of God. We of the present older generation are not afraid, as our parents and grandparents always were afraid. It is not a marked feature of religious life today that we work out our own salvation with fear and trembling (Philippians 2:12), or that we offer service well-pleasing to God with godly fear and awe (Hebrews 12:28), or that we order our lives, whilst we live here, in fear (1 Peter 1:17); and I doubt whether to most Europeans today the words of Joseph to his brethren, 'This do, and live; for I fear God'[1] would at once give the natural and obvious reason for his forbearance towards them. And it will scarcely be suggested that this has come about, because we have attained the perfect love which casts out fear. The Christian doctrine of eternal life, which is indissolubly connected with that of the Lord's resurrection, is, in the true sense of the word, a tremendous and, on one side, a terrible truth; if we do not know for ourselves that this is so, we are far astray. And if the belief should ever come to be widely held that St. Mark may have ended his book deliberately at Chapter 16, Verse 8, I should like to think that such a recognition might have its part to play in recalling men and women to the truth that the dread as well as the love of God is an essential

[1] Genesis 42:18

note of our religion, which sounds loudly in the New Testament as well as in the Old, and in no book of the New Testament more strongly than in the Gospel according to St. Mark. And St. Mark's conclusion, stylistically harsh and abrupt though it may seem to us and doubtless is, may be as appropriate for him, as the delivery of 'the marching orders of the Church' (as the Duke of Wellington described Matt. 28:19 f.) on the mountain in Galilee is for St. Matthew, and the idyll of the life of the first disciples in Jerusalem is for St. Luke.

From: *The Gospel Message of St. Mark*

(Clarendon Press, 1950, p. 97)

St. Philip and St. James, Apostles – May 1

Following Christ

SØREN KIERKEGAARD

My hearer! If you imagine a youth who stands at his life's beginning, where many ways open before him, asking himself which course he might wish to enter upon: is it not true that he then inquires carefully where the individual ways lead, or, what amounts to the same thing, he seeks to learn who has earlier walked this way. Then we mention to him the celebrated, the acclaimed, the glorious names of those whose memory is preserved among men. At first we perhaps mention several, so that the choice may have some relation to the youth's potentialities, so the wealth of advice proffered may be excessive. But even if he, impelled by an inward urge, makes a lesser choice, at last there comes to be for him only one. The only one, the one which in his eyes and according to his belief is the most advantageous of all. Then his heart beats violently, when he enthusiastically mentions this name, to him the only name, and says: 'This is the way I will go, for this is the way He walked!'

We shall not divert our attention or waste time by mentioning such names; for there is indeed only one name in heaven and on earth, one alone, and consequently but one way to choose – if a man is to choose earnestly and choose rightly. There may indeed be several ways, since a man is given a choice; but there must be only one way to choose if the earnestness of eternity is to rest upon the choice. . . .

There is only one name in heaven and on earth, only one way, only one pattern. He who chooses to follow Christ, chooses the name which is above all names, the pattern which is highly exalted above all heavens, but at the same time so human that it can be a pattern for a human being, so that it is named and will be named in heaven and on earth, in both places as the highest. For there are examples whose names are only mentioned on earth, but the highest, the only one, must precisely have this exclusive quality whereby it is indeed recognizable as the only one: that it is named both in heaven and on earth. This name is the name of our Lord Jesus Christ. . . .

Is it so glorious a thing to eat on silver when others go hungry; to dwell in palaces when so many are homeless; to be the scholar which no simple man can become; to have a name that in a sense excludes thousands and thousands: is that so glorious? And if this, the *envious distinction of the earthly life*, were the highest, would it not be inhuman and life unendurable for the fortunate! How different, on the contrary, when the only joy consists in following Christ. Greater joy cannot be vouchsafed than this: to be able to become the highest; and this exalted joy cannot be made freer, more blessed, more secure than it is through the glad thought of a *merciful heaven*: that every man can do this.

From: *The Gospel of Suffering*

(Augsburg Publishing House, 1948, pp. 14–16)

St. Barnabas the Apostle – June 11

Unworldliness

CHARLES GORE

'Lay not up for yourselves treasures upon the earth, where moth and rust doth consume, and where thieves dig through and steal: but lay up for yourselves treasures in heaven, where neither moth nor rust doth consume, and where thieves do not break through nor steal: for where thy treasure is, there will thy heart be also.'

In the days when our Lord spoke these words people mostly preserved their money and other treasure by concealing it, as in many parts of Europe they do still. Thus the task of thieves was, in the main, to 'dig through' into places in houses or fields where treasure was likely to be hidden. This is the meaning of our Lord's metaphor. We are to lay up our store in heaven, where no thief can get at it, and where no natural process of corruption can affect it. Now heaven is

God's throne. It is where His will works centrally and peacefully; and in the kingdom of heaven, because, through a visible society in the world, God is there specially known and recognized, His good will towards man is consequently at work with a special freedom and fullness.

If then you are asked, what is it to lay up treasure in heaven, I think you may answer with great security: To lay up treasure in heaven is to do acts which promote, or belong to, the kingdom of God; and what our Lord assures us of is that any act of our hands, any thought of our heart, any word of our lips, which promotes the divine kingdom by the ordering whether of our own life or of the world outside – all such activity, though it may seem for the moment to be lost, is really stored up in the divine treasure-house; and when the heavenly city, the New Jerusalem, shall at last appear, that honest effort of ours, which seemed so ineffectual, shall be found to be a brick built into that eternal and celestial fabric.

And our Lord gives the answer to a difficulty continually perplexing honest Christians – How am I to learn to *love* God? I want to do my duty, but I do not feel as if I love God. Our Lord gives the answer, 'Where your treasure is, there will your heart be also.' Act for God: do and say the things that He wills: direct your thoughts and intentions God-ward; and depend upon it, in the slow process of nature all that belongs to you – your instincts, your intelligence, your affections, your feelings – will gradually follow along the line of your action. Act for God: you are already *showing* love to Him and you will learn to *feel* it.

From: *The Sermon on the Mount*

(John Murray, 1897, pp. 142–4)

The Nativity of St. John Baptist – June 24

Minister of God

W. C. E. NEWBOLT

Time was when a man went from college to encounter the difficulties of ministerial life, and to develop his capacities, pre-eminently as a gentleman; to add a desirable acquaintance to the society of the neighbourhood; to be a good man to ask out to dinner, or to associate with the squire. Time was when a man went from college to make himself acceptable in the character of a scholar; to view everything from an intellectual standpoint, and to mingle in parochial affairs and personal difficulties, tinged with that complexion and absorbed in those pursuits, in the abundant case of a neglected parish. Time was when a man went to commend himself by conducting his actions as a pioneer of improvement; a martyr, if need be, to sanitary reform, to intellectual culture, and material improvement. All, be it noticed, excellent ideals in their way – ideals which one can so easily bring one's self to believe are most suited to the circumstances of the case, and most congenial to the feelings of those with whom we have to do. A man may so easily bring himself to believe that he is putting forward his best self, his self of influence and of power, by being in society a man of society, in touch with the world; or that a learned leisure is of infinite profit in an age prodigal of energy, and a spendthrift in immatured schemes; or that the position of respect which he holds on Boards and Committees does show that, after all, more than anything else, men appreciate the clever administrator and the good man of business. But there is a startling amount of the spirit of the old prophet still in the world. He draws the man of God down from his high ideal; he brings him back; he makes him eat bread and drink water in the forbidden place, and return by the prohibited way. He makes him break his vow, and lose his high ideal, and then mourns over his inconsistency, and laments his downfall: 'Alas, my brother!' Look again, is there not a wistful longing for something higher? Does not Herod respect and admire the steadfastness of St. John Baptist, even while he is keeping him in prison? Does not Ahab have a sort of lingering respect for Micaiah, uncompromising and unyielding though he be? Is there not a fascination about a St. Paul which even Felix and Agrippa cannot resist? 'As ministers of God.' This is, after all, what men want. This is the clerical self which most commands respect. Think only of such various and separated instances as Savonarola, John Wesley, and the Père Lacordaire; and then, as we recognize the fascination of a high ideal, let us ask ourselves whether on the lowest ground it does not answer to be what we profess to be, ministers of God; and put forward a self which commands the respect due to that honoured title.

From: *Speculum Sacerdotum*

(Longmans, 1894, pp. 3–5)

St. Peter the Apostle – June 29

The Restoration of Peter

WILLIAM TEMPLE

The Lord has by a 'sign' illustrated the blessing which rests on work done in obedience to His command. He has refreshed His friends with sustenance which is, in part, the product of their own labour. Then He turns to the eager-hearted follower whose loyalty so sadly failed as a result of the self-will that was intermingled with it. He had once said, 'Although all shall be offended, yet will not I'; he had claimed a devotion more sure than that of his fellow-disciples. Does he claim that still? *Simon, son of John, lovest thou me more than these?* Peter says nothing of the comparison with others; on that score he can make no claim. Nor does he claim to love his Lord with that self-forgetful love which Christ had made known to men and to stand for which the Greek word – Agape – had been drawn out of its commonplace obscurity. Human love is a tainted thing, tinged with lust or with the possessiveness which is self-will and is the spring of jealousy. The words commonly used for love are not free from those associations. So this word which had no bad suggestiveness because it had none at all was used to stand for the pure and the holy love of God as Christ disclosed it, to gather from that disclosure its associations and suggestions. Peter will not use this word of himself; he uses the word of simple friendship; *Yea, Lord, thou knowest that I am thy friend.* That at least, in spite of everything, he can claim. Because he can make that claim, the commission can be given: *Feed my lambs.*

Then the Lord repeats the question, but this time without any addition of comparisons. Whether more or less than others, does Peter love his Lord? *Simon, son of John, lovest thou me?* Peter still gives the same answer: *Yea, Lord, thou knowest that I am thy friend.* And again the commission is given: *Tend my sheep.*

Once more the Lord questions Peter, and this time he changes the form of question and adopts Peter's own word: *Simon, son of John, art thou my friend?* Is even that true? Peter was grieved, not only because, recalling the threefold denial, the Lord puts His question for the third time, but also because this time He questions even that lesser claim which Peter had made. He pleads not only the Lord's unerring knowledge of what is in him, but his own manifest sincerity: *Lord thou knowest all things; thou seest that I am thy friend.*

Thou seest; elsewhere I have translated this Greek word 'recognize'. In the other two answers, and here in the first phrase, Peter uses the word that stands for knowledge of facts or truths; here he uses the word for acquaintance and appreciation. Before the Lord is His devoted, loyal and deeply penitent disciple: *thou seest that I am thy friend.*

We too have often failed our Lord; we stand before Him ashamed and penitent. Can we say with Peter's confidence *Thou seest that I am thy friend*? If we can, the commission to do the Lord's work may be given to us. We may not be able to say that we love Him with love like that which He has shown to us; but we must be able to say 'I am thy friend'. We must have taken our stand on His side, with full intention to be constant in our devotion. We may fail through weakness; but if that be all we shall hear Him saying, *Let not your hearts be troubled. Trust God and trust me.* If we can sincerely say we are His friends, He is ready to let us serve Him by serving His people.

From: *Readings in St. John's Gospel*

(Macmillan Press, 1970, pp. 384–6)

The Visitation of the Blessed Virgin Mary – July 2

Mater Christi

MOTHER ST. PAUL

When the Angel left her, Mary's thoughts seem to have been fixed, not, as we should have expected, on the part of the heavenly message which concerned herself, but on what had been incidentally revealed to her about her cousin Elizabeth. What a total oblivion of self there is in Mary and what charity! She picks out just the little bit of the message that concerns somebody else, decides that it is not for nothing that she has been told this – it may be that her cousin has need of her; and so, instead of giving herself up to dwelling on the great things that have been said and done to her, she rises up in those days and goes into the hill country, with haste, to pay a visit of charity. And she takes Jesus with her.

Mary is my model, and I can surely find some lessons to study here. One is that charity passes before everything, even sometimes before spiritual exercises and contemplation and meditation, going to Mass and Benediction. I see too that though I must be ever mindful of

God's benefits, I need not dwell too much – if at all – on the interior graces He has given to my soul; on any words of praise – though they may have come almost directly from Himself; on any piece of work that He has effected through my instrumentality. It is far more wholesome to be rising up to go to the next duty, starting forth into the hill country of difficulties, if need be, and thus taking my thoughts off myself by doing something for somebody else. I shall not, by thus acting, lose any of the graces or any of the sweetness, for I shall take Jesus with me, and together we shall face the difficulties of the next bit of life's journey.

From: *Mater Christi*

(Longmans, 1937, pp. 30–1)

St. Mary Magdalen – July 22

Blessed are the Pure in Heart

CHARLES GORE

'Blessed are the pure in heart: for they shall see God.'

If we are to take part in the kingdom, there must be singleness of purpose. Purity of heart is, or course, continually taken in its narrower meaning of absence of sensual defilement and pollution. That is an important part of purity; and may I say a word about the pursuit of purity in this narrower sense? A great many people are distressed by impure temptations, and they very frequently fail to make progress with them for one reason, namely, that while they are anxious to get rid of sin in this one respect, they are not trying after goodness as a whole. Uncleanness of life and heart they dislike. It weighs upon their conscience and destroys their self-respect. But they have no similar horror of pride, or irreverence, or uncharity. People very often say that it is impossible to lead a 'pure' life. The Christian minister is not pledged to deny this, if a man will not try to be religious all round, to be Christ-like altogether. For the way to get over uncleanness is, in innumerable cases, not to fight against that only, but to contend for positive holiness all round, for Christ-likeness, for purity of heart in the sense in which Christ used the expression, in the sense in which in the 51st Psalm a clean heart is coupled with a 'right spirit' – that is, a will set straight towards God, or simplicity of purpose. There is an old Latin proverb – 'Unless the vessel is clean, whatever you pour into it turns sour.' It is so with the human will. Unless the human will is directed straight for God, whatever you put into the life of religious and moral effort has a root of bitterness and sourness in it which spoils the whole life. Our Lord means 'Blessed are the single-minded', for they, though as yet they may be far from seeing God, though as yet they may not believe a single article of the Christian Creed, yet at last shall attain the perfect vision; yes, as surely as God is true, they shall be satisfied in their every capacity for truth and beauty and goodness; they shall behold God.

From: *The Sermon on the Mount*

(John Murray, 1897, pp. 40–2)

St. James the Apostle – July 25

Discipleship

A. H. MCNEILE

Two pairs of brothers were in their boats by the lakeside when Jesus of Nazareth passed along the beach, and said 'Follow Me.' Another man was sitting at his counter in the little *douane* near by, and He said to him also 'Follow Me.' Others were engaged in we know not what occupations, when they also were called. And one and all arose and followed Him. They were called to become disciples.

Now when we study this word in the New Testament a remarkable fact comes to our notice. The twelve men whom Jesus called, and others who surrendered themselves to Him when He was on earth, are described as 'disciples' some 280 times by the writers of the Gospels and the Acts. But in the Epistles the word never occurs. Not once did St. Paul, St. Peter, and the other Epistle-writers, take this name to themselves. I like to think that they did not dare to; it was too high an honour. It seems strange at first sight that in spite of this St. Peter in his first Epistle, and St. Paul over and over again, calls himself an 'apostle'. One might think that 'apostle' was an even higher word than 'disciple'. But it is not really; after all, it only means 'sent'. God says to this man Go, and he goeth, and to another Come, and he cometh, and to His slave, Do this, and he doeth it; – merely sent to do a piece of work. The writer of 2 Peter knew this well enough when he began with the words 'Simon Peter, a slave and an apostle of Jesus Christ'.

What makes this word 'disciple' so great that not one of them would use it? Look at St. Ignatius, sending farewell letters to his friends in various Churches, as he was conducted along the weary journey to martyrdom, 'by land and by sea, by night and by day, being bound amidst ten leopards, even a company of soldiers, who only wax worse when they are kindly treated'. And he writes: 'I myself also, although I am in bonds and can comprehend heavenly things . . . I am not yet by reason of this a disciple.' He expected, and longed for martyrdom, 'if so be I may through suffering attain unto God, that I may be found a disciple through your intercession'. 'I was hoping through your prayers to succeed in fighting with wild beasts in Rome, that by so succeeding I might have power to be a disciple.' 'Even though I am in bonds for the Name's sake, I am not yet perfected in Jesus Christ; for I am now [only] beginning to be a disciple.' It is clear what he thought of the word: it meant one who is perfected, one who *has learnt*. And the evangelists, looking back at the lives and deaths of the first Christians, could apply to them the word which they never used of themselves. In the Fourth Gospel the thought is brought out clearly: 'Herein is My Father glorified, that ye bear much fruit; and [so] become disciples of Mine.'[1] The word, then, does not mean simply a learner; it puts before us an ideal, a far-off honour for which to strive and labour and yearn – to become finally men who have learnt, men who know.

From: *Discipleship*

(S.P.C.K., 1917, pp. 1–3)

The Transfiguration of Our Lord – August 6

Transfiguration

MICHAEL RAMSEY

The festival . . . gathers up and suggests a wealth of the central themes of Christianity. The union of Cross and glory, the lordship of Jesus amongst the living and the dead, the creative role of prayer, the fulfilment of law and prophecy, the relation of the two covenants and the transformation of man and the world are all included. Western Christianity has dwelt upon the practical theme of the event as the preparation of the disciples for the Passion. . . . Eastern Christi-

[1] John xv:8.

anity has dwelt upon the power of God to transform man and the cosmos by Christ. Students of religious psychology have dwelt upon the mystical experience of the disciples at a time of spiritual tension and its symbolic expression. Modern biographers of Jesus have dwelt upon the event as a crisis in the growth of his mission. Here indeed is something for everyone.

It is small wonder that this festival holds its own amongst Christian festivals, and indeed finds its authority and significance enhanced by the ecumenical trends of today. But how does it relate to the hard facts of the modern world?

In his work *A Study of History* Arnold Toynbee included a discussion of the possibilities open to those who live in a 'declining civilization'. He distinguished four attitudes which he described as archaism, futurism, detachment, transfiguration. *Archaism* is the attempt to revert to a past tradition and restore it; *futurism* is the attempt to substitute for the present order a new order utterly different from it, to be achieved probably by violence; *detachment* is to despair of the political and social order as unredeemable and to retreat into an other-worldly salvation apart from it (we might feel that 'escapism' would be a better word for this). Rejecting these doctrines, Toynbee commended another way which he called *transfiguration*, which he defined thus: 'to bring the total situation, as we ourselves participate in it, into a larger context which gives it a new meaning'.

Leaping back across the centuries from Toynbee to the Gospel story, is it fanciful to see how these attitudes could have had a place in the mind of the disciples of Jesus at the time of the Transfiguration? Archaism: how good it would be to return to the success days of the ministry of Jesus, with the sick healed and the crowds thronging him with popularity and the promise of the new order really coming, before the talk about suffering and death had started. Escapism: how good it would be to linger on the mountain in a dream-world of glory with Jesus, Moses and Elijah and the heavenly radiance, leaving pains and trials at the bottom of the mountain. Futurism: how good it would be to take a leap forward beyond time and history into an apocalyptic reign with Jesus in glory. But, no, the way was transfiguration. And when Jesus went up the mount to be transfigured he did not leave behind the conflicts of his mission, the pains of humanity and the agonies he had yet to face. No, he carried these with him, to the mountain, so that when he was transfigured all these were transfigured with him. It was the transfiguration of *the whole Christ*, in all that he had suffered and was going to suffer.

Glory for the Christian is never a glory 'apart'. Human life, just as it is, is the stuff from which glory is made, by the bringing of situations just as they are, into a context in which they became changed from top to bottom. . . . Transfiguration, as an event, a doctrine and a philosophy, may be the point at which the Christian gospel does not bypass our contemporary world but rather touches it with force and relevance.

From: *The Glory of God and the Transfiguration of Christ* by A. M. Ramsey

    (Longmans, 1949)

St. Bartholomew the Apostle – August 24

The Two Ways

CHARLES GORE

'Enter ye in by the narrow gate: for wide is the gate, and broad is the way, that leadeth to destruction, and many be they that enter in thereby. For narrow is the gate, and straitened the way, that leadeth unto life, and few be they that find it.'

This is the 'doctrine of the two ways'. Human instinct has seized on the metaphor in many parts of the world; the easy way of self-pleasing, the difficult way of duty. It speaks home to every heart, to every intelligence, and nothing needs to be said about it. But I would ask your attention to one question which in our time arises instantly as we read these words – Are we to suppose that our Lord is here saying that at the last issue many will be 'lost' and few 'saved'? Is this the meaning of 'Few be they that find it'?

To this question we may reply thus: On one occasion the disciples categorically asked our Lord, 'Are there few that are being saved?' and our Lord replied, 'Strive to enter in by the narrow door.' And on another occasion Peter asked the question about John, 'What shall this man do?' and was answered, 'What is that to thee? Follow thou Me.' Beyond all question, our Lord does not intend us to know the answer to the questions which our curiosity raises as to the ultimate destinies of men. He fixes our attention, we may say, on three great principles: the character of God our Father, and His impartial, individual, disciplinary love: the final and universal victory of His kingdom over all resisting forces within and without: the critical character of our present life with its capacities for good or for evil, and the limitless consequences for good or evil which flow from the present attitude of each individual towards his personal responsibilities.

It is not unfair to translate our Lord's words here, 'Many there be that *are entering* the broad way; few there be that *are finding* the narrow way.' Thus they embody what is always found to be true in the experience of men. Always to one who wants to do his duty, it will become plain in the long run that he has to be prepared to stand alone, or at any rate to go against the majority. He cannot tell the opportunities and responsibilities that others may have. He knows that God is infinitely considerate, and will do the best possible for every soul that He has created; but he can, he does, know his own reponsibility and his own duty, and in following that he will have to bear the burden of going with the few and watching the spectacle, so depressing or staggering to the imagination, of the multitude running to do evil.

From: *The Sermon on the Mount*

(John Murray, 1897, pp. 174–6)

The Beheading of St. John Baptist – August 29

Endurance

W. C. E. NEWBOLT

With some people there is a craving for tenderness. The experience of a parish priest, who had to cast away his much-cherished popularity in going against the evil lives and low standard of the parish, has been beautifully described in a well-known story. 'With a power of persistence, which had been often blamed as obstinacy, he had an acute sensibility to the very hatred or ridicule he did not flinch from provoking. Every form of disapproval jarred him painfully; and though he fronted his opponents manfully, and often with considerable warmth of temper, he had no pugnacious pleasure in the contest. It was one of the weaknesses of his nature to be too keenly alive to every harsh wind of opinion; to wince under the frowns of the foolish; to be irritated by the injustice of those who could not possibly have the elements indispensable for judging him rightly; and with all this acute sensibility to blame, this dependence on sympathy, he had for years been constrained into a position of antagonism. He had often been thankful to an old woman for saying, "God bless you", to a little child for smiling at him; to a dog for submitting to be patted by him.' This craving for sympathy, for kindness, if it be a fault, surely is a very slight one. It carried with it deep pain, and many a heartache, as the word has to be spoken, the action done, the concession refused, at the price of a present smile, but of future remorse, and what has been described as 'the untold anguish of a dishonoured conscience'. And yet how frequently and how unexpectedly the decision has to be made! Need Daniel carry his opposition so far as to kneel down, when he is thwarting the wishes of the king, in putting up his petitions to God? There is nothing essential in a posture, or vital in a mere piece of ritual. Is it worth while to throw away his splendid position and his great influence with the king for an irritating detail and an ostentatious item of defiance? Is it necessary for St. John Baptist always to allude to the king's private disgrace? It might ruin his chance of ultimate influence, and establish an irritation, and preclude all hopes of future usefulness; it might be even thought unmannerly, as well as unstatesmanlike to persist in a protest, wearisome from its monotony, ineffective from its constant repetition, 'It is not lawful for thee to have thy brother's wife'. . . .

Yes, it is hard to bear the cold looks, the impatient scorn, the smart epigram, the cheap wit, the falling away of friends, the collapse of support, the withdrawal of subscriptions, the letter to the newspaper, the harsh names, the ungenerous suspicions. And, perhaps worse than all these, is the sense of loneliness, which has crushed many a man to the earth. To stand alone argues self-reliance; it may mean self-conceit. We mean it for steadfastness of purpose; is it obstinacy? We are standing out for principle; does that mean love of our own way? And there pours in from every side the pitiless refrain, Why do you refuse to act like other people? Why? Because we have caught a glimpse of the higher peak, white and glorious against the unclouded blue; because the mists, as they drive down the mountain-side, have parted just for a moment, and showed us the path, wet and slippery, fossed with precipices, battlemented with crags, and swept with the storm, but still a path, and above it the blue sky. . . .

Christ has asked for martyrs in all ages, and in all ages He has found them.

From: *Speculum Sacerdotum*

(Longmans, 1894)

St. Matthew the Apostle – September 21

By Honour and Dishonour

W. C. E. NEWBOLT

Here is another medium of display in which the minister of God can manifest his true nature – the alternations of honour and dishonour. 'Dishonour'[1] has an ominous sound; it seems to suggest almost loss of privilege, social or political ostracism. And there is a remarkable interpretation of a somewhat obscure passage in the Epistle of St. James, which represents the writer as speaking of these ups and downs of life as the object-matter of temptation, on which the Christian must be tried. To find himself as a brother of low degree suddenly exalted, or as a rich man suddenly brought low, is in either case a trial to be delighted in, as testing a man's real strength. The ups and downs of life are full of difficulty, as they cause it to contract and expand, like an iron bridge under the vicissitudes of weather. So the elation of prosperity and the depression of adversity are trials in which the minister of God displays himself; able to bear, able to adapt himself, as one who has been heard according to the fullness of that petition so often on his lips, 'In all time of our tribulation; in all time of our wealth, good Lord, deliver us.' . . .

'Honour and dishonour', going hand-in-hand for the most part, singly at times – these in some measure await us all. It is not really of so much consequence that we should ask ourselves, '*Where* shall I be' in God's field, or 'What shall I *do*', as 'What shall I *be*?' It is a wonder of some great steam-hammer that it is so beautifully adjusted in its delicate mechanism that it can crack the slightest shell, or hammer out the huge slab of iron which is to protect a ship of war. It requires an equal force within, held in check by the restraint of God, to live the life of dishonour, unknown, unregarded, with the pent-up energy still fresh and ready to do God's service, as it does to lead the life of power, supported by the praise of men, and the approving plaudits of the world, to be the honour of the parish, the noted man in the diocese, the ornament of the Church, to be that most difficult thing, to play that most arduous part, the minister of God in honour.

Holy Scripture is full of warnings addressed to those who carry a commission from God. There are few pictures so sad as that of wise

[1] ʼΑτιμία

Solomon, whose judgement was so famous, whose proverbs were so terse, whose wisdom was so notorious – temple-builder, honoured by visions of God, consulted by kings, and loaded with riches and splendour – sitting in the gloom of a moral night, which hides from us all the glory which characterized the opening of his prosperous reign. He is a type of the dangers which beset the minister of God in honour; while, on the other hand, the man of God out of Judah, suddenly called upon to do a work of valour, and speak a word from God, who successfully resisted the wrath of the king, and refused his hollow hospitality, who was on his way home, having done a difficult work well, is shown to us torn by a lion, laid in a grave unnoticed and nameless, with an epitaph as pitiable as the 'miserrimus' grave in the cloisters at Worcester – 'The man of God, who was disobedient unto the Word of the Lord.' He is a type to us of the man of God in dishonour, who forgot under the shelter of the old prophet's roof, in the humble hospitality which refreshed him weary with his difficult task, the uncompromising obedience which God requires to His most minute orders in those who attempt to serve Him. There he lies, an example to us of the dangers which beset a man of God who thinks himself to be off duty; a man who was faithful in much, but faithless in what was least. Ah! how many single talents which were meant to find their way to the bank are buried by those who do not know their value in the sight of God! Honour and dishonour! God's will must be done in both; both act as a touchstone of worth and a criterion of merit; in both there are opportunities for the minister of God to show his real nature.

From: *Speculum Sacerdotum*

(Longmans, 1894)

St. Michael and All Angels – September 29

A Rumour of Angels

PETER L. BERGER

'Everything is full of gods,' exclaimed Thales of Miletus. Biblical monotheism swept away the gods in the glorification of the awesome majesty of the One, but the fullness that overwhelmed Thales continued to live on for a long time in the figures of the angels, those beings of light who are witness to the fullness of the divine glory. In the prophetic visions they surround the throne of God. Again and again, in the pages of both the Old and New Testaments, they appear as messengers (*angeloi*) of this God, signalizing His transcendence as well as His presence in the world of man. Above all, angels signal God's concern for this world, both in judgement and in redemption. Nothing is left out of this concern. As a rabbinical writer put it, 'There's not a stalk on earth that has not its (protecting or guardian) angel in heaven.' In the religious view of reality all phenomena point toward that which transcends them, and this transcendence actively impinges from all sides on the empirical sphere of human existence.

It was only with the onset of secularization that the divine fullness began to recede, until the point was reached when the empirical sphere became both all-encompassing and perfectly closed in upon itself. At that point man was truly alone in reality. We have come a long way from the gods and from the angels. The breaches of this-worldly reality which these mighty figures embodied have increasingly vanished from our consciousness as serious possibilities. They linger on as fairy tales, nostalgias, perhaps as vague symbols of some sort. A few years ago, a priest working in a slum section of a European city was asked why he was doing it, and replied, 'So that the rumour of God may not disappear completely.' The word aptly expresses what the signals of transcendence have become in our situation – rumours – and not very reputable rumours at that.

. . . A rediscovery of the supernatural will be, above all, a regaining of openness in our perception of reality. It will not only be, as theologians influenced by existentialism have greatly overemphasized, an overcoming of tragedy. Perhaps more importantly it will be an overcoming of triviality. In openness to the signals of transcendence the true proportions of our experience are rediscovered. This is the comic relief of redemption; it makes possible for us to laugh and to play with a new fullness. This in no way implies a remoteness from the moral challenges of the moment, but rather the most careful attention to each human gesture that we encounter or that we may be called upon to perform in the everyday dramas of human life – literally, an 'infinite care' in the affairs of men – just because, in the words of the New Testament writer, it is in the midst of these affairs that 'some have entertained angels unawares'.[1]

From: *A Rumour of Angels*

(Pelican Books, 1971, pp. 118–20)

[1] Hebrews 13:2.

St. Luke the Evangelist – October 18

The Author of 'Luke'

G. B. CAIRD

A study of [St. Luke's] Gospel enables us to describe in some detail the man who wrote it. He was a second-generation Christian who had had ample opportunities of associating with those who had first-hand knowledge of the gospel story. He was an educated man who could adapt his Greek diction to different occasions, writing some-times formal, classical prose, sometimes a racy narrative style in the vernacular of his own day, and sometimes the semitic 'Bible Greek' in which the Septuagint was written. His command of Greek, his constant interest in Gentiles, and his avoidance of matter of purely Jewish interest may be taken as indications that he himself was a Gentile, but he was one of those Gentiles who were deeply versed in the Greek Old Testament and in the ways of the synagogue. He had something of the poet in his make-up and an artist's ability to depict in vivid pen-portraits the men and women who inhabit his pages. He delighted in marvels and was a little inclined to emphasize the miraculous element in his story. He was more interested in people than in ideas. He had a lively social conscience and an inexhaustible sympathy for other people's troubles.

To the evidence of the Gospel must be added that of Acts. For in Acts there are certain passages where the narrator switches abruptly from the third person to the first person plural,[1] and these 'we' sec-tions can be plausibly explained only on the assumption that the author is using his own style indistinguishable from the style of the rest of the book. If, then, we suppose that the author was using as one of his sources a diary written by a companion of Paul, we must add that he rewrote it so thoroughly as to eliminate all traces of its original style and yet so carelessly that he did not always remember to make the change from first to third person. The simpler explana-tion is that the author was using his own diary, and allowed the first person to stand in order to indicate at what points he himself had been an eyewitness; and in that case it follows that the author was a companion of Paul. . . .

What then was the author's name? The uniform belief of ancient

[1] Acts 16:10–17; 20:6–21:18; 27:1–28:16.

writers is that he was Luke, the doctor whom Paul mentions as his companion and colleague. . . .[1]

At one time it was claimed that the use of medical terms in these books was striking enough to prove that their author was a doctor . . . but perhaps the most that can properly be claimed is that the language used in Luke-Acts to describe ailments and cures is compatible with the ancient tradition that the author was a doctor.

From: *Saint Luke*

(Penguin, 1965, pp. 15–17)

St. Simon and St. Jude – October 28

Discipleship

A. H. MCNEILE

In 2 Timothy ii:21 a Christian is described as 'a vessel unto honour, sanctified, useful for the Master, prepared unto every good work'. . . .

'A vessel *unto honour*.' By adding 'unto honour' St. Paul at once leaves the metaphor of vessel far behind. To a vessel or tool, as such, no honour can be given. We have the honour, of which we have already spoken, of being human. We are earthen vessels; born of the First man we are of the earth, earthy. But we contain the life of the Second Man, the Lord from heaven; we are the highest created instruments of God's Self-expression. So we need a word which will preserve the thought of utter humility, together with the fact that we are human; a word which can represent *living tools* of God. St. Peter gives us a similar combination of fact and metaphor when he speaks of Christians as 'living stones'. But that which will best suit our purpose is the word 'slave'.

St. Paul calls himself in five of his epistles 'the slave of Jesus Christ' or 'of God'. And other writers do the same; we find it in the epistles of St. James, St. Peter, and St. Jude. They all gloried in it – the glory of humility and the glory of being human. To St. Paul it was a peculiar dignity that he was able to say, 'I bear about in my body the brands – the slave-marks – of the Lord Jesus.' The humility is glorious just because a human being can render it voluntarily. He is an active, and not a passive, tool of God. The Old Testament writer who soared to the highest point of inspired genius was the prophet

[1] Col. 4:14; Philem. 24; 2 Tim. 4:11.

who pictured the ideal Israel as the 'Servant – the slave – of Jehovah'. And the New Testament seer, rapt in the mystic vision of the heavenly Jerusalem, delights in speaking of the Christian Church, the New Israel, as God's slaves. 'Hurt not the earth, nor the sea, nor the trees, till we have sealed the slaves of our God in their foreheads.' 'Praise our God, all ye His slaves.' 'His slaves shall serve Him, and they shall see His face, and His name shall be in their foreheads.' And our thoughts can travel from all these saints of God to the greatest of them: 'He hath regarded the lowliness of His slave.' 'Behold, the slave of the Lord; be it unto me according to Thy word.' And once more, our thoughts can take wing, and soar up from the mother to her Child: 'He emptied Himself, taking the form of a slave, being made in the likeness of men.' Are we not right in saying that a slave is 'a vessel unto honour'?

From: *Discipleship*

(S.P.C.K., 1917, pp. 59, 63–5)

All Saints – November 1

The Universal Society

B. F. WESTCOTT

If the outward were the measure of the Church of Christ, we might, as we have seen, well despair. But side by side with us, when we fondly think, like Elijah or Elijah's servant, that we stand alone, are countless multitudes whom we know not, angels whom we have no power to discern, children of God whom we have not learnt to recognize. We have come to the kingdom of God, peopled with armies of angels and men working for us and with us because they are working for Him. And though we cannot grasp the fullness of the truth, and free ourselves from the fetters of sense, yet we can, in the light of the Incarnation, feel the fact of this unseen fellowship; we can feel that heaven has been re-opened to us by Christ; that the hosts who were separated from Israel at Sinai by the fire and the darkness are now joined with us under our Saviour King, ascending and descending upon the Son of man; that no external tests are final in spiritual things; that while we are separated one from another by barriers which we dare not overpass, by difference of opinion which we dare not conceal or extenuate, there still may be a deeper-lying bond in righteousness, peace, and joy in the Holy Ghost, the apostolic notes of the kingdom of God, which nothing that is of earth can for ever overpower.

Such convictions are sufficient to bring calm to the believer in the sad conflicts of a restless age, widely different from the blind complacency which is able to forget the larger sorrows of the world in the confidence of selfish security, and from the superficial indifference which regards diversities as trivial which for good or evil modify the temporal workings of faith. They enable us to preserve a true balance between the elements of our life. They teach us to maintain the grave, if limited, issues of the forms in which men receive the truth, and to vindicate for the Spirit perfect freedom and absolute sovereignty. They guard us from that deceitful impatience which is eager to anticipate the last results of the discipline of the world and gain outward unity by compromise, which is hasty to abandon treasures of our inheritance because we have forgotten or misunderstood their use. They inspire us with the ennobling hope that in the wisdom of God we shall become one, not by narrowing and defining the Faith which is committed to us, but by rising, through the help of the Spirit, to a worthier sense of its immeasurable grandeur.

And yet more than this: they quicken our common life with a vital apprehension of the powers of the unseen order; they break the tyranny of a one-sided materialism; they proclaim that a belief in natural law is essentially a belief in a present God; they take possession of a region of being which answers to the capacities of the soul; they encourage us to bring our ordinary thoughts and feelings into the light of our eternal destiny, and add to them that idea of incalculable issues which must belong to all that is human.

At the same time there is an element of awe in this revelation of the fullness of spiritual force active about us, of this association with invisible fellow-workers, of this communion with Him who *is a consuming fire*. And the writer of the Epistle [to the Hebrews] does not shrink from dwelling on the sterner aspect of his teaching. He insists on the heavier responsibility which attaches to those who have larger knowledge. He calls for the exertion, the courage, the thoughtful endurance, the watchful purity, which correspond with the truths that he has laid open.

From: *Christus Consummator* by Brooke Foss Westcott

(London, Macmillan, 1886, pp. 58–60)

St. Andrew the Apostle – November 30

The Church of England at the Pan-Anglican Conference, 1910

H. SCOTT HOLLAND

Romance! We [clergy] don't look like it. It is, no doubt, our coyness that hinders us from displaying this character of ours with better effect. We hush it all up in gaiters and buttons. We creep about in obscure and ugly disguises. The last epithet that even our best friends would think of applying to those who are known as the dignified Clergy, would be 'romantic'. No! Stuffy: fusty: portentous: – all this we are: but not picturesque. We do not wear the air of having often looked through

'Magic casements opening on the foam
Of perilous seas, in faerie lands forlorn.'

No one would look for us in that sort of spot: or expect to find us engaged in any such occupation. We are very obvious: very ordinary: very usual: very commonplace: rather heavy and tiresome: a bit slow in the wind: with a touch of wet-blanket somewhere about us.

And that is why the Pan-Anglican business was so significant. Suddenly, we all rubbed our eyes, to find that something was up of quite another order. Strange things were all about us. Strange beings from strange places swarmed round every corner. Their titles stretched our spelling powers to breaking point. We had long ceased to remember whether these Dioceses, with their outlandish names, are in Australia or California. Is 'Oluwole' a name or a place? Who can say? Anyhow, there is not one island in the far seas that one or all these men had not touched at: there is not a river that they had not forded: there is not a veldt so wide and desolate that they had failed to cross it: there is no ocean that they had not sailed: there is no people, black, brown, yellow or green, that they had not intimately greeted. They murmured weird sounds from unknown languages: they clicked: they snorted: they dropped liquid vocables, like rain. They carried about in their names and in their talk, the fragrance of historic memories that had been to us fabulous, but which they had taken possession of. India, Persia, China, and all the wonders of Pacific Island, were to them familiar ground. They had been rocked in bullock carts: wrecked at sea: half-drowned in floods and fords:

all but eaten alive by men and beasts. And here they were: and they were ours: and they made themselves quite at home. There was a Canadian Bishop who relieved the tedium of a Lambeth Conference by dropping in, during lunch-time, at a rifle-range to indulge his favourite tastes, by shooting at tin bears down a tube: and hitting at every shot. Probably at certain hours in the day, all those gentlemen who were in the habit of taking sliding headers down the shoots in the Westminster Baths were members of the Episcopal Bench.

Ah! And it was very real, this romance. As we looked at those men among us then, we recalled Archdeacon Johnson, blind and worn in Nyassa: and the body of Chancey Maples under the lake water: and Bishop Hannington dying under the malarian tyranny: and the white body of Patteson floating out in the lone boat, with the martyr-palms, laid by those who killed him, crossed on his breast. And many a lonely grave of those well known to us, hidden away in far corners of African jungles, came back on the imagination. Here was adventure: here was romance.

And the odd, and the comforting thing is this – that these returning heroes of ours – these, our braves – looked, after all, very like us. You could not tell us apart.

It is this English church, snug and smug among the hedgerows, that has done it. That is the astonishing thing. It has thrown feelers out so far and wide. It has overleaped the paddock fence. It has flung out its frontier line. It has set sail with every wind that blows; and planted its feet on every shore that ocean washes. Who would have dreamed it of her? She hardly believes it herself. She finds it difficult to remember as she sits tied up in Elizabethan red-tape; and smothered under the convention of Establishment; and fat with dignities; and very scant of breath. Yet it is all true. For here were the adventurers whom she had sent out, trooping home to din the story into her dim, deaf ears.

Quoted in Roger Lloyd's *The Church of England: 1900–1965*.
(SCM Press, 1966, pp. 194–5)

From: *A Bundle of Memories*

(Wells, Gardner Darton, 1915, pp. 231–3)

St. Thomas the Apostle – December 21

The Appearance to Thomas

WILLIAM TEMPLE

Doubting Thomas received the 'sign' which was refused to enquiring Pharisees.[1] Why are they differently treated? Of course it is because the Pharisees did not want to believe, and if they had been convinced by a 'sign from heaven' they would have been unwilling adherents, not truly disciples at all. To give them the sign would be to yield to the temptation typified by the throwing of Himself down from the pinnacle of the Temple. Their demand proceeded from ill-will; it was necessary first to cure that ill-will. Nothing can be more remote from discipleship than a man who should suppose the Gospel to be true while wishing that it were not.

The doubt of Thomas, on the other hand, proceeded from loyalty and good-will. He was utterly devoted. It was he who had said *let us also go that we may die with him.*[2] But he was rather literal-minded; it was he who said *We know not whither thou goest: how know we the way?*[3] He could not dare to believe the tremendous news; and, after all, the other disciples were equally unable to believe at first.[4] He was not present when on the evening of the first Easter Day the Lord appeared to the ten apostles and, perhaps, to other disciples assembled with them; and when they tell him, he still refuses to believe. It is natural to the prosaic temperament to demand certainty as a condition of self-committal. His negative is very strong: *unless I see in his hands the print of the nails and put my finger into the print of the nails, and put my hand into his side, I shall in nowise believe – or – there is no chance of my believing.* Such vigour of disbelief plainly represents a strong urge to believe, held down by common sense and its habitual dread of disillusionment.

The Lord waits till all the associations of the earlier scene can again be present. Again it is the first day of the week – the resurrection-day. Again the disciples are assembled behind closed doors. Again the Lord suddenly stands in the midst with His salutation *Peace to you.* Then at once He turns to Thomas and shows His knowledge of His disciple's heart. Thomas is offered precisely the test which

[1] e.g. St. Mark viii:11, 12.
[2] St. John xi:16.
[3] St. John xiv:5.
[4] St. Luke xxiv:11.

he had demanded; but he does not avail himself of it. He does not touch the marks of the wounds; but at once he leaps to the first confession of true Christian faith: *My Lord and my God.*

The disciples could not maintain themselves at that level. The full doctrine of the Deity of Jesus is not apparent in the speeches recorded in the Acts. But St. Stephen grasped this truth devotionally, when he commended his spirit to the Lord Jesus as to God;[1] and there was, apparently, no sense that St. Paul was departing from the original Gospel, as he developed his Christology. The Church of Jerusalem was perplexed and troubled about him in many ways, but not in this. Gradually we watch the Church moving towards a well-grounded assurance of that truth which St. Thomas reached in the exaltation of his sudden deliverance from obstinate gloom to radiant faith.

From: *Readings in St. John's Gospel*

(Macmillan, 1970, pp. 370–2)

St. Stephen – December 26

Courage in Suffering

SØREN KIERKEGAARD

A youth has been instructed in the true and the good, in loving the good for the sake of the truth, and in fleeing the very appearance of evil. But now the world shows him the opposite. There is an *opposite*, which we may call that of impudence; there are men who reverse their ideas, and, as the Apostle says, '*set their glory in their shame*', '*boast of their disgrace*'. A youth must see it with horror; they not only do evil, but they do not even hide it; they not only do not conceal it, but they make it manifest; they seek the light, although we usually believe that evil avoids the light; they lift up their eyes and are recognized just by this act, although we usually think that an evil conscience casts down its eyes; not only do they make the evil manifest, but they boast of doing so, and 'approve of those who do it'.[2]

But there is still another way in which the world may show the opposite of what the unsophisticated youth had believed; there is

---

[1] Acts vii:59.

[2] Romans 1:32.

another inversion which certainly contains the highest exaltation, even if it presents so terrible a slight that the youth shudders because it is out of harmony with his beautiful ideas. It happens when the good must suffer in the world for the sake of the truth; when the world appears not to be worthy of the good; when the righteous have no reward, moreover are rewarded with insult and persecution; when the confusion at last becomes so great that men think to please God by persecuting the witnesses of the truth; that is, when the good is forced to call derision an honour; is forced, in an opposite sense, with the everlasting emphasis of truth, to find his honour in his disgrace. Such things certainly seldom occur to a youth; a youth has certainly seldom been able to imagine such things; usually and naturally a youth has that lovable credulity, but he does not apprehend anything like this.

Hence, when this happens, when his ideals are shaken in an overturning more terrible than an earthquake, when the truth is hated and its witnesses persecuted, then what? Must the witness succumb to the world? Yes. But is everything therefore lost? No, on the contrary. We are ourselves satisfied, and therefore we need no proof. For if this were not the case, then neither is such a person a witness for the truth. Hence, we are assured that every such one has preserved the memory of youth, even up to the last moment, about what the youth expected, and that therefore he has tested himself and the relationship before God, as to whether the fault might not be in him, whether it were not possible that it might be as the youth had expected, which he now perhaps desired most of all for the sake of the world – that truth does have its victory and the good its reward in the world. But when he then reassures himself that he is not to blame, and assures himself that from now on he is responsible if he does not act: then courage rises with overwhelming power, then he turns the relationship about, and marvellously transforms the shame into honour, takes pride in being thus derided by the world, 'boasts of his persecutions and his chains', praises God that 'it is permitted to him to suffer in this way'. This *turning about is the conversion of courage*; it is also the reverse of what an unsophisticated youth had expected to see in the world. Woe to the one who presumptuously, precipitately and tempestuously brings this horror of confusion into the more peaceful relationship. But woe, too, to the one who, if it becomes necessary, lacks the courage to reverse everything a second time, if it is done wrong the first time! Woe to him! It is hard to bear the persecution of the world; it is, however, even harder to bear the responsibility of eternity for not having acted, to stand abashed in eternity, because he had not through God won the courage to transform the disgrace into honour.

The Apostles did this, but they did it through SUFFERING.

From: *The Gospel of Suffering*

(Augsburg Publishing House, 1948, pp. 148–50)

St. John the Evangelist – December 27

The Vocation of John

WILLIAM TEMPLE

St. Peter has received his commission and his call; it is a call to follow by difficult stages to the complete offering of the will that was by nature so self-assertive. Close beside the Lord is the Beloved Disciple. Is there any call for him? The Lord, it would seem, has illustrated the command *Follow me* by the gesture of moving away from the main body of the disciples, and as Peter followed, the Beloved Disciple moved with him. So Peter turns to 'follow', and his attention is caught by the presence of this one of all their company whom they knew to be the most intimate.

As the Lord moves, the Beloved Disciple has moved too; it was natural that one so intimate as the incident at the Last Supper proves him to have been, should keep close to his Master without any special command. But Peter's curiosity is aroused. His own future has been declared; what of John's?

The Lord does not answer speculative questions or satisfy curiosity. To the question 'Are they few that be saved?' His answer was 'Strive to enter in by the narrow door.'[1] So when St. Peter asks about the future in store for his fellow-disciple, the reply is *If I will that he abide while I am coming, what is that to thee? Do thou follow me.* Our duty is to obey, without waiting to know what orders or promises may be given to others.

Incidentally the recalling of this episode makes it possible to explain and dissipate the rumour that St. John would survive till the expected Second Coming. Nothing of the kind had been promised. All that was said was that even if this were the Lord's intention for St. John, this was no business of St. Peter's; his business was plain: *Do thou follow me.*

[1] Luke xiii: 23–4

Abide while I am coming. This translation exaggerates the suggestion of the original, but the suggestion is there. The Coming of the Lord is, from the time of the Passion, permanent present fact. 'He cometh with the clouds'; that is present. 'Every eye shall see him'; that is future.

So the story of this Gospel ends with a little group standing apart from the company of the disciples. It consists of three: the Lord of love; the disciple in whom self would be offered; and the disciple in whom self would be forgotten.

If we are to enter into the Life to which the Lord Jesus invites us, the self in us must be eliminated as a factor in the determination of conduct; if possible let it be so effaced by love that it is forgotten; if that may not be, let it be offered. For if we are to *come to the Father,* self must be either offered or forgotten.

From: *Readings in St. John's Gospel*

(Macmillan, 1970, pp. 388–90)

The Innocents – December 28

Christus Consummator

B. F. WESTCOTT

Time has not softened the sharpness of the impression which is made upon thoughtful spectators by the sight of the sorrows of life. If the contrast between man made *a little lower than angels* – nay literally *a little less than God* – and man as man had made him, was startling at the time when the Apostle wrote, it has not grown less impressive since. Larger knowledge of man's capacities and of his growth, of his endowments and of his conquests, has only given intensity to the colours in which poets and moralists have portrayed the conflict in his nature and in his life. Whether we look within or without, we cannot refuse to acknowledge both the element of nobility in man which bears witness to his Divine origin, and also the element of selfishness which betrays his falls. Every philosophy of humanity which leaves out of account the one or the other is shattered by experience. The loftiest enthusiasm leaves a place in its reconstruction of society where superstition may attach itself. Out of the darkest depths of crime not seldom flashes a light of self-sacrifice,

like the prayer of the rich man for his brethren when he was in tor-
ments, which shews that all is not lost. . . . We trace back, till thought
fails, the long line of ages through which the earth was prepared to
be our dwelling-place, but we refuse to accept time as a measure of
the soul. We recognize without reserve the influence upon us of our
ancestry and our environment, but we refuse to distrust the immedi-
are consciousness of our personal responsibility. We do not hide
from ourselves any of the evils which darken the face of the world,
but we do not dissemble our kindred with the worst and lowest,
whose life enters into our lives at a thousand points. We acknowledge
that *the whole creation groaneth and travaileth in pain together until
now*, but we believe also that these travail pains prepare the joy of a
new birth. We make no effort to cast off the riddles or the burdens
of our earthly state, but we cling all the while to the highest thoughts
which we have known as the signs of God's purpose for ourselves
and for our fellow-men. We allow that man and men are uncrowned
or discrowned in the midst of their domain, but we hold that they
cannot be put off the prerogatives of their birth. We ask, as prophet
and apostle asked: *What*, O Lord, *is man that Thou art mindful of
him? or the son of man that Thou visitest him?* without any expectation
that we shall find an answer to the questions; but none the less we
proclaim what we know, and confess that He is mindful of us, that
He has visited us, that *the Word became flesh and tabernacled among
us, full of grace and truth.*

And indeed this Gospel reconciles the antagonisms of life. The
fact of the Incarnation shews the possibilities of our nature as God
made it. The fact of the Passion shews the issues of sin, which came
from the self-assertion of the creature. The fact of the Resurrection
shews the triumph of love through death. Christ, in a word, fulfilled
man's destiny, fellowship with God, by the way of sorrow; and the
Divine voice appeals to us to recognize the fitness of the road. *It
became Him* – most marvellous phrase – *It became Him for whom are
all things, and through whom are all things, in bringing many sons unto
glory to make the Author of their salvation perfect through sufferings.*

From: *Christus Consummator*

(Macmillan, 1886, pp. 21–4)